Narratives from the Crib

EDITED BY

Katherine Nelson

HARVARD UNIVERSITY PRESS

Cambridge, Massachusetts

London, England · 1989

Library of Congress Cataloging-in-Publication Data

Narratives from the crib / edited by Katherine Nelson.
    p. cm.
    Bibliography: p.
    Includes index.
    ISBN 0-674-60118-1 (alk. paper)
    1. Language acquisition.   2. Monologue.   3. Discourse analysis,
Narrative.   4. Child psychology.   I. Nelson, Katherine.
P118.N37 1989   88-28455
401'.9—dc19   CIP

Preface

This book represents the results of an unusual collaborative project, a project focusing on what a 2-year-old child, Emily, said to herself when she was alone in her crib at naptime or at night. The authors of these chapters have listened to the tapes of Emily's crib speech, studied the transcripts, and reflected, each from a different perspective, on the meaning and significance of Emily's talk to herself when alone.

The collection of data for this project was inspired in a particular way by Ruth Weir's (1962) study of her son Anthony's crib monologues. Weir concentrated on the linguistic form of Anthony's talk, but his references to daily events were at least as provocative as his practice of language forms. Roman Jakobson concluded his foreword to Weir's book with the following comment:

> Anthony's bedtime play with language as a condensed summary of his day imperatively calls for further investigation—how far such self-educational linguistic games are usual among dozing children. Yet however prominent is the metalingual function in Ruth Weir's records, she is right to consider the copresence of other functions. In particular, the last and longest of Anthony's "paragraphs" discussed by his mother, with its eight times recurring leitmotiv "Daddy dance," is not only an elaborate lesson in grammar but also a moving and poignant psychoanalytic document, exploiting the child's whole inventory of expressive devices, and above all it is a true and beautiful poetic composition tantamount to the masterpieces of infant art— verbal and pictorial.

Here Jakobson rightly stressed the multiple functions of the monologues and suggested that one might be able to view the inner life of the child through them. What interested me most about this possibility was their function of providing a "condensed summary of the day." If one could compare such a summary with an "objective" account from the parents (while recognizing that the putatively objective situation might be different for parent and child), one might be able to gain real insight into what features of an experience were memorable for a young child, how the child organized them, and how they might be distorted from the adult point of view.

Episodic memory in early childhood is of particular interest because of the phenomenon of infantile or childhood amnesia, discussed by Freud, Schachtel, Neisser, and many others. The vast majority of people can remember episodes from their childhood back to the age of 3 to 5 but can remember little or nothing from before that age. When I began collecting data, there were virtually no studies of episodic memory in early childhood, and thus no evidence relating to autobiographical memory during the period of childhood amnesia. It seemed that a fruitful way to pursue the topic would be to study what very young children remembered of their own life experiences. Ruth Weir's study suggested a method for doing so: record pre-sleep monologues and analyze them in relation to the child's experience as reported by her parents.

At the time when Emily's parents agreed to participate in the study of early childhood memory I had no idea how fascinating Emily's monologues would prove to be along so many different dimensions. Emily is the first-born child of academic parents, a bright, highly verbal child. She reportedly engaged in crib babble even before she could talk. By the time the recordings began, at 21 months, her language skills were considerably advanced for her age (for a detailed description of her speech at 21–22 months see the Introduction). Over a fifteen-month period her parents periodically placed a cassette recorder under her crib at naptime or at bedtime. The resulting tapes and transcripts form the basis for the work presented in this book.

Originally I focused on analyzing Emily's "memory talk," and this analysis enabled me to address questions about the beginnings of autobiographical memory and the puzzle of infantile amnesia (see Nelson 1984; 1985; 1988; in press). At the same time I was intrigued by the contrast between Emily's long and richly textured monologues and her short and spare contributions to pre-bed dialogues with her parents. What might be the source and significance of such monologues from the perspective of linguistic and cognitive development?

In the fall of 1982 a small group of researchers concerned with the beginnings of language, particularly with its sociocultural bases, began meeting regularly in New York to discuss issues of common interest. The original participants included Jerome Bruner, John Dore, Carol Feldman, Daniel Stern, Rita Watson, and me. We were joined occasionally during that first year by Roy Pea, Susan Sugarman, William Hirst, Catherine Snow, and others. During the second year Julie Gerhardt was a frequent participant. (Elena Levy and Joan Lucariello joined the project at a later stage.) At the outset I offered the Emily tapes and transcripts as a provocative data set to consider. This data set became the focus of our discussions over the next two years. Each participant in what we came to call the New York Language Acquisition Group (NYLAG) took away from the discussions—and contributed to them—his or her own viewpoint on the problems posed by the data.

During the first year our meetings ranged widely over a variety of issues. Among the most compelling were the following questions: What are the functions of private or inner speech as revealed in crib speech? Linguistic practice, cognitive representation, self-regulatory efforts, role-playing were among the suggested functions. What are the routes into constituting the inner reality of the self? How is recipient design (or "taking account of the listener") manifested, and how does it differ between dialogue and monologue? Is there an implicit, noninterpretive, nonthreatening other, a "play" or imaginary other in these monologues? Are crib monologues a function looking for a form? Are they different from adult monologues? To what extent do specific speech forms in Emily's use of language mirror routinized dialogue contexts and particular speech forms in her parents' language? How are topics established and maintained in the monologues and the dialogues?

In order to bring some more coherent focus to our questions, in December 1983 we presented a set of papers to the New York Child Language Group (NYCLG)—an informal group of researchers from the New York area who meet semiannually to present and discuss ongoing research. For this occasion we decided to concentrate on a small portion of the data, the period from 22½ to 23½ months. We chose this period because it appeared to be a time of important changes and developments both in Emily's life and in her language. In the middle of that month her brother was born, and during that month she began to acquire control of new grammatical devices, particularly verb morphology, and more coherent connected discourse structure. The papers we presented formed the first versions of several of the chapters in this book.

The response that greeted these papers indicated that the data were of considerable interest to a wide audience, and encouraged us to extend our analyses. Moreover, we realized that although each of us approached the data from a somewhat different viewpoint there were common themes running through our work that could be brought together to shed light on what had come to seem a basic (if not the crucial) question: Why did Emily engage in monologue? The many answers to this question are contained in the chapters that follow. We offer the book to readers in the hope that it will reflect some of the excitement and wonder that we have felt in confronting the solitary musings of one 2-year-old, and will provoke questions and provide insights into the developing language and thought of the young child.

Our greatest debt in this work is to Emily's parents, who collected the data, made rough transcriptions of the tapes, supplied information about Emily's life and experiences, and generously allowed us to use all this information in constructing our accounts of what Emily's talk was all about. Equally important, of course, was Emily herself at age 2, providing us with so many provocative examples of the very young creative mind at work. We gratefully dedicate the book to Emily and her parents.

We are indebted to participants in our informal seminar meetings in 1982–83 and 1983–84 for insightful comments during the gestation of these ideas. In particular, we wish to remember Alison Gopnick, Bill Hirst, Roy Pea, Catherine Snow, and Susan Sugarman. We also thank the members of the New York Child Language Group who have twice listened to our presentations and offered comments and questions about the data and our conclusions. And we gratefully acknowledge the contribution of Margo Morse, who provided the first full transcription of the data and assisted in some of the early analyses. The work was supported in part by NSF grant BNS-8208904 and by NIH grant HD07196.

Katherine Nelson

Contents

Narratives from the Crib

Introduction

Monologues in the Crib

Katherine Nelson

Why does a child engage in monologue? What is its function for her? What role does it play, if any, in the development of her language or thought? What role does it play in the construction of her view of self in relation to others? How does it differ in function and form from dialogic speech? These questions define the themes of this book, which is centrally concerned with the relation of language and thought in development. The pre-sleep monologues of a 2-year-old child, Emily, are the focus of our analyses.

In recent years a consensus has formed among students of child language that beginning speech emerges in the context of communicative efforts between parents and children, and that it reflects these communicative purposes. Why then does a child just entering into the linguistic community engage in noncommunicative monologues? Can the study of noncommunicative monologues shed light on communicative speech, on language development, on cognitive development? Our studies of Emily's monologues have convinced us that it can, and we invite the reader to follow the varying paths our arguments take through the challenging and frequently delightful byways of our recordings.

Before I describe the data, our subject, and the relation of these data to other research, it is important to note a few points about the enterprise as a whole. The work presented in this book is a collaborative project—but the nature of the collaboration is somewhat unusual. Most of the authors of these chapters (Bruner, Dore, Feldman, Nelson, Stern, and Watson) were members of a group that met monthly for two years and focused on issues brought out by the data. The questions in the first paragraph—and other questions—were discussed from many different directions, and many possible answers were proposed and elaborated. All members of our group had a scholarly commitment to the study of child language, but each approached it from a somewhat different angle. Four of the six were primarily identified as developmental psychologists, one was a linguist, and one was a psychiatrist. A burgeoning interest within the group was the structure of discourse, and in particular narrative, and discussions of narrative features in the monologues became a particular focus. Although all of the chapters are based on analyses of the same data set, the analyses were carried out independently and with different theoretical questions in mind. Thus the book as a whole represents an attempt to describe and explain the many facets of these unusual data, while the individual pieces are informed by, but not dictated by, our group discussions. It is our conviction that this data base is virtually inexhaustible; although we present here nine different ways of looking at it, there is yet more to be uncovered. No one chapter, or even one book, can capture the full richness of these monologues.

Does a single case merit the treatment we have given this one? After all, how generalizable are conclusions based on data from one child, who may be special in ways not documented? We have two points to make in response to these questions: (1) Although the data are from a single child, they were gathered longitudinally over fifteen months, and thus encompass considerable developmental change. Studies of an individual's development over an important life period have their own value and can inform studies of larger samples as well. (2) Much of what we describe here has never before been reported, or at least not subjected to detailed analysis, and regardless of how generalizable the details may be, the existence of some of the phenomena is important enough to warrant attention. We take it for granted that any interpretations we make of the present data are subject to future verification or rejection on the basis of further research. Indeed we hope that they will inspire other researchers to gather similar data, or to approach the issues we raise from other directions.

The Emily Tapes

Our data consist of tape recordings made over a fifteen-month period when Emily was between the ages of 21;7 (21 months, 7 days) and 36;9. The recordings include Emily's dialogues with her parents before bed, as well as her talk when alone. My arrangement with Emily's parents at the beginning of the project was that mother or father would place a cassette recorder near enough to the crib to pick up the child's speech at times when they felt she would be likely to talk to herself before sleep.[1] I did not suggest any set number of times per week, believing it was the quality of talk rather than its frequency that was important. At the beginning four to six recordings were made each week. After each recording session Emily's mother listened to the tapes and made a rough transcription, noting any references to prior experiences and clarifying their context. For example, in an early transcript Emily referred to a cocktail party in conjunction with her grandmother's babysitting for her. Her parents had told her that her grandmother was to babysit that afternoon. Although they were not going to a cocktail party that day, they had attended one a week earlier, at which time her grandmother had stayed with her. The mother's notes made it clear that this conjunction of ideas was not supplied by something said by the parents before they left the room that day but by Emily herself.

My contribution to data collection was simply to supply tapes, pick them up, and question uninterpretable passages. I then made a transcription of all passages that referenced memory in some way, as my initial interest in the data was as evidence of early episodic memory. As it happened, most transcripts included some talk between parents and child, but initially these dialogues were used only to provide context for the monologues.

Transcribing crib speech poses special difficulties over and above those usually encountered in decoding the speech of very young children. There is no immediate context to provide clues to the meaning of a word or sentence. There is no discourse partner to provide an interpretation or to give feedback. Techniques such as slowing down the tapes may be helpful in disambiguating features such as verb endings, but cannot always clarify what a word target might be if the phonological form deviates significantly from the standard. Thus Emily's mother's willingness to listen to the tapes and make a first transcription proved to be an enormous contribution, even though that transcription often varied in detail from what a careful transcriber later produced. The mother could provide clues to what Emily was talking about, and could interpret Emily's words in terms of the phonology she was used to hearing. Even so, there remains legitimate disagreement among listeners as to particular phonemes, syllables, whole words, and even in some cases whole phrases or sentences. Eventually a research assistant transcribed the entire corpus. In the first two months of the recording Emily's articulation was quite imprecise, making transcription very difficult. By 23 months word targets were clear most of the time, although endings were often ambiguous. Beginning at about 25 months reliable transcriptions could be made with approximately as much ease as for ordinary conversational recordings from preschoolers. Even when we were able to retranscribe and arbitrate conflicting versions, legitimate doubts remained for some passages. The compromise we reached was to attempt to verify the transcription of any passages that were crucial to a particular analysis. Where differences of interpretation arose among the investigators, a common solution was agreed upon, in most cases.[2]

The total data set consists of 122 tape-recorded sessions; over half (68) were recorded in the first five months, the rest equally divided between the second five (26) and the last five months (28). Thus the data are heavily weighted toward the early period, and this fact is reflected in the analyses. The sessions are not by any means equivalent in terms of length or content of recording. Most sessions include some dialogue between parents (usually the father) and child before they (he) left the room at naptime or at night. Some sessions include little or no monologic speech, as Emily appears to fall asleep immediately. Others include half an hour or more of monologue, but in many of these cases bursts of talk are interspersed with long periods of silence.

When one first approaches these data the most striking feature is the contrast between Emily's monologic speech and her speech in the context of dialogue with her parents. This contrast is focused on in a variety of ways in the chapters to follow (see especially Chapters 6 and 7). What one is not initially prepared for in the monologues is the long sequences of comments on a single topic, strung together more or less coherently almost from the beginning (see Chapters 1 and 4 for discussion of development along this dimension). One usually finds transcripts of 2-year-olds' speech in the form of single brief utterances (one to five words) responding to a question or comment from an adult. Emily's dialogic contributions are similar in kind, although, as described below, her linguistic abilities are in general advanced for her age. It seems very clear from our transcripts that monologue and dialogue are very different types of discourse and that these different types are revealed in discourse structure, grammar, lexicon, and selection of syntactic form (on this point see especially Chapter 5). The way in which words are strung together makes it difficult to apply the usual notion of "utterance" to these monologues. Chunks of speech may include a few words, a phrase, a clause, or several clauses.[3] Pause length has been our primary guide to the division of the monologues into segments, but we adopted no single guideline for this purpose. The division of a given monologue into basic units may occasionally differ from one author to the next, but this should not be a problem unless a particular claim hinges on the boundary between units.

The following conventions are used throughout in our transcriptions:

( ) indicates that the word or phrase enclosed is a best guess but an uncertain transcription
(?) indicates an uninterpretable word
(???) indicates more than one uninterpretable word
[ ] indicates an interpolation by the researchers
... marks a pause
italics are used for intonational stress
hyphens between the letters of a word indicate that it is drawn out in pronunciation.

Who Is Emily?

Emily is the first-born child of university professors. At the time of this study she lived in a large, comfortable house in an upper-middle-class urban neighborhood that included many children of different ages. Emily's parents both worked full time, but as is the fortunate case with academics, their time was flexible, so they could spend more time with her during the day than is possible for most full-time professionals. Nonetheless, Emily had been in a neighborhood home day-care arrangement from early infancy. Her mother substitute was called Tanta, and it can be seen in the transcripts that Tanta played a major role in Emily's life. A number of other children attended day-care with Emily, in particular her close friend Carl. Tanta's own teen-age children, Jeannie and Annie, frequently helped to care for the younger ones, and they too make their appearance in the monologues. Emily's maternal grandmother (called Mormor) lived nearby and sometimes babysat. When Emily was 23 months old her baby brother, Stephen, was born. At 31 months she began to attend nursery school two or three times a week alternately with staying with Tanta. These then were the major characters, settings, and happenings of Emily's life, forming the context for her talk.

Emily's Discourse

What sort of discourse does Emily engage in? The dialogues seem clearly to belong to the general class of conversational discourse. They display consistent and well-ordered turn-taking, focus on a topic or topics, contain semantically and syntactically coherent question-answer sequences, and so on. Characterizing the monologues is less obvious, and is part of the analytic task. Both variation in structure and variation in substance may lead to distinctions among genres, and the covariation between structure and substance may verify such distinctions as are made.

As a first cut, several different genres may be identified on the basis of their form. These are examined more closely in the following chapters. One is what Gerhardt (Chapter 5) refers to as "enactment sequences," which involve language used to bring about action. These occur when Emily is actively playing with her dolls and stuffed animals (referred to as her "friends"), her language being embedded in ongoing play. This genre resembles conversational speech, although it often occurs in long uninterrupted sequences as she describes to her friends what she and they are doing (for example, "I put blanket on baby . . . change baby's diaper"). This type of talk, which occurs most frequently in the earliest transcripts, is carried on in a low tone, accompanied by much movement and noise of objects being moved about. It is very difficult to transcribe and has for the most part been ignored in our analyses.

A second genre can be characterized as narrative or proto-narrative. In these sections Emily recounts in story-like form either something that has happened, something she has been told is going to happen, a story from one of her books, or an imaginary happening. These narrative-like portions are formulated as temporal-causal sequences. They may be very brief ("Carl come after my nap") or extended to 150 words or more. Both long and brief examples occur from the earliest sessions. This genre is the focus of the bulk of our analyses. The degree to which these sections resemble adult narratives is the topic of several chapters, and the implications of this genre for understanding the relation between thought and language in development is also taken up by several authors.

A third genre may be distinguished in which instances are not temporally organized but rather are organized around some central problem or rule (see Chapter 3). These may be compared to an expository format; for Emily they tend to be less compactly structured than the temporal narrative types.

Is there poetry here, as Jakobson (1962) discerned in Anthony's monologues? Certainly there is word play; and there are also bits and pieces of songs and nursery rhymes. My general impression, though, is that Emily may be more of a novelist or historian than a poet (but see also Chapter 2).

A word of warning: We have not attempted to agree on a classification of the monologues into different types of genres. Thus different authors may make their cuts differently, and genres defined in one chapter (as here) may not be the same genres referred to in another. All authors are in agreement, however, that the monologues reflect several types of discourse, corresponding at least roughly to those described here.

Emily's Language

In the chapters and appendixes we present numerous examples from Emily's monologues and dialogues at different times during the observation period. The reader will gain a good sense of the flavor of her speech from these, although it is impossible to convey the quality of her intonational patterns in this way, and these patterns provide important clues to her meaning and also impose upon the listener a sense of narrative form.

One question that inevitably arises is how Emily compares in language development with other children of her age. It is obvious from the examples we give that her linguistic skills were greater than those of the average 2-year-old. But although she talked early, her course of early development did not appear to be unusual: she used single words before two-word constructions, for example. To compare her language use with that of other children, I have analyzed her language for the first six weeks of recording, when she was 21 to 22½ months of age. I present this analysis for developmental psycholinguists who may be interested in the details of her linguistic skills. Other readers may want to skip this description and move on to the section on implications.

For this purpose all of the interpretable utterances in both monologue and dialogue were analyzed. To get a rough idea of the level of

Emily's language skills and to have a basis upon which to evaluate her relative developmental progress, we calculated a Mean Length of Utterance (MLU) for both monologue and dialogue. This index is widely used as a measure of development in the early language acquisition period, although, as many authors have cautioned, it is a rough measure at best. The assumption behind it is that as grammatical competence progresses the length of sentences increases. This assumption is generally held to be reasonable in the early phases of development, when the child is moving from two-word sentences combining two nouns or a noun and a verb to the expansion of noun phrases and the acquisition of grammatical morphemes such as auxiliary verbs, articles, and prepositions. However, past the early months of grammatical development the index is less consistently associated with grammatical competence, although it continues to be a reliable index of sentence length.

Brown (1973) set forth general rules for counting morphemes in child utterances, which we followed with some exceptions, based on evidence that Emily contrasted certain forms, for example *can* and the negative *can't*. Fragments of utterances in the monologues and utterances containing more than one uninterpretable word were not included in the count, nor were "yes-no" responses to questions or direct repetitions in the dialogues. Division into utterances in the monologues was based on the intonational and pause boundaries identified by the transcribers. No claim is made that these boundaries can be considered comparable to utterance boundaries in dialogic contexts. However, the system is functional for the present purpose.

The dialogues included 235 usable utterances during this period, for which the MLU was 3.61 (s.d. = 1.76). Of 243 usable utterances in the monologues, the MLU was 5.40 (s.d. = 2.43). The longest utterance in the dialogues was 11 morphemes ("baby have crying and we can't go in there"). The longest utterances in the monologues consisted of 14 morphemes. There were two of these ("then when Daddy done getting Mommy pretty soon then gets Emmy up"; "so Daddy not coming and Mommy not coming and I not sleep"). Thus it appears that Emily's utterances were considerably longer in the monologues than when she was interacting with her parents.[4]

Regardless of context, these estimates place Emily at a very advanced stage of development, according to Brown's (1973) scheme, in which an MLU of 4 morphemes places a child in Stage 5, at which point basic grammatical development is pretty much completed. At that stage, achieved by most children at 3 to 4 years of age, grammatical functors (inflections and closed-class words such as prepositions) have been acquired, the syntax of questions and negatives has been mastered, and complex sentences, including embedded forms, compounds, and relatives, are used. Bloom and Lahey (1978) lay out a more complex scheme, less tied to specific MLU numbers and more sensitive to the semantics of the particular developments. They avoid matching particular ages with MLU ranges, but they do indicate that their subjects at 25 months had an average MLU of 2.54 (range = 2.30–2.83). Thus by either comparison Emily is considerably in advance of most children in her age-group. But she is not unique; other children with such advanced language skills at 2 years have been documented (see, for example, Nelson 1973).

It is instructive to look more closely at the characteristics of Emily's language at this point. As the examples above indicate, Emily does not yet have a fully grammatical system, in spite of the complexity of her constructions. What is missing from her grammar, and what is present? The following analysis is based primarily on her monologic speech.

Consider first the grammatical functors that, according to Brown, begin to be acquired in Stage 2 and are completed by Stage 4. *Prepositions* are present. Eight different types appear in many different contexts, including *in, on,* and *under,* the crucial ones in Brown's table, as well as *to, of, with, for,* and *after. Present progressive:* the ending *-ing* is present on many verbs during this period; 11 verb types are so marked. Brown's criterion for acquisition was use of a form in 90 percent of its required contexts, although it is now generally recognized that identifying required contexts is not always possible and may reflect subjective interpretation. There are only 4 cases where the present progressive is clearly required and is missing, although many cases of the unmarked verb might be better expressed with *-ing.* (A better criterion would be productivity as marked by contrastive use with other forms, as discussed in Chapter 5.) *Irregular past* is marked on 10 verb types in 46 cases, with only 3 cases where it is clearly missing, although again the context often does not make it clear whether the past is required or not. This count may be overgenerous because it is often difficult to distinguish forms clearly; for example, "can" and "came" are difficult to distinguish in some contexts. In any event, there is no indication that the past is used contrastively during this period; both present and past occur in the same sentential contexts. *Modals* are present in 28 cases and include *won't, can, can't,* and *have to.* On the basis of this analysis, it appears that Emily has progressed a good way toward mastering the grammatical morphemes.

There are three such forms that are questionable or borderline, however, either because the data are insufficient or where the presence of a form appears to be optional. *Plurals* appear in only 7 cases with 4 types. It is indeterminable whether there are cases where they are omitted. Similarly, *possessive 's* is present in 2 cases and clearly missing in 5. *Articles* are frequent—36 cases—but in 27 cases they are clearly missing. Thus for these forms Emily appears to be in the process of development, but mastery is not yet complete.

Other grammatical functors are missing from Emily's grammar almost completely. These include the *third-person singular -s* (9 positive cases, 62 negative); the *copula* (3 +, 13 −); the *auxiliary* (24 +, 52 −); and the *regular past -ed* (only 2 questionable cases). It is important to note that the missing auxiliary is always *be* or *do;* the forms that are present are negative contractions (*don't, won't, didn't, can't*). Emily appears to be at an early stage in the acquisition of these grammatically important forms, in spite of her high MLU. Indeed, her degree of mastery of these forms seems to be quite comparable to that of other children of her age or slightly older. For example, the past inflections appear for most children sometime between 18 and 27 months (Weist 1986). But of the achievements that Bloom and Lahey place in their Phases 3 to 5 (MLU < 3.0), Emily still lacks the copula, the possessive *'s,* and the third-person *-s;* and there is questionable or no data on the plural *-s,* the use of quantity words (*some, many, all*), and the dative.

In contrast, Emily had achieved by 22½ months all of the new forms specified by Bloom and Lahey for their Phases 6 and 7, including the coordination of clauses, complex clauses, and modals. And of the achievements of Phase 8, she used the time specification *when,* the wh-question *why,* and the modal *have to,* although still missing the progressive *be,* the past *-ed,* and the third-person *-s* from that phase. In the dialogues only she uses questions (*where, why,* and *what*). Negative constructions vary, with 28 correct uses with *don't, won't, can't,* and *didn't* but 14 incorrect constructions using *no* or *not.*

It is noteworthy that Emily constructs complex sentences at this early point. As the two examples quoted earlier indicate, she coordinates clauses using the conjunctions *and, cause, so, then, but,* and *when,* with one use of *before* ("naptime before Daddy came home"). She also coordinates noun phrases and verb phrases (13 instances) and produces subordinate clauses (7) and complex verb phrases. Of the latter, the majority (35) are conjunctions of two verbs where the appropriate form would be verb plus infinitive but *to* is missing ("I getting play with big kids").

It is also worth noting that in contrast to the children observed by Bloom, Lifter,and Hafitz (1980) Emily uses some temporal adverbs, including *now, pretty soon,* and *this afternoon,* even though her verb morphology for expressing temporal concepts is still largely undeveloped. She also connects clauses with *when* and *then* (a practice that is examined more closely in Chapter 5).

It is clear from this analysis that Emily's unusually long utterances reflect an ability to use complex syntactic structures rather than a mastery of the fine points of grammatical morphology. Her morphology lags behind her lexical and syntactic development. This is evident also from the functors that are present (primarily lexical forms such as prepositions and modals) in contrast to those that are absent (inflections on nouns and verbs). In brief, Emily coordinates before she modulates.

Implications of the Grammatical Analysis

From this analysis, Emily's grammatical development appears to be unusual in that her complex sentence constructions emerge prior to her morphology; according to both Brown (1973) and Bloom and Lahey (1978), this is the reverse of what is generally observed. Of course her development of complex sentences is not complete by age 2. Notably, she lacks the *to* infinitive form, and she frequently stumbles in trying to conjoin two clauses. But clearly, her aim in the monologues is to connect propositions, and her achievements in this line are remarkable.

It is important to note that in the dialogues during this period there are only two cases of sentence coordination and no examples of subordination or relativization. In the dialogues complex verb phrases are limited to "want to V" (9 cases), and the use of past tense occurs only twice, on irregular verbs. Thus the dialogues reveal a much less unusual picture of development than do the monologues. On the evidence from the dialogues alone, we would conclude that Emily was advanced, but not different from other children in her course of development.

What are we to make of this discrepancy between the dialogues and the monologues, and of the deviation from the usual pattern of development in the monologues? To forecast the conclusions drawn in subsequent chapters, we believe that Emily's purpose in engaging in monologic speech—to make sense of action sequences—drives the development of the narrative form. What Emily is trying to express in her monologues can be expressed only in connected discourse, which requires the grammatical devices documented here. The ability to string together phrases and clauses, both in adjoining sentences and in coordinated sentences, and to use appropriate lexical terms for expressing relationships, enables the child to talk about events in terms of sequences of related actions. Indeed this is what makes it possible for us to interpret her talk in terms of narrative structures. Without this linguistic capability she would not be able to convey an understanding of events in terms of temporal-causal sequence, or (later) to express notions of intention and of possibility and necessity. In short, her grammatical capacity is a reflection of her discourse capacity. The grammatical forms present in her speech reflect the requirements of discourse; those which are undeveloped appear to be less crucial to the construction of extended discourse (see Chapters 5 and 8).

On the evidence from the transcripts Emily appears to be an unusual child not only in her linguistic abilities but in her capacity for understanding, for listening to and remembering stories, and for imagining, making inferences, solving problems. We are faced, then, with the nagging question of whether her advanced linguistic abilities made possible cognitive understanding or whether the need or desire to express complex relations led to the mastery of the appropriate linguistic forms. This question will be deferred until more of the data have been laid out and discussed in later chapters.

The data from Emily's transcripts have enabled us to generate interesting hypotheses about the development of thought and language. We would expect the general thrust of development to be consistent for many children, although the specifics of development might not be. Whether the type of development we see revealed in the monologues also occurs in children who do not engage in crib talk we can only guess at at this point. We believe these findings are important and provocative enough to warrant more studies of a similar kind.

The Study of Crib Speech

Weir's monograph (1962) reporting on her son Anthony's crib speech is now a classic. It is also still among the few publications in this area. In his foreword to Weir's book, George Miller expressed surprise that more child-language researchers had not studied crib speech, given its richness as a source of data. He assumed that once they were made aware of this source they would be eager to follow it up with further studies. Twenty-five years later it must be noted that this was not the case. Why not?

Two of the reasons Miller suggested for the dearth of studies before Weir's still seem relevant. First, at that time language development was thought to depend upon environmental supports. Few people today are still persuaded by the behavioral models that were commonly accepted then. Nonetheless, most contemporary child language studies continue to emphasize the social and interactive support of language partners, primarily parents, in promoting language development. And even those who hold the view that language development depends only minimally on environmental input have not focused on crib speech, probably for the second reason Miller noted.

This second reason is the sheer magnitude of the undertaking. Weir's painstakingly detailed phonological and grammatical analyses of nine language samples provoked Miller to comment: "When I project this to include the full description of language learning in a single child over a period of several years, it grows to staggering size. And when I project that further to include several aspects of the child's development, or to include the verbal development of several children, the whole enterprise seems literally monstrous" (Miller 1962, 16). Miller noted that psychologists tend to avoid such problems by focusing on specific questions or hypotheses that can be tested by reasonable sets of data. "But," he continued, "part of the danger of this economy . . . is that our hypotheses often blind us to obvious facts that are not entailed by the particular hypotheses we are testing." Researchers in the past twenty-five years have not found a way out of this dilemma.

Weir provided a complete description of her son's crib talk, based on nine recordings made when he was between 28 and 30 months of age. She analyzed his intonation patterns, phonology, morphology, syntax, and discourse functions. A second major study of crib speech was carried out by Kuczaj (1983) with a more restricted goal. He studied the speech of fourteen children in both social and crib-speech contexts over varying periods between 15 and 30 months. His primary focus was on a comparison of the two contexts as settings for the kind of grammatical practice that Weir had identified, and his main analyses centered on the patterns of repeating, breaking up, or building up the immediately prior sentence, practices he assumed to underlie the formulation and organization of syntactic knowledge.

Our own study differs from those of Weir and Kuczaj in significant ways.[5] The earlier studies focused on synchronic linguistic descriptions of crib speech and language practice, primarily grammatical. Although Kuczaj's study included longitudinal observations, his concern was not with changes over time, but rather with the comparison of social-context speech and crib speech. In contrast, our focus here is on developments of discourse forms and functions over a fifteen-month period as revealed in crib speech. To the extent that we examine grammatical forms, we do so in the context of their discourse functions (Chapters 4 and 5) or their conceptual relations (Chapter 8). The facts that Emily's language was considerably advanced at 2 years and that she continued to engage in crib monologues until her third birthday no doubt explain the unique character of these data. Both Weir and Kuczaj report that crib speech declines after 28 to 30 months in most children; given the relatively primitive language at the command of the average 2½-year-old, it should not be surprising that the monologues produced at this age tend to be of little interest except as examples of grammatical practice. But the differences between Emily and the children studied by Weir and Kuczaj raise a host of (at present unanswerable) questions: Why do most children stop engaging in crib talk at 2½? Why did Emily continue the practice? What relation does crib talk have to private or inner speech as conceptualized by Vygotsky (1962, 1987)?

We are well aware that a complete description of the data from the Emily tapes, such as that undertaken by Weir, would be a project of staggering size. We have not undertaken anything like Weir's type of analysis. Partly this is a matter of our own theoretical interests. Partly it follows what appeared to be Emily's focus: she seemed to be less interested in linguistic practice than was Anthony. Rather she seemed to be interested in *using* language for various purposes while she was alone, and it is these purposes that we have tried to examine. We offer our study, then, as a follow-up to Weir's, but not as a replication. We hope that this contribution may encourage a renewed interest in crib speech as a source of data on children's language, twenty-seven years after Weir's initial demonstration of its importance.

Functions of Crib Speech

Most studies of early language development take for granted that the child's speech is grounded in the context of an interactive situation, one focused on the here and now. Indeed, the importance of the support provided by the communicative context has been emphasized in other works by most of the contributors to this book. Moreover, discourse analyses in general assume that speakers are attempting to organize their discourse for the benefit of their hearers (Brown and Yule 1983). What then are we to make of a situation where there is no interlocutor and thus no hearer and no communicative support, indeed no apparent contextual support at all for what is said?

A speech situation without communicative context has unique characteristics, presenting both positive and negative features in comparison with conversational interactions. On the one hand, there is no support offered from a conversational partner to scaffold the child's talk (Bruner 1983), setting up topics, filling in omitted portions, interpreting intentions. On the other hand, the speaker does not have to respond appropriately and felicitously to comments of another or to attend to the perspective of a listener, thus is freer than she is in a dialogic situation to lead the talk into topics and ways of speaking to her own liking. Lack of support is also lack of constraint, and as we shall see, the importance of the latter characteristic has been underestimated in child-language studies heretofore. An alternative view might be that in her monologues Emily plays the roles of both speaker and hearer, thus providing her own communicative context. This view would have interesting implications for understanding her organization of the discourse. But whatever view one takes on this issue, it is clear that the existence of the monologues requires that one expand one's thinking about early language beyond the context of the interactive here and now to include the there and then and even the nonexistent.

Weir devoted a large part of her book to discourse analysis in terms of the six functions of speech identified by Jakobson (1960).[6] She delineated "paragraphs" in Anthony's monologues—long strings of utterances that seemed to be connected in topic and prosodic characteristics, the longest 61 units in length. These may be considered equivalent to Emily's "episodes," described in Chapter 1 and other chapters. There are certain differences between Anthony's paragraphs and Emily's, however. First, Anthony was at a much earlier point in language development at 28 months than was Emily even at 21 to 22 months. His "units" tended to be between 1 and 4 words in length, whereas Emily's average 5.4. More important, Anthony seemed more intent than Emily on producing variations on particular structures, or associations between words and word sounds. Weir noted that paragraphs with the primary function of narrative were infrequent, and she provided only one example. In contrast, Emily seems to be intent on producing narratives as at least one of the major discourse functions of her crib talk.

Both Weir and Kuczaj emphasized the function of crib monologues as practice spaces, practice carried out in play. Weir stated: "the child's play also has sense: the pleasure of play is structured so that it serves as a linguistic exercise. The role of content in most cases is subordinated to linguistic form, or the content serves the form" (p. 144). Although this statement may hold for some of our data, clearly much of the time for Emily the form serves the content and not the reverse. Indeed, we claim with reason that Emily's development of complex language occurred in the service of her intention to construct complex connected discourse.

Halliday's (1975) typology of the functions of child speech, based on the analysis of the beginning speech of his own son, Nigel, seems more apt for the present purpose than Weir's or Kuczaj's description of crib speech. Halliday divides functions into two broad classes, mathetic and pragmatic, roughly similar to the mature functions of ideational and interpersonal, respectively, the latter two functions said to be jointly encoded in every adult utterance (together with the textual function binding discourse together). Halliday described the course of early development in terms of a progression from pragmatic (instrumental, regulatory, expressive) to mathetic (personal, pretend, heuristic) functions. Heuristic is the most significant one here: in this mode the child uses language to sort out how the world is, what categories can be constructed from it, how to explain its phenomena. It is not particularly surprising that in the present samples of speech for self pragmatic functions play little part. Rather, Emily's speech is primarily mathetic—heuristic—serving the evident purpose of representing and sorting out her experience, using language to make sense. Representation is usually thought of by linguists and philosophers as the primary function of language, and it has entered into analyses of early child speech mainly in terms of mappings between words and the world, whereas most studies of child speech have been focused on pragmatic exchanges. Halliday's analysis made the point that language may be employed from very early on as a tool for the child to represent, to categorize, to explain, as a way of coming to know about the world. Emily's monologues are clear examples of this point, but go beyond it. Halliday's analyses were based on interactive speech; Emily engages in heuristic speech *for herself alone*. Thus language for her is clearly serving a cognitive (or in Halliday's terms a mathetic) function independent of any communicative purpose.[7]

Crib Speech: Egocentric or Private?

Although crib speech itself has not been the focus of many developmental studies, there is ample precedent in developmental psychology for the study of children's nonsocial speech. Piaget's (1926) early work characterized much of preschool children's speech in social situations as egocentric: monologic speech that was not addressed to a listener or did not take the perspective of the listener into account. In Piaget's view speech began as speech for self and subsequently became socialized. This characterization has been subjected to much critical analysis and has not fared well over the succeeding six decades.

The major view opposing Piaget's characterization of egocentric speech was set forth by Vygotsky (1962; 1987; original 1934). What Piaget had characterized as egocentric speech by young children, Vygotsky saw as private speech: speech directed to self and serving a self-regulatory function. In his conception, speech began as a social medium and became internalized as inner speech, that is, verbalized thought. External private speech was but a developmental way-station along the path from social speech to inner speech. Vygotsky and his colleagues carried out a number of experiments to demonstrate the functional value of private speech, and research within this tradition has continued to the present day.

Although Vygotsky's conception of the role of private speech is highly provocative, with its reference to the relation between language and thought, its usefulness to us in thinking about the function of crib speech in general and Emily's monologues in particular is limited. There are three reasons for this. First, Vygotsky (following Piaget) viewed egocentric or private speech as emerging at about the age of 3 years and coming to an end at about 7 years. Our own data, however, begin much earlier than this.[8] Our first transcripts are from 21 months, but Emily by that age had already been talking to herself for several months.

Second, and more critical than age of onset, is Vygotsky's view that private speech reflected the emergence of a new self-regulatory function (Wertsch 1985b). While the Emily transcripts include hints of self-regulation, this does not seem to be the primary function of her monologues, as the following chapters document.[9] When self-regulatory admonitions do appear, they tend to be based rather directly on parental talk (for example, "big girls don't cry"). This observation fits well with Vygotsky's view that all higher mental functions exist first on the social plane and then on the intrapsychological plane. However, such self-addressed rules and regulations form only a small part of the total data. The total set of transcripts clearly indicates that Emily's crib speech primarily serves other functions than self-regulation (but see Chapter 8).

Third, Vygotsky believed that egocentric speech was undifferentiated from social speech when it first emerged, thereafter undergoing differentiation to become inner speech with its own function. This presumed lack of differentiation was the basis for several demonstrations that at early ages egocentric speech was depressed in the same contexts in which social speech was depressed, such as in the presence of noise or in interaction with deaf children. But the hypothesis of undifferentiation clearly does not hold for Emily's speech. Her speech is not depressed in the absence of an active interlocutor. Moreover, as shown in the previous section and in the chapters to follow, it is clearly differentiated from interactive speech in both form and function.

Thus Vygotsky's conception of private speech is not apt for the type of speech we are considering in this book. There is a further problem in applying this general conception to our data. Vygotsky saw a continuum of discourse genres from the most complete, explicit representation of a message appropriate to scientific discourse with unacquainted others through dialogue with familiars using abbreviated forms. In this view the "very essence of dialogue" is "that it encourages deletion of those portions of the message that have been mentioned" (Wertsch 1985a, 58) because both partners in the discourse can assume prior knowledge of those portions. But inner speech goes further in its abbreviation, being a fragmentary form in comparison to external speech, "preserving the predicate and associated parts of the sentence at the expense of deleting the subject and other words associated with it" (Vygotsky, quoted in Wertsch 1985a, 60). This presents an interesting progression from maximum explicitness in formal speech to maximum abbreviation in inner speech. Crib speech, if it is a form of private speech, should, according to this analysis, fall far on the abbreviated side of this dimension. Although to some degree Emily's self-talk is abbreviated, and therefore difficult to follow and interpret, it is in many ways more complex and explicit than her dialogic speech. It does not seem to fall neatly into a slot along the dimension defined by Vygotsky. We need to understand why a child represents her thoughts so completely and explicitly and when she finds it possible to abbreviate.

Up to this point, Vygotsky has given the most complete account of the function of speech for self. There is virtually nothing in the developmental literature to suggest an alternative to his conception, and we seem to be left without a theoretical limb to hang our studies on.

In the two years our group—the New York Language Acquisition Group (NYLAG)—spent discussing the significance of the Emily data, we might have been expected to uncover a unifying theory, either given in previous work or constructed anew. In point of fact we did not, although many possibilities were considered and there was a brief moment when we seemed to be closing in on a common conception. In the end, however, we agreed that closure was not desirable and that there was value in maintaining diversity of views. Our decision is reflected in this book: each of the contributors has considered the data from a somewhat different theoretical angle, proposing analyses and explanations drawn from the fields of developmental psychology, philosophy, discourse analysis, pragmatics, psychoanalysis, and poetics, among others. Monologic speech, like language itself, must be considered multifunctional and multidetermined. Thus one theoretical scheme cannot be expected to explain all of its forms and functions. The kaleidoscopic view of developing language and mind resulting from our collaboration permits us to ask what central functions are served by monologic speech, and together we have produced a multifaceted picture of its many functions.

It should be noted that not all children engage in crib monologues. Thus consideration of what functions such speech serves for Emily necessarily raises the question of whether it facilitates particular kinds of development—cognitive, emotional, or expressive. The contributors can be forgiven for speculating that the monologues are developmentally productive in various ways. At the same time, it must be borne in mind that there may be multiple routes toward any developmental achievement. Thus, whereas monologic speech may be developmentally functional for those who engage in it, this does not necessarily imply that those who do not are disadvantaged in some way.

World, Language, and Self in Monologue

One common theme that emerges from the chapters of this book is that Emily's talk to herself appears to serve the function of representing and making sense of her experience, both direct active experience and that filtered through parental (or other) language. Through representing and interpreting in words Emily manages to organize, generalize, categorize, narrativize, and thus ultimately to clarify what may originally have been problematic or troublesome. Three general domains of experience can be discerned here. First, there is the world of people and things, activities in which Emily participates, past episodes and future anticipations. All of these she needs to understand if she is to take her part successfully within that world (which incidentally changes in important ways over the course of this study). Second, there is the task of mastering the language itself through representing and interpreting in linguistic and narrative forms. As I indicated earlier, Emily has made great progress in this direction by the time our story opens, but she has far to go in making language work for her in constructing, interpreting, problem-solving, and fantasizing activities. And third, there is the discovery of herself as a thinking, feeling, acting person in the world of other people who think, feel, act, and interact with her. We have taken these three domains—separable only for the purposes of exposition—as a framework for the arrangement of chapters. Although each chapter must consider aspects of all three domains at once, each focuses primarily on one or another of them.

Part I includes three chapters concerned with the representation and interpretation of the world of experience. In Chapter 1, I present an analysis of the monologues in terms of their content and structure. The premise of this chapter is that Emily is using language to represent what she has experienced, or what she has been told may happen, and eventually to speculate on what may come about on the basis of her prior experience and inference. Although the analysis focuses on representation of events,[10] it also considers changes in the structure of the monologues, which reveal changes in the way Emily interprets events and in her picture of the world.

In Chapter 2, Bruner and Lucariello consider the monologues as narratives constructing a life story. Their analysis concerns the use of different narrative devices in composing the monologues at different developmental points. They find change over time in the direction of more explicit sequential and causal structure, more stance marking, the use of more general themes, and more complex use of multiple narrative markers. A major point of the chapter is the surprising degree of competence Emily exhibits in the monologues in the use of these relatively sophisticated narrative devices.

Feldman in Chapter 3 also considers the monologues as narrative, but her focus is on their function in problem solving. She selects a number of cases that exemplify an increasing ability to pose problems encountered in the world, to examine the problems in narrative terms, and to come to some resolution of the problems. The surprise here is seeing the early cognitive work of problem solving carried on in the context of a highly elaborate system of speech for the self. Eventually Emily becomes capable of inserting fantasy elements into these problem-solving narrative patterns. At this point she can pose problems in invented worlds. Feldman suggests that this is the beginning of theoretical thinking.

Part II concerns monologues as a problem space for the development of linguistic forms and devices. In Chapter 4, Levy traces the acquisition of cohesive discourse devices in the construction of monologue, in particular the developing use of anaphoric and cataphoric pronouns to tie the structure of a narrative piece together. She shows that Emily displays by 2½ years considerable facility in using pronominal reference to produce cohesive discourse, whereas previous literature has suggested that such use is delayed until the school years (Karmiloff-Smith 1986). Her analysis raises the question of whether examination of extended discourse among preschool children might not provide evidence of generally greater ability to use complex language at an early age than has been observed in studies of adult-child conversations.

Gerhardt presents in Chapter 5 a detailed examination of the development of verb morphology (past, present, progressive forms), relating their development to differential uses in different pragmatic, discourse contexts. This analysis has important bearing on questions raised in the child language literature as to the meaning of present, past, and progressive forms for children who are just acquiring them. A primary question in the literature is: do children understand that the past-tense marker *-ed* refers to events in the past, or do they understand it to refer to the completion of action? This issue is considered anew from the point of view of the child's understanding of the composition of action frames, and a pragmatic rather than a semantic solution is proposed. The discussion, however, moves beyond the confines of this rather narrow question, considering the possible discourse function of different forms in different contexts in relation to their development. This chapter is a model of a rare form of developmental analysis: tracing changes in a system that seems to have psychological validity for the child over a brief period of time (six weeks in this case). This type of minilongitudinal analysis is especially valuable in identifying the psychological process of change within a system or a domain.

In Chapter 6 Dore looks at the forms of the monologues in relation to forms presented in the dialogues. His claim, based on the work of the Russian semiotician Bakhtin, is that the monologues can be understood as "reenvoicement" of the dialogues with the father. This claim has broad implications: whereas other authors see the child as creatively constructing representations, interpretations, narratives, problem solutions, Dore sees her as being "taken over by" her father's language. This is one of those points on which we have agreed to disagree. It seems likely that a final understanding of the monologues and their meaning would have to take into account both the reproductive and the creative forms and the way in which they develop over time.

Finally, Part III is concerned with the development of the self in the social world. In Chapter 7 Watson provides an analysis of Emily's part in the dialogue between father and daughter that takes place before he leaves her alone in her crib. The dialogue is always highly structured, although it changes with time. Watson's examination of it at one point shows how Emily and her father work together to construct a format within which her goal (keeping father in the room) becomes a subordinate part of the routine leading to her father's goal (to get her to bed peacefully and to leave the room). Over time Emily attains control over the routine and manages to regulate the leavetaking to a high degree herself. Watson suggests that this joint-regulation format is indicative of the social origin of self-regulation, which emerges in a different form in the monologues.

In Chapter 8 I present a dual analysis: first, of Emily's changing use of self-reference (alternatively Emmy, my, and I), and second, of her developing understanding of temporal concepts. Both of these continue, on another level and with different emphases, the analyses worked through for a one-month period in Gerhardt's chapter. The focus of the chapter is on Emily's developing sense of herself as an active agent in a temporally organized social world. The analysis also reveals her ability (unexpected on the basis of prior research) to construct temporal relations among speech time, reference time, and event time in extended discourse by the age of 2½. Again, this suggests the importance of studying children's extended-discourse skills at an earlier age than previous research has done. The implication of many of these chapters is that we may find, not just for Emily but for children in general, devices (and concepts) on the connected-discourse level that are not apparent on the sentence level. This possibility clearly needs to be followed up.

Finally, in Chapter 9 Stern reflects on the data from a psychoanalytic point of view. He notes that major life themes are not the focus of Emily's monologues, and he considers the implications of this finding for psychoanalytic theory. Making explicit many themes that are implicit in the previous chapters, he considers what role the monologues may play in the creation of a "narrative self" and a "reconstructable past."

What we present here, then, is a variety of views into the developing mind of a 2-year-old. A fascinating panorama unfolded before us as we became immersed in the data, and we invite readers to share our fascination and to join in our speculations about the emerging relation between language and thought.

Part I

Constructing a World

Chapter 1

Monologue as Representation of Real-Life Experience

Katherine Nelson

Emily's talk to herself in her crib conveys to most listeners a strong sense that she is giving an account of her life, as she understands it at the time, an account that changes over time as her experience in the world changes and expands. In this chapter I consider her talk about how things are in her world, how they may be, and how they should be, with the aim of discerning developmental trends in her expanding knowledge base and in her capacity to represent that knowledge linguistically.

My particular interest here is in her ability to represent the events in which she participates. My earlier research with preschool children showed that very young children form general event representations that structure their understanding of everyday experience (Nelson 1986). The Emily data present an opportunity to trace the evolution of such representations over time and to observe changes in their content and structure during an important period in early development.

The general assumption behind my analyses is that Emily is engaged in mentally constructing an understandable world within which she can begin to take her place (see also Chapters 2 and 3). To make sense of her experience, she narrates accounts of important happenings, those which have taken place, which may take place, and (of increasing importance) which should take place. In so doing she apparently creates a coherent mental world that supports her interpretation of and activity in the real world. From this perspective it is of interest to trace the way her own experience combines with her parents' verbal accounting of events within an increasingly integrated and organized narrative[1] representation of these events.

The analyses to follow focus on two aspects of the data—theme (what Emily talks about) and organization (how the talk is sequenced)—and on the relation between the two. Does different content invoke different monologic organization, such that different genres emerge (for example, episodic recounts and exposition of general rules); or does a single type of organization develop as the child masters conventional ways of organizing discourse? To address these questions I first characterize the themes that appear in Emily's monologues. Next I examine the content of the monologues more closely, tracing changes in emphasis over time and noting the relation of those changes to changes in Emily's real-life experiences. After that I look at the organizing structure of her narratives, variations in structure by theme, and changes in structure over the observation period. These analyses of content and structure result in a description of the evolution and differentiation of Emily's developing representation of the events of her world.

Monologic Themes

Consideration of Emily's talk in terms of general event themes will provide a basis for later discussion of sources of information, changes in content, and modes of organizing. One clear theme is "what happened." Evidence of episodic memory is present in the earliest transcripts in the form of references to past episodes from her life, although at first these appear primarily as fragments (see examples to follow).[2] By 2 years of age Emily has mastered the grammatical and lexical forms that make it clear that she distinguishes past and future, so we can reliably identify certain passages as episodic recounts. Recounting at 2 years is marked by use of the past tense[3] and temporal adverbs such as *yesterday* and sequencers such as *and then, after,* and *so.* We use both reference to past (attested to by mother's notes) and past marking to identify memory talk.

A second frequent theme is "what is going to happen." Again this theme occurs from the beginning, although not clearly differentiated in form from past or present. In the early months it appears primarily as repetition of phrases Emily's father or mother has used to convey what will happen after her nap or the next day. Over time it seems to be derived also from Emily's own increasingly well organized knowledge of routines. These themes are also organized as temporal sequences, and are identified by future indicators such as *after my nap* or *tomorrow morning* and by the future progressive (*are going* or *gonna*), rarely by the *will* form.

A third type of temporally organized topic is "what happens" or "what should happen" in general. For example, at 2 years Emily formulates a general account of when diapers are worn and when pajamas are worn. These sequences are marked by the use of the simple present tense and the frequent use of the pronouns *we* and *you* as actor-subjects. Such uses accord with those found in the recounts of preschoolers reporting on knowledge of general event routines (Nelson 1978, 1986).

Still a fourth sequentially organized type, not included in the present analysis, is the reciting of stories based on books that have been read to her. While these are organized and marked similarly to episodic recounts (and may be interspersed with them) the actors are drawn from story characters rather than from Emily and her family and friends. They also increasingly employ a dramatic narrative prosodic frame, which is less marked in episodic recounts. By the end of the period of observation Emily has begun to construct stories of her own, based on those she has heard and involving sometimes real friends, sometimes story characters. These sequences are difficult to distinguish at times from either episodic recounts or book-based stories.

In addition to these temporally sequenced protonarratives or narrative types, there are monologues that are not organized in terms of a temporal sequence. Some of these are concerned generally with problems posed by events or language that is not fully understood. They involve such questions as "what might happen" (but is uncertain), "why did *x* happen?" (or will it happen again?), "what did Mommy/Daddy/other say/do and what did it mean?" These are marked by phrases such as *maybe* and *I don't know.* There are also nontemporal excerpts that are apparently problem resolutions or formulas, categorizations, and rules. These are generally brief and frequently evaluative, marked by deontic modals and catenatives, sometimes based on parental rules ("big girls don't cry") and sometimes on Emily's own inferences (see Episode 1.8 later in this chapter: "If ever we go to the airport we have to get some luggage"; see also Chapter 3 for further discussion of problem solving).

The three general themes I will be concerned with here are (1) what happened in the past, (2) what will happen in the future, and (3) how events are organized in general. Where relevant, problems, problem resolutions, and rules are included under theme (3). For convenience I call these general themes (1) memory (or past talk), (2) anticipation (or future talk), and (3) general (or routine talk).

These three themes play major roles in Emily's mental construction of her world. To construct a mental world it is important to know how things generally go (routines), and thus (at least partially on the basis of that knowledge) what one can expect in the future. To construct a model of how things are in general that is predictive of similar experiences in the future one must know what has happened in the past in similar circumstances. This dependent relation between past, general, and future events becomes apparent as we look more closely at the data. Moreover, we see that Emily's emerging ability to use the descriptions presented by others—and not only her direct experience—as the basis for prediction plays an increasingly important role.

Thematic Analysis

For the initial analysis of these three general themes, we coded all of the transcripts, including both dialogue and monologue, for their presence. The transcripts of recording sessions were considered to consist of episodes of talk, an episode being defined as a sequence of uninterrupted talk focused on a single topic. A pause of more than a few seconds, or the intrusion of a different topic, marked the end of one episode and the beginning of another.

Each episode was coded as memory, anticipation, or general formulation. For an episode to be coded as *memory,* the context or mother's notes had to provide evidence that a specific happening in the past might have provided the basis for the recall. Memories were additionally coded as either *specific* or *novel,* novel referring to an event that was experienced only once, and specific to an occurrence of a recurrent event.[4] *Anticipations* were episodes focused on a coming event, whether one Emily's parents had told her about or one she anticipated on the basis of general knowledge. *General* episodes were focused on general action sequences (behavioral scripts), rules, or inferences about how things should be (norms). It was not possible to construct mutually exclusive categories of these themes, since a given stream of talk might include both specific memory references and anticipations or routines, even though the topic (such as breakfast) was the same. In particular, routines and anticipations often overlap, as can be seen in the examples to follow.

The frequency with which Emily's talk focused on these general themes is of interest in indicating how her knowledge of the world evolved over the fifteen months of the study, and how the work involved was divided between the dialogue and monologue. This analysis is designed to provide preliminary answers to these questions: Did her parents set the agenda for Emily's talk about her world, or did her talk focus on topics that reflected concerns independent of parental talk? How did she make use of parental input?

For the purposes of this analysis, we identified the number of episodes of each type of talk in both dialogue and monologue.[5] Table 1.1 presents the data in terms of number of episodes per recording session. (Recall that the number of recording sessions in the first half of the study was nearly double that in the second half.) In this table, frequencies greater than 0.5 (indicating 1 or more episodes in every 2 sessions or more) are in boldface for ease of interpretation.

Considering the themes of the monologues, we see that in the earliest period anticipations and general episodes are more frequent than memories, but that memories are more frequent at every point but one after that time. Memories show a general rise through the peak at 27–28 months, and then rise again from a low point at 29–30 months to another high point at 35–36 months.[6] General and anticipation talk show a decline over the first year but rise again at 31–32 months and then fall off to zero in the last four months.

In contrast to the monologues, the most frequent type of parent-child dialogue was anticipatory at all periods, with very little discussion of specific memories or routines. Indeed, from about 23 months "what's going to happen after your nap (or tomorrow)" became a

Table 1.1. Relative frequency of anticipations, routines and specific memories in dialogue (D) and monologue (M): number of episodes per recording session.

Age (months)	Anticipation		Routine		Memory	
	D	M	D	M	D	M
21–22	.48	**1.07**	.33	**.87**	.27	**.67**
23–24	**.54**	.48	.29	**.54**	.29	**1.03**
25–26	**.50**	.18	.09	.45	.09	**.59**
27–28	**1.30**	.30	0	.20	**.60**	**1.20**
29–30	**.50**	.36	.14	.14	.07	.14
31–32	.30	**.50**	.20	**.50**	0	**.90**
33–34	0	0	0	0	.21	**.79**
35–36	**.50**	0	.33	0	.33	**1.17**

Note: Frequencies of .5 and greater are in boldface to highlight changes over time and between contexts.

pre-bed routine, with frequent repetitions demanded by Emily. To a large extent, then, the themes of the dialogues (talk with parents) and those of the monologues (talk alone) at any given period complemented each other, rather than focusing on the same themes at the same time. In general, while parents focused on anticipations, Emily focused on memories. There were many occasions for repetition in the monologue of a topic that had been the focus of a dialogue, as subsequent analyses and chapters will show. Nonetheless, what Emily appeared to find it important to talk about to herself was to a considerable extent independent of what her parents talked to her about before bed. Only with regard to memory talk does the correlation of thematic frequency in dialogue and monologue approach significance ($r = .66$, $p < .05$; general $r = .47$; anticipations $r = .11$).

The figures in Table 1.1 give only a general review of the emphases of Emily's concerns. A more detailed consideration of the content of both the dialogues and the monologues provides greater insight into the "why" of the monologues.

Memories

Although there was a positive correlation between the occurrence of memory talk in the dialogues and in the monologues over time, as Table 1.1 shows, there was relatively little specific memory talk in the dialogues overall; of all the memory episodes recorded only 22 percent occurred in dialogues, and of these a large portion concerned the location of objects. Typically, Emily would ask for a toy or a book and then tell her parents where to find it. There was, however, a period at 27–28 months when her father recounted the day's events to her as a pre-bed routine, and Emily contributed to these recounts. But even though memory talk in the monologues was also at a high point during this period, there was only one recorded case in which material from the day's recount in the dialogue was repeated in the monologue. That is, even during this period, memory talk in the monologue was never simply a repetition of what her parents talked about. If, as I have suggested, Emily was using monologic talk to construct a mental representation of reality through the linguistic representation of experience, we may speculate that when her parents discussed with her an event she had experienced, that experience received sufficient attention that she did not then need to recapitulate it in her own talk in order to understand it and integrate it into her model of events.

The memories Emily talked about to herself involved both truly novel experiences and simple variations of everyday routine events, and the distinction between these two types is of interest in revealing what she found it important to dwell on. A focus on routine events might suggest that she was building up general event representations, which we have found to be central to the representational systems of young children (Nelson 1978, 1986), whereas recounting novel events might suggest that she was rehearsing autobiographically significant memories. A number of events that most observers would probably consider novel occurred in her life during the period of recording—trips to visit relatives, holidays, the birth of her brother, her own birthday, the beginning of nursery school.

Although Emily did recall some infrequent events in the monologues, they did not include these major life events. An early example is her talk about one of the family cars being broken (see Episode 1.1 in the Appendix to this chapter), which referred to an episode that had happened two months before its first appearance in the monologues, and which reappeared in the monologues four more times over the first five months. Emily's bedroom had been changed two months before the baby's arrival so that the baby could have the room closest to the parents. She talked about this incident three times, but did not in our data talk about the birth or the sudden appearance of the baby when she was 23 months old, although several recordings were made during the week of his homecoming. There were other relatively novel memories that appeared once only: a trip to the library on the bus; watching a tow truck tow away a car; a dream about an alligator; getting her own TV; a clown at a birthday party. Sickness, medicine, and doctor visits were referred to eight times over the first five months but not thereafter. (This period covered the winter months, when Emily, like most young children, had her share of colds and sore throats.) In contrast, holidays, excursions, and visits to relatives, with brief exceptions, were not the topic of memory talk. Rather, what she remembered tended for the most part to be specific variations on daily routines, and the content of these memories changed over time as her life arrangements changed. Beds and sleeping arrangements were prime topics in the early months, as were visits to stores and the eating of different foods. These topics disappeared in the later transcripts, which instead involved friends, happenings at nursery school, stories retold from books, incidents from the premonologue interaction with her parents, and her father's activities, such as his running in races.

My general hypothesis here is that Emily's monologues were motivated at least in part by the effort to construct a coherent representation of her experience. It seems reasonable, then, to conclude that the early topics of sleep, food, and doctor visits became well integrated into her general knowledge system by 2½ years and thereafter were no longer especially notable or memorable. After this point she no longer needed to talk about these routine topics in order to organize them or understand them. Instead, incidents involving other people—children at nursery school, friends at her babysitter's, Daddy—became prominent topics in the monologues. This change coincided with Emily's entering nursery school at 31 months, an experience that was sufficiently different from her previous family daycare arrangement that it led to a new flurry of memory talk (as seen in Table 1.1 at 31–32 months).

Anticipations

Consider next the topics that fall under anticipation of coming events. As Table 1.1 shows, anticipatory talk was quite frequent in the dialogues, but there was little correlation between such episodes in the dialogues and in the monologues. Emily's parents habitually talked about coming events as a pre-bed routine, and a majority—56 percent—of all anticipation episodes occurred in the dialogues. This was not true for the early months (21–24 months), however, when most anticipatory talk was found in the monologues. For example, Emily frequently repeated phrases such as "Daddy come, Emmy up," which had the flavor of a kind of self-reassurance, repeating Daddy's phrases in Daddy's absence.

In contrast to the case with memory talk, which was rarely carried over from dialogue to monologue, Emily frequently attempted to repeat what her parents had told her about what would happen after nap or the next day. An early instance of this (at age 23;6) is shown in Episode 1.2 in the Appendix. In this example, her father repeated his account of getting an intercom three times at Emily's request. In the monologue she then immediately tried to repeat what he had said. The missing pieces and inferences are interesting. She is unable to remember the name of the intercom, and she seems to believe that it is to be plugged into Stephen (like a pacifier?), and that when it is he will cry. After two attempts to get this account right she moves on to mention other things to be bought at Childworld, beyond those mentioned by her father. These include a new infant seat because the one at Tanta's is broken. Thus, although initially this episode depends very closely on what her father has told her, she elaborates it from her general knowledge of what needs to be bought and where things are bought. Here we see specific memory (for the broken infant seat), general knowledge (of buying things in stores), and anticipation of tomorrow's activities all merging into a *plan* that includes her father's proposal but goes beyond it. I do not mean to imply that Emily consciously intends to carry out this plan. Indeed, she cannot, as she does not have the necessary control over events. But her talk expands on Daddy's plan, and thus may become part of her representation of that plan.

This episode brings out two important points. First, whereas Emily's memories are not reflective of parental pre-bed talk, her anticipations do tend to be based on parental talk. Thus we might expect to observe differences between the ways the two themes are organized. Second, using parental explanations as the basis for constructing a representation of events is not a straightforward process for Emily. Although she is able to repeat part of what her father has told her, she apparently is not able to integrate the novel material successfully into her own conception of events. The interplay between mediated knowledge (from parental talk) and unmediated knowledge (based on direct experience) is vividly displayed in these monologues.

At about 2 years Emily began to use her memory of past events to speculate about the future. The tow truck excerpt (Episode 1.3) is representative. In the dialogue just preceding this monologue Emily proposes that an incident remembered from the day's experiences might happen again ("maybe that tow truck tow another car"), and her mother agrees this may indeed happen ("maybe that tow truck will come back"). This episode thus begins in the dialogue but is continued and elaborated upon in the monologue.

A similar example (Episode 1.4) from the same period further illustrates Emily's ability to project the future on the basis of past experience. In the dialogue preceding this episode her mother mentioned going to the doctor the next day. Although they had visited the doctor several times in recent months, Emily had never been to the doctor in her pajamas. From her talk in this excerpt ("maybe the doctor take my jamas") we infer that she well understood the relation between doctors and taking clothes off. She apparently struggled to integrate this knowledge with her present state of dress, even though past experience might have indicated that she would wear day clothes to visit the doctor. Her repetitive "maybe take my jamas off" suggests the emergence of an ability to make inferences based on prior experience.

The argument goes as follows. Emily has built up knowledge about the event of going to the doctor from her several previous experiences of that event. Part of the event is taking off her clothes. She has understood from her parents' talk that they will go to the doctor after her nap that day. She is wearing her pajamas. Ergo her pajamas will come off when she goes to the doctor. There is of course a flaw in this reasoning. She has failed to take into account other facets of the doctor event, namely that she wears day clothes to visit the doctor. She has also failed to coordinate the "getting up from nap" script—which would dictate that her pajamas should be changed to day clothes—with the doctor script. Thus she has more to master in using event representations as the basis for inferences about future happenings. Nonetheless, the basic mechanisms for such operations seem well in place for her by 2 years.

Episode 1.5, from 28 months, provides further testimony to Emily's increasing ability to formulate plans that integrate what her parents tell her with her own general and specific knowledge. Again, before leaving the room her father had repeated three or more times in different versions his account of what they would do the next day. In the monologue Emily begins with a statement based on this account ("we are going to the ocean"), and immediately thereafter launches into speculation about the particulars of what might be going to happen. For example, the ocean is far away, maybe a couple of blocks (actually more than ten miles), the hot dogs will be in a fridge, they will have to take the car with the car seats, and so on. Although her father's account included details such as hot dogs, he did not mention refrigerators or car seats. According to her mother's report, Emily had had no previous experience with the beach, nor had she ever eaten a hot dog. Her parents had said nothing about which car would be used for the beach expedition, and her speculation was in fact incorrect, but the basis for it was logical: her mother reported that the car seats had been moved from one car to the other that day.

We see here an advance in Emily's ability to use and coordinate event representations to make inferences about future happenings. In this case she has taken the account provided by her father and constructed a representation that still needs some filling in of details, which she proceeds to supply by plausible guesses based on experience with similar items (for example, other food items in the case of hot dogs). She then coordinates the representation of a recent past event—moving the car seats—with the new mediated representation of the expected future event to make the inference that they will have to take the car that now has the car seats in it. The unstated assumption behind this inference, based on prior experience and probably on parental injunctions as well, is that the children go in cars with car seats. Thus by this age she is taking her parents' talk as the basis for constructing a picture of future events, but building into that picture logical inferences based on her own prior knowledge of how things are. That her inferences are pragmatically incorrect is unimportant; they are nonetheless logical.[7] This passage also suggests that she finds it satisfying to construct and elaborate a coherent account of how things are, based on various sources of information—her own experience, parental input, and logical inference.

As already noted, many of her inferences, although logical, are contrary to fact. What happens to the coherent constructed account when her expectations are not validated? I have searched in vain for evidence in the monologues that Emily might reconstruct the account of an experience after the fact to accommodate such contradictions. For example, on the Sunday night of the weekend of the beach episode, another monologue was recorded, but it included no memory talk at all, no effort to integrate the novel happenings of the weekend into some general knowledge base or specific memory store.

It was in fact generally the case that relatively novel material was much more likely to be discussed in the monologue in *anticipation* of an event rather than after the fact. Perhaps Emily did not notice the contradictions between her projected future and the actual occurrence of events and thus needed no accommodation. Such an explanation might account for the many inaccuracies that are often found in episodes remembered from early childhood; that is, inaccurate projections or misunderstandings of verbal reports might distort the memory of an experience. Or perhaps Emily saw the contradictions as but minor perturbations in the anticipated account, and perhaps her well-founded expectation provided a sufficient basis for the representation of the event to take its place in her knowledge system without her contemplating it further. While the data are provocative of speculation, they provide no decisive evidence on this question.

General Accounts

As is evident in Table 1.1, anticipatory talk and talk about general knowledge are closely related, rising and falling together over time (r = .89, p < .01). A closer consideration of general topics is called for if we are to understand this relation. Often it is difficult to decide whether to classify an episode as anticipatory or general or both. In the early months there are fragmentary references to sleeping and waking, apparently reflecting Emily's attempt to come to grips with her sleeping and waking routines and the rules that govern them. By 23 months she has begun to formulate variations on the daily and weekly schedules, such as the fact that sometimes she stays with her grandmother and sometimes with her babysitter. It should be recalled that Emily's routine was complicated, with both parents working, her weekdays spent with her babysitter Tanta or her grandmother Mormor, and her evenings and weekends spent with her parents. Thus there was a great deal for her to mull over and get straight with respect to these matters.

Understanding events involves not only understanding what usually happens (the canonical script) but also understanding variations that may be expected and recognizing when something is out of place or novel. Working toward this type of understanding takes up a good deal of Emily's talk throughout the year, but especially in the early months when the topics are sleeping, eating, what to wear, and who takes care of her, and again after she starts nursery school when both the routine and the people involved are changed. Thus the rise and fall and rise again of both anticipations and routines in her monologues are understandable. After she masters the basics of how life goes in the early months, such talk drops out, but it comes to the fore again when her life changes and she must add to and modify her evolving experiential model.

A clear example of her formulation of "how things go" is shown in the Appendix in Episode 1.6, from 24 months. Here what to wear, what to do, and with whom to do it are set forth in the fashion of norms. This example suggests that Emily moves readily from the epistemic to the deontic, from her understanding of *what is* to *what should be,* by formulating general rules and norms. This tendency is increasingly apparent in the further examples over the period of her third year.

That "what happens when" continued to be a central concern is evident in Episode 1.7, from 28 months. Her parents at this time were helping her to learn the days of the week and distinguished weekends as "Mommy and Daddy" days, Sunday as "waffle day" (the day waffles were served for breakfast). In the episode, she makes an effort to distinguish between two types of buses, based on a distinction, discussed earlier with her mother, between city (blue) buses and school (yellow) buses, the latter coming only on weekdays.

It might seem that the problem of distinguishing between types of buses is of minor import to theoretical issues of cognitive development. But note what this example implies about Emily's growing understanding of how the world works. First, Emily is extending her concern with her own personal routine to a normative account of objective events in the real world that are only observed. Despite her talk about going on buses, she had only once—months earlier—been on a bus, and had never been on a yellow school bus. Note too that this formulation is possible only because it has been talked about with an adult who can explain the regularities of days of the week and events associated with them. Without language and the help of an older person it would no doubt take Emily many months to understand the regularities of the appearance of different buses, if she ever managed it at all. Thus we see that the boundaries of Emily's representation of her world have expanded beyond her direct experience, and that her mental model of the real world increasingly depends upon mediated knowledge, information conveyed to her by parents and others. How she integrates this information into her knowledge system is only partially determined by how it is conveyed to her, however, as these examples clearly indicate.

It is noteworthy that Emily formulated norms based on novel experiences as well as routine ones, as shown in Episode 1.8, from 30 months, after her plane trips during the summer. As noted earlier, she did not talk about her trips as memories, but, as this example shows, she integrated experiences from them into her general knowledge as the basis for formulating rules and norms. Note here the modal of necessity: "hafta take something for the airport, to the airport or you can't go." It is most unlikely that parents or others had described airplane travel in this way. Rather, it appears that Emily has used the representation of an experienced event as the basis for inferring a necessary relationship between one element of the event (luggage) and another (going on the plane). Again she has leapt from the epistemic to the deontic. Now it happens again that she is wrong: the relation between airplanes and luggage is contingent, not logically necessary. Her inferences are too strong for the real world. Further experience will teach her that empirical regularities alone are not sufficient bases for making logical deductions. Nonetheless, like the rest of us, she will go on drawing conclusions on the basis of past experience, but perhaps more cautiously.

Emily's ability to use repeated experience as the basis for forming representations of expected events was well established by 32 months, as Episode 1.9 shows. This passage was produced on a Thursday evening and, according to her mother's report, it was an accurate account of the Friday routine. This example illustrates as well the methodological problems of distinguishing between general and anticipation themes. Knowledge of routines allows a person to accurately predict what will happen in an event (see Abelson 1982; Nelson 1986; Nelson and Gruendel 1981; Schank and Abelson 1977). The importance of this type of knowledge for the child, and its utility in predicting the future, are nowhere better illustrated than in this lengthy episode, in which she recounts in detail the activities, people, places, and things that can be expected on the following day.

The accurate ordering of events in this account is flawless. The ability of young children to sequence events has been demonstrated repeatedly in recent years (Nelson 1978; Nelson and Gruendel 1981; Fivush and Mandler 1986; Bauer and Shore 1987), in contrast to earlier claims by Piaget, among others, that young children were incapable of constructing ordered sequences. Thus Emily's capacity to reconstruct the day's events in order no longer comes as a surprise. Nonetheless, the long series of events in this episode demonstrates this capacity to a far greater degree than previous research has documented.

The wording of the passage may raise questions as to whether it is an imitation of parental talk ("and here comes Carl in here"). Of course many of Emily's verbal representations may include bits taken directly from what she has heard others say. There is, however, no direct model for this production in the present data, and there is no reason to believe that the entire passage was modeled on adult talk (but see Chapter 6 for a different view). Rather, there is good reason to believe, on the basis of internal evidence, mother's report, and other episodes (such as Episode 1.5), that Emily combines information from direct experience, parental talk, and inference to construct her representations. In the case of the Friday routine, little inference or reliance on parental report is needed because she is representing an event she has herself repeatedly experienced.

In the examples of general episodes considered thus far there are two distinct types of topics, one involving a well-established sequence of events, such as the Friday routine, and the other involving norms and general rules, such as which buses come on which days and the rule about luggage at airports. The latter types appear to be inferences derived from the former; they are expository rather than narrative in form. The original category of general-knowledge monologues, then, cannot be expected to reveal a single coherent type of organization. For this reason, in the analysis of structure I will consider the anticipation of routines in conjunction with anticipations. I will not consider further the construction of rules and norms; they are discussed in different ways in Chapters 2, 3, and 5.

Summary

From this analysis of content it is apparent that the major topics and themes of Emily's talk involve the effort to make sense of her experience, to construct a model of the world that will permit her to anticipate what will happen and thus enable her to take her part in events effectively. Her parents actively assist her in this by their extensive talk about what will happen, while Emily contributes an independent account of what has happened. The child needs to talk about what *has* happened because—together with parental explanations—it serves as a foundation for an understanding of what *will* happen. Norms and scripts are built from what has happened and been understood previously, and once constructed, they take their place in the general knowledge model and the child no longer seems to need to discuss them. This explanation accounts for the fact that in the last two months of the study Emily's routine and anticipatory talk drop out completely. By then she has mastered her new (nursery school) experience, and more interesting topics—memories, fantasies, retold stories—take the place of dull daily accounts in her monologues.

Monologue Structure

The analysis of content highlighted the central role in Emily's monologues of sequential narrative accounts of events. It also brought out
an interesting divergence between the sources of that content. Memory narratives appeared to derive primarily from Emily's own interest
in a past experience, while anticipatory narratives derived in large
part from parental input, with contributions—increasingly frequent
and important over time—from Emily's own general knowledge and
inferences. This difference raises questions as to whether the two
types of narratives differ in organization—whether anticipations are
better organized than memories, for example—and whether narrative
organization changes over time for one or both types.

For the present analysis, the central issue about organization or
structure is that of the ordering of events. To represent an event accurately one must represent its component actions in their correct
sequence. As already noted, 3- and 4-year-old children are quite good
at this. We have seen in the episodes presented thus far that at least
by 32 months Emily too is capable of describing events in their correct temporal order. In this section I analyze the means by which she
structures her accounts to reveal their order, how these change over
time, and how they vary with different themes.

As a first step we need to identify a basic unit of analysis, a matter
that is taken for granted in the analysis of dialogue, but that is not
straightforward for monologue, as indicated in the Introduction. The
monologues consist of many long passages of continuous streams of
talk, as well as fragments and disjointed phrases, and it is not immediately apparent how these may be segmented into utterances. Neither the sentence, the clause, nor the proposition serves well as a basic
unit. When one listens to the tapes, however, it is clear from the intonational pattern that Emily does segment her talk into units of different size, similar in many ways to those used by adults. The transcribers intuitively used these patterns to break up their transcriptions
into phrases and sentences.

Following up these intuitions, for this analysis I relied on the system of segmentation described by Chafe (1980, 1986), based on the
notion of an intonation unit (IU). According to Chafe, an intonation
unit (termed an "idea unit," 1980) is a sequence of words combined
under a single, coherent intonation contour. It is about two seconds

in length and in English contains about six words. A basic intonation unit, then, is produced in a single breath-group.[8] Chafe found that the intonation unit used in narrative discourse does not reliably mark clause boundaries but may mark phrases, false starts, interjections, and other incomplete syntactic units. He has analyzed speech production by adults and children, both in story-production tasks and in natural conversation, in terms of IUs. Because of its applicability to sustained discourse similar to that of the monologues, I applied his analysis to the Emily data.

Chafe also identifies intermediate structural units (typically three IUs in length) that combine to make up a total episode, called here "IU strings." Chafe (1980) hypothesized that young children might produce short strings of one or two IUs, each with sentence closure, or long strings of IUs with closure only at the end of the episode. He proposed that intermediate closure was something that had to be learned. Thus, among other things, the Emily data provide us with a test of this idea. Does Emily utilize IUs the way adults do, or does she follow either of the suggested immature patterns? Does she learn to structure her narratives with intermediate closure? Of central importance here, can the pattern of IUs and closures reveal structural dimensions of development or of thematic genres?

For this analysis I selected six transcripts of memory episodes and six of anticipation episodes. They were distributed across the period of transcription from 21 to 33 months, with twice as many from the first six months (eight) as from the later (four). An equal number of past and future episodes were chosen from each period. This distribution reflected the frequency of transcribing at different periods, as well as the frequency of different themes (see Table 1.1). In selecting episodes I looked for ones that represented at least one type of the "best" organization revealed during a given period. Thus these episodes are not representative of the monologues as a whole but of the most coherent organization Emily appeared to be capable of at a given age.

Each episode selected was retranscribed to reflect the intonation pattern based on Chafe's description. Segmentation was guided by pause length and intonation contour. IUs may have falling, rising, rising-falling, or sustained (neither rising nor falling) intonation. In the transcripts these are indicated with question marks (rising), commas (falling or rising-falling), or ellipses (sustained). Brief pauses within an intonation contour are indicated by two ellipsis dots. Spaced letters and italics, respectively, indicate drawn out and emphasized words or syllables. When a passage comes to sentence-final closure, with falling pitch followed by a pause of two seconds or more, it is marked with a period.

Although this system is workable, it is far from algorithmic. Decisions on segmentation are based on a combination of pause, intonation, and clause structure taken together. In defense of the system, it must be said that no more straightforward way of determining units exists for data of this kind. Further, decisions about major divisions such as sentence-final closure are almost never in doubt. Rather, disagreements about segmenting involve decisions such as whether a hesitation indicates an IU break or only a short pause within an IU. For these reasons the quantitative data reported in Table 1.2 should be viewed as approximations rather than as hard and fast numerical descriptions.

Table 1.2. Descriptive data on memory and anticipation episodes.

Age	Length of episode (IUs)	MLIU	Mean string	Longest string	IUs per proposition
Memory episodes					
21;07	32	4.25	3.2	7	3.2
21;13	50	4.44	2.9	9	1.79
23;06	39	4.59	3.0	13	2.16
24;13	36	4.86	1.42	6	1.56
32;08	41	5.14	2.6	5	2.15
33;09	13	6.85	4.3	8	1.18
Mean		5.02	2.90		2.01
s.d.		(.95)	(.93)		(.69)
Anticipation episodes					
22;23	8	5.62	8.0	8	1.33
23;15	20	5.35	5.0	12	1.54
24;01	30	5.37	4.3	6	2.00
24;08	13	6.05	2.3	6	2.43
28;0	38	6.10	4.8	13	1.70
32;0	63	6.19	9.0	21	1.80
Mean		5.79	5.56		1.80
s.d.		(.35)	(2.49)		(.38)

IU Analysis

My main use of the IU system was to examine how Emily's memory and anticipation narratives were organized at different ages; this analysis is presented in the next section. First, to provide an overview of how the episodes as a whole were constructed in terms of IUs, and of whether their construction differed for different types and at different ages, I present some quantitative summaries of the data.

The passages selected ranged in length from 13 to 50 IUs. Mean length of IU (MLIU) was measured in terms of morphemes.[9] I also calculated the mean length of IU strings between sentence closures, and recorded the maximum length. In addition, I analyzed each episode in terms of the propositions expressed in each identifiable clause, to determine whether the narrative progressed in sequence or whether certain ideas were repetitively expressed. A count of the number of propositions in a narrative in relation to the number of IUs thus provided a measure of narrative efficiency.[10]

Table 1.2 gives basic descriptive data on the episodes of the two types—memory and anticipation—and at different points in development. As is apparent in this table, there is a positive correlation of age with length of IU ($r = .648$, $p < .01$). Chafe found adult IUs to average 6 words in length. Taking into account that IUs here are measured in morphemes rather than words, it appears that even by 33 months Emily's units were probably not as long as adults' tend to be, but the difference is not great (MLIU in morphemes $= 5.4$). On the other hand, her intermediate units (number of IUs per sentence-final closure, or string length) averaged somewhat longer (at 4.23) than the average of 3 that Chafe reported for adults. There was no significant correlation of string length with age, however, nor, surprisingly, of IUs per proposition (efficiency) with age, although both measures were in the expected direction. Number of IUs per proposition averaged 1.9.[11]

As shown in Table 1.2, there were differences in these indices between narratives concerning past events (memory) and those concerned with the future (anticipation). MLIUs of the anticipatory episodes were longer than those of the memory episodes ($t = 3.04$, $p < .05$). Mean length of IU strings also differed, with future narratives longer than past ($t = 1.95$, $p < .10$). Together, these figures indicate that IU strings in the anticipatory passages were more than twice as long as those in the memory passages (32.19 for future,

14.55 for past). There was no difference, however, between the two types of episodes on the IUs per proposition (efficiency) measure. These figures suggest that there is some difference between narratives concerned with the future and those concerned with the past, but they reveal little about either the actual structure of such narratives or the underlying processes that could lead to such a difference. To shed light on these issues, I next examine the sequential construction of the narratives.

Sequential Construction of Narratives

To provide a picture of the productive process, I devised a method of graphing the progression of the narratives in terms of the propositions expressed in each succeeding intonation unit. A number of these graphs are presented here to illustrate the skeletal structure of the episode as it unfolds through time and to portray developmental differences in the structures. In each graph, distinct propositions are numbered across the abscissa in the order in which they were produced in the narrative (not necessarily in the correct order within the event reported, as will be shown). IUs are numbered from top to bottom in the order in which they were produced. Full stops (sentence-final closure) are indicated by circles. Connective terms are placed on the lines connecting IUs, before the IU that began with the connective. For example, in Figure 1.1 the first *so* appears on the line connecting IUs 11 and 12, where IU 12 is "So Mommy Daddy go in their their car." In these diagrams progression to new information is indicated by lines from left to right, returns to old information by lines from right to left, and immediate repetition of information by vertical lines. These can be characterized respectively as progression, regression, and stasis—or as advances, returns, and standstills.

Memory Episodes

Figure 1.1 graphs Episode 1.1, in which Emily at 21;7 describes a remembered event when the family car was broken. As the figure indicates, this episode uses 32 IUs to express 10 propositions (IU/proposition ratio = 3.2). The figure is dominated by vertical and right-to-left lines. There are 5 returns to previously expressed propositions. Moreover, one proposition is repeated 10 times, including 4 returns. This proposition ("car broken") is clearly what the narrative

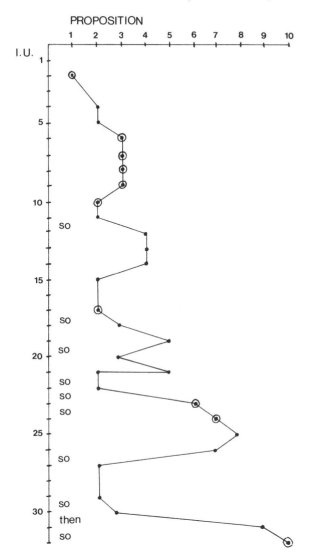

Figure 1.1. Structure of Episode 1.1.

is about, and it is expressed in part very early at IUs 4 and 5. (Earlier IUs, while within the same productive episode of connected talk, do not relate to the main theme.) The rest of what Emily wants to say on the topic is apparently focused around this one proposition, so she keeps returning to it, adding only that Mommy and Daddy had to use another car and "fix" the car. Finally, with IU 23 she moves on to new territory: "Daddy went to the meeting, Emmy put the (circles), Daddy stop it." These propositions all appear to be connected (perhaps in her view causally) to the broken car, which is returned to in IU 27. Finally, she asserts that another car (the green car) is broken, and ends firmly with "so my go to nap."

It is impossible to know what actually happened in this incident or what relation any of Emily's statements have to the objective "true" situation or to her memory of the situation (insofar as this can be considered independently of the verbal recount). Regardless of whether the event represented in her talk reflects a real happening or some sort of fantasy, we can consider whether it is expressed coherently. What are of interest are the possibilities for narrative development that this structure suggests.

First, there is a kind of coherence in the first 22 IUs in that they are all on a single topic, the broken car, and propositions about that situation are set forth, repeated, and elaborated. Indeed, this whole section up through 22 can be considered as setting up the background situation against which the foreground narrative can be expounded. In the last third of the narrative new information is added, and even though the word presented here as "circles" is not readily interpreted, the story line has a certain clarity, is connected to the main topic by a return at 27, and is given a coda at the end, indicating the end of that particular story. All in all, Emily seems to have acquired some of the rudiments of storytelling at this point—a theme statement, setting statements, use of repetition, an ending—even though her narrative has more of a circular than a linear structure. Still, there is very little actual content expressed in this episode; it seems to be a rather impoverished narrative (Peterson and McCabe 1983). As for the central question of narrative sequencing, the episode gives us little evidence because it includes so few actions to be linked.[12]

From the beginning Emily's narratives were sprinkled with connectives such as *so, then, and, when, and then, but* (all these by 23 months), and later *though, just, see, where*. But these do not at first seem to mark actual event sequences. In this first monologue there is an average of one connective (all but one of these is *so*) for every three IUs. One might expect to find that these are placed so as to move the narrative forward, but 4 of the 11 introduce either returns or standstills. They do seem to be placed in such a way as to connect IUs within an intermediate string, however. With one exception, one-unit strings (of which there are 6) are not introduced with *so*. This turns out to be a general finding: in the later narratives standstills are virtually absent, but when they do occur they are not introduced by connectives. Thus it appears that Emily has some intuitive sense of what connectives (or at least *so*) are useful for: connecting interrelated propositions. However, she has not yet acquired the semantics of *so*, nor has she constructed a contrastive system of connectives. I will return to these developments later.

Consider another example classified as memory from the same age period (21;13), Episode 1.10 (see Appendix), graphed in Figure 1.2. In this episode Emily is apparently concerned with happenings associated with Daddy doing the washing in the basement. There is a larger ratio of propositions to IUs in this passage (50/28 = 1.79) and the IU/closure rate (length of string) is 2.9, equivalent to Chafe's adult length (and similar to the previous example). This narrative also seems to open with a thematic statement: "That Daddy brings down basement washing," a proposition that is repeated with minor variations 4 times over the first 12 IUs, forming the somewhat static pattern shown on the graph. Thereafter, in contrast to the first episode, the narrative progresses through an additional 23 propositions with few returns, all but one of the returns within three propositions, and with no repetition of the original theme statement. The repetition ratio (7/50 = .14) is very similar to that of the first example (5/32 = .16), but the fact that the returns are for the most part very short in the second case gives this ratio a different interpretation. A better comparison might be the "progression ratio," the proportion of advancing IUs per episode, which is .34 for the first episode and .54 for the second. Thus this narrative appears to have a very different—and apparently more mature—structure from the earlier one: more linear than circular, as depicted in the graph.

As in the first example, there are many lexical connectives in this episode—19 for 50 IUs—including an instance of *before* and one of *then*, thus also contributing to the sense that this passage expresses a sequential temporal progression. However, these observations may be misleading. If we look closely at the content of the propositions conjoined, this sense of sequence and coherence is lost. The new propositions that follow on the "Daddy washing" theme include references to changing the baby, going to sleep, Daddy making pretty, coming home, seeing truck, and other less interpretable statements. Indeed, many of these, although sprinkled throughout with *and* and *so,* and despite their appearance in a lengthy uninterrupted monologue, ap-

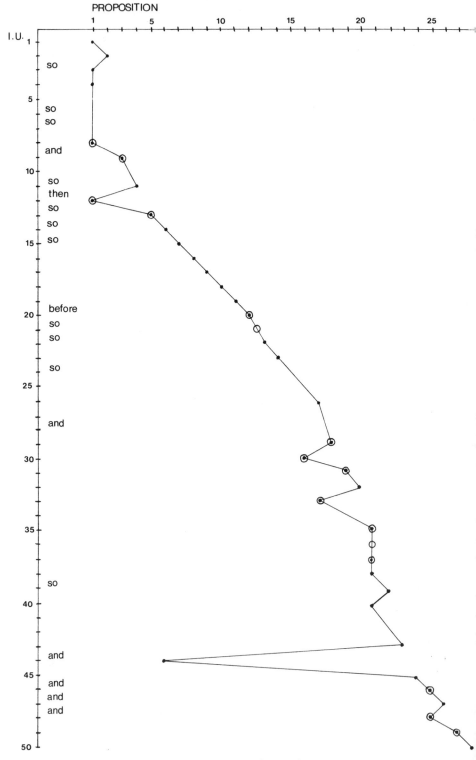

Figure 1.2. Structure of Episode 1.10.

pear to be unconnected fragments. A vague theme that occurs throughout is Daddy's activities, but whether these are sequentially ordered in Emily's representation seems doubtful, and they are interspersed with Emily's own activities, whether associated or not.

Thus reading the passage for semantic coherence gives a very different impression from the one given by the comparison of its structural characteristics. Nonetheless, we should not lose sight of the fact that this monologue does display many characteristics of the sequentially organized narratives of adults. The patterning in terms of IUs combined into intermediate structural units defined by clause-final closure, the use of lexical connectives to join statements, the introductory topic statement, and even a final commentary ("that okay") indicate that even though Emily has failed to produce a coherent temporally organized narrative, she has acquired many of the structural units and linguistic devices that will eventually enable her to construct such a narrative around a coherently understood event. Putting together the achievements of these first two examples, we may speculate that in the first she has the semantics of the narrative under fair control, with less competence at providing progressive structure, while in the latter she has better control over the structure but little control over the content.

A different pattern is seen in the narrative of Episode 1.11 (see Appendix), graphed in Figure 1.3. In this memory excerpt from 23 months Emily recalls a happening from earlier in the day (but referred to as "yesterday"). The same event is recounted 5 times with variations, accounting for the high regression ratio (11 returns out of 39 IUs = .28). Unlike the previous examples, however, this structure shows little stasis. The progression ratio (22/39 = .56) is as high as in the previous example in spite of the fact that the IU/proposition ratio is also high: 2.16. Some of the returns do not reflect actual regressions in the reporting of the event, but are rather the result of adding new propositions to the previous account (for example, "and in Tanta house" at IU 17) at an appropriately early point in the event being narrated. Again, as in the first two narratives, the mean length of strings is 3, equivalent to the adult value reported by Chafe. If we considered each attempt at a recount as a single short narrative, then, this episode would appear to be an advance over the previous ones in that it combines semantic coherence with progressive structure.

There are some additional noteworthy features about this narrative. As in the previous episodes, many connectives are used through-

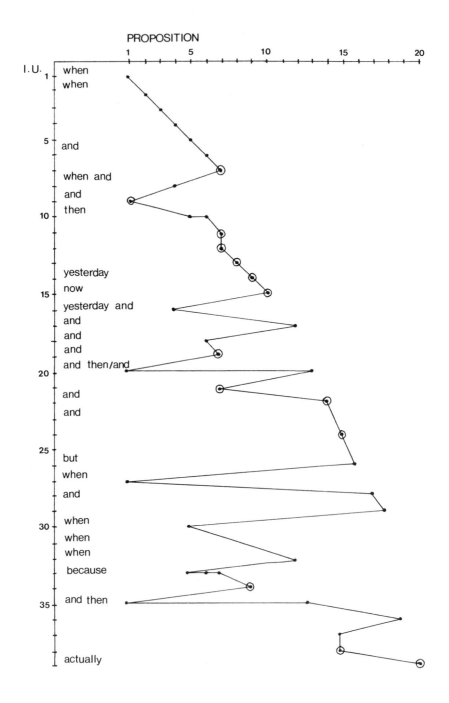

Figure 1.3. Structure of Episode 1.11.

out, including *when, then, and then, because, yesterday, now,* and *actually,* each used at an appropriate point in the narrative (with the noted exception that *yesterday* refers to an earlier point in the same day). Although the placement of the connectives in the graphs appears to be haphazard with respect to the progression of the narrative, reading the episode for sense indicates that with few exceptions *when* and *and then* are used to indicate sequential temporal relations. The use of *because* ("because time go home") and *actually* ("actually actually Mommy did it"—true according to Emily's mother) is especially notable. It would be rash to claim that Emily has the concepts of causality and truth value and their linguistic expressions under control at this point, but clearly something is guiding their use at appropriate points and not at inappropriate ones. This accurate use may be compared to the inaccurate timing of *yesterday,* or to the indiscriminate use of *so* in the first example.

The fact that *so* is not one of the connectives used in this episode is not coincidental. It reflects a typical pattern in the acquisition of these terms. In the early transcripts *so* is used frequently, as we saw in Figure 1.2, reaching a high point in an episode from 21;13 containing 20 instances of *so.* But after that age *so* drops out of the monologues almost entirely, with only 3 scattered uses over the next three months, the last at 22;31. *So* appears again as one among many connectives at 24;8 and continues thereafter to be used sparingly in contexts that suggest causality or contingency. This term was apparently first learned with some notion of its appropriate syntactic context (to introduce a clause) and was then used indiscriminately and with great frequency in such contexts for a time. It then dropped from usage entirely for a period of months before reappearing with apparent semantic content that contrasted with other connectives used in similar syntactic contexts. This developmental pattern of use is indicative of the complex relation between syntax, semantics, and discourse pragmatics that drives the development of the child's linguistic system. (These relations are discussed revealingly in Chapter 5.)

The circularity exhibited in Figure 1.3 may be interpreted in terms of Emily's attempt to express a coherent memory, including the complex relations of simultaneity and sequentiality, and to get it right. This represents a considerable advance over the previous examples. It contrasts both with the coherent topic but static structure of the first narrative and with the mechanically advanced but semantically incoherent second narrative. Here Emily visibly struggles to integrate con-

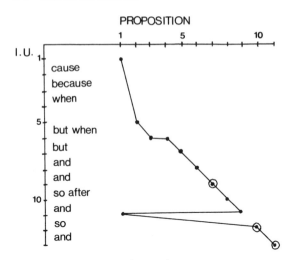

Figure 1.4. Structure of Episode 1.12.

tent and structure and in the end seems to succeed. It is at this point—
at about 23 months—that she seems to achieve an integration of the
form and content of the sequentially organized narrative. From this
point she can begin to master the many linguistic devices that will
enable her to formulate her narratives in a way that more adequately
expresses her intentions.

Consider one more example of a memory narrative, this one from
almost a year later at 33 months, Episode 1.12 (see Appendix),
graphed in Figure 1.4. Here the progression is almost perfect, except
for the false starts over the first 4 IUs. The one return is not an interruption of the narrative flow, but rather comes about because Emily
begins the narrative with a statement of its outcome ("we bought a
baby"), which could be considered a topic statement or title (see
Brown and Yule 1983).

There are only 2 intermediate closures in this brief (13 IUs) narrative, yielding a relatively high string length (4.33). Still, it cannot be
characterized as immature in Chafe's sense, since it consists neither of
single closed IUs nor of one long uninterrupted string. Despite the
false starts at the beginning, the narrative is very efficient with an IU/
proposition ratio of 1.18. Eight IUs begin with a connective, and except for the use of *but* in preference to *and*, which is difficult to explain, these are used conventionally. Note especially "so after we were
finished with the store" which places the central event in appropriate

temporal reference to the background event. Here Emily displays her ability to manipulate speech time, reference time, and event time in relation to one another, a capability that is generally placed at a much later age (see Chapters 5 and 8 for further discussion).

This excerpt then represents Emily's most successful construction of a memory narrative. Possibly because it is so brief and because it is based on a clear recent episode, it is very clearly structured. At the same time, it includes complex temporal and causal relations conventionally expressed. The sequential structure of event narratives is well mastered by 33 months and reflects a considerable advance over the structures of the previous year.

Anticipation Episodes

Figure 1.5 shows a graph of the "Childworld" monologue (Episode 1.2) from the same time period as the "getting up" episode (1.11) at 23 months. Unlike the memory episode, this narrative progresses

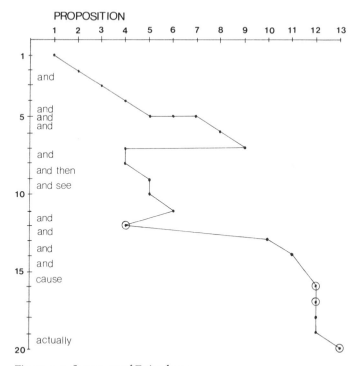

Figure 1.5. Structure of Episode 1.2.

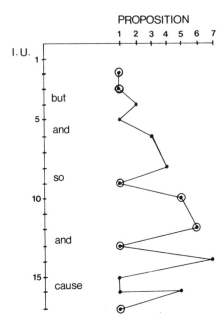

Figure 1.6. Structure of Episode 1.4.

quite directly over 13 propositions, with only 2 returns (regression ratio = .10; progression ratio = .70; IU/proposition ratio = 1.54). As discussed earlier, the general theme is buying things at Childworld, but the focus changes midway from diapers and intercom to broken infant seat, and this change is reflected in the two parts visible on the graph. In other respects, the structure is similar to contemporaneous memory episodes, with 13 out of 20 IUs connected with conjunctions, including *cause* and *actually*, again expressing causality and truth validity in what appear to be appropriate relations.

A different picture is shown in Figure 1.6, from 24 months, in which Emily talks about her coming trip to the doctor (Episode 1.4). Here the structure is quite circular, with 5 returns out of 17 (regression ratio = .29; progression ratio = only .41; IU/proposition ratio = 2.43). There are few connectives in this narrative (5, or fewer than one in three), and only two of them are used progressively. In addition, *maybe* is used 4 times to introduce a proposition, reflecting the problematic character of this narrative. Although, as I indicated earlier, this narrative is based on information gained from pre-bed talk with her parents, Emily's speculations about what might happen make it a less than straightforward account of what will take place.

Figure 1.7 graphs one of the most progressive and efficient narra-

PROPOSITION

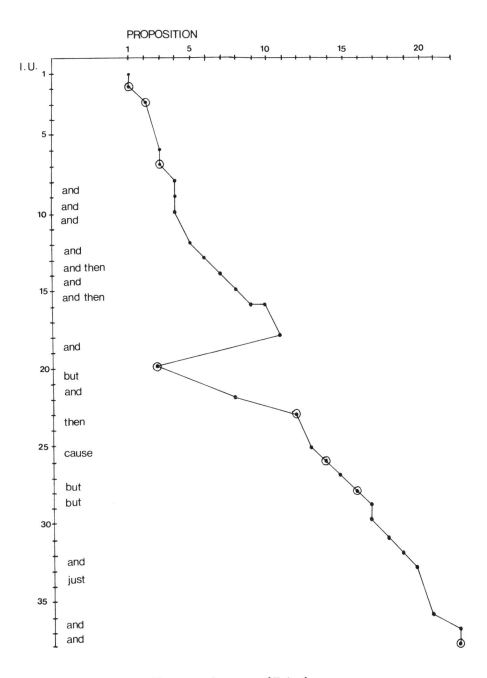

Figure 1.7. Structure of Episode 1.5.

tives, Episode 1.5, discussed earlier in terms of Emily's speculation (at age 28;0) on the coming trip to the beach. Here the regression ratio is only 1/38 or .03 and the progression ratio is 22/38 or .58. The IU/proposition ratio is 1.7 and the string length is 4.75. Connectives are used liberally—20 of them—with one use of *cause* to express causality. All of these measures indicate a coherent cohesive account using forms and constructions that adults might use to express similar thoughts. Like Episode 1.2 this episode follows a parental account repeated a number of times, which provided the basic information upon which Emily's elaboration and speculation is based. Nonetheless, Emily introduces many additional points from her own inferences, as she did in Episode 1.4. But by 28 months she seems to be able to integrate them into the story her father has told her without the hesitations and repetitiousness of the previous example.

Finally, consider again Episode 1.9, concerned with the Friday routine at 32 months, graphed in Figure 1.8. Although (as in Episode 1.11) this event is recounted more than once, there are only 5 returns (regression ratio = .08; progression ratio = .51; IU/proposition ratio = 1.9), indicating an efficient, progressive narrative. The string length here is quite long: 9.0 with a maximum of 21. This example suggests that when Emily has a good representation of what she wants to say she extends her string of unclosed IUs considerably.[13]

Two out of every three IUs (40/63) in this narrative are introduced by a connective, but these are not used with much discrimination, consisting almost entirely of *and, and then,* and *then.* The one *because* may represent a false start ("Because sometimes I go to nursery school cause its a nursery school day"), and the two "buts" are not clearly motivated. However, as in the contemporaneous memory narrative (Figure 1.4) there are indications of a sophisticated understanding of temporal relations, with reference time ("when we get there") established separately from event time and speech time (see Chapter 8). Like the expression of causality and truth validity, the manipulation of temporal relationships is required in the construction of a complex sequentially organized narrative. But such manipulation is unlikely to be noted in ordinary dyadic discourse between adult and child, when the emphasis is on talk about the here and now. Thus the early acquisition of such ordering devices in children's interactive speech may be undocumented only because the occasions for their use are infrequent in most situations in which child language is recorded (see French and Nelson 1985 for data and discussion of this point).

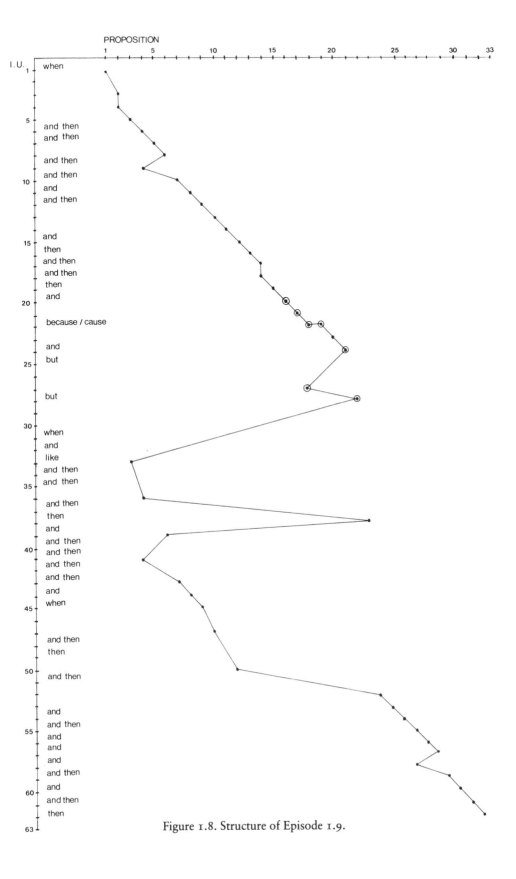

Figure 1.8. Structure of Episode 1.9.

Conclusion

Developmental Differences

In the first section of this chapter I discussed the content of the monologues in terms of the changing emphasis, over the course of the fifteen months of taping, on themes of anticipation, memory, and general event knowledge. All themes appeared at all points, but over time the emphasis shifted from one to another and back again, as Emily's life circumstances changed and she appeared to need or want to talk about what had happened, what might happen, or what should happen. In particular, there was a notable shift first to memory talk and then to anticipatory and general knowledge talk after her entry into nursery school.

There were also discernible changes over time in the organization of her monologues. As revealed in the analyses in the second half of this chapter, the basic units of her monologues lengthened, as did the length of the intermediate organizing units (represented by sentence-final intonation), although there was more variability in this index over time. There also appeared to be a general trend toward a more efficient, more linear, less circular (repetitious) narrative, with fewer IUs used to express a single proposition.

Quite early in the course of our observation (at 2·3 months) Emily appeared to integrate the ability to focus on a central topic and the relation of information about that topic with the ability to construct a cohesive and progressive organization, using basic narrative techniques such as topic sentences, sequencers, and summaries. Most notable of the factors considered here (others will be discussed in later chapters) was the increasingly conventional and contrastive use of connectives; at the outset they were used indiscriminately, but at the end of the study they were deployed with considerable finesse to express temporality, causality, truth value, contingency, and uncertainty. By the end of the study Emily was also able to express relative time, and to differentiate and coordinate reference time, event time, and speech time. Thus over the course of the study Emily gained control of numerous discourse devices that enabled her to produce a coherent, sequentially organized narrative on one of her chosen topics.

Thematic Differences

The primary differences identified between memory and anticipation episodes were in length of MLIU and mean length of strings. An initial overview revealed no consistent difference between the two types in the use of lexical connectives, adverbials, or verb forms, and a look at structural patterns showed variations over time but no variations consistently associated with thematic differences. For example, the progression and regression ratios do not vary consistently with theme type. What, then, explains the observed difference in overall string length?

The individual narratives strongly suggest that the longer MLIUs and strings appear in anticipatory narratives that are firmly based on recent parental discussions, as for example the Childworld and beach episodes (Episodes 1.2 and 1.5), or on well-established and therefore well-represented routines, as in the Friday episode (Episode 1.9). In contrast, memories that are not clearly represented or well understood, and anticipatory episodes reflecting Emily's independent speculations or attempts to achieve a coherent account, tend to circle around specific issues, returning again and again to a central proposition and reformulating it. This is seen particularly in the doctor episode (Episode 1.6) and in the "Mormor get me" episode (Episode 1.3). This type of structure tends to disappear over time, however, as Emily becomes better able to represent events and to express them in a progressive narrative structure.[14]

This description depends upon the interpretation of the short strings (1 or 2 IUs) as representing static or problem points, and the longer strings as expressing well-represented schemas or ideas, which can be maintained in consciousness as single mid-size chunks while the individual component ideas are expressed in intonation units (Chafe 1980). This conceptualization fits Chafe's hypothesis quite well even though the data do not reflect either of his proposed developmental patterns. Although the present analysis is only suggestive on this point, it does provide a method of analysis that might be applied to other narrative data collected from young children.

The interpretation of linearity in the episodes analyzed seems reasonably straightforward after the early months when the integration of form and content is achieved. When the narrative moves forward progressively in linear fashion, the teller seems to have good control over the event that is being recounted.[15] When the narrative circles around, continuously returning to an earlier point, it appears to indicate one of three things: Either the underlying episode is not coherently understood, so that linear ordering is not possible. Or the circularity indicates a recurrent attempt at coherent organization, an attempt to transform an underlying episodic representation into a well-formed verbal account, which meets with difficulty along the way. Or, finally, the circularity may indicate a verbal attempt at solving a puzzle, as for example, what will happen at the doctor's. If there is no underlying episodic representation, but only a number of possibilities generated by prior experience, an anticipatory account may involve a series of different solutions, returning continually to a beginning point to construct the different accounts. Circularity can be seen then in terms of progress toward the development of coherent, reliable event structures and not necessarily in terms of incoherent representations.

It is worth dwelling on the finding that anticipatory episodes based on parental accounts (even though Emily does not repeat them exactly) reveal a better-organized, progressive structure consisting of longer IUs and strings. This suggests that the verbal representations of her parents can be directly used by Emily in her own representations, and that these provide fewer problems for verbal organization than does her own direct experience. When a child attempts to formulate a narrative based on her own direct experience, she must struggle to put things in order and to express the relationships among events in the way they happened. We saw this particularly in Episode 1.11, in which Emily goes over the same memory five times with variations. The transformation from nonverbal to verbal representation is obviously not an easy one. But when she has a parental account to build on, it is apparently easier to insert new information—even nonverbal information such as where the car seats are—into the verbal account. The parent's verbal account has provided the framework to which further material can be attached.

However, it must also be noted that the parental account, although easily repeated, may not be as easily understood. Recall Emily's difficulty in integrating her father's account of going to Childworld to buy an intercom (Episode 1.2) into her own knowledge system. It is apparent that she becomes better over time at integrating information mediated through others' verbal representations, but it would be a mistake to believe that because she can repeat an account and use it as a framework for her own representation she always understands it in the way the adult intended.

Implications

Over time, the organization of Emily's narrative monologues moves in the direction of adult models. There is no external push in this direction—Emily can talk to herself in any way that she pleases. But her monologic forms not only become better organized over time but also reveal more elaborate and advanced grammatical constructions than do her dialogic contributions. The central mystery is why this is so: not only why she talks to herself, but why she talks the way she does, developing increasingly complex and coherent forms.

I propose that Emily talks as she does because she is attempting to construct a representation of events in language. Implicit in the discussion thus far has been the assumption that she has a nonlinguistic representation of her own direct experience, and that through her monologues she translates that experience, as it were, into verbal—specifically, sequential narrative—form. Parental talk impinges on the prelinguistic representation, providing a verbal framework which Emily can put to her own use in elaborating her event representations, which constitute her mental model of the real world. The result of the integration of parental input and child representation in verbal form is the monologic organization I have explored in this chapter.

I further propose that Emily talks about events in different ways at different ages because different narrative forms and linguistic devices enable her to represent the relations within events more accurately, and that accurate representations are important to her for her growing understanding of how the world is and should be, this understanding in turn enabling her to gain some control over her own activities and to take part competently in interactions with others. More than this, she uses the constructed representations to derive other sorts of knowledge and beliefs—rules for how things should be done, inferences as to how things will be. What I have sketched here, then, is a picture of a child building a mental model of the world that represents reality as she understands it on the basis of her own direct experience of events and the verbally presented representations of her parents. As we have seen, this model of the world is a continuously evolving knowledge system with remarkable power.

Appendix

EPISODE I.I (21;7)

1. What do my,
2. Emmy get (tooky)
3. the the booty,

    4. the broke,
    5. Car broke,
    6. the . . . Emmy can't go in the car.
    7. Go in green car.
    8. No.
    9. Emmy go in the car.
    10. Broken. Broken.
    11. Their car broken,
    12. so Mommy Daddy go in their their car,
    13. Emmy Daddy go in the car,
    14. Emmy Daddy Mommy go in the car,
    15. broke,
    16. Da . . da, the car . . .
    17. their, their, car broken.
    18. So go in the green car,
    19. fix the car broken,
    20. so go in the green car . . .
    21. car fix their car broke,
    22. so their car broke . . .
    23. so my daddy went in the meeting in c- in the, in the car.
    24. So Emmy put the (circles) in the, (w-) in the way.
    25. Daddy stop it, in the (circles) over there . . .
    26. Emmy put over there,
    27. so car broke,
    28. Car B[last name],
    29. car broken,
    30. So have go in the green car,
    31. the, then, green car broken,
    32. so my go to nap.

EPISODE 1.2 (23;15)

    1. I member the . . .
    2. I went to sleep . . .
    3. and Daddy said . . .
    4. buy diapers for Stephen and Emmy . . .
    5. and buy something for Stephen plug in and say ahhh . . .
    6. and put the in . . .
    7. on Saturday go Childworld buy diaper for Emmy . . .
    8. and diaper for the baby . . .
    9. and then buy something for the . . .
    10. and . . . see . . . for . . . that . . . baby . . .
    11. plug in . . .

12. and get diapers for *any*body.
13. and buy more that that day at Childworld . . .
14. and buy croutes . . .
15. and maybe Childworld . . .
16. cause the one that broken at Tanta's.
17. The one that's broken.
18. The one that's broken here,
19. the . . . the infant seat . . .
20. Dada actually at home.

EPISODE 1.3 (24;1)

1. Maybe the tow truck come back,
2. and then tow truck nother car (?) . .
3. maybe my tand by the tow truck with the (ho-) . .
4. maybe tow, the tow, tow, (woo-) h-,
5. go back and then yellow car come (back).
6. And then leave the blue car.
7. The it's broken.
8. Now the (big) tow-tow truck back with the blue car . . .
9. and then my Tanta get Mormor,
10. and, and maybe Tanta saw the tow truck,
11. and Mormor.
12. Maybe this broken my . . .
13. and then we go back to Tanta.
14. And then we go back Tan- . .
15. maybe Daddy come back here . .
16. we go back my . .
17. and then . . .
18. the tow truck come back and tow nother car . . .
19. and then come back tow different kind . . car
20. But then we,
21. this go to my house,
22. and we come back.
23. And then . . different time . . .
24. somebody come and get . .
25. the little.
26. No one with, keep the (whether anyone) like the (with) and put (with)
27. and come in the house . .
28. and then the tow truck come back . . .
29. for little car . . .
30. but then . . .

EPISODE 1.4 (24;8)

1. Maybe the doctor,
2. took my jamas [very soft] I don't know.
3. Maybe, maybe we take my jamas off.
4. But, I leave my diaper,
5. take my jamas off,
6. and leave them off,
7. at the doc-,
8. my have get my check up,
9. so we take my jamas off.
10. My don't know this looking all better.
11. (??) doctor, doc,
12. the boys take back home.
13. The, and we maybe take my jamas off.
14. I don't know what we do with my . . .
15. maybe the doctor take my jamas,
16. my jamas off cause my maybe get check up,
17. have to to take my jamas.

EPISODE 1.5 (28;0)

1. We are gonna . . .
2. at the ocean.
3. Ocean is a little far away.
4. baw, baw buh [etc.]
5. far away . . .
6. I think it's . . .
7. couple blocks . . away.
8. Maybe it's down, downtown,
9. and across the ocean,
10. and down the river,
11. and maybe it's in,
12. the hot dogs will be in a fridge,
13. and the fridge (would) be in the water over by a shore,
14. and then we could go in,
15. and get a hot dog and bring it out to the river,
16. and then sharks go in the river and bite me,
17. in the ocean,
18. we go into the ocean,
19. and ocean be over by . . .
20. I think a couple of blocks away.

21. But we could be,
22. and we could find any hot dogs,
23. um the hot dogs gonna be for the for the beach.
24. Then the bridge is gonna,
25. we'll have to go in the green car,
26. cause that's where the car seats are.
27. Um, I can be in the red car, but,
28. see, I be in the green car.
29. But you know who's going to be in the green car . . .
30. both children . . .
31. I'm going to be in the green car in my car seat,
32. he's gonna be . . .
33. and nobody's gonna be,
34. just . . . you know,
35. these people,
36. we don't know,
37. and too far away from the beach,
38. and two things.

EPISODE 1.6 (24;4)

1. I can't go down the basement with jamas on.
2. I sleep with jamas.
3. Okay sleep with jamas.
4. In the night time my only put big girl pants on.
5. But in the morning we put jamas on.
6. But, and the morning gets up . . of the room.
7. But, afternoon my wake up and play.
8. Play with Mommy, Daddy . .

EPISODE 1.7 (28;0)

1. Yellow buses.
2. 1 2 3 4 days we have yellow buses,
3. but not 5 4 5 4 5 have blue buses.
4. I like . .
5. these days we're going to have the yellow buses,
6. and the,
7. right now, it's Thursday,
8. and Friday,
9. and S-, S- . . .
10. and Sunday,
11. so it's, um . . . a yellow bus . . . day.

12. And on Friday and Sunday it's blue day,
13. so I going on yellow and a blue.
14. One day going on a yellow bus and one day going on a blue bus.
15. When Mormor comes,
16. one day we'll maybe yellow bus that day,
17. and just, n- now . . .
18. once I am going on, one,
19. again,
20. I know,
21. I'm going on a yellow bus,
22. this day,
23. but on a weekends,
24. when we have the waffle day,
25. and we,
26. it's not . . .
27. what the . . .
28. it's a blue, yellow bus day.
29. And we're gonna walk downstairs as . . .
30. I finished.
31. On blue bus days we just get blue.
32. I can see yellow and I can see . . . black.

EPISODE 1.8 (28;18)

1. If ever we go to the airport we have to get some luggage.
2. If have to go to the airport,
3. hafta take something for the airport,
4. to the airport or you can't go.
5. Need your own special bus . . .
6. (carry me)
7. and they z-o-o-m, o-o-m.
8. Zoom!
9. Zoom!
10. Zoom!
11. Zoom!

EPISODE 1.9 (32;0)

1. Tomorrow, when we wake up from bed,
2. first me and Daddy and Mommy,
3. you, eat breakfast . .
4. eat breakfast,
5. like we *usually* do,

6. and then we're going to p-l-a-y,
7. and then soon as Daddy comes,
8. Carl's going to come over,
9. and then we're going to play a little while,
10. and then Carl and Emily are both going down the car with somebody,
11. and we're going to ride to nursery school,
12. and then we when we get there,
13. we're all going to get out of the car,
14. go in to nursery school,
15. and Daddy's going to give us kisses,
16. then go,
17. and then say,
18. and then we will say goodbye,
19. then he's going to work,
20. and we're going to play at nursery school.
21. Won't that be funny?
22. Because sometimes I go to nursery school cause it's a nursery school day.
23. Sometimes I stay with Tanta all week,
24. and sometimes we play mom and dad.
25. But usually,
26. sometimes I um,
27. oh go to nursery school.
28. But today I'm going to nursery school in the morning.
29. In the morning,
30. Daddy in the,
31. when,
32. and *usual*,
33. we're going to eat breakfast like we usually do,
34. and then we're going to . . .
35. and *then* we're going to . . .
36. *play,*
37. and then we're,
38. then the doorbell's going to ring,
39. and here comes Carl in here,
40. and then Carl,
41. and then we are all going to play,
42. and then wha-,
43. and then go in the car with somebody,
44. and drive to nursery,
45. when we get to nursery school,
46. we're to,

47. *all* going to get out of the car . . .
48. and then we're going to ummm . . .
49. I think then we're going to . . .
50. they're going to give us kisses . . .
51. and t-h-e-n,
52. she's going to go to work,
53. with somebody with her,
54. and meet her new students,
55. and then she's going to pick us up,
56. and work,
57. and Daddy's going to bring us,
58. and Mommy's going to pick us up,
59. a-n-d then she's going home,
60. and we're going to go to nap,
61. and t-h-e-n when you awake,
62. then we are going to-o-o . . . school. .
63. uh, uh [monologue tapers off]

EPISODE I.10 (21;13)

1. That Daddy brings down basement washing,
2. I can hold Emmy,
3. so, Daddy brings down the,
4. the washing on the basement,
5. washing,
6. so my can,
7. so why, the, the, the,
8. na- daddy brings washing.
9. And not down, um, um, um. .
10. Emmy, Emmy, Emmy da- and the (?) in the (?).
11. So, so Emmy change right there, baby,
12. then my daddy bring them that time.
13. So, naptime, go to sleep. (wah-ten).
14. So my came,
15. so why my daddy will take . . .
16. I can get my daddy,
17. my daddy (make me pretty),
18. Emmy daddy came home,
19. see Emmy, daddy, Emmy daddy don't go in wa-,
20. naptime before Emmy came home, Emmy.
21. So my daddy (???).
22. So, Emmy (miss cellar),
23. not this baby,

24. so my daddy went on a big free washing,
25. I can wake the Emmy,
26. my daddy coming by pretty soon,
27. my baby, and gonna . . .
28. and Emmy daddy came right . . .
29. not go in wa- . . mmm y-e-t.
30. I came waking Emmy.
31. I don't why my daddy came.
32. I want to get a minute . . .
33. Um . . My, my daddy coming.
34. (Walk) . . .
35. get my.
36. Emily.
37. Get me up.
38. Up . . .
39. so-o . . . Emmy went down the, down cellar,
40. oh my get me, oh my,
41. Mommy and Daddy just di-,
42. Emmy di-,
43. Mommy, my coming,
44. and my came . . .
45. I came see (Cahty),
46. and see truck.
47. And Daddy came see truck,
48. and my came see truck.
49. That . . . that . . . okay.
50. K-a-y, my came back . . .

EPISODE 1.11 (23;8)

1. When Mormor get me,
2. when Mormor make pretty,
3. Mommy had a help,
4. my sleep,
5. Mommy came,
6. and Mommy get,
7. get up, time go home.
8. When my slep and,
9. and, Mormor came.
10. Then Mommy coming then get up,
11. time to go ho-o-ome.
12. Time to go home.
13. Drink p-water [Perrier].

14. Yesterday did that.
15. Now Emmy sleeping in regular bed.
16. Yesterday my slept, and say um,
17. and in Tanta house,
18. And Mommy woke my up,
19. And go, time to go home.
20. And then Mormor came and Mormor said . . .
21. time t' go home.
22. And Daddy bring p-water.
23. And yesterday, Mommy and Mormor and . . .
24. Daddy bring my in my regular bed. [long pause]
25. I can (?) Mommy,
26. but my (in) Daddy and Mommy's . . .
27. when Mormor came in,
28. and Mommy (got) it,
29. make my bed . . .
30. when, when Mommy came in,
31. when my bed,
32. when, when I sleeping Tanta house . . .
33. Mommy came wake my up because to go home,
34. drink p-water.
35. And then Mormor [speaks quickly] came and Mormor said
36. time to drink p-water . . . [long pause]
37. Daddy, Mommy, Daddy put my into bed,
38. in my regular bed.
39. Actually, actually Mommy did it.

EPISODE 1.12 (33;9)

1. We *bought* a baby,
2. . . . cause,
3. . . . the, well because,
4. when she, well,
5. we *thought* it was for Christmas,
6. but *when* we went to the s-s-store we didn't have our jacket on,
7. but I saw some dolly,
8. and I *yelled* at my mother and said
9. I want one of those dolly.
10. So *after* we were finished with the store,
11. we went over to the dolly and she *bought* me one.
12. So I have one.
13. And I need a (broke).

Chapter 2

Monologue as Narrative Recreation of the World

Jerome Bruner and Joan Lucariello

We shall be examining Emily's monologues with one particular object in mind, though we shall be forced to take detours along the way. Our object is to explore how and with what possible purpose Emily moves in her monologues from simple expository accounts of particular events to more embellished narrative accounts of the things that happen in her world. We shall, accordingly, examine narrative features of her language growth over the period in which she was recorded, while concurrently speculating about the functions served by her crib soliloquies. If we succeed at all in relating her language to our speculations about the functions of her monologues, we hope our efforts will have the effect of establishing a new working hypothesis about the relations among language, thought, affect, and action during early development.[1]

Our first question is inevitable. Why, indeed, might *any* of us at *any* age bother to speak to ourselves at all?

At least two different types of hypotheses have been proposed in the last half-century to account for this Hamlet-like phenomenon. The first is typified by Dewey's (1958) discussion of language as a vehicle (if not *the* vehicle) by which we bring order into our thoughts about things. The brunt of Dewey's argument was that language is an instrument for segmenting, ordering, predicating about, categorizing, and so on, that, when applied to experience, yields increased cognitive coherence and power in the organization of that experience. A first version of this view is attributable to Peirce (1960), whose discussion of the role of symbolic interpretants in the organization of knowledge was the foundation of virtually all later views. A "strong" form of this view—introduced by von Humboldt (1885) and later developed by Whorf (1956)—holds that language is *constitutive* of thought if not of experience itself. That is to say, the very form of human thought is imposed upon it by the nature of language. On this view, and quite counterintuitively, we should expect a fair amount of soliloquy to occur in the course of everyday thinking, for we are often in need of the kind of ordering that language can provide. The absence of such soliloquy in adults is attributed to the gradual "internalization" of speech as we grow older: language eventually becomes inherent in or inextricable from thought. Children must initially sort out their worlds by outer speech, in dialogue with others. Internalization is achieved only by dint of long practice. Soliloquy is conceived of, in this view, as a stage or process midway between the regulation of thought by overt speech and its regulation in the adult by inner speech.

The most explicit advocate of this view was Vygotsky (1962). His reasoning was that, initially, thought and speech are independent of each other, two separate "streams," in his metaphor. Mental growth consists in "fusing" speech and thought so that eventually thinking itself becomes inextricable from our lexicon, from our grammar, and even from the history of our language. Language for Vygostky is *constitutive* of thought in its fully developed human form, in spite of the fact that thought begins as an autonomous activity. By appropriating the instrument of language to the uses of thought in this progression, the child links herself to the culture's storehouse of knowledge and procedures. By using language—whether in dialogue, monologue, or inner speech—the child is able to move beyond her socially unaided powers of thought into a world where, as it were, she can first borrow the skills of the language by having an adult for a partner in dialogue, and then finally appropriate them through internalization.

In the main, this view has emphasized the cognitive side of development, in the sense that it has been instantiated by such phenomena as the organization of perception, of memory, and of thought. Vygotsky had little to say about the incorporation of affect into mental life generally, or about the integration of affect, cognition, and action and how these are brought into concert by the use of language.[2] Recall that Vygotsky's most celebrated examples on the subject of language and thought were drawn either from mathematics or from Marxist political theory, both distinctly nonaffective or at least impersonal domains.

A second, alternative hypothesis has been implicit in the more recent writings of scholars outside main-line academic psychology. This hypothesis speaks more directly to the role of narrative in the regulation of thought. It can be derived from work in anthropology (for example, Turner 1975; Hallowell 1960), in "revisionist" psychoanalytic theory (Spence 1982; Schafer 1981; Stern 1985), and in literary theory (Burke 1945). This is not the place for a review of that work, and the reader is referred to Bruner (1986) for a more detailed account. What we shall try to do here is to sketch briefly the elements of such a hypothesis with relevance to our immediate concern: the growth of narrative discourse and its uses in thought—narrative thought. The view we are setting forth is not meant to deny the cogency of Vygotsky's work, but to enrich and augment it by assigning a special status to narrative in the integration of affect, cognition, and action. Indeed, even Vygotsky (1987) urges that the distinctive character of human affect is that it is "central": connected to other higher mental activities rather than operating in a peripherally isolated way, as in the James-Lange theory.

The hypothesis we derive from this work rests on the propositions that early in life thought, action, and feeling are relatively undifferentiated, that one of the first "developmental tasks" is to bring some order into this tumult, and that language—particularly narrative discourse—is a prime means for doing so. Talking, on this view, is a way of imposing on experience some organized differentiation between what, in adult parlance, we refer to as action, cognition, and feeling. It is not by accident that early language use, given this early lack of differentiation, is often syncretic (Werner 1948), or is characterized by what Freud (1956) called the omnipotence of thought, in which the child believes that thinking or feeling something is tantamount to doing it, or that—as Piaget (1955) has taught us—the child has difficulty in "decentering," in distinguishing an inner perspective from an outer one. Grace deLaguna (1927) put the matter well six decades ago, commenting that in early child speech it was impossible to interpret what the child was saying without taking into account what the child was concurrently doing and feeling. One use of language, then, is to help the child develop through practice sufficiently decontextualized procedures so that speaking becomes differentiated from action and affect. The child gradually learns to use speech in a manner that makes it comprehensible independently of what is going on at the moment of speech. The developmental task of differentiation is never fully completed, as we know from Austin's (1962) discussion of performatives and from the work of sociolinguists (such as Silverstein 1985).

The means for the child's more reliably distinguishing what she does from what she feels from what she knows or experiences about the world is, we believe, inherent in the structure of narrative discourse. We shall turn to that matter shortly. But there is also a sense in which language use *in general* contributes to this end. For language, it seems, helps to "cool" or reduce some of the uncertainty and emotionality in the child's world just by its displaced mode of representing that world in memory and thought. By doing so, it removes that world from the arena of immediate commitment. In Ella Fitzgerald's immortal phrase, "talking about it ain't doing it." Some recent research suggests that even earliest language use may have such a "cooling function." Bloom (1987) and her colleagues have recently taught us that early speech and early language acquisition are most likely to occur under cool conditions: under circumstances that are neither very exigent nor very emotionally arousing. The world as represented or recoded in language is a world that, so to speak, has been cooled in the making, in the very process of translation into a symbolic form. Writers as various as Dollard and Miller (1950), Luria (1961), and Pavlov (1929) have all made the same point in different ways. For Pavlov, for example, the Second Signal System, the world turned into language, provided a basis for reflection and thereby freed humans from immediate emotional and overt response to stimuli. The relevance of "cooling" to Emmy's monologues and particularly to her most evolved narratives will be clearer presently.

The claim that narrative is the "natural" instrument for aiding us in differentiating action, affect, and cognition rests on a view of the inherent structure of narrative as a mode of discourse. It has been said that narrative is the appropriate folk description of human action. The claim is based on the fact that narrative is an elaboration and extension of the arguments of action that many linguists (such as Fillmore 1968) believe to be the semantic base of human grammar. Burke, in his classic *Grammar of Motives* (1945), notes that at a minimum, narrative requires an Actor, an Action, a Goal or intention, a Scene, and an Instrumentality. These provide the skeleton of Burke's "pentad." The "drama" of narrative emerges from an imbalance between elements in the pentad. Rather than the "drama" of narrative, we prefer to speak of the "trouble" that is always implicit or explicit in narrative. Actions do not reach goals, scenes and agents do not match, instruments and goals are out of kilter, and so on. The narrative is a vehicle for characterizing, exploring, preventing, brooding about, redressing, or recounting the consequences of "trouble." We shall have more to say about the "elaborations and extensions" that carry narrative beyond the arguments of action.

The Russian Formalists and particularly Propp (1968) add an important element to this minimal description of narrative. They argue that narratives as such have a top-down structure. That is to say, the constituents of a story are "functions" of the story structure as a whole. In their words a story is *about* something: it bespeaks a timeless gist or moral, what the Russians call its *fabula*—ambition thwarted by vanity, self-defeating greed, lost love. The constituents or "functions" of the story are the means whereby the fabula is worked out or realized as a sequentially organized tale. As Propp notes, there are many functionally substitutable alternative constituents by which this sequencing can be effected. A particular story may require a hero on a rescue mission, but many kinds of heroes will serve and many different missions will fill the bill. In this sense, narratives are in some sense abstract, or in Karl Marx's colorful phrase, they *ascend* to the particular as an instantiation of the general. They exhibit an "ordinariness" or a timelessness that makes their theme sufficiently universal as to be readily recognizable.

Contemporary theorists of narrative note one other feature of developed stories. Given that they deal with trouble or, at least, the unexpectable, they are normative. As Todorov (1977), Hayden White (1981), and Turner (1982) note, a developed narrative always contains implicitly or explicitly some element of normativeness or of appropriateness. We shall call this characteristic its *canonicality*. This is what is implied by the trouble that is the engine of narrative: the trouble is a violation of the legitimate, the expectable, the appropriate. And the outcome of the story depends upon seeing legitimacy either maintained, restored, or redefined.

Narrative, moreover, always involves a stance or perspective on the part of the narrator. In the narratives of classic myth and folklore, there was a convention of marking stance as if the narrator were virtually divine: omniscient, omnipresent, and directly in touch with the ontology of the story. The convention became so entrenched that it came, in time, to be the unmarked case in storytelling. In more recent narrative fiction, the narrator's stance has been more explicitly marked, and in modernist and postmodernist fiction or even in

Woody Allen films, in addition to the protagonists in the story having points of view or perspectives, the narrator does as well—if only the stance of epistemic uncertainty. It is generally agreed among modern theorists that no description of narrative is complete without reference to stance, that stories (to put it technically) are relativized with respect to the perspective of the narrator. This means that any developed narrative must have, as Greimas and Courtes (1976) put it, a double landscape: one landscape of the world of action depicted in the story, the other of the world of consciousness in the minds both of protagonists and narrator. It is this double landscape that lends perspective to story. The landscape of consciousness, of course, cannot be defined without reference to the intentions and to the reflections of the cast of characters.

One final point relates to the sequential ordering of the fabula in the form of a story or *sjuzet*. As narrative elaboration develops, it requires a richer or "thicker" variety of sequencing. All natural languages are rich in sequencing devices: tense and aspect marking, time deixis, anaphora, conjunctives, prepositions. But for a story to achieve dramatic necessity, it needs some means of raising sequences from the happenstantial to the causal or necessary. This can be done either directly, by the use of causal constructions, or by triggering causal presuppositions, as in "The king died and the queen mourned." In any case, wherever there is developed narrative, there will be richer causal sequencing, achieved by means direct or indirect. It is this implicit causal feature that creates and sustains the top-down structure of narrative to which Propp referred.

Now we may return to our central point: the manner in which the elaboration of narrative makes possible the differentiation and reintegration of thought, action, and affect in the child. The point that needs underlining is that narrative involves an elaboration on action. This elaboration consists in placing action in relation to the thoughts and feelings of the protagonists (and of the narrator as well, in some implicit way). How is this accomplished?

For one thing, the arguments of action are captured in terms of the dramatic pentad, which specifies the agent of the action, the intention that motivates her, as well as any instruments of action that may be involved. This structure provides the means whereby one can depict imbalances among the elements of the pentad. Imbalances expressed narratively as crises or troubles are what make for gripping stories. Developed stories also specify causal relations among actions or among actions and their outcomes, moving the occurrence of events from the happenstantial to the necessary.

Even further elaborations on the arguments of action are inherent in the narrative form. These elaborations introduce thought and feeling into the arena of action. For example, expressions concerning the regularity or canonicality of actions or events within a story introduce perspective into the story by presupposing not only what has occurred but what ought to have occurred. If the expectations are emotionally charged, the kind of perspectival twist that such canonicality introduces charges the story still more strongly with affective loading. In effect, then, a story contains both an epistemic stance with respect to what occurs, and a deontic stance with respect to what should occur or what is valued (see White 1981). A developed narrative, then, is not simply an account of what happened, but implies much more about the psychological perspectives taken toward those happenings.

Accordingly, one deep reason why we tell stories to ourselves (or to our confessor or to our analyst or to our confidant) is precisely to "make sense" of what we are encountering in the course of living—through narrative elaborations of the natural arguments of action. The reason that Emily narrates "out loud" in monologue may simply be that she does not yet have the inner-speech fluency to do so in her head. Later we shall deal with the question of why it is that one is impelled not only to tell stories that make sense, but to tell them *well*.

Keeping in mind all the foregoing considerations, we set out to analyze Emily's monologues in a manner that would capture their developing narrative elaborations. To begin with, we chose to examine utterances that are about events in which Emily had herself participated, or ones in which she expected or wanted to participate. This selected set of utterances was guaranteed to be not only about Emily's world but about the world in which she took a role as actor. Moreover, we eliminated talk that accompanied present ongoing activity, even if it was narrative-like, for our objective was to analyze the way Emily represented her world of happenings and actions, removed from the arena of ongoing action. By the same token, we eliminated any talk that was addressed directly to her dolls or other toys in the course of ongoing action. Talk derived from the immediately preceding dialogue with her parents or from storybooks was also eliminated, since these represented, so to speak, "borrowed" representations rather than her own. Additionally, since we wanted to focus on Emily's understanding of her "actual" world, uniquely fantasy monologues were eliminated from the sample.

We divided the remaining narratives into "episodes," each of which we then subjected to analysis. The transcripts of Emily's crib speech were divided into naturally occurring bouts of talk, marked by the presence of initial and terminal pauses longer than five seconds. Within these bouts, we defined episodes as talk referring to coherent activity. The coherent activity could be a single act, such as her father's eating dessert, or it could be a thematically connected set of acts such as an account of her morning routine involving getting up, getting dressed, going downstairs, and so on. A naturally occurring bout could incorporate more than one episode. Within a bout, talk about the same activity might not be continuous; that is, after a start, some unrelated talk might appear, with the original topic then being picked up again. In such cases, all talk about the same activity was counted as a single episode. If, however, the same action or set of actions was repeated in a later bout of speech, it was counted as another episode.

Since our object was to sample Emily's monologues over the entire period in which she was studied (roughly between her second and third birthdays), we concentrated on three separate time periods. The first was at roughly 22–23 months, during which there were eighteen recorded episodes that met our criteria. By that age, her talk about her activities was sufficiently comprehensible and coherent to be readily analyzable. Our efforts to analyze her action narratives in the previous month had been thwarted by her lack of fluency. The second period was (again roughly) at 28–29 months, when seven appropriate episodes were recorded. Though the episodes were few, they were richly elaborated. The final period was at 32–33 months, when there were recorded ten particularly rich and extended episodes. In the end, we combined the two later periods and compared early episodes (22–23 months) with later ones (28–29, 32–33 months).

The specific category scheme we employ in our analysis follows directly from our discussion thus far. For example, on the basis of what we have said, one needs to know to what degree and in what form narrative accounts of Emily's own experience are *sequenced* rather than recounted in a patchwork of images or referred to synecdochically. For sequencing tells us whether there is an effort being made to introduce order into experience. Sequencing may be managed by various devices. Linguistically, the simplest form of connectivity is provided by the use of the conjunction *and,* as in "And Emmy slept the hallway, and (my) pretty, and throw the baby." At a next level, a more temporally directed connective is used, usually in the form *then* or *and then* or *when . . . then,* as in "When Daddy come, then Daddy get Emmy, then Daddy wake Emmy up then." Another way of achieving greater sequence connectivity is through the use of such temporal adverbials as *before* and *after* or temporal framers such as *yesterday* or *tomorrow* or *pretty soon.* Finally, sequential connectivity can be achieved by the use of causal expressions, as in "Daddy moved Emmy in this room cause the baby sleeping in own room." The principal causal expressions used by Emily were *because* and *so.*

A second dimension has to do with the *canonical* or noncanonical status of an action being described. By this we mean basically the process of organizing one's representations of the world into expected, ordinary, appropriate events. Once canonicality is achieved, the child can then note which happenings are in violation of the cannon, and which in conformity with it. Ordinary or canonical events are noted in adult speech by the use of unmarked forms, extraordinary ones by marked forms. Now, the young child does not yet have a clear sense of what is normal and expectable and what is bizarre or strange—particularly during those times when adults control the sequencing and shaping of events. Much of the child's cognitive activity consists in trying to figure out what indeed is canonical, and what is out of the ordinary. We have tried to detect these efforts in Emily's monologues.

One method is by noting her use of recurrence expressions such as *again* and frequency expressions such as *once, one time,* and *sometimes.* These, we believe, express her effort to sort out steady and reliable events from those which are rare or unpredictable. Another method is to count instances of acknowledged or imputed variability (in contrast to steadiness) in the occurrence of events. Expressions include *or* and *but,* as in "Emmy get up and go Mormor . . . Tanta's house or Mormor" or "Her daddy or mommy will stay the whole time, but my mommy and daddy don't." A third expression of this search for canonicality is by the use of such appropriateness terms as *not supposed to, usually,* and *regular,* as in "He's not supposed to have dessert" or "We're going to eat breakfast like we usually do." Finally, there is a fourth mode of expressing canonicality: through marking necessity. An example is, "If ever we go to the airport, we have to get some luggage." We refer to these four modes of making the distinction between canonical and noncanonical as *frequency* marking, *variability* marking, *appropriateness* marking, and *necessity* marking.

A third narrative dimension of interest is the management of *intentionality* in narrative accounts: the extent to which the narrator attributes the course of action to an initial intention on the part of an agent (in this case Emily herself). The illocutionary marking of intention in child speech, as we know from Astington's (1988) recent study, is fairly late in appearing and, indeed, it is quite rare in Emily's speech. Yet its occurrence in less formal ways is an important sign of her development. It should also be noted that in the history of literary forms, the emergence of intention as central to the recounting of action is similarly late (see, for example, Propp 1968; Bruner 1986).

A fourth aspect of narrative is *perspective:* expressing one's stance toward what is being represented in the narrative. There are many linguistic devices and tropes by which perspective or stance can be indicated. We have particularly emphasized a set of these that are within the capability of a young child. Among them are markers of uncertainty: doubt about the performance or outcome of an action An example is "then Daddy maybe perhaps and hold Emmy." A second and related expression is through the use of epistemic marking, as in "I don't know about Lance and Danny come." A third is by the use of affective marking, as in "Danny wasn't frightened when the clown came down." Closely related to these is the expression of perspective through the use of emphasis. It takes the form of introducing a redundant and semantically unnecessary term when referring to a person or object or action involved in a narrative recounting. An obvious example is "and here comes Carl in here." There is also a form of perspective that is temporal—perhaps best called time perspective. In effect, it is Emily's notion of the time frame in terms of which events are to be assessed, as in utterances like "We're going to play a little while" or "Her daddy or mommy will stay the whole time."

Finally, with respect to perspective, monologues may show an awareness of the relation between the narrator's account and the points of view and acts of the protagonists whose deeds are being described. An example: "I'll *ask* Tanta if Lance and Danny come." We also included instances in which Emily reported almost verbatim what one of the protagonists in her narrative had said or might say, as if to distinguish their point of view from her own. An example: "And Mommy said 'Get up, time to go home.'" We believe these forms of expression to be efforts to add metacommentary to the on-going discourse.

Before turning to the results of the analysis, we may summarize the foregoing discussion in an outline:

> Dimension 1. *Sequence*
> Conjunctivity marking
> Temporality marking
> Causality marking
> Dimension 2. *Canonicality*
> Frequency marking
> Variability marking
> Necessity marking
> Appropriateness marking
> Dimension 3. *Intentionality*
> Indicating actor's intention
> Dimension 4. *Perspective*
> Uncertainty marking
> Affectivity marking
> Epistemic marking
> Emphasis marking
> Time-perspective marking
> Narrator-protagonist metacommentary

Now to consider Emily's soliloquies and the shapes that they take. We will comment upon each of the dimensions in turn.

Sequence

We look first at the development of Emily's ability to deal with the narrative sequencing of the events in which she has been involved, or in which she anticipates being involved, or which she considers as possible events in which she might be involved. Not surprisingly, there is a notable progress from the early period (age 22–23 months) to the later period (28–33 months) in her forms of marking. Table 2.1 contains data on the three forms of connectives per episode of narration. The most striking change from the early to the later period is in the use of causal connectives. In the early period, sequence is primarily expressed by the use of conjunctivity and various temporal markings. Later, causality becomes a major mode of sequencing.

Table 2.1. Percentage of episodes in monologues containing various forms of sequence marking.

Marking	22–23 months	28–33 months
None	12%	18%
Conjunctive	50	53
Temporal	72	71
Causal	11	47
Number of episodes	18	17

Some examples will help to give the flavor of the change. Here is a monologue at 22 months:

> when Daddy comes then Daddy come and
> get Emmy then, when Daddy done getting
> Mommy pretty soon then gets Emmy up
> Daddy comes and play with me when up.   (22;5)

The chief sequencing work is being done by *and, when/then,* and the mapping of the utterance on the order of events. Or, about two weeks later, she soliloquizes:

> when Daddy come then Daddy get Emmy
> then Daddy wake Emmy up
> then, then . . . then Carl come play
> Emmy not right now
> Emmy sleep, Emmy sleep(ing) . . .
> next year, next year Carl come
> and the the baby come.   (22;20)

These examples illustrate that in her early monologues Emmy is principally preoccupied with getting temporal order right: what happens first, what next, and what finally. It is also typical of these episodes that they concentrate on family routines. The second example involves the imposition of temporal ordering over a more varied set of events extending into the more distant future (signaled by *next year*), including an event she is anticipating with some anxiety—the birth of a sibling.

Later that month, we see a transformation in her expression of temporal ordering. She has invented or picked up a form of reprise in which a key topic ("when Daddy comes") is forefronted, tonally emphasized, and repeated as in the stanzas of a saga. The final reprise even has a form of terminal denouement.

and . . . when Daddy comes
  I put that (there)
  then my eat my breakfast
  and Daddy make my bed
  Emmy (all right)
  and then maybe, maybe . . .
when Daddy comes
  Dad
  and then not Emmy now putting anything
  Emmy just leaving the tools on my jamas
  singing to my head and my um
  and my (other day)
  and my this right there . . .
and when Daddy comes
  up Emmy sleeping on this.
when Daddy comes up
  then Daddy get Emmy and bring my (water)
  (bring down) in my (waffles)
then Daddy maybe perhaps and
  and hold Emmy . . . in
  that not now
Emmy sleepyhead.   (23;2)

There are several other narratives in the weeks following that use the reprise form. In the first of them, the key topic is a set of variations on the initial "when my woke up." Note that this time it is delivered in the past tense.

when my woke up
  then Daddy come
  my went out and took the boat [crib liner] out
  and took Emmy out in . . .
  Emmy (crash) the boat
when my woke up
  Emmy took the boat out
  now the boat in my
  in the (friends)
  I take the [inaudible]
when my get up.   (23;6)

Toward the end of the early period, *causality* begins to mark Emily's sequencing efforts. Here is a striking example:

Daddy didn't bring in the baby room
cause the baby [inaudible] and diapers the baby room

> but Daddy (moved) Emmy in this room
> cause the baby sleeping in (own) room
> Daddy brought this in the (ma-goo)
> Emmy sleeping in this (magoo-goo)
> cause the (bassinet) in the baby in there
> then Emmy's stay other room
> that's where the baby
> this is Emmy room
> this where Emmy sleeps.   (23;11)

This episode is one of the last of the early period. It is rather like a "review" of the new regime that follows her brother's birth. It begins in the past, and uses a reiterative scheme for its development. Compare it with an episode from the later period:

> Carl and Emily . . . see Carol, see Car- . . .
> (her) mommy and dad, Carol's mom and dad
> all leave, and she's going to
> then she'll cry
> and (call/cry) for Betty.
> So (?) Her daddy or mommy will . . . stay
> the whole time . . .
> but my mommy and daddy don't.
> They just tell me what's happening
> and then go right to work,
> cause I don't, cause I don't, cause I don't cry.   (32;4)

This time, Emily seems to be emphasizing causality, and the example illustrates how her soliloquies in the later period incorporate not only family routines but the new scene of the nursery school and playmates.

Another way to characterize Emily's mastery of narrative sequencing is by noting her simultaneous use of different kinds of connectives in the earlier and later periods. To be sure, the later episodes are longer (on average 72 words for later, 45 for earlier episodes). But it is interesting, nonetheless, that more than a third of her later episodes show triple sequential markers, while only a tenth of the earlier ones do.

Canonicality

In general, then, Emily is mastering the linguistic means for cementing her narrative accounts with rich and appropriate connective devices.

Table 2.2. Percentage of episodes containing various forms of canonical marking.

Marking	22–23 months	28–33 months
None	67%	47%
Frequency	22	24
Variability	11	29
Necessity	—	18
Appropriateness	6	18
Number of episodes	18	17

But at the same time, to shift to our second dimension of narrative marking, canonicality, she is also struggling to sort out the expectable from the nonexpectable in the events she is relating. Table 2.2 reveals that in the earlier episodes canonicality markings are few and simple. An example from this early period, using frequency marking, is the following:

> Then Emily got the blanket
> and set the dinner
> Emmy ate one time
> and one time Emmy sick.
> Emmy wanted dinner
> Emmy [inaudible]
> and Emmy ate the ice
> and took dinner.   (23;6)

As with the acquisition and use of sequencing expressions, so with canonicality: there is a slow but sure progression toward richer and more varied marking of individual episodes, so that about a quarter of the later episodes involve multiple marking, whereas only one of the earlier episodes does. And just as expressions of causality emerge as the dominant, later form for binding sequences, expressions of necessity and appropriateness emerge as Emily's more advanced form of indicating canonicality. Now things have "gotta" be of a certain kind, or are "supposed to be" in a certain way.

The following episode is typical of the multiple canonicality marking of the later period.

> If ever we go to the airport,
> we have to get some luggage.
> If have to go to the airport,

> hafta take something for the airport, to the airport
> or you can't go.
> Need your own special bus (carry me)
> and they z-o-o-m, o-o-m, zoom, zoom, zoom. Zoom.   (28;18)

This particular monologue was precipitated, as one would guess, by an airplane trip to visit her grandmother. Its confusion of antecedent and consequent logical conditions will surely be familiar to anybody who has listened much to 2- and 3-year-old discourse. But her insistence on imposing them does illustrate her concern with establishing canonicality in her experience.

A little while later her sense of appropriateness surfaces in another context:

> One day Daddy was eating dessert.
> He's not supposed to have dessert . . .
> Dessert, dessert, des-o-kay, dessert.   (28;18)

Her narrative world is not only becoming causal but also marked by necessary conventions where events are concerned. Causality, necessity, and appropriateness are taking command of her narratives, whereas in the earlier period conjunction, frequency, and contingency marked most of her narrative telling.

Intentionality

There is only one instance in our records of Emily's noting intention in any way, and it happens to be in the earlier period, when she says "Emmy (try) go in the library." We are inclined to believe that the distancing required to comment on intentionality is not yet within her reach.

Perspective

The data on Emily's perspective-taking in her soliloquies are presented in Table 2.3. What is striking is that the great majority of her narratives in the early episodes have no perspectival marking at all. Only about a third show any evidence of perspective taking.

Here is an instance of rather primitive emphasis marking (use of *all*) from this period. This example is interesting structurally, because the thematic key phrases are marked by the use of verbs, with the following unmarked predicate phrases being loosely strung to them.

Table 2.3. Percentage of episodes containing various forms of
perspectival marking.

Marking	22–23 months	28–33 months
None	67%	29%
Uncertainty	17	18
Affectivity	—	35
Epistemic	11	41
Emphasis	11	41
Time perspective	6	18
Metacommentary	17	29
Number of episodes	18	17

> Yesterday my left all the blankets
>   and on the wall
>   and on the floor
>   and in the dining room . . . table
>   with the baby
>   and in the hallway like my pretty
> and Emmy slept the hallway
>   and (my) pretty
> and throw the baby. (23;6)

And later in the same session, she marks her stance not by the use of
tropes but by a simple narrative.

> Baby back home and I play and play and play
> and then Emmy went to sleep
> and play on the blanket.
> And one day Emmy sleeping no good
> Emmy last, Emmy . . .
> Daddy hold my tightly and tightly
> Then my play, play and won't bite. (23;6)

But starting five months later, more than two-thirds of the episodes
are stance marked. Stance or perspective is one of the ways Emily is
able to mark the affect she feels toward her stories—not only by direct notation in affective verbs, but in many other subtle ways. It is of
great interest to us, given what we have said about the uses of narrative in soliloquies, that there is such a striking increase in stance
marking during the third year of Emily's life. It is a reasonable hypothesis that as Emily begins to get her world structured into necessary, appropriate, and causal sequences, she is doing so partly with

the aim of putting herself affectively and perspectively into the narratives she is constructing. Here surely is tantalizing evidence of the function of narrative as crucial to the integration of events, actions, and feelings into a common structure. Note especially in Table 2.3 the sharp increases in such stance markings as affectivity, epistemics, and time perspective. Her later narratives are expressing not only what caused what and what was appropriate and necessary, but above all how Emily thought and felt about what she thought was going on. Here is a striking instance from 32 months that incorporates virtually all of the stance markings to which we referred earlier.

> Tomorrow when we wake up from bed, first me and Daddy and Mommy, you, eat breakfast eat breakfast, like we *usually* do, and then we're going to p-l-a-y, and then soon as Daddy comes, Carl's going to come over, and then we're going to play a little while. And then Carl and Emily are both going down the car with somebody, and we're going to ride to nursery school [whispered], and then we when we *get* there, we're *all* going to get *out* of the car, go *in*to nursery school, and Daddy's going to give us kisses, then go, and then say, and then we will say good*bye,* then he's going to work, and we're going to play at *nur*sery school. Won't that be funny? Because sometimes I go to *nur*sery school cause its a nursery school day. Sometimes I stay with Tanta all week. And sometimes we play mom and dad. But usually, sometimes, I um, oh go to nursery school. But today I'm going to nursery school in the morning. In the morning, Daddy in the, when, and *usual,* we're going to eat breakfast like we usually do, and then we're going to . . . and then we're going to . . . *play.* And then we're, then the doorbell's going to ring, and here comes Carl in here, and then Carl, and then we are all going to play, and then wha . . . And then go in the car with somebody and drive to nursery. When we get to nursery school, we're to, *all* going to get out of the car . . . and then we're going to ummm, I think then we're going to . . . they're going to give us kisses. And t-h-e-n she's [probably her mother] going to *go* to work, with somebody with her, and meet her new students, and then she's going to pick us up, and work, and Daddy's going to bring us, and Mommy's going to pick us up, and work, a-n-d then she's going home, and we're going to go to nap. And t-h-e-n when you awake, then we are going to-o-o school. Uh, uh. (32;0)

This example exhibits strikingly and fully Emily's new concerns with causality, canonicality, and stance. It is a sequenced account of her style of life in a capsule. Her mother notes that the description is a variant of Emily's Friday routine. For all that, it is a remarkable example of world making, for it is plainly no particular Friday, but rather some appropriate day, one in which events dovetail predictably, appropriately, with proper affect and action, and with enough disfluency to suggest that Emmy was choosing among options. Rather than using the tropes of repetition now, she uses tonal emphasis, prolongation of key words, and a kind of "reenactment" reminiscent of the we-are-there cinéma verité (with her friend Carl practically narrated through the door as he enters). As if to emphasize that she has everything "down pat," she delivers the monologue in a rhythmic, almost singsong way. And in the course of the soliloquy, she even feels free to comment on the drollness of the course that events are taking ("Won't that be funny").

Here again there is multiple marking in the episodes of the later period, with nearly a third of later and virtually none of the earlier episodes containing three to four such simultaneous markings.

Elaborating on the act of narration by showing an awareness of the relation between the narrator's account and the point of view of the protagonists is what we earlier referred to as metacommentary. Metacommentary is another means of stance taking. It uses indirect speech as a way of representing the points of view of protagonists and narrator—as when Emily indicates what she or somebody else has said or will say. There is a small increase in instances of metacommentary from the early to the later period (see Table 2.3). An example from the later period will help to give the flavor of her usage:

> We *bought* a baby . . .
> cause . . .
> the, well because
> when she, well
> we *thought* it was for Christmas,
> but *when* we went to the s-s-store
> we didn't have our jacket on.
> But I saw some dolly
> and I *yelled* at my mother
> and said "I want one of those dolly."
> So *after* we were finished with the store,
> we went over to the dolly,
> and she *bought* me one.
> So I have one.   (33;9)

Dimensional Multiplicity

There is an interesting way of measuring Emily's growing control in the narrative recital of the events through which she is living. We can count the number of episodes, early and late, that show a *strong* narrative marking (that is, the presence of two in three of the following: causality in sequence, necessity or appropriateness in canonicality, any perspectival marking). When we do this, we find that in the early episodes only one in eighteen is so marked, in contrast to nearly one in three later.

It struck us as we read the transcripts that there seemed to be one other form of narrative marking that was characteristic of Emily. We could distinguish, in her talk about events, instances that were quite clearly marked for tense—past and future—and ones in which there seemed to be no tense marking or something like a "timeless present." The more timeless accounts had about them the character of "gists" or general representations of the state of things rather than mere recountings of episodes in her life. It is a distinction reminiscent of the one made by the Russian Formalists between a "timeless" fabula and the textual mode for expressing it. That is to say, one can characterize states of the world by placing them in time, or by characterizing them more abstractly. The distinction is captured by the contrast "On Sunday we got up late" versus "On Sundays we get up late."

We searched for evidence of this distinction in Emily's soliloquies. Was it associated in any way with the use of those other forms of narrative markings with which we were concerned in the preceding section? To put it in the most general terms, if narrative discourse is an integrated discourse strategy it should exhibit a concurrent use not only of narrative elaborations like stance marking, canonicality, and so on, but also of timelessness. Would this be evident in the soliloquies of a child between the ages of 2 and 3?

We had better give some illustrations of timeless and tense-marked utterances in Emily's soliloquies. Here is a tense-marked example from the early period in the past tense: "Daddy did make some cornbread for Emmy have." And two instances of future marking: "Pretty soon Emmy get up and go Mormor"; "Maybe afternoon when my wake up." And finally some timeless instances:

> when you wake up, but on Sunday morning
> sometime we wake up, morning but

sometimes we wake up, the time is uh
sometimes we wake up morning.

Consider first the frequency of present, past, and timeless tense markings in the early and later monologues. The data are presented in Table 2.4. Emily's later narratives are more "timeless" than her early ones. Moreover, her use of future markings declines at the same time, and one might speculate whether in place of trying to predict particular future events, she is now dealing instead with timeless characterizations about how the world might be or ought to be.

Now we may ask about the marking of sequence, canonicality, and perspective in tense-marked and timeless episodes. The data are in Table 2.5, which sets forth the account without regard to age. A glance at the table makes it plain that narrative markers are far more common in timeless episodes than in tense-marked ones. Of the 13 narrative markers, 11 occur more than 20 percent of the time in the timeless episodes, in contrast to 5 for past-tense episodes and 4 for future-tense episodes.

Does this pattern hold for both early and late monologues? To ascertain the answer to this question, we must first compare the incidence of narrative markers in Emily's timeless accounts in the early and late period, a comparison set forth in Table 2.6. Causality, canonicality, and perspective all increase dramatically from the early to the late timeless soliloquies. Causal marking jumps from none in the early period to two-thirds of the episodes in the later one. The canonical marker of variability jumps from none to more than half. Perspectival marking of affectivity, epistemics, and emphasis also show very large increases. And metacommentary jumps from none earlier to a third of the episodes later.

What about the narrative elaboration of tense-marked and timeless

Table 2.4. Percentage of episodes containing utterances with various forms of time marking.

Marking	22–23 months	28–33 months
Past	39%	31%
Future	28	13
Timeless	33	56
Number of episodes	18	16[a]

a. One episode was indeterminate.

Table 2.5. Percentage of episodes with three types of time marking containing various narrative markers.

Marking	Future	Past	Timeless
Sequence			
Conjunctivity	57%	42%	53%
Temporality	86	58	73
Causality	14	25	40
Canonicality			
Frequency	—	17	40
Variability	14	8	33
Necessity	14	—	13
Appropriateness	—	17	13
Perspective			
Uncertainty	29	—	27
Affectivity	—	17	27
Epistemic	14	25	33
Emphasis	—	17	44
Time perspective	—	—	27
Metacommentary	29	25	20
Number of episodes	7	12	15

episodes in earlier and later soliloquies? Tense-marked topics show little change or growth over time, as can be seen in Table 2.7. At the start and at the close of Emily's third year, tense-marked topics are simply not much elaborated narratively. Contrariwise, timeless episodes, hardly elaborated at all in the earlier period, come to be heavily elaborated by narrative marking in the later period. This suggests that the full elaboration of narrative, with both narrative marking and timelessness, does not appear until the end of her third year.

What this amounts to, then, is that there is an integration of marking in more mature narration: the timeless gist is combined with the variety of narrative markers that elaborate upon action and put it in a subjective context. Together, they conspire to make a "good story." It is striking that we find all these rudiments present in the narratives of a child as young as Emily.

We have set forth a view of the nature of narrative that is consistent with the claim that narrativization provides a means, early in life, for the child to accomplish one of her first "developmental tasks": to

Table 2.6. Percentage of timeless topics containing narrative marking in early and late monologues.

Marking	22–23 months	28–33 months
Sequence		
Conjunctivity	33%	67%
Temporality	83	67
Causality	—	67
Canonicality		
Frequency	33	44
Variability	—	56
Necessity	—	22
Appropriateness	—	22
Perspective		
Uncertainty	17	33
Affectivity	—	47
Epistemic	—	56
Emphasis	17	67
Time perspective	17	33
Metacommentary	—	33
Number of topics	6	9

differentiate and then reintegrate action, affect, and cognition. We have tried to spell out how such narrative construction transforms accounts of particular human actions, and in doing so, we have set forth five relevant processes (we call them dimensions) that might be involved in the transformation: strong sequencing, canonicalization, stance marking, intentionalization, and metacommentary. To this we have added a sixth, timelessness. These are not intended to exhaust the list of processes that are involved; others (not found in early childhood) are described elsewhere (Bruner 1986).

The developmental task to which we refer is resolved in two striking ways. The first way is through the creation of well-wrought accounts of the events through which one has passed—particularly those events which are likely to arouse some affect, such as the birth of a younger sibling or entry into nursery school. It is not these events per se that must be mastered, but the routine life into which these events intrude—meals, transportation arrangements, babysitters, friends. Emily is greatly concerned to get ordinary life under control while "all hell is breaking loose" around her. It is much as Stern

Table 2.7. Percentage of future and past topics containing narrative marking in early and late monologues.

Marking	22–23 months	28–33 months
Sequence		
Conjunctivity	50%	42%
Temporality	67	71
Causality	17	29
Canonicality		
Frequency	17	—
Variability	17	—
Necessity	—	14
Appropriateness	8	14
Perspective		
Uncertainty	17	—
Affectivity	—	29
Epistemic	17	29
Emphasis	8	14
Time perspective	—	—
Metacommentary	25	29
Number of topics	12	7

(1985) remarks about early development: it is not just the great traumatic events that preoccupy the child, but the actual process of daily life in the midst of important events.

Emily learns how to tell about these events in her soliloquies in a way that captures their sequencing and gives a sense of how usual or unusual they are, what stance she takes toward them, what her intentions were at the time, and how she reflects upon them. She also takes such events "out of time" by putting them in a timeless form. What she accomplishes can almost be called a triumph of ordinariness, a kind of routinization in story. For the fact is that most of her narrative elaborations are not directly about the great dramas in her life: coping with the arrival of a baby brother, or learning how to get on with the new acquaintances at nursery school. They are, rather, about that actual process of living noted above. She is concerned about her bed and changing table, about her prerogatives at mealtime, about when she will be picked up at school and by whom, about what friends she can count on for a visit.

The second thing Emily accomplishes is a cooling of events. She manages not only to convert her world into manageable narrative but also to do so on her own terms—alone, in her crib, and without intervention by adults or anybody else. She has begun not only to master her developmental task but to master it *on her own*. This does not mean that she does not borrow linguistic forms and even literary devices from her parents' talk (as Dore remarks in Chapter 6), but that she borrows them and makes them her own. It is very much like T. S. Eliot's famous quip that poor poets borrow from better ones but good poets steal from them. Indeed, whatever Emily takes from parental discourse, she takes for good: she steals rather than borrows. Perhaps, in the final analysis, that is what solid development consists of.

Chapter 3

Monologue as Problem-Solving Narrative

Carol Fleisher Feldman

I am going to make a case that Emily's principal purpose is to make sense of events past, present, and future, reported and experienced, actual and hypothetical, real and fictional. That is, Emily is driven by a need to explain or to interpret (for a discussion of this distinction, see Feldman and Bruner 1987) those putative facts which she feels to be unclear. To put it more boldly, she develops linguistic procedures for framing matters that she doesn't know something crucial about— how, when, who, what, or even why. These linguistic procedures organize the unknown by giving it one or another kind of narrative pattern, placing it into one or another kind of narrative frame.

In Chapter 2, Bruner and Lucariello discuss one such frame—the *temporal narrative*—that Emily uses to establish the patterns of events in her daily life. There is a second narrative frame that I want to discuss here—the *problem-solving narrative*. Emily produces problem-solving narratives when she is faced with a puzzle—a contradiction or some state of affairs that she doesn't know something about. Often, she arrives at her time alone in bed with an unsolved puzzle in hand and goes to work on it in monologue. Like the temporal narratives, problem-solving narratives have distinctive linguistic features. I will discuss them more fully later; for the moment let me just say that they include especially the language of logical inference (*but, so, not, because*) and qualifications of knowledge states (*maybe, probably, certainly*). In these narratives, Emily's principal purpose is to formulate more clearly a disturbingly unclear idea. They pose a puzzle at the beginning (often as a statement beginning "I don't know," or as a contradiction). Often, then, there is a series of statements beginning with *but, maybe, because* that have the pattern of logical reasoning. They often end with Emily's resolving the disturbing puzzle for herself.

Obviously I have let a lot of rabbits out of the hat all at once, and I'll not be able to catch them all. But let me chase one or two. First, am I treating language as if it were one and the same as thinking and/or thinking as if it were language? Yes, and no. Yes in this sense: a child talking to herself about things she doesn't know is engaged in a kind of problem solving while she talks. It is important to note that talk for the self need not always be ideational—a pure expression of thought for the self. Emily could be telling her dolls stories about fictional characters, or reciting the alphabet to herself, or replaying her conversations with her parents so as to keep them "with" her, or practicing phonology, or singing songs. Indeed she does all of these things some of the time. But her problem-solving talk *is* ideational, for while she is trying to solve puzzles she is "thinking out loud." The forms of thought she engages in involve an abstraction from particulars to relationships—that is, they are highly semiotic. It is hard to imagine how thought of this kind could occur without, or even exist apart from, language (if not natural language, then some other semiotic system).

But in another sense thinking is *not* the same as the language in which it is expressed. For as soon as we ask *how* Emily deals with intellectual puzzles, we are going to want to refer to language, or rather to certain powerful interpretive features of language, as the instrument by means of which her thinking is accomplished. One way to frame the relationship between language and thought here is to say that Emily achieves certain *cognitive goals* by certain *linguistic means*. In this sense, then, thinking is not the same as language, but rather is undertaken with the assistance of language.

Beginning at about 22 months and continuing until about 28 months, Emily is heavily engaged in problem-solving talk. Problem-solving narratives continue to occur to 32 months, and they may continue beyond that time, indeed may go underground to become "inner speech," but the simple problem-solving narrative occurs with less frequency after 28 months, when it begins to give way to a problem-solving narrative form that includes fantasy elements as well. The great burst of cognitive activity at 22–28 months may be triggered by Emily's emerging linguistic ability itself. For now that she has a semiotic system that can be used as an instrument for the construction of patterned meanings that interpret particular impressions, the very existence of that system may make a less interpreted version of the world unacceptably chaotic. So her creation of the problem-solving narrative at this moment may be attributable to the simultaneous discovery of thinking and of the semiotic possibilities of language, each of which, in a sense, emerges separately at this age, even if, in another sense, neither can exist without the other.

But since we have only one child to study, we cannot rule out another possibility: that the discovery of the problem-solving narrative is triggered by the distress of confusion occasioned by the birth of Emily's brother. Her bedtime puzzles may be substitutes for the one big puzzle about why this interloper is permitted in her house, even in what were formerly her room and her bed. With this last matter she is actively engaged in the dialogues, but, interestingly, she never discusses it in the problem-solving formats that she uses to discuss other less important problems. But the question of why she produces these narratives at this age is one we will not be able to resolve here. For my present purposes it will suffice simply to raise some of the possibilities inherent in Emily's situation.

Emily is astonishingly duller in her dialogues than in monologue. Objectively measured, her dialogic speech is, as we have seen in the Introduction, grammatically less sophisticated than her monologic speech, and the MLU is shorter. As we shall see, her dialogic and monologic utterances also differ vastly in the richness of their pragmatic and narrative marking. In general, her speech to herself is so much richer and more complex that it has made all of us, as students of language development, begin to wonder whether the picture of language acquisition offered in the literature to date does not underrepresent the actual patterns of the linguistic knowledge of the young child. For once the lights are out and her parents leave the room, Emily reveals a stunning mastery of language forms we would never have suspected from her dialogic speech.

In particular, to give a complicated story a simple initial gloss, Emily shifts from simple proposition to pragmatically framed proposition—that is, from utterances composed of bare propositions to those in which propositions are given along with instructions for how they are seen or are to be taken. And she shifts from single propositions to sequences of propositions strung together with suitable connectives—that is, from getting just the facts to putting the facts together into stories.

Perhaps her parents, as dialogue partners, in effect supply the pragmatic framing for Emily's utterances as well as their own. The nature of the particular language game played seems to be largely under their control—which is to say that they provide the frame. Emily need not supply one, and perhaps she cannot either, whether because they will not permit it or because the intellectual tasks involved in fitting her replies to another person's frames may themselves be so difficult that they take all her available effort and skill.

Dialogue with her parents gives her a fixed frame within which she must insert categorically appropriate completions. In order to compose a reply that her parents will accept, she has to fit her replies to the patterns supplied in her parents' speech: *pragmatic* patterns such as the speech act, the *syntactic* frame within which she is expected to offer comments on her parent's topic, and *semantic* constraints. In this manner, then, the production of dialogic speech may make at least as heavy an intellectual demand as does the production of monologue because her utterance must attend to so many exterior constraints, even though the language she actually produces in the dialogic situation is so much simpler than her monologic speech.

Moreover, the simpler language produced in dialogue may be teaching her forms of linguistic control that are necessary for the more enriched productions of monologue. One way to look at this is to say that dialogue provides a context in which the procedures for constructing propositions can be practiced. Without this practice and the control of propositional construction that results, Emily's kind of monologic narrative might not be possible. For the monologic genres make use of propositions by framing them pragmatically and composing them narratively in characteristic ways.

What is puzzling here is that Emily's patterns of speech production violate certain basic shibboleths about language development. Unexpectedly, Emily's problem-solving talk for herself is pragmatically marked, even narratively framed. We might have expected problem-solving talk in speech for the self to be reduced in pragmatic features—to be a language of pure propositions, as Chomsky (1975) suggests, or even a language of only the predicates of propositions, as Vygotsky (1962) suggests. For according to Chomsky and Vygotsky, respectively, pragmatic features and even sentence subjects are included in an utterance chiefly to accommodate the information needs of an interlocutor not identical with the speaker. But here problem-solving talk for the *self* is seen to arise in pragmatically rich, story-like frames. Can it be that reasoning actually depends upon or grows out of its putative antithesis, the story forms of language? I believe that, at least for Emily at age 3, it does.

Three Kinds of Talk

The problem-solving narratives are one of two main narrative types in Emily's monologues. The other is the temporal narratives described in Chapter 2. If one counts well-formed, extended monologic sequences of these two types, a total of 42 are obtained.[1] The two types occur in this sample with exactly equal frequency: there are 21 sequences of each.

Both types of monologic narrative contrast with Emily's speech in dialogue. Both monologic types contain a great deal of pragmatic marking; the dialogues contain very little. These differences are reflected in word counts. Approximately 600 words of each narrative type were compared with an equal number of words of ordinary dialogue.[2] Pragmatic markers constitute only 4 percent of the words in the dialogue sample, while they constitute 12 percent and 14 percent of the temporal and problem-solving narratives, respectively. Table 3.1 shows these patterns.

The pragmatic markers most typical of the temporal narratives are temporal patterning devices—*(and) then, (and) when, before, later, tomorrow, usually, sometimes.* Emily's effort in the temporal narratives seems to be directed toward getting remote events organized into an ordered and connected sequence. In contrast, the pragmatic markers most typical of the problem-solving mode are the logical connectives (*but, not, so, because*). These too give individual elements order and connection, but it is an order found in reason rather than in nature. Problem-solving narratives are also typified by epistemic ad-

Table 3.1. Number of pragmatic markers by genre.

	Problem-solving monologue	Temporal monologue	Dialogue with parents
Number of words	634	640	599
Number of pragmatic markers	88	78	24
% of pragmatic markers	14%	12%	4%

Table 3.2. Types of pragmatic marker by genre.

	Genre					
	Problem-solving monologue		Temporal monologue		Dialogue with parents	
Stance marker	#	%	#	%	#	%
Mental verbs						
think, know	13	15	14	18	0	0
Epistemic adverbs						
maybe, actually	19	22	5	6	1	4
Temporal						
again, soon, today	4	4	40	51	8	33
Logical						
but, so, because	29	33	11	14	12	50
Modals						
can, could	14	16	1	1	3	13
Attention focusing						
now, see, look	9	10	7	10	0	0

verbs (*maybe, actually, probably, certainly*), and modal verbs (*can, could*). Mental verbs (*think, know,* and especially *don't know*) are common but are as common in temporal narratives. For a comparison of the frequencies of these features in the two narrative types, see Table 3.2.

As examples, contrast two mature narratives: a temporal narrative reviewing the day, with its *when-then* patterns, and a problem-solving narrative. First, here is the temporal narrative:

> In the morning, Daddy in the, when, and usual we're going to eat breakfast like we usually do, and then we're going to . . . and then we're going to . . . play, and then we're, then the doorbell's going to ring and here comes Carl in here, and then Carl, and then we're all going to play, and then (with), and then go in the car with somebody and drive to nursery. When we get to nursery school we're all going to get out of the car . . . and then we're going to ummm . . . I think then we're going to . . . they're going to give us kisses . . . and then she's going to go to work with somebody with her, and meet her new students, and then she's going to pick us up and work and Daddy's going to bring us, and Mommy's going to pick us up. (32;0)

Now we come to the problem-solving narrative. It is phrased as a premise leading to a conclusion (beginning with *so*), then to a *but* that begins a new conclusion ("my parents leave") with its premise set off by a *because*.

> Carol's mom and dad all leave, and she's going to, then she'll cry and (call/cry) for Betty so (?) her daddy or mommy will . . . stay the whole time . . . but my mommy and daddy don't. They just tell me what's happening and then go right to work. Cause I don't cause I don't cause I don't cry.   (32;4)

Occasionally, a problem-solving narrative is nested inside a temporal one. The forms are not always pure.

The narrative types are like formats in Bruner's (1983) sense in that they provide a framework within which a certain kind of thinking is made possible. The two narrative types offer the support that comes of being highly patterned in the way they are constructed by the solo speaker. In this respect they differ from dialogic formats, which are maintained by the joint efforts of parent and child. But for the child just learning how to talk and to think they are similar to dialogue in that they offer a patterned frame that assists in the organization of particular propositions. If, as I have argued, Emily's dialogues with her parents provide a format that aids the acquisition of propositions and the rules for their construction, then the more heavily narrativized formats of monologue can be seen as providing a scaffold for the acquisition of patterns of organization (temporal or logical) that depend upon perspective. Moreover, the patterns of the narrative types give each type a distinctive organization that suggests an analogy to the more literary narrative types that are referred to as *genres*.

But the two types of narrative are different in some important respects. Temporal narratives appear both in dialogue and in monologue. Emily's parents seem to give her the tools for the construction of such narratives—as Nelson also observes in Chapter 1. In contrast, the problem-solving narratives, with one exception initiated by Emily herself, do not appear in the early dialogues, at least not in the dialogues that we have before us. She seems to invent the problem-solving narrative herself, and it appears first in, and for nearly a year thereafter exists almost entirely in, speech for herself. The problem-solving narrative, then, seems to begin as private speech. It does become social later, for it eventually begins to appear in dialogue with her parents, as I will show. But this is at a much later time—at about 33 months—and by the time this happens, the problem-solving type of narrative has undergone very considerable development both in strictly cognitive or logical complexity and in including elements of fantasy play.

As I mentioned, problem-solving talk occurs in dialogue only once in the early months of this sample, at 22 months, and it is Emily who initiates it. In this episode, she is preoccupied with something she doesn't know—the name of "Judy's neighbor."

> E: (When) my go Tanta house then my ask Tanta about Judy's (neighbor/name was). I don't know about what Judy's (neighbor/name was).
> M: Is it maybe Julie Nelson? Is that right?
> E: Yeah.
> M: Is that right?
> E: *Nelson.*
> M: Yeah, I think that maybe that's right, I think I remember that.
> F: Julie *Nel*son.
> E: Maybe Judy c-, go call up Carl, look like Nelson cause don't look like Nelson, Carl don't, so that, Tanta said that's, Judy is (Carl), not, friend that Nelson, Judy Nelson at, at Tanta and Judy in Nelson, you, the that? I going over Judy's neighbors don't know. At Tanta what name, Judy was I don't know.
> M: Yeah, I don't know either.
> F: Yeah.
> M: Good-night Emmy. Have a good night's sleep.
> F: You say good morning,
> E: Remember Tanta (tomorrow) ask Tanta what Judy (name was).
> M: Yeah, we'll ask her that.
> F: [simultaneously with M] That would be a good idea, Sweetie.
> M: Yeah, I'm sure that Tanta knows.
> F: Okay.
> E: When my go Tanta, (and) my wake up, then Emmy fly go Tanta he did (about) Judy (name was) I don't know.
> M: Right.
> [M and F exit]
> E: My daddy my da-da . . . da-, remember . . . and then Da- goes Mormor ask. (22;21)

Problem-Solving Narratives

I should like now to focus more closely on the construction of problem-solving narratives in monologue. At the back of my mind is a notion like Nelson Goodman's (1978) view that we make worlds not with bricks but with symbols, and that the central cognitive task of childhood is the task of learning how to make worlds, chiefly with the linguistic tool kit of culture.

Problem-solving monologues always involve the statement of a puzzle and an effort to resolve it. They can begin with a flatly asserted fact that provides the setup or premise for the puzzle, or they can begin with the puzzle itself. The puzzle may be presented as a contradiction, such as "Annie say no, Emmy say yes. Tanta say no, Tanta say yes." Or, it can be presented more explicitly, either with mental verbs as in "I don't know which boy," or with such discourse markers as "that's funny" or "why is that?" Indeed, by the time Emily is 2 years old she has a surprisingly large set of relevant pragmatic devices available to her. Interestingly, at the start the only common mental verb, *know*, usually appears in the statement "I don't know."

Every puzzle involves a challenge to some stipulation of a steady state. There is at least an analogy to a crucial feature of the better-formed narratives of adult literary fiction. Bruner (1986), following Burke (1945), describes narrative as consisting of a pentad composed of an Actor, an Action, an Instrument, a Setting, and a Goal. To this pentad, Bruner adds the essential narrative trigger: trouble. Emily's intellectual puzzles take place against a pentadic background of someone trying to do something with something for a purpose, more or less completely specified, and into that frame she introduces the trouble, whether in the form of a contradiction or of a statement of "I don't know." The skilled adult narrative restores a steady state by resolving the trouble. Emily cannot always do this successfully. But reading these transcripts, one gets very strongly the impression that this is what she is *trying* to do.

Her puzzle solutions readily yield to an analysis in terms of the tools of logical reasoning. It is not necessary to say that she "has" these logical concepts herself, consciously or even unconsciously. Rather, a consideration of the logical patterns that we can discover in her attempts at resolution may be a useful way for *us*, as scientists, to organize her talk into patterns. (See Feldman and Toulmin 1976 for an extended discussion of the limitations on "psychologizing" scientific patterns of analysis.)

In this spirit, Emily's solutions can be seen as including cognitive processes of correspondence, classification, inference, and identity in the interval from 22–28 months and beyond. She uses the language of correspondence ("Annie has one Jeannie has the other"), of classification ("some men can go in the footrace"), of inference ("I don't know why . . . because") and of identity ("that's not my daddy"). But these are not perfect subcategories. They are merely a way of looking at how cognitive characteristics emerge at this time, and a rough way of glossing cognitive patterning.

And this is not the end of the story. For once these forms appear, they are reconstrued and the problem-solving genre develops into a pretend-play problem-solving genre where puzzles are placed into playful and fantastic narratives. These later monologues keep the same patterns of reasoning but import fantasy characters and events into them. This last transition is the one that is of real interest, for it suggests that the problem-solving pattern that emerges in narrative then undergoes more sophisticated development in the context of playful narrative invention. This important shift begins to take place for Emily at about 28 months and seems to be triggered by mastery of the basic problem-solving narrative form, a mastery that liberates her to play with reasoning, to reason about fictional and invented worlds. Moreover, as these fantasy problem-solving monologues appear, the unfanciful problem-solving monologues begin to disappear, and by 32 months they have become very uncommon.

Let me offer a conjecture, one that I will try to illustrate below: narrative frames provide a distancing device that makes possible both the reasoning patterns of the earlier problem-solving monologues and the fantasy play of the later ones. By using narrative frames, Emily is able to extricate herself from the stream of her ongoing activity and to stand outside it as an observer—to separate the events reported from her perspective about them.

Problem-solving procedures arise in a crucible of narrative. The narrative is at first a problem-solving tool that makes puzzles approachable by providing a means for interpretation and analysis. Later the same narratives provide a locus for play and invention as their scope is extended beyond the exigencies of the here and now. Narrative frames then may offer a distancing device, an analytic tool, in the service of both logical and playful reflection.

Cognitive Complexity in Unfanciful Narratives

The effort to explain the self, to resolve the trouble, to solve puzzles, is the business of problem-solving monologues. Beginning at about 24 months Emily produces numerous problem-solving narratives that have a seemingly well defined cognitive pattern. Between 24 and 28 months one can find narratives whose cognitive constituent is correspondence, others whose cognitive constituent is classification, and others whose cognitive constituent is inference or identity.

The first set of examples I will give involves problems of correspondence. The first four narratives are from a single night. In this one the correspondence is that Annie has one, Jeannie has another:

> Maybe when my go to Tanta's might get some soap to put on my hands . . . some . . . some (with) wa-, some from Annie. Probably, and probably Jeannie have different (color). Probably Annie have Jeannie. Jeannie went to the store. I don't know (which) one. But Jeannie put some on my bed . . . Not that one, I can get hurt.   (24;2)

In the next, it is that Annie babysits for Stephen, Jeannie for me:

> Annie babysit for Stephen . . . And Jeannie babysit for my. And Daddy my, Mommy . . . how about babysit for different one. How bout Daddy babysit for, for, for Danny. Mommy babysit for for, for Arthur . . . Ah, Mommy babysit for Arthur, the two for o-, other kids. And Arthur and Danny. Arthur and Danny. Arthur and Da . . . ny . . . what. Look. Look at that . . . Arthur. Danny. Arthur and Danny. Arthur. Danny. [repeats 4 more times]   (24;2)

Here, Danny was on the horse, Arthur on the bike:

> I put . . . Danny my can put my horse. And Arthur put like one bike. That . . . Danny said no. I can't get on bicyc-. Arthur said no. Danny said yes. I can go my horse, but not on his bike. But but yes, yes you can go . . . go in the bike. Getting on the horse. But but Danny said no my can't go on the, but Mormor came to watch my horse . . . (24;2)

In the next, Emily was taking one boy, not the other:

> One day . . . Arthur, Arthur was in my, my was taking somebody. But . . . somebody was in way. But somebody came back today. Taking (un-do) . . . A different kind of boy was coming. What a bo-.   (24;2)

In the next example, from the next day, Emily poses the puzzle early and clearly, with "I don't know what boy bring book tomorrow," and makes a long and serious effort at resolution that fizzles out at the end. The correspondence here is who is bringing the book.

> I don't want to like the Hansel and Gretel book . . . Mommy, Dad . . . (who) . . . maybe Carl turn, or maybe Emmy turn, or maybe Stephen turn, or maybe Lance turn or Danny turn. I don't, I don't know

what boy bring book tomorrow. Maybe Lance. I don't know (whether), which boy bring book today. Maybe Danny or maybe Carl, maybe my, maybe Lance, maybe (too-wee). How about Lance bring book . . . Carl bring book . . . one . . . boy's (Jewish) . . . and one (tell) a lie . . . Carl brought Dr. Seuss book for my . . . Carl turn bring (c-) what if (for) doing. What if (for) Carl bring Dr. Seuss book for my. Maybe my get Dr. Seuss book from Carl, maybe . . . the bear book to my. And Carl maybe bring no, maybe c-, maybe bring me . . . the book. Maybe . . . boy book it . . . maybe(???) I had a bottle . . . where is it? (24;3)

On the same day Emily produces a narrative that includes the correspondence Annie says *no* and I say *yes:*

Emmy sleeping. Or E-, Emmy and Jeannie say got no wa-, Annie say no. Tantas, ta- Annie say no. Emmy say yes. Emmy say yes. Tanta say no. Tanta say yes. I singing my daddy in, no (singing) my, Jeannie, Tanta . . . say no. (Jeannie) say yes. Tanta there, have a (happy) and the kids say yes. Andy and y-, yes. And my daddy and mommy say yes. Daddy yes. I say, say yes. (24;3)

One day later she produces four problem-solving monologues in one night. They can be seen as exemplifying a transition from correspondence to classification. In the first, a narrative of correspondence, Mormor bought the cheetah and someone bought the tiger:

Where the put, the cheetah. Mormor bought it. But the tiger got something home . . . But the . . . tiger got m-, Emmy bo-, eh, Mormor bought the, the cheetah. (Ya) foot Emily. But I don't know who bought, bought the tiger. Maybe Mormor or Daddy or Mommy. Mormor bought the cheetah. I don't know what kids bought the ti- . . . maybe . . . M-, Mormor bought the cheetah. That's what Mormor bought. The cheetah. And Emily, Emmy bought tiger . . . (24;4)

The next narrative is concerned with the correspondence what fell down, but it seems more complex in its range of accounts, for it also undertakes to explain how the bed got broken.

In the bed falling down. Actually the bed broken. Huh, huuh, Daddy funny. The bed broken. Anybody can put it away. Emmy go to sleep. Maybe the baby and the mommy buy different crib. Maybe do that cause the other one broken. What be the tree fell down. Could be. I don't know which. Maybe tree fell down and broke that crib. I don't know what thing fell down. In the ho-, broke the crib . . . The crib did it . . . the tree did it. The crib. But I don't know which kind of lady bought the crib . . . But that one fell down. That crib must been, that tree must been, broke that tree. That must fell down. I don't know what lady bought it. But the lady went to get this new crib. But then this is one was, bring it back (seat) . . . And the you not supposed broke the tree. (Broke) up. (24;4)

The next two monologues compare two things, with Emily observing likeness between them. In the first, which is a kind of sound play, she compares two words:

I know, a-ah, the . . . raccoon (pa-ke). So . . . rac*coon*. So big, big rac- . . . coon. Not rick. Rick, rac-, rac-, rac*coon*. Not rick. That raccoon. Not like rick. But Monday raccoon. Rick like rac-. . . coon. Rac-coon. Raccoon . . . Not rick. Rick like rac-*coon*. But rick like this is gonna find rac-coon. But raccoon like rick-c-coon . . . Raccoon . . . (24;4)

In the last one Emily not only compares two kinds of fruit to see if they are alike (as she does with the sounds *rick* and *rack* above) but also gives a color criterion for distinguishing them. Distinguishing between two members of a class and giving a criterion for that distinction seems to me a procedure that can be reasonably described as exemplifying classification. This then is the first example of classification:

Banana (pear) . . . and apple and a baba, pear and a apple. This pear like a bana. Bana and the pear. Bana and the pear and the apple. The red thing the pear, but the red thing, the apple. Pear, pear, pear, pear and the pear, pear, pear and pear. A pear and a apricot. And this (ban) ah (mic) said that one. (Mac) said that one. (24;4)

The next two examples, from around the same time, illustrate an especially interesting kind of classification, classification into real and nonreal exemplars of something. The something in the first case is "my daddy." In the second, it is moles. (In this special kind of classification exercise, one can also think one sees the discovery of the identity of Daddy in the first case and of moles in the second.)[3]

This is the kind of daddy (???) and this is the kind of daddy, that's . . . Mommy (were) Daddy . . . that was who name is . . . Daddy (??) but this is not my daddy cause it's funny Mommy gave that Daddy. (24;23)

Next the mole:

I don't like the mole . . . But my mostly like the mole, but not really like the mole. I (tell) it the, mmm (good). I was a mole. And my . . .

didn't like the baby. More like a mole. The baby don't know how to the baby don't know how, make a mole. But the baby mostly makes mole, but not really was a mole. (24;7)

In the following two examples, from three months later, classification seems more complex. In both these cases classes are hooked up with reasons (*'cause*). What makes them seem more complex is their being part of an inferential process.

> Now I don't want it smaller cause see it has longer string. This one is better cause it has smaller string like Danny's but they had smaller string and I don't know what size. But Mommy said big. (27;28)

> We'll have to go in the green car cause that's where the car seats are. I can be in the red car but, see, I be in the green car, but you know who's going to be in the green car. Both children, I'm going to be in the green car in my car seat, he's going to be, and nobody is going to be jus-... (27;28)

Sometimes a particularly vexed topic provides repeated opportunities for posing a problem and giving it various resolutions. One such case is the footrace. It occurs twice—first as an anticipated event, later as past event. Emily is about four months older here than in the previous examples. Both these monologues are good examples of the developed, cognitively complex form of problem-solving narrative in the variant that does not include elements of play. The first monologue begins as a temporal narrative that establishes the steady state against which the problem arises. The problem is whether Emily can run in the footrace. It begins this way:

> Panny, nanny, canny, panny, Jimmy, Nelson, Christopher ... and Danny's mommy and daddy are going to be in the footrace. Danny and Arthur ... Danny ... and ... Danny's daddy and Danny and Arthur ... are going to watch the footrace. Danny's daddy's going to run ... and his mommy, and Danny, and Arthur are going to do, I don't ... watching, watching, too. And then ... I want to have the footrace ... I'm going to have the footrace. My mom and dad's going to be there ... My mom and dad are just going to watch me, but they ... my ... they're going to watch, right on the sidewalk there, now while I have the footrace then when I get done, then Arthur will do it and then when Arthur gets done, child, men won't you watch, and kids will run in the footrace. (32;5)

Emily then addresses the problem in a problem-solving format, using terms that resemble the logic of classes. She continues:

Well, some men will run in the footrace and some kids will run in the footrace. But not too many kids can run in the footrace, just a couple of kids like Arthur and Danny and me can run by ourselves, while my mommy and daddy will wait and I'll run by myself and Arthur and Danny will, and all the kids will run with their daddies. Okay? ... And mommies, too. And some kids get to run by theirselves and some kids can't like Sara and Jimmy, their mommy has to go with them. (??) No. Sure! Arthur and Danny ... can, Arthur will not be with anybody and Danny will be with somebody, I don't know who, maybe his daddy or his mommy will take care of Danny, but Arthur sure won't do it by himself. But there are two tries. Emily and Arthur will do it first. Two kids at a time, Arthur and Emily do it first and then we hold hands, I don't think Arthur wants to hold hands but I hold hands ... All of, Danny, Arthur, Emily and all us kids can do it ... the mens, too. (32;5)

The next monologue is the follow-up three days later. The steady state here is that Daddy could not run in the footrace. Her puzzle is abstract: "I don't know why that is." Reasons are given. But there is a happier day coming when both she and he will run, and reasons why she will. This passage is not just cognitively complex but also sophisticated in its language. It has a tidy and intricate pattern of puzzles posed, considerations raised, and solution achieved. She musters the tools of language in the service of her logical puzzle—*I don't know why, maybe, I think that's why, so, has to, can, could, no no, have to, but.* And she musters other discourse features in the service of giving that puzzle a narrative shape—reported speech of her own and of others, changes of "voice" from participant to narrator, dialogic patterns, audience replies (*it's nice, hooray*). Her skillful use of all these linguistic features contributes to its being a *good* problem-solving narrative.

Today Daddy went, trying to get into the race but the people said no so he, he has to watch it on television. I don't know why that is, maybe cause there's too many people. I think that's why, why he couldn't go in it. ... So he has to watch it on television ... on Halloween day, then he can run a race and I can watch him. I wish I could watch him. But they said no no no. Daddy Daddy Daddy! ... No no, no no. Have to have to watch on television. But on Halloween Day he can run, run a race. Tomorrow (he'll) run (???) He says yes. Hooray! My mom and dad and a man says "you can run in the footrace," and I said "that's nice of you. I want to." So next week I'm going to ... run to the footrace and, and run in the footrace cause they said I could. (It's nice) a week or so, Sunday and Saturday and Monday and Tuesday I'm going to run in the footrace because that's fun . . . Oh, Tuesday, that's Carl's birthday . . . (??) before, it was the footrace. The . . . Saturday and Sunday eeooo. Wednesday and Thursday and Friday. (32;8)

By 32 months, Emily is able to produce sophisticated problem-solving narratives—problem-solving narratives that show linguistic sophistication in their narrative patterning and cognitive coherence. This is what I mean by "well-formedness" for a problem-solving narrative.

The Move to Pretend Play

I have argued that the same narrative frame that permits the analysis of mundane problems permits Emily to move to the higher ground of invention once she has mastered the basic tools of analysis. At 28 months, she moves to pretend play with the first monologue with an *invented* puzzle. The "two Chris" problem first appears as a mundane problem in dialogue. It reappears in monologue two weeks later as an instance of pretend play, entirely transformed. Here is the mundane dialogic problem:

E: And there was two (babies) one for Chris and one for Peter . . .
    two (babies) one for Peter and one for (?). Two . . .
F: Two Chrises, that's right, there were two Chrises.
E: No! There isn't two Chrises! There is only Peter, there is only one
    Chris.
F: One Chris and one Peter? (28;0)

Two and a half weeks later, Emily converts this topic into a fantasy problem-solving narrative, as follows:

Take a nap now, Chris. Chris nap-nap Chris. Good nap-nap, Chris. (And Daddy's coming, yeah.) Emily (???) She's in (??) No I'm Carl, it's Emily that sleeps, I'm no, there are two Chrises, I'm Emily, no, um I'm Carl . . . and Chris is my mother here and there's another Chris at Carl's house, there's one Chris for me . . . (???) and there's one Chris for the other Carl, the regular Carl, (it's) really Carl Rechtshaffen. Oh my oh my oh my oh . . . (28;18)[4]

The next example transforms mundane problem-solving matter into problem-solving matter with pretend play. (Emily's mother commented on this monologue, "We worked tonight on numbers—if I have 5 apples and give you 1, how many do I have left, etc. We did not work with giraffes.")

Suppose I have giraffe. Suppose I have giraffe to Dad. Suppose we give giraffes to me and Joshie and Carl and Emily. If I did that, five, five things. First me. Okay. Five.   (30;3)

The next example, from two months later, is another transformation of dialogic material into pretend play in monologue later on the same day. In the dialogue Emily's father talks about brushing her teeth; in the monologue she converts this to talk about doing it for her stuffed animal.

F: Well, I shaved this morning so it's not too bad . . . you try tomorrow morning, before I shave, it'll be scratchier.
E: What did you put, why did you put . . . your why did you put your finger in your eye?
F: Wasn't in my eye, hon, I was just trying to move my contact lens around. I got some toothpaste in my eye when I was brushing your teeth [laughs]. Some toothpaste splattered up and hit me in the eye when I was brushing your teeth.

Here is the monologue:

When I wash, brushing the Dino's teeth this morning I got a little in my eye. I need to get it out. There you are. Pretty soon I'm going to put contact lenses on in the morning. You put contact lenses on inside my eye.   (32;10)

The next example is our best one of a problem-solving monologue with pretend play. It has the rich logical structure of the best of the problem-solving monologues (directed to solving a space shortage), organized around materials of great fancifulness—all her friends sleeping in her room on the ceiling and having a picnic there. She begins the topic in the prior dialogue where her mother's fanciful contributions were suggestive of the possibilities Emily developed in the subsequent monologue:

E: You have some so(???) what (happened) to me while a (worry) my books. I I got to sleep on my (?) room. And, we and you guys could sleep in my room, and Stephen too.
F: We would have a lot of people in here, wouldn't we? How about . . . can we bring Mormor in here, too? Can Mormor sleep in here?
E: And so . . . can everybody.
F: Everybody can sleep in here.
M: [simultaneously] And Uncle Don could sleep on the ceiling.
F: Well, in the meantime, have a good nap. Have a good night, hon, sleep, hon.

The monologue follows:

> Sleep good. And so sleep (a lot) right there. Mommy there. Daddy
> there. And Mormor there. Stephen there, and . . . Carl there and
> Daddy. And Stephen I c-, Carl wa-, come there. Carl was in there
> (wa-catch-in) cause his mommy and daddy . . . fell down so, so he
> got to sleep in my bed with me. And also he's been sleep . . . way up
> in the ceiling. Sleeping (with Stephen) . . . (u-up) . . . Mormor . . . You
> can sleep on the ceiling a little bit away from Uncle Don and Carl . . .
> cause . . . cause I wanna . . . (play with) Uncle Don. He's (lacking . . .
> this one) . . . sleeping right on the gr-a-ass. And then . . . sleeping on
> the ground. And Carl coming, and (wonderful). Carl brought along
> two bags. One for um, one for candy for Uncle Don, and one for
> grapes for him . . . You know why the (up). I don't have anything
> because I'm going to sleep. Just the other people brought a picnic, but
> they don't put it, so they put it, the bags, up there. So they could sleep
> and see the . . .   (32;25)

By 33 months, Emily has become an artful constructor of children's
stories and, simultaneously, their appreciative audience. In this monologue, fantasy material from a book is mixed with problem-solving
day matter about crossing streets:

> Un-u-sual animals. Unusual animals. Now that's a nice book. That
> and that . . . and that. I like that book cause it's (easy to read). There's
> a platypus. There's a platypus. Long tail and a beak that's just like
> the duck. Duck bill . . . and he always swims and they eats plants. He
> likes to play with (?) is right there. And he swims in the water and he
> does . . . the only thing he doesn't . . . he doesn't eat plants . . . Now
> this one eats plants. These always eats plants, but he knows he not
> supposed to go in the street, and only his father (??) his mom said
> that . . . what his mom okay to go in the street. Mormor said that
> and I don't . . . and even I know . . . that I do. But now (he's fine).
> But mommy and daddy and (father) thought about it and said "I
> don't think it's okay cause your Mormor says it's not okay," so they
> zoomed away and he got in the street. That's okay okay okay. No-
> body was in the (street). He just did it. Oh that was a nice
> story. (33;14)

By 32–33 months, then, Emily has well-developed narrative procedures for dealing with abstraction and invention. As we have seen,
these procedures include extending the problem-solving genre to include fanciful and playful material. Once armed with this way of
dealing with what Goodman would call the "irreal," Emily is ready
to take on the world of abstract objects. The passage that follows is

the first discussion of an inner state as an object. (Of course, inner states have been employed earlier as a way of looking at the world.)

> I'm sick . . . a pain somewhere. I can't touch (pain). Can't touch my pain. Can't touch my nick. Can't touch me anywhere cause I'm . . . don't feel so good . . . as you do.   (33;15)

At about the same age, Emmy produces a monologue that includes the instructions for how to construct monologues for fantasy play:

> So they can be . . . (to Da-da). And anything they wanna be . . . bisons . . . or anything. Bunny rabbits. Bunny rabbits they could be, or anything. They could, but there's no bunny rabbit.   (33;1)

At the same time, fantasy worlds also begin to enter her dialogues with others. But notice how limited her language is when it occurs within a dialogue with one of her parents when compared with the language she uses in her monologues. The language she brings to dialogues with parents is virtually devoid of logical, narrative, or even pragmatic marking. Perhaps dialogue with parents is a frame for the organization of propositional constituents and at this age, one excludes the other. The dialogic frame seems to *replace* the narrative frame by providing an alternative shape or set of constraints, as I discussed earlier. The bareness of the following sequence is best seen in contrast with the rich talk in the monologue about sleeping on the ceiling at 32;25.

> E: You know what bear did today?
> M: What did he do?
> E: He, he um, paint.
> M: He painted. Did he make a mess?
> E: And he . . . now he put his hands in there.
> M: Oh, he didn't? Oh, Ras-cal . . . Okay, lie down.
> E: And he got a lot of paint over there.
> M: I'd like you to tell me . . .
> E: [over M] He got it on everything.
> M: Okay. Now you lie down and go to sleep and tell the story to Dino and the bear. That will be fine.
> E: No.
> M: Goodnight. I love you.
> E: No!   (33;15)

Let me stop here and consider the range of Emily's linguistic products at 32 months. First, there is dialogue. Her dialogic speech is still largely made up of bald propositions without narrative markings.

Into this dialogue she has begun to import the fantasy talk she has acquired in the context of the heavily narrativized speech for the self that she uses in monologue. The narrative patterns of monologue seem to have given her a scaffold for the move to analysis and invention. But dialogue is apparently providing patterns of another kind, which may teach her not only how to construct propositions but also how to be metacognitive by turning around on a proposition just constructed and commenting on it. With her parents in dialogue, Emily acquires the ability not just to comment on former topics but also, by 32 months, to comment on former comments, to turn former comments into topics, a process that I have discussed elsewhere (Feldman 1988) as "ontic dumping." This is perhaps a mechanism for the acquisition of metacognitive processes.

Second, there is monologue. In her speech for herself, there are, by 32 months, very distinctive genre-like patterns. There are first the problem-solving narratives of fantasy that we have just examined. Second, she continues, though with lesser frequency, to tell pure problem-solving narratives. Third, there are temporal narratives which, by this age, habitually distinguish between the usual or canonical and the unusual or particular. By 32 months, these last two narrative types are highly patterned and very different from one another. By this age, we may be justified in considering them to be true genres. One example of each follows, to round out the picture of Emily's range of narrative abilities at 32–33 months.

First, a beautifully formed, extended problem-solving narrative:

> Today it's beau-, it's night time it's dark out. [sings] It's a beautiful day. Tomorrow it's going to be . . . day. Tanta day. Tanta day. All the kids come just home. Carl, Carl, Carl, Danny, Lance . . . Janet. I don't (know) about Lance or Jack. I know Janet and Carl (kids). Carl and Danny. Danny and Carl and Janet come. I don't know about Lance . . . and um . . . Jackie. If they don't come Lance and Jackie maybe they, maybe their mommy and daddy won't work. I think they like to be home, but are certainly unable and Carl . . . and Janet and Dan. I don't (offer/know) and Jack . . . Jackie and Lance. I don't know are coming. I'll ask Tanta if Lance and Jackie are c- cause I don't know about Lance and Jackie come. I sure know Danny and Lance . . . and um, Carl are coming. I don't know about Lance and Jackie . . . Carl is coming, and Jack, and um, Jack's coming. And Lance, and Danny and L-, and Carl went too. I know that. What time does Jackie and Lance . . . I think they go . . . think . . . If they don't maybe that will be the case that (their) mommy and daddy don't need to work. But I

> (won't) . . . and Danny, and um, Janet and um, Carl (could) come . . .
> Okay, just Jackie and Lance, okay? (32;26)

Next a temporal narrative of habit and convention:

> Just before breakfast I changed all of my clothes. Just before break-
> fast . . . put on my clothes. See in, when I first get out of bed and I
> . . . get out of my room and I go in Mommy and Daddy's bedroom
> and . . . play awhile. And then it's breakfast. So Stevie and Emily get
> on their clothes and go down for breakfast . . . See. And I choose
> what I want, cheese omelet or eggs . . . eggs . . . cheese omelet or
> yogurt. So I do that, and then . . . and then I, and then when Carl
> come we play awhile, and . . . and then we get in the car and zoom
> to nursery school . . . then when we in the (???) someone going to be
> there. I don't know who's there. Who, who, who. I think someone
> person who brings, and she's going to . . . parent-teacher . . . the per-
> son who brings me to school is going (a) . . . (go back to
> sleep). (33;4)

Conclusion

The language of Emily's monologues at age 2–3 years is pragmatically much richer than her dialogic language in its linguistic patterning. By 32 months, it is apparent that she has two distinct monologic genres: temporal narratives and narratives of problem solving. It is the second of these that has concerned us in this chapter.

The problem-solving genre is directed to the solution of epistemic puzzles, and makes use of markers of argumentation, possibility, and modality. From 24 to 32 months, it undergoes two changes. First, there is an increase in cognitive power or complexity to include arguments that have the form of correspondence, classification, inference, and identity. Second, there is a shift from the mundane to the fanciful. I conjecture that the narrative frame provides a mechanism that permits Emily to take a detached, reflective point of view first for logic-like analysis and later for invention.

The argument suggests, first, that it is the telling of stories, to oneself in this case, that makes possible the reflective activities of analysis and later of invention. It also suggests a common origin in story forms for two activities that are not usually seen as related in development: problem solving and fantasy. They seem to begin in the same narrative frames.

The speech patterns that have been best described in the literature up to now are largely derived from dialogue. These prove in our data to be a nonrepresentative sample of the full range of speech products at this age, for at least this one child and, we may speculate, for other children who talk to themselves when alone. And this should give us caution. We must wonder, moreover, about the importance of speech-for-self in development generally, and in the development of reflection or interpretation in particular. For we encounter such reflection principally in Emily's crib speech, and it seems essential for her construal of the world.

Speech-for-self seems to provide the medium within which Emily develops her ability to take a perspective and to think interpretively. Her problem-solving narratives seem to be a step along the path to interpretive thinking. There is a sharp contrast between the linguistic skills Emily deploys in these narratives and the linguistic skills she deploys in dialogue with her father. As I have discussed here and elsewhere (Feldman 1988), the heavily controlled productions of dialogue, where Emily is required to produce appropriate comments for her father's topics, seem to support an entirely different line of acquisition. In monologue, Emily produces topic-comment structures that are elaborated upon pragmatically to give her perspective on the world. In dialogues with her father, rather, she is involved in the conventional game of providing culturally appropriate and pragmatically unmarked comments on the topics her father chooses to launch. It is *her* world that constitutes the domain of monologue, her *father's* that provides the basis for dialogic discourse. It may be in this respect that monologic speech is a necessary step toward Emily's construction of her own working representation of the world. How children who do *not* engage in speech-for-self accomplish this feat of "personalized construction of the world" remains an open question.

Part II

Constructing a Language

Chapter 4

Monologue as Development of the Text-Forming Function of Language

Elena Levy

Indexicality in language is an issue that has been addressed in large part through studies of children's speech. Most of these studies have focused on exophoric reference, or the use of language to index aspects of the nonlinguistic context of speaking (Halliday and Hasan 1976). Far less research has examined the development of endophoric reference, or the cohesive component of language, in which language is used to index language itself. In focusing on exophoric reference, developmental studies have tended to overlook the acquisition of discourse skills by children; that is, children's developing ability to sustain discourse about things not present in the nonlinguistic context—things whose existence and identity have been created through the act of speaking itself (Silverstein 1985; Wertsch 1985b).

Of those developmental studies which have focused on units of speech larger than the clause, studies of children's monologues indicate that cohesive (that is, anaphoric) pronouns are not used appropriately until a relatively late age. Specifically, it appears that children do not use pronouns cohesively to create "thematic subjects" in discourse until at least the age of 5 (Karmiloff-Smith 1980, 1985, 1986). This appears to be a frontier age from a psycholinguistic point of view; a time at which a fundamental reorganization of the cognitive-linguistic system takes place, along with a corresponding advance in the mastery of discourse skills.

Findings such as these are suggestive of a functional split between preschool and later years—that the former are devoted to intrasentential grammatical relations and the latter to extrasentential discourse skills—but this is clearly not the case. Grammatical relations continue to develop after the age of 5 (Karmiloff-Smith 1986), and discourse relations have roots in earlier years: "If age 5 does represent the beginning of a new period in language development, in my view it is because of the *gradual functional shift* from using linguistic categories in processing juxtaposed utterances to their use as organizers of coherent and cohesive text" (Karmiloff-Smith 1986, 474; italics added).

Observations of young children's speech point toward roots of endophoric reference in dialogue. When children in the one-word stage participate in dialogue, for example, their utterances tend to denote that which cannot be presupposed on the basis of other participants' remarks; in other words, their single-word utterances tend to mark new information (Greenfield 1979; Keenan and Schieffelin 1976).

In light of this research concerning one-year-old children's participation in dialogue on the one hand and older children's narrations on the other, Emily's crib talk provides an opportunity for viewing developments in the cohesive system during the intervening period. From the start of the recordings, when she is 21 months old, Emily uses the forms of endophoric reference (Nelson and Levy 1987), as the following productions—(1) at 21 months and (2) at 23 months— demonstrate:

(1)   broccoli soup carrots cause rice
      baby eat *that*

(2)   when my slep
      and and Mormor came
      then Mommy coming
      then get up
      time to go home
      time to go home
      drink p-water [Perrier]
      yesterday did *that*

The use of pronouns with interpretable textual antecedents continues throughout the recordings. Over time, however, the distributional relationship of pronouns with respect to their surrounding context changes. For one thing, pronouns start to occur in coreferential chains, with each pronoun in a series occurring in a different intraclausal context, as in example (3), produced toward the end of the recorded period at 34;8:

(3)   but I don't know what happened to the dumpster
      it was at the church parking lot
      and all the big boys were jumping in *it*

I don't know what happened
it mustav been moved someway

In this passage, the child uses pronouns in the text-forming function of maintaining reference. Since language is used here to create its own context, the child can "operate on a new category of objects: objects whose existence and identity are created through speech" (Wertsch 1985b, 150).

The use of pronouns as cohesive devices in these spontaneously produced monologues suggests that Emily's intersentential cohesive system—the set of options available to her for linking sentences together—matures along with her intrasentential grammatical system. In this chapter I am concerned with tracing the path of this development—specifically, of the cohesive use of pronouns—during the fifteen-month period covered by the Emily data. To this end, I map out changes in Emily's use of the pronouns *it* and *that* with respect to relationships between pronominal form and discourse context. Before turning to these observations, I discuss the larger pragmatic functions served by cohesive pronouns in the creation of large discourse units.

Cohesive Function of Pronouns

When pronouns serve a cohesive function, their denotational value relies on relationships of temporal (and in written language, spatial) contiguity with some aspect of the larger linguistic context in which they occur: "'third person anaphors' present a denotatum only by virtue of the previous or subsequent presentation of that denotatum in some relevantly-same stretch of structured linguistic signal" (Silverstein 1987). Because denotational value relies on such relationships of copresence, pronouns used as cohesive devices serve as indexical signs—more precisely, as intratextual indices, or instances of endophoric reference.

Specifically, a pronoun's denotatum is picked out by virtue of "a special asymmetric relationship" (Silverstein 1987) of indexical presupposition and/or entailment between pronoun and linguistic context. The italicized pronoun in (4) functions as a presupposing index, where appropriate use of the pronoun requires that conditions for satisfaction of the reference are set up by *earlier* linguistic context.

(4)   The man looked behind him. Then *he* started to run.

This use of the pronoun constitutes an example of anaphora. The pronoun in (5), in contrast, is an example of cataphora, where interpretation of the pronoun depends on a relationship of indexical entailment with respect to the subsequent context in which the pronoun occurs:

(5)   Let me tell you *this*: I'm not happy with the way things are going.

These examples stand in contrast to pronouns uses as extratextual indices, or exophoric usages, in which aspects of the nonlinguistic context are presupposed at the moment of speaking. In (6), for example, the italicized pronoun indexes a sound that occurs in close (spatial and temporal) proximity to the utterance:

(6)   [sound of books falling] Did you hear *that*?

From the point of view of the ongoing construction of discourse, coherent conversation is built out of extended chains of endophoric reference, as in the following example (from Levy 1984):

(7)   *the father*$_i$ pretended that *the guy*$_j$ who was English was American
      ah *he*$_i$ pretended all evening
      in *his*$_i$ conversation *he*$_i$ talked about coming across the water and *he*$_i$
          whenever *he*$_i$ would say an English phrase like slang something
      uh *he*$_i$ would translate it for *the guy*$_j$ . . .

In this passage, each pronoun in the series picks out its referent by indexically presupposing aspects of earlier language use. These pronouns constitute, then, a coreferential chain.

Note that in this passage the italicized pronouns form a nominal chain, in that each pronoun in the series indexes an earlier noun phrase. In contrast to this, most instances of speaking show the use of pronouns to index a variety of linguistic units, such as broader grammatical constituents (for example, full verb phrases), whole clauses, series of clauses, or long, unspecified segments of earlier text (Schiffman 1985). Broadly classifying these anaphoric functions, we can make a distinction between *nominal reference,* in which the pronoun's antecedent is a noun phrase, and *predicational reference,* in which the pronoun is used to index at least the predication of an earlier clause. Passage (8), taken from a naturally occurring multiparty conversation, illustrates some of these options:

(8)   J: Well I just hope that—I hope that that machine doesn't come up
          for bid for the rest of the gang and I get to run *it* all that time.
      D: Well I'm I'm well *that*'d be to your advantage, *that*'s for damn
          sure.
      J: *It* certainly would.

D: You know if you could run *that* for the rest of the season *that* would conclude *it* well. I just I mean . . .

J: I'm afraid that *it* won't happen. Jessel looks like's gonna take the saw at least for now.

As this passage shows, the pronouns *it* and *that* can be used in both nominal and predicational functions.

Complexive Nature of Discourse

In (8) the use of pronouns in their two anaphoric functions helps achieve a larger social-pragmatic goal: that of keeping the conversation alive, rather than pushing the communication forward toward a specific informational goal. In this light, note similarities between processes involved in the construction of the passage in (8) and processes characteristic of children's thought, that is, processes underlying children's creative behavior. An unplanned conversation, such as (8), can be characterized to a large extent as complexively based behavior. This can be seen by analogy to Vygotsky's (1962, 1978) blocks task. Asking children to group blocks together on the basis of perceived similarity, Vygotsky found that the choice of each successive block depended on perceived features of a single block chosen earlier. Each step thus relied on features of a single earlier step. Vygotsky characterized this as behavior based on complexive processes. A chain complex, for example, is "a dynamic, temporal unification of isolated elements in a unified chain and a transfer of meaning through the elements of that chain . . . Each element in the chain is united with that which precedes it and with that which follows it . . . Each [element] belongs to the complex because it shares some feature with some other element" (Vygotsky 1987, 139–140).

In contrast to this, conceptually based behavior requires an ability to "rise above" (ibid., 156) discrete elements of a task: "It presupposes the isolation and abstraction of separate elements [and] the ability to view these isolated, abstracted elements independently of the concrete and empirical connections in which they are given" (ibid., 156). While conceptual processes are involved in planned, goal-directed aspects of behavior, complexive thinking requires only that each step in a constructive process rely on perceived features of an earlier step. As a result, a construction produced in this way need not have a "structural center" (ibid., 139).

As passage (8) suggests, adult discourse can be viewed to a large extent as complexively based behavior. That is, to the extent that the choice of each utterance in discourse relies on features of an earlier utterance, the constructive process is a complexive one. To the extent that pronouns are used to index earlier speech, they serve as tools in this process.

It is important to note that this does not imply that discourse constructed on a complexive basis lacks overall thematic structure. Rather, to the extent that discourse is constructed on a complexive basis, thematic structure emerges *in retrospect*. In unplanned conversations, global hierarchical properties—such as the embedding of subthemes within larger themes, the subordination of minor characters and events to main characters and events, and so on—emerge in the course of speaking itself. It is in this sense, at the level of discourse, that "meaning cannot be separated from acts of . . . speaking; it is constituted *in* these acts" (McNeill 1988).

Pronouns, in particular, play the following role in this process. From the point of view of larger pragmatic function, pronouns do not simply index earlier segments of speech, but in addition each pronoun marks its referent as relatively "presupposable" information; that is, as topic of its own clause. The rest of each clause then serves as a comment on that topic. To the extent that discourse is constructed on a complexive basis, global thematic structure emerges from the linear thinking of individual topic-comment constructions—where, all other things being equal, that which is pronominalized frequently at the local clausal level emerges over time as thematic at the global discourse level.

This can be seen in passage (7) above, where the character marked frequently with pronouns, character i, emerges over time as globally thematic. Similarly in (8), the proposition "J can run his machine all summer" becomes globally thematic, through sheer frequency of mention with pronominal forms.

Crib Talk as Complexive Behavior

In her early study of crib talk, Weir (1962) characterized her son Anthony's monologues as complexive in nature. Passage (9) is characteristic of monologues produced by Anthony between the ages of 28 and 30 months:[1]

(9)   1. hi big Bob
      2. that's Bob (2x)

3. big Bob
4. little Bob
5. big and little
6. little Bobby
7. little Nancy
8. big Nancy
9. big Bob and Nancy and Bobby
10. and Bob
11. and two, three Bobbys
12. three Bobbys
13. four Bobbys
14. six
15. tell the night, Bobby
16. big Bob
17. big Bob not home

Weir comments on the first part of this passage:

> The first line is simply a greeting intended for a real person who is not present, but whom the child sees rather frequently. *Big Bob* is preferred by Anthony to *Bob* alone, probably because of alliteration. Line (2), repeated twice, identifies the person, and two of the repetitions of line (3) serve to clarify who it is, returning to the alliteration. In the third repetition the intonation is changed to a rising contour, showing the adjectives in still another function as they contrast with *little* in line (4). There is no such person as *little Bob,* the origin of this phrase could be the child's wish to make *Bob little,* but he has now engaged in a practice session of adjectival substitution, using the antonyms *big* and *little,* as they appear in line (5) as the synthesis from the previous thesis *big* and antithesis *little.* In line (6) *little Bobby* could just be mention of the child's name, but line (7), *little Nancy,* when no such person exists, shows clearly that the substitution game continues, as line (8) also shows.   (1962, 119)

Note the complexive nature of this constructive process. Throughout the passage the choice of each utterance is based on both retaining some features of a single earlier utterance (for example, in line 4 retaining *Bob* from line 3) and changing other features along a single dimension (for example, changing *big* in 3 to *little* in 4). The discourse is thus built on the basis of paired associations, or paired constructions. In Jakobson's (1962) terms, these various forms "attract each other."

The dimension along which paired associations are made itself changes in the course of speaking. At times the links between utterances are made on the basis of semantic properties of words (such as the antonymic relationship of *big* to *little*), and at times on the basis of phonological properties (such as adding *not home* to *big Bob*).[2]

Weir found that linkages were most frequently based on phonological and other nonreferential properties of utterances. Rarely were they made on the basis of referential relationships. This "lowering of the referential function" served the broader goal of bringing other functions—in particular the metalinguistic one—to the forefront. In this light Anthony's monologues can be described as "practice sessions," or "self-educational linguistic games" (Jakobson 1962).

Pronouns in Anthony's Speech

Weir noted a high frequency of pronominal forms in Anthony's speech. The word *it* occurred 103 times, *that* 121 times. It is likely that many of these usages were exophoric in nature. However, Weir also found that pronouns occurred frequently in distributional relationships such as those in (10), where they alternated with more explicit forms within the same verbal context:

(10)   take the monkey   stop it
       take *it*   stop the ball
                             stop *it*

It is clear that on Weir's account the link between a pronoun and its textual antecedent need not be referential in nature. Consider, for example, passage (11), in which, as Weir puts it, "prenominal substitutions are the underlying theme":

(11)   1. find it
           2. with juice
           3. drink it (2x)
           4. juice
           5. that's the right way
           6. right way
           7. where you going
           8. I'm going
           9. shoe fixed
          10. talk to Mommy
          11. shoe fixed
          12. see Antho
          13. Anthony
          14. good night

15. see morrow morning
16. shoe fixed (4x)
17. fix it (3x)
18. shoe fixed
19. it took it
20. bring it back
21. took them
22. took it down (4x)
23. he took it (2x)

In this passage, pronouns are produced to match the pattern of the imperative that occurs in line 1. In line 2, "*juice* evokes *drink* in line (3) which together with *it* repeats the pattern of line (1)." Similarly for the pronoun in (17): The appearance of *shoe fixed* in line 16 "is once more a good occasion to return to the imperative and substitution exercise, with the resulting *fix it* repeated three times in line (17), also forming the usual paired association." Again in line 20, Anthony "returns to the imperative pattern with the pronoun *it*, and the pattern of line (1)" (Weir 1962, 132). Each of these pairs of utterances, then, is a "paired association" made on a nonreferential basis.

Pronouns in Emily's Speech

As I have pointed out, pronouns occur early in both Anthony's and Emily's monologic speech; both children clearly have the forms of endophoric reference available to them from a very early age. It is clear, however, that these early uses need not serve an anaphoric function.

But by the end of the period in which Emily's monologues were recorded, pronouns do appear to serve a coreferential function, as cohesive devices. In (12), for example, produced at 33;14, links between pronouns and antecedents appear to be made on a referential basis:

(12)   but he knows he's not supposed to go in the street
        and only his father (says *it*'s okay in the s-)
        his mom says (*this/that*)
        what his mom say?
        okay to go in the street
        his mormor says *that*
        and I don't
        even I know

and I still
but now he's fine
his mommy and daddy and (father) thought about *it*
and said I don't think *it*'s okay cause your mormor says *it*'s not okay
so they zoomed away
and he got in the street
that's okay okay okay
nobody was in the street   (33;14)

During the period of the recordings, then, the cohesive function of these forms starts to emerge.

This is the problem I will focus on in Emily's speech: the emerging use of pronouns as intratextual indices, and corresponding to this, mastery of the formal means for making language serve as its own context. Toward this end, I will look at the changing contexts in which Emily uses the pronouns *it* and *that*. Before turning to these distributional relationships, however, I will examine general characteristics of Emily's monologues and the relationship of the monologues to her parents' pre-bedtime speech.

Emily's Monologues

Unlike Anthony's speech, many of Emily's monologues, especially those occurring toward the beginning of the recorded period, consist of repetitions (or near-repetitions) of patterns spanning a number of clauses (see Chapter 1). Passage (13) is an example from the first few months of the recordings, 23;8 (discourse units are separated by space).

(13)   when Mormor get me
        when Mormor make pretty
        Mommy had a help
        my sleep
        Mommy came
        and Mommy get get up
        time go home

        when my slep
        and and Mormor came
        then Mommy coming
        then get up
        time to go home
        time to go home

drink p-water
yesterday did that

now Emmy sleeping in regular bed
yesterday my slept
and say um
and in Tanta house
and Mommy woke my up
and go
time to go home

and then Mormor came
and Mormor said
time (dgo) home
and Daddy bring p-water
and yesterday Mommy and Mormor and Daddy bring my in my
    regular bed
[10-second pause]

I can (?) Mommy
but my in Daddy and Mommy's
when Mormor came in
and Mommy got it
make my bed
when when Mommy came in
when my bed

when when I sleeping Tanta house
Mommy came wake my up
because time to go home
drink p-water
[7-second pause]
(dinner)
Daddy Mommy Daddy put my into bed in my regular bed
actually actually Mommy did it.

Note that each unit in this passage appears as a linear list of activities; thus overall the passage, like many of Emily's early monologues, appears to consist of repetitions of such lists. It is important to note that the linear effect is created, in part, by the absence of pronominal chains; as a result no single proposition assumes prominence over others as globally thematic.

In contrast to the early monologues, many of the later ones have a different overall character. Passage (12) above, for example, appears to have a rudimentary sort of hierarchical organization. In particular, a single proposition, "going in the street," assumes thematic prominence over others. This effect is created in large part through repeated pronominal coreferences—after the initial introduction of the proposition with full explicit form ("to go in the street").

Similarity to Father's Speech

There is a striking similarity between much of Emily's speech, especially those passages consisting of lists of reported activities, such as (13), and that of her father's pre-bedtime routines. Specifically, her father's recorded speech tends to consist of lists of reported events (which describe what Emily has done earlier in the day, will do after she wakes up, and so on). At Emily's request, her father often repeats these lists a number of times, as in (14). (Ellipses indicate that at least one interspeaker turn exchange has been omitted from the transcription.)

(14) F: And you know what?
           We're going to talk about tomorrow! . . .
      F: Well we're going to get up tomorrow morning
           and that's a nobody day!
           And we're going to get up . . .
      F: And we're going to have breakfast
           and then play outside in the yard . . .
      F: And nobody is going to mow the lawn tomorrow morning
           and anyone can help
           and after that we are going to go on an excursion to see some
             antique stores . . .
      F: Well and after then we're going to come back and have lunch
           and then you're going to have nap
           and then after your nap we're going to have hot dog at the ocean
             with the Smiths
           and Mr. and Mrs. Smith and and their kids and a bunch of other
             kids are going to have hot dogs at the ocean . . .
      E: Tell me again! . . .
      F: Okay [quickly]
           but tomorrow is a nobody day
           and we're going to get up, and have breakfast, and mow the
             lawn, go to an antique store, have a nap, and go to the ocean
             and have some hot dogs.

Furthermore, the lists tend to be "packaged" with such discourse-bounding devices as "you know what" and "go to bed." Here are three examples:

(15)   F: I'll tell you what we're going to do tomorrow . . .
            and you know what? . . .
            [list of activities]
            You know what Stephen's going to do?

       F: First thing you're going to do . . .
            but you know what?
            [list of activities]
            If you don't go to sleep
            we won't be able to do those things.

       F: You know what we're going to do?
            [list of activities]
            And now go to bed.

Thus the father's discourse tends to show patterns such as:

$$\begin{Bmatrix} \text{you know what} \\ \text{(I'll tell you) what we're going to do} \\ \text{(first thing)} \qquad \text{you're going to do} \end{Bmatrix}$$

$$\begin{Bmatrix} \text{[activity]} \\ \text{[activity]} \end{Bmatrix}$$

$$\begin{Bmatrix} \text{. . . go to sleep} \\ \text{. . . go to bed} \end{Bmatrix}$$

Passage (16) illustrates a strong similarity between this discourse pattern and that found in Emily's speech. In fact (16), taken from Emily's monologues at age 24;23, consists of four partial repetitions of this pattern.

(16)   *(then) you know what we do*
       we (make) (?) house
       and then we [pause]
       and then (then we make) (?) . . .

       then what we do
       we can (go) play with (the) dollhouse
       and when we('ve) done that
       I can play

       and you know what we do when I play
       we do something 'pecial
       we get juice
       we get (jui-)

       (and then) you know what we do
       we going outside
       and look at the flower

and not now
and now we just *going to bed*
afternoon we do that
do all (those) kinda thing
right now it's bedtime . . .

The similarity in structure between Emily's and her father's discourse patterns, then, suggests that the formal devices Emily uses are
strongly influenced by her father's speech; her father tends to package
information into units consisting of lists of activities bounded by formulaic phrases, and Emily tends to do the same.[3]

Contextual Distributions of *It* and *That*

I turn now to changes in Emily's use of pronouns during the course
of the recordings, concentrating on the two pronominal forms *it* and
that. As noted above, both of these forms can be used in both nominal
and predicational functions. Specifically, I look at all nonexophoric
uses of these pronouns occurring during the entire fifteen-month period of the recordings. Each instance is categorized as either nominal
or predicational reference (or as lacking an interpretable antecedent).
It is important to emphasize that coding decisions were based on
adult standards of interpretation. Thus in the following discussion,
the terms "nominal reference" and "predicational reference" reflect
adult interpretation of the forms; the use of these terms does not imply that their adult functions are served in Emily's speech.

It *and* That *with Nominal Antecedents*

For the pronouns *it* and *that*, all instances of nominal reference that
occur in the recordings appear in the Appendix to this chapter. These
are pronouns with clearly interpretable nominal antecedents. Table
4.1 shows the distribution of these instances by month of the study.

I will look first at instances occurring early in the monologues.
Keep in mind that while from an adult point of view these forms have
textual antecedents, there is no evidence that they in fact serve such a
function for the child. Rather, seemingly endophoric usages may result from interclausal linkages that are primarily nonreferential in nature.

Many of the earliest instances of pronouns appear without interpretable antecedents:

Table 4.1. Frequency of anaphoric reference by month of study.

	Month														
	1	2	3	4	5	6	7	8	9	10	11	12	13	14	15
Nominal	2	—	2	11	2	1	—	4	—	—	2	5	3	3	—
Predicational															
+do	—	—	4	5	—	2	—	12	—	1	—	5	1	—	—
−do	—	—	—	—	—	—	—	1	—	—	—	7	5	—	—

(17)   put it over there   (21;9)

Daddy stop it in the (circles) over there   (21;7)

Emmy gotta . . . stop it   (21;7)

I can see my daddy get it from the down the washing   (21;13)

These instances show no evidence that the pronoun is distinguishable from its co-occurring verb; in other words, there is no evidence that verb and pronoun have been acquired as separate units.

In those instances which do have interpretable antecedents, the anaphoric (referential) appearance of the pronouns may reflect paired associations between a verbal unit and aspects of a prior utterance, where the verbal unit consists of both verb and pronoun. In (18), for example, any (or all) of the lexical items in the first utterance may attract the verbal unit "eat that."

(18)   broccoli soup carrots cause rice
       baby eat that

A second interpretation of the linkage between pronoun and antecedent arises from the relationship between Emily's speech and that of her father. Specifically, the similarity between Emily's and her father's discourse units leads to the question of to what extent Emily's speech reflects imitation of larger segments of discourse, units that include both pronoun and antecedent. In this light, consider passage (19):

(19)   hide the bottle
       where is *it*?

This appears to represent a linguistic game, a speech pattern Emily has heard a number of times. It is likely in this light that she has acquired the pronoun-antecedent pair as part of a single unit. (For related discussion see Chapter 6.)

The extent to which imitation contributes to the construction of the monologues cannot be determined without a full corpus of input to Emily's speech. It is sufficient for this discussion, however, to point out that neither of the above interpretations suggests that pronouns in the early monologues serve a true anaphoric function.

Later passages appear to be different in character from these early ones. As Table 4.1 shows, an especially high frequency of pronouns with nominal antecedents appears in the fourth month of the study (when Emily is 24 months old). A look at these monologues illuminates this frequency distribution: two different monologues in this month show noun substitution patterns, in which pronouns alternate with fuller noun phrases. As in Anthony's speech, these forms alternate within similar (sometimes identical) clausal contexts. At 24;4 for example, the following contrasts occur:

(20)   Mormor bought *it*
        bo but Mormor bought *the cheetah*
        Mormor bought *the cheetah*
        Mormor bought *the cheetah*
        that's what Mormor bought *the cheetah*

        I don't know which kind of lady bought *the crib*
        I don't know what lady bought *it.*

        the tree fell down
        tree fell down
        what tree fell down
        that one fell down
        that must fell down[4]

Consistent with Weir's account of similar passages in Anthony's speech, the construction of these passages can be accounted for in terms of complexive procedures; specifically, in terms of those involved in the construction of "chain" complexes. Thus the construction of a given utterance (such as "I don't know what lady bought it") is based on an earlier utterance ("I don't know which kind of lady bought the crib"), where certain features of the earlier utterance (the initial nominal and verbal elements) are retained while other features (the latter nominal) are changed.

Again, one need not posit a referential basis to the link between pronoun and antecedent. Rather, it is plausible that these passages are generated on the basis of pragmatic rules of use, derived from distributional relationships between pronoun and antecedent in adult speech. Thus, the appropriate use of pronouns may be based on paired associations between pronoun and antecedent, where the links are nonreferential in nature: in this case, based on co-occurrence relationships between forms observed in adult speech (for example, the observation that pronouns and fuller nouns tend to appear near one another in time in similar verbal-clausal contexts).

It is not necessary that the child create a novel utterance in each case; rather, a somewhat less creative process can account for these constructions. Specifically, passages like those in (20) may be produced by the juxtaposition of pairs of utterances, *both* of which have been previously heard in adult speech. (For example, both "Mormor bought it" and "Mormor bought the cheetah" may have been heard previously.) If this is the case, the seemingly anaphoric nature of the pronouns may result from the child's reproducing each utterance as heard and creatively juxtaposing pairs of utterances in time. Since on this interpretation the (re)production of one utterance evokes another, this type of constructive process remains a complexive one.

On either interpretation, the process underlying the production of these noun-substitution exercises at 24;4 is more creative than imitation of both pronoun and antecedent. Neither account, however, requires a referential linkage between the two utterances. (On the second account imitation is restricted to the level of the clause.)

An additional feature of this monologue should be noted here. In the first and third segments of (20), pronouns occur in two separate clauses. Since they occur in similar clausal contexts, they are interpretable from an adult point of view as coreferential. This distributional relationship between pronouns and context lends to the monologue a somewhat less linear character than that of the earlier monologues.

The next passage that contains the nominal form of reference, occurring at 24;13, is similar in many respects to this earlier one. It has characteristics in general of a chain sequence, and in particular of a noun substitution exercise. (Again, the full monologue appears in the Appendix.)

(21)   my broke my t-
       (re)pairman fix *it*
       maybe (re)pairman fix *that*
       fix *it*
       . . . . .
       fix *the car*

As in passage (20), (21) shows alternations between pronouns and fuller noun phrases (NPs) within the same verbal context. In this case, alternation occurs between the pronouns *it* and *that*, as well as between pronouns and more explicit forms (*the car*). The occurrence of a series of pronouns within the same verbal context again lends to these forms the appearance of coreferentiality.

The monologues in the fourth month, then, appear primarily complexive in nature. These monologues, like Anthony's, have the character of "self-educational linguistic games." In contrast, the later ones are increasingly narrative-like; increasingly, they present a sense of "communicative dynamism," in which a story line progresses over time (Firbas 1971; Danes 1974).

A monologue at 25;8, for example, shows a full NP alternating with a series of pronouns, each this time occurring within a *different* verbal context.

(22)   probably Mommy takes the corder out of my room cause I don't
            want (*it*)
        but right now we need to put *it* in my room
        but I like *it* in my room when I go to bed
        but not for my nap.

The referring forms that constitute this chain clearly appear to be coreferential. Note that reference is appropriately introduced with a full NP, "the corder." All of these phenomena—the occurrence of a coreferential chain of pronouns, appropriately preceded by a full NP, with each pronoun occurring in a different verbal context—contribute to the narrative-like character of the passage.

Two months later, at 28;0, a chain of coreferential pronouns occurs for the first time in subject position.

(23)   we are gonna at the ocean
        ocean is a little far away . . . far away
        I think *it*'s a couple blocks away
        maybe *it*'s down downtown and across the ocean and down the
            river
        and maybe *it*'s in . . .

Pronouns again occur in different clausal contexts: both pronouns that appear in completed clauses occur with different predicates. As in the earlier passage, the series is appropriately preceded by a fuller NP.

At 31;3, a passage with a clear story line appears.

(24)   Peter . . . (gave) his car
       I bought *it* (??)
       and he loved *it*
       then he honked kong honked
       got out of the car car
       drived to
       got into the car.

In this segment, the referent is again introduced with a specific noun. Reference is appropriately maintained through the use of a coreferential chain of pronouns. Each pronoun in the series occurs in a different verbal context ("bought it," "loved it") as do the coreferential specific nouns that follow ("got out of the car car," "got into the car").

The same points can be made for the remaining passages. At 32;8, for example, a long narrative-like passage again occurs, in which pronouns are introduced with fuller NPs.

(25)   today Daddy went trying to get into the race
       but the people said no
       so he has to watch *it* on television
       . . . . .
       but he couldn't go in *it*
       so he has to watch *it* on television.

At 33;21 a pronoun is appropriately used to index both preceding and following linguistic context. It is thus an instance of both anaphoric and cataphoric reference.

(26)   and they were walking to school
       she talks about *it*
       she said I don't think I wanna go to school.

This segment is part of a much longer, wandering narrative, much of which is fabricated by Emily. In this light, it is likely that the pronoun in (26) is used creatively—that is, in a novel context—with respect to both prior and subsequent speech. It is unlikely that a pragmatic rule of use would account for the pronoun's occurrence. This instance strongly suggests, then, that the pronoun in fact is used as a referential device.

Finally, at 34;8 coreferential pronouns are used in a variety of verbal contexts, in both subject and predicate position.

(27)   but I don't know what happened to the dumpster
       it was at the church parking lot

and all the big boys were jumping in *it*
I don't know what happened
it mustav been moved someway.

This demonstrates increased flexibility with the use of pronominal forms.

CHANGES IN EMILY'S USE OF NOMINAL REFERENCE

Pronouns interpretable as indexing an earlier nominal occur as early as 32;8. During the course of the recordings, the monologues show an overall increase in length of pronominal chains. The earliest instances, starting at 32;8, consist of a single instance of a pronoun. Several months later, chains of length two occur, followed in a few weeks by longer pronominal chains.

In the early passages, pronouns occur in similar clausal (and identical verbal) contexts, the similarity lending to these forms the appearance of coreferentiality. At first, single pronouns alternate with fuller NPs ("bought it" versus "bought the cheetah"; "the tree fell down" versus "that must fell down"). Later two different pronouns alternate with each other as well as with fuller NPs—but still within the same verbal context ("fix it" versus "fix that" versus "fixes her TV"). After this, coreferential pronouns start to occur within different verbal contexts, with the pronominal series appropriately preceded by fuller NPs. These form-context (that is, distributional) relationships begin to lend to the monologues a narrative-like quality. During the rest of the recorded period the monologues become increasingly narrative-like.

In the earlier monologues most pronouns occur in predicate position in their respective clauses. It is not until 28;0 that a chain of subject pronouns occurs, and only at 34;8 do coreferential pronouns alternate between subject and predicate position.

These observations suggest increasingly creative uses of pronouns during the course of the recordings. While pronouns appear in appropriate usage throughout the full fifteen-month period, I have argued that appropriate usage need not reflect mastery of the anaphoric function of the forms. Rather, seemingly anaphoric usages may in fact be based on less creative processes, involving imitation and paired associations. In the former case, both pronoun and antecedent are reproduced as part of a larger unit, as in (28):

(28)   hide the bottle
       where is *it*?

In the latter case, appropriate usage is based on either (a) semantic relations between the pronoun's co-occurring verb and some aspect of an earlier utterance (where the pronoun is part of the lexical verb), as in (29), or (b) pragmatic, distributional relations between pronoun and antecedent, as observed in adult speech (for example, the observation that pronouns tend to follow fuller NPs), as in (30).

(29) broccoli soup carrots cause rice
      baby eat *that*

(30) I don't know which kind of lady bought the crib
      I don't know what lady bought *it*.

Toward the end of the recorded period, coreferential chains of pronouns appear to be used in novel contexts, usages that appear in fact to be based on referential links between pronoun and textual antecedent.

It *and* That *with Predicational Antecedents*

The Appendix shows all instances of predicational reference that occur in the recordings. These are pronouns that, by adult standards, index either an earlier predication or a larger unit of text (one that includes at least a single predication). As Table 4.1 shows, most instances of this type of reference occur with the verb *do* (as either *do it* or *do that*). In fact, all but one instance of predicational reference through the eleventh month of the study are of this form. It is only in the twelfth month that pronouns appear with predicational antecedents with verbs other than *do*.

Let us look first at the contextual distributions of *do it* and *do that*. The first monologue shows a pattern that holds throughout most of the rest of the recordings: *do it* and *do that* are distributed differently with respect to earlier linguistic context. Consider passage (31), from 23;8:

(31) when my slep
      and and Mormor came
      then Mommy coming
      then get up
      time to go home
      time to go home
      drink p-water
      yesterday did *that*

      . . . . .

> Daddy Mommy Daddy put my into bed in my regular bed
> actually actually Mommy did *it*.

Here the first pronominal construction, *did that*, is interpretable as indexing a number of earlier clauses (from "when my slep" to "drink p-water"). It is thus interpretable as indexing an entire discourse unit. The second construction, in contrast, can be interpreted as indexing only the immediately preceding predicate ("put my into bed in my regular bed"). In this case, the subject nominal in the later utterance, *Mommy*, is chosen from one of several alternatives in the earlier clause ("Daddy Mommy Daddy").

This difference holds for the most part throughout the rest of the recorded period. *Do that* tends to index (from an adult point of view) large segments of text (see Appendix, passages at 23;8, 23;10, 24;23, and 33;4), while *do it* indexes only a single prior predicate, with its co-occurring subject nominal chosen from a number of earlier mentioned alternatives (see passages at 23;8, 24;4, 26;16, and 32;5). The question arises of to what extent these usages are based on imitative procedures and to what extent on mastery of the adult functions of the forms. As in the case of nominal reference, the use of the *do it* and *do that* constructions need not imply full control of their adult functions. Rather, seemingly anaphoric uses may again result from non-referential links between clauses; specifically from imitation or paired associations based on pragmatic rules of use.

DO IT

The first occurrence of the *do it* construction is at 23;8, in the passage reproduced in (31) above. At this date, the occurrence of several relatively sophisticated lexical items (such as "regular bed" and "actually") suggests that there may in fact be an imitative component to this early use. In this view, pronoun and antecedent are acquired and reproduced as part of a single discourse unit. An alternate interpretation involving somewhat more creative processes again involves rules of use based on distributional relationships between form and context in adult speech. On this second account, the use of *do it* reflects a process of complexive substitution in which construction of the later utterance depends on properties of the earlier one (that is, certain features of the earlier utterance are retained and others changed). Specifically, *do it* substitutes for the immediately preceding verb phrase, while the subject nominal, *Mommy*, is simply chosen from several alternatives also in the immediately preceding clause. Neither interpretation requires that Emily have mastery over the function of this form as a referential index device, or that it in fact has any semantic (referential) value at all.

At 24;4, this construction occurs twice in succession, in each case preceded by a subject nominal chosen from previously occurring alternatives (*tree, crib*):

(32)   I don't know what tree fell down
        who broke the crib
        the crib *did it*
        the tree *did it*
        the crib

It is unlikely that these alternations are constructed on a strictly imitative basis. The passage, in fact, does not "make sense" from a referential point of view; interpretation of the pronominal forms is not fully unambiguous. (Note that this passage occurs at the same date at which complexive substitution occurs for nominal reference.)

Two months later, at 26;16, two successive instances of *do it* again occur:

(33)   Daddy will put the light on uhn yeah
        . . . . .
        cause Mommy can't *do it* well
        so Daddy will *do it* when he gets home.

The distribution of forms here is similar to that of the passage in (32). Both reflect the following pattern:

        NP + explicit predicate
        NP + *do it*
        NP + *do it*.

In contrast to the earlier case, however, the pronouns here are clearly interpretable as coreferential.

The next (and last) appearance of the *do it* construction, from 32;5, follows a similar format:

(34)   but Arthur sure won't *do it* by himself
        but there are two tries
        Emily and Arthur will *do it* first
        two kids at a time
        Arthur and Emily *do it* first
        and then we hold hands

> I don't think Arthur wants to hold hands
> but I hold hands
> all of Danny Emily Arthur and all the kids can *do it*

Note that for the last three instances at least one subject nominal repeats an earlier NP. The extent to which these usages are imitative versus creative is unclear.

DO THAT

Similar arguments can be made for processes underlying the *do that* construction; seemingly anaphoric uses may result from nonreferential links between clauses. From a strictly imitative point of view, appropriate use of the construction arises from imitation of individual tokens of discourse, where pronoun and antecedent are acquired and reproduced as part of a larger discourse unit. On a second, less extreme account, links between pronoun and antecedent are based on pragmatic rules of use derived from distributional relationships in adult speech—in this case on the observation that *do that* tends to be used as a follow-up to lists of reported activities. These two accounts differ in that the latter assumes mastery of a more general function of the forms as discourse-bounding devices.

There is some suggestion that distributionally based rules of use are derived in part from the dyadic pre-bedtime routines in which Emily participates. As noted above, in the course of these routines Emily's father packages lists of activities with such discourse markers as "you know what we're going to do" and "now go to bed." At 23;2, note in particular that he concludes his remarks using a "do + demonstrative" construction, "do those things":

(35)   first thing you're going to do . . .
       but you know what?
       [list of activities]
       if you don't go to sleep
       we won't be able to do those things.

One can conjecture that similar units are concluded at times with the closely related *do that* construction ("if you don't go to sleep we won't be able to do that"). At 24;23 Emily, in fact, juxtaposes the latter construction with a phrase similar to that in (35): "afternoon we do that do all (those) kinda things":

(36)   *(then) you know what we do*
       we (make) (?) house

and then we [pause]
and then (then we make) [unintelligible]

then what we do
we can (go) play with (the) dollhouse
and when we('ve) done that
I can play

and you know what we do when I play
we do something 'pecial
we get juice
we get (jui-)

(and then) you know what we do
we going outside
and look at the flower
and not now
and now we just going to bed
afternoon we do that
do all (those) kinda thing
right now it's bedtime.

These observations, along with the observation that *do that* tends to be used as a conventional discourse-bounding device in adult speech, suggest that Emily has heard this construction used as a pragmatic boundary marker—specifically one that follows a list of reported activities. Given this assumption, it is plausible that her appropriate use of the construction is based on a rule of use derived from observations of distributional relations in adult speech, perhaps influenced in particular by her father's pre-bedtime routines.

Neither account of the appropriate use of pronouns, whether based on imitative processes or pragmatic rules of use, requires that the linkage between pronoun and antecedent be referential in nature. That is, neither account requires mastery of the cohesive function of the forms, in which appropriate referential usage relies on presuppositions derived from earlier text.

Finally, note the occurrence of the *do that* construction in a different contextual (distributional) relationship. At 28;21 this construction occurs twelve times, in each case indexing a single prior clause. At least four of these instances are coreferential.

IT AND THAT WITH VERBS OTHER THAN DO
At 32;0 the first instance of predicational reference with a verb other than *do* appears.

(37)   tomorrow we wake up from bed
    first me and Daddy and Mommy you eat breakfast
    eat breakfast like we usually do
    and then we're going to play
    and then soon as Dad comes Carl's going to come over
    and then we're going to play a little while
    and then Carl and Emily are both going down the car with some-
        body
    and we're going to ride to nursery school
    and then we when we get there we're all going to get out of the car
        go in to nursery school
    and Daddy's going to give us kisses
    then go
    and then say and then we will say goodbye
    then he's going to work
    and we're going to play at nursery school
    won't *that* be funny?

This monologue consists of two repetitions of a pattern, where each sequence reports a routine series of events in Emily's life (see Chapters 1 and 2). It is important to note that the pronoun occurs at the end of one such unit. As with instances of *do that* noted above, this pronominal usage can be viewed as a discourse boundary marker.

Two other monologues contain predicational uses of *it* and *that* with verbs other than *do*. At 32;8 *it* occurs once, and *that* three times, with the verb *to be* and predicational adjectives.

(38)   today Daddy went trying to get into the race
    but the people said no
    so he has to watch it on television
    I don't know why *that* is
    maybe cause there too many people
    I think *that* is why why
    . . . . .
    hooray my mom and dad and a man says you can run in the foot-
        race
    and I said *that*'s nice of you, I want to
    so next week I'm going to run to the foot
    and and run in the footrace
    cause they said I could
    it's nice . . .

This passage appears to have been fabricated in large part by Emily. To the extent that she uses pronouns in novel contexts, and given that their use cannot be accounted for by distributionally based rules of use, one can argue that they in fact serve an anaphoric function.

Finally, at 33;14 a relatively long coreferential chain occurs, in which at least five pronouns are interpretable as referring to the proposition "going in the street":

(39) but he knows he's not supposed to go in the street
      and only his father (says *it*'s okay in the s-)
      his mom says (*this*/*that*)
      what his mom say?
      okay to go in the street
      his mormor says *that*
      and I don't
      even I know
      and I still
      but now he's fine
      his mommy and daddy and (father) thought about *it*
      and said I don't think *it*'s okay cause your mormor says *it*'s not
            okay
      so they zoomed away
      and he got in the street
      that's okay okay okay
      nobody was in the street.

Pronouns occur here in two different verbal contexts: with the verbs *to say* and *to be*. The same argument can be made as for the preceding passage. This passage is clearly fabricated to a large extent, and pronominal usages cannot be accounted for by pragmatic rules of use. Thus the pronouns appear to have referential value, serving as intratextual indices (as cases of endophoric reference).

The distribution of forms in this passage—of coreferring pronouns occurring in different intraclausal contexts—helps create a relatively complex thematic structure. Through sheer frequency of mention, a single proposition assumes prominence over others.

From a formal point of view, pronouns occurring in the latter category appear with two different classes of verbs. As subjects, they co-occur with the verb *to be* and predicate adjectives:

      that/*it* is funny (32;0)
            why (32;8)
            why why (32;8)
            nice of you (32;8)
            nice (32;8)

fun   (32;8)
okay   (33;14)
okay   (33;14)
okay   (33;14)
okay okay okay   (33;14).

As predicates, pronouns serve as complements of verbs of speaking and cognition:

I don't like it   (28;21)
I know that   (32;37)
Mormor says that   (33;14)
his mommy and daddy and (father) thought about it   (33;14).

CHANGES IN EMILY'S USE OF PREDICATIONAL REFERENCE

Thus far we have observed the following relationships between form and context in Emily's speech. Pronouns interpretable as indexing a predication or larger unit of text occur as early as 23;28. Through 32 months, such usages occur only with the verb *do*. Of these instances, *do it* and *do that* (and the related form *that's what x do*) show different distributional properties: *do it* tends to co-occur with a subject nominal representing one of several alternatives occurring in an immediately preceding utterance, while *do that* tends to follow a list of reported activities. As a result of these co-occurrence relationships, the *do it* construction is interpretable as indexing a single predication (in an immediately preceding clause), while the *do that* construction appears, for the most part, to index a series of earlier clauses.

After 32 months, most instances of predicational *it* and *that* occur with verbs other than *do*. They occur first in subject position with the verb *to be* and predicate adjectives, and later as complements of verbs of speaking or cognition. In the final monologue in the series, pronouns with predicational antecedents occur in both of these intraclausal contexts; in this case pronouns alternate between subject and predicate position.

For predicational reference as for nominal reference, the length of pronominal chains increases during the course of the recordings. At first, pronouns occur in chains of length one (that is, single instances of pronouns with interpretable antecedents). This is followed by the appearance of pairs of pronouns. Since they appear both in succession and within the same verbal context, these forms are interpretable as coreferential.

(40)   the crib *did it*
       the tree *did it*

(41)   Daddy will put the light on
       cause Mommy can't *do it* well
       so Daddy will *do it* when he gets home.

Finally, longer chains of pronouns occur:

(42)   what his mom say?
       okay to go in the street
       his mormor says *that*
       and I don't
       even I know
       and I still
       but now he's fine
       his mommy and daddy and (father) thought about *it*
       and said I don't think *it*'s okay cause your mormor says *it*'s not
           okay.

Throughout the monologues, some links between pronoun and antecedent appear to be nonreferential in nature; specifically, based on imitation or distributionally based rules of use. In the former case the seemingly appropriate use of pronouns results from imitation (or near-imitation) of both pronoun and antecedent. In the latter case, the use of pronouns is based on pragmatic rules of use derived from distributional relationships observed in adult speech; for example, based on the observations that *do it* tends to occur with a subject nominal chosen from several alternatives occurring in an earlier utterance, and that *do that* often follows lists of reported activities. Neither of these accounts requires that pronouns have referential value.

As with nominal reference, it appears that by the end of the recorded period predicational pronouns are used in a more creative way, appearing in novel contexts, in relationships that do not appear to be based on pragmatic rules of use. By the end of the recordings, then, series of pronouns appear in fact to constitute coreferential chains.

Summary: Nominal and Predicational Reference

Observations of nominal and predicational reference suggest a gradually increasing sophistication in Emily's use of the pronouns *it* and *that,* with respect to the length of the chains in which they occur, their co-occurring verbs, and surface case-marking (that is, intraclausal position).

Many of the early instances of pronouns have no interpretable antecedents, nor do they appear to be used exophorically. In the first monologue in the recordings, at 21;8, single instances of pronouns start to occur in appropriate contexts. These are pronouns with clearly interpretable nominal antecedents. Pronouns with interpretable predicational antecedents start to occur two months later, at 23;8. After these early occurrences, parallel patterns continue for nominal and predicational reference.

For both types of reference, passages appear in the fourth month of the study in which two separate pronouns occur, each in a separate clause, and each appearing in its respective clause with the same verb:

> Mormor bought *it*
> *that*'s what Mormor bought
>
> the crib did *it*
> the tree did *it*.

After this, somewhat longer series begin to occur in which each pronoun again appears, in its respective clause, within the same verbal context. These longer same-verb chains appear several months earlier for nominal than for predicational reference:

> fix *it*
> fix *that*
> fix *it*   (24;13)
>
> why do you do *that*
> I think you maybe wanna do *that*
> why did you two do *that*   (28;19)

Finally, for both nominal and predicational reference, clearly coreferential pronouns begin to appear in different verbal contexts:

> I don't want *it*
> we need to put *it*
> I like *it*
>
> his mormor says *that*
> his mommy and daddy and (father) thought about *it*
> I don't think *it*'s ok.

This change with respect to predicational reference lags considerably behind the same change for nominal reference.

For both types of reference, most early instances appear in the clausal predicate. Subject chains of coreferential pronouns do not appear for nominal reference until 27;7, and for predicational reference until 32;8. Chains in which pronouns alternate between subject and predicate position occur only in the last few months of the recordings (33;14 for predicational and 34;8 for nominal reference):

> his mormor says *that*
> his mommy and daddy and (father) thought about *it*
> and said I don't think *it*'s okay cause your Mormor says *it*'s not
>   okay (33;14)

> *it* was at the church parking lot
> all the big boys were jumping in *it*
> *it* mustav been moved someway (34;8)

Thus nominal and predicational reference follow similar patterns of increasing length of pronominal chains, progression from same to different co-occurring verbs within these chains, and progression from predicate to subject to subject-predicate chains. For the most part, changes in predicational reference lag behind those in nominal reference.

FUNCTIONAL IMPLICATIONS
From a functional point of view these observations suggest a gradual change in Emily's mastery of the cohesive function of pronouns. The early monologues provide no evidence that the link between a pronoun and its interpretable antecedent is referential in nature. Rather, appropriate uses of pronouns seem to be based on such nonreferential processes as imitation of discourse units containing both pronoun and antecedent, as in (43), or paired associations between the verb that co-occurs with the pronoun and some earlier segment of speech, as in (44):

(43)   hide the bottle
       where is *it?*

(44)   broccoli soup carrots cause rice
       baby eat *that.*

In the latter case, some aspect of an earlier utterance evokes a verb + pronoun unit. In both cases it appears that pronouns are part of the lexical verb, a conjecture that is supported by the observation that many of the earliest instances of pronouns lack interpretable antecedents.[5]

In Emily's later monologues, one cannot account for the appropriate use of pronouns on the basis of paired associations derived from distributional relationships observed in adult speech. For nominal reference these pragmatic rules of use are based on the observation that pronouns and more explicit nouns tend to occur in close temporal proximity within similar or identical clausal contexts (more precisely, that verb + NP units tend to occur near verb + pronoun units). Such a pragmatic rule is sufficient to generate same-verb chains of nominal reference, as in

> I don't know which kind of lady bought the crib
> I don't know what lady bought *it*.

For predicational reference, appropriate instances of *do it* can be generated by pragmatic rules based on the observation that this construction tends to occur with a subject nominal that repeats one of several nominals in an earlier clause. The resulting discourse pattern consists of alternations between *do it* and a fuller predicate, as well as alternations between different subject nominals, as in

> I don't know what tree fell down
> the crib did *it*
> the tree did *it*.

Appropriate uses of *do that* and *that's what x do* can be generated by a rule of use based on the observation that these constructions tend to follow lists of reported activities, such as those produced by Emily's father as part of a pre-bedtime routine. For the *do that* construction, the resulting pattern consists of alternations between lists of activities and *do that*, as in

> we can (go) play with the dollhouse
> and when we've *done that* . . .
> we going outside and look at the flower . . .
> afternoon we *do that*.

In any of these processes, the link between pronominal form and textual antecedent is nonreferential in nature.

By the end of the recorded period, in contrast, at least some links between pronoun and antecedent appear to be made on a referential basis, where pronouns and earlier segments of speech (other pronouns, specific nouns, predicates, full clauses) occur in coreferring relationships. The appropriate use of pronouns in novel contexts—in instances that cannot be accounted for by general rules of use—suggests that Emily's mastery of the anaphoric function of pronouns progresses during the course of the recordings. Gradually, she appears to acquire the adult function of pronouns as devices whose denotational value is based on presuppositions derived from earlier text.

Monologues as Developmental Workspace

Given that the cohesive function of pronouns evolves during the course of the recordings, the question arises whether Emily's crib talk provides a workspace for this development, as implied by Weir (1962). I focus for this discussion on Emily's pronominal substitution patterns: those segments of her monologues in which pronouns alternate with fuller NPs and other forms, as in (45).

(45)   Mormor bought *it*
        Mormor bought the cheetah

        I don't know which kind of lady bought the crib
        I don't know what lady bought *it*

        fix *it*
        fix *that*
        fixes the car.

Weir presents similar passages from Anthony's speech, such as (46):

(46)   take the monkey
        take *it*.

For Weir, such passages constitute metalinguistic exercises: "pronominal substitution exercises . . . occupy the child a good deal . . . The great number of pronominal substitution exercises . . . point to the fact that these are genuine learning exercises" (1962, 110). On this account, alternations such as those in (45) and (46) constitute "practice" rather than mere "play."

This perspective, along with the observations of Emily's monologues, leads to a question of developmental process: Given that passages such as those in (45) and (46) are produced on a nonreferential basis, does the resulting arrangement of forms (for example, of pronouns and more explicit nouns) contribute to the emergence of a referential link between pronoun and contextually occurring noun?

It is plausible that such metalinguistic procedures—in which similar, but not identical, constructions are juxtaposed—result in the forefronting of *contrasts* between utterances for the child. From this point of view, the highlighting of formal distinctions affects the child's participation in later social interactions. For example, the juxtaposition of specific NPs (such as *the crib*) and pronouns (*it*) in the child's monologic speech may facilitate focus on this contrast in later adult speech. Thus the highlighting of formal distinctions may influence the child's attention to functional distinctions, in this case directing attention toward the semantic-referential sameness of pronoun and contextually occurring noun.

This proposal is illustrated in example (47), taken from a mother-child interaction quoted by Wertsch and Stone (1985). The child, age 2½, has been instructed to complete a "copy" puzzle in accordance with a "model" puzzle.

(47)   C: (C glances at the pieces pile; C looks at the copy puzzle; C picks up the orange piece from the pieces pile.) Now where do you think *the orange one* goes?
       M: Where does *it* go on the other truck? (C looks at the model puzzle.)
       C: Right there. (C points to the orange piece in the model puzzle.) *The orange one* goes right there.

Note that here noun-pronoun alternations cross speaker boundaries, and each nominal occurs within a similar intraclausal context. In accordance with the above account, one can propose that similar alternations in monologue lead to a refocusing of the child's attention in social situations. More specifically, the forefronting of formal distinctions in a monologic setting may lead the child to focus, in subsequent social interaction, on both verbal and nonverbal contextual cues (such as the semantics of co-occurring verbs, direction of eye gaze and finger points); these cues in turn aid the child in resolving the pronominal reference, and thus in interpreting the pronoun's coreferential relationship with other nominal forms. As a result, pronoun and nominal antecedent come to "mean the same thing."

By this account, then, formal distinctions highlighted in monologue are assessed from a functional point of view in subsequent dialogue; in other words, functional distinctions *emerge from* formal distinctions practiced in monologue. It is in this sense that noun-pronoun substitution exercises may contribute to the discourse-cohesive function of the forms.

The same points can be made for alternations between pronouns and larger units of text (those including predications). The passage at 24;23, for example, consists of four repetitions of the pattern

(and then you know) what we do
[list of activities]
(we do that)

where each list of reported activities is preceded by *what we do,* and two units conclude with *do that.* Like noun-pronoun alternations, this segment can be viewed as a pronominal substitution exercise: in this case similar pronominal constructions (*we've done that* and *we do that*) substitute for two different discourse units. Thus the monologue contains alternations between pronouns and larger segments of discourse. In the model proposed above, these alternations serve to highlight formal distinctions, leading to a refocusing of attention in subsequent dialogue, and thus contributing to mastery of the referential function of these pronominal constructions.[6]

Consistent with Weir's (1962) analysis, on this account as well Emily's pronominal substitutions constitute practice rather than (or in addition to) mere play. I have suggested that the process of appropriating pronominal forms as cohesive devices first involves the appropriation of larger discourse patterns—either on a strictly imitative basis or on the basis of distributionally based rules of use. The discourse segments that result from these procedures provide a basis for the working out of semantic-referential relationships between forms.

Finally, it is useful to compare Emily's discourse to that of children in a later stage of development. The children studied by Karmiloff-Smith (1980, 1985, 1986), for example, show greater mastery of discourse skills that involve the use of a "thematic subject constraint" to guide the choice of pronouns or fuller NPs. To the extent that acts of speaking are guided by such constraints, the speaker has achieved greater ability to sustain cohesive discourse about topics whose existence and identity are created through the act of speaking itself (Silverstein 1985; Wertsch 1985b; Levy 1987).

Emily's monologues, in contrast, remain essentially complexive in nature. I have suggested that in her speech thematic structure is created in retrospect, emerging in part from the use of pronominal coreferences, which lend thematic prominence to the pronoun's referent. Thus just as in adult speech thematic structure emerges from the linking of utterances with one another, in Emily's speech themes are created as utterances are spontaneously linked together. At the level of discourse, "generating the linguistic form of utterances is a kind of thinking itself" (McNeill 1988).

The fact that Emily creates monologues with apparent thematic structure does not mean that she is "aware of" that structure, nor that her productions are consistently guided by global thematic constraints. The question remains whether the mastery of these abilities is influenced by earlier complexively based procedures—whether in this sense the development of the cohesive system paves the way for further cognitive-linguistic developments.

Appendix

(21;8)
[talking to doll, "baby"]
baby no in night
cause baby crying
baby in might
baby in might
my baby no in my car
my baby in my
baby no eat supper in in in this
no eat broccoli no
so my baby have dinner
then baby get sick
baby no eat dinner
broccoli soup carrots cause rice
baby eat *that*
baby no in night
broccoli broccoli soup carrots cabbage
no baby sleeping
so why baby eat
then baby get sick
Emmy no eat dinner
broccoli soup cause
no baby sleeping
baby sleeping all night

(21;13)
Da- Da- Daddy Daddy no (wakey) Emmy
don't wake Emmy up
(?) Emmy Emmy wake
afternoon Emmy wake up
then Mormor come
now Emmy afternoon
Emmy sleep

afternoon Daddy coming pretty soon
Emmy go to sleep
then Mormor come
that get Emmy
then get Emmy
then Mormor get Emmy out
sleep
then then Emmy no go sleep
Mormor coming
I be really dry
Emmy wake
Emmy woke up
Emmy get uh huh
Emmy woke up
Emmy get
Emmy woke up

(23;8)
when Mormor get me
when Mormor make pretty
Mommy had a help
my sleep
Mommy came
and Mommy get get up
time go home
when my slep
and and Mormor came
then Mommy coming
then get up
time to go home
time to go home
drink p-water [Perrier]
yesterday did *that*
now Emmy sleeping in regular bed
yesterday my slept
and say um
and in Tanta house
and Mommy woke my up
and go
time to go home
and then Mormor came
and Mormor said
time (dgo) home

and Daddy bring p-water
and yesterday Mommy and Mormor and Daddy bring my in my
      regular bed
[10-second pause]
I can (?) Mommy
but my in Daddy and Mommy's
when Mormor came in
and Mommy got it
make my bed
when when Mommy came in
when my bed
when when I sleeping Tanta house
Mommy came wake my up
because time to go home
drink p-water
. . . . .
Daddy Mommy Daddy put my into bed in my regular bed
actually actually Mommy did *it*

(23;10)
lessons
get lessons
and come back
that napping
the Babar lessons
that what Babar do.

(23;11)
one morning when Emmy go Morm in the daytime
that's what Emmy do sometime.

(23;11)
and my get that diaper
and put *it* on

(23;11)
there Emmy's that other room
that's where the baby

(24;3)
hide the bottle
where is *it?*

(24;4)
where the put the this cheetah
Mormor bought *it*
but the tiger got something home
but the tiger got m Emmy
bo but Mormor bought the cheetah
ya foot Emily
but I don't know who bo bought the tiger
Mommy Mormor or Daddy or Mommy
Mormor bought the cheetah
I don't know what kids bought the ti-
Mormor bought the cheetah
that's what Mormor bought the cheetah
what (?) the tree fell down
could be
I don't know which
maybe tree fell down and broke that crib
I don't know what tree fell down
who broke the crib
the crib did *it*
the tree did *it*
the crib
but I don't know which kind of lady bought the crib
but that one fell down
that one was (?)
that tree must then broke that crib
that must fell down
I don't know what lady bought *it*
but the lady went to get this new crib
but then this is one
bring it back (keep)
and ah you know sup broke the tree
(?) the lady did not

(24;8)
everybody sat like a bear
go
probly I sat on Mormor's lap
and we went to the library
probably *that*'s what we did
probably we did we did

(24;13)
my broke my t-
(re)pairman fix *it*
maybe (re)pairman fix *that*
fix *it*
[low voice] (Poppy that)
fix the car
car not broken
but the T-TV broke
other peop-
then
but telling me
the boy boy called
(she's gonna go in my ? now
she go he- to see other town)
there and that one there
Emmy's repairman fixes her TV for her
but the boys the boy goes
that's his TV
why can't go my play get his TV?
Doctor (Margot) some tee times
that boy goes my bed that
someone watches TV
but the boy was bro- [whispers] broken broken
have a tank
I broken
but the boy passed up the passed
so my sleeping
. . . . .
though I don't want to watch little kitty
so the repairman fix *it*
and my went upstairs to listen to other TV
and not broke other tee
listen TV upstairs on the floor
and Dad turn off *it*
and my watchin (moose)

(24;15)
I call my bed [unintelligible]
that's what Emily calls *it*

(24;23)
(then) you know what we do

we (make) (?) house
and then we
[pause]
and then (then we make) (?)
[unintelligible]
then what we do
we can (go) play with (the) dollhouse
and when we('ve) done *that*
I can play
and you know what we do when I play
we do something pecial
we get juice
we get (jui-)
(and then) you know what we do
we going outside
and look at the flower
and not now
and now we just going to bed
afternoon we do *that*
do all (those) kinda thing
right now it's bedtime

(25;8)
probably Mommy takes the corder out of my room cause I don't
    want (*it*)
but right now we need to put *it* in my room
but I like *it* in my room when I go to bed
but not for my nap

(26;16)
Daddy will put the light on uhn yeah
(she looks like a wet too)
cause Mommy can't do *it* well
so Daddy will do *it* when he gets home

(26;28)
Emmy would take the paper off of the
and give *it* to Mother

(28;0)
we are gonna at the ocean
ocean is a little far away
. . . . .

far away
I think *it*'s a couple blocks away
maybe *it*'s down downtown and across the ocean and down the
      river
and maybe *it*'s in
the hot dogs was be in a fridge
and the fridge (would) be in the water over by a shore
and then we could go in and get a hot dog and bring it out to the
      river
and then (sharks) go in the river and (bite) me in the ocean
and ocean be over by I think a couple of blocks away
and we could be
and we could find any hot dogs
um the hot dogs gonna be for the for the beach
then the bridge is gonna
we'll have to go in the green car
cause *that*'s where the car seats are

(28;21)
and we don't do it that much
but sometimes you go rinky-dinky all over the house
and do *that*
and go running away
and Stephen says I don't like *it*
why do you do *that* says Pooh-Bear
and my mom says you you look like a
and that's why you yeah
and that's why
why don't you go (walking with your bear)?
why why why why
why did you do *that*? [5 times]
why did you go flying about getting out of bed?
why do you do *that*?
I'm afraid you can't run round cause you're in bed
up and you wake up
why do you go running around when Stephen is
why do you do *that*?
I think you maybe wanna do *that*
but you can't
over and over you can't
I know you can't have matches match
you can't go with him in his (playpen)
one blanket two blankets bear blankets
why were you running around in Stephen's room

and the other room and another room?
children what are you doing?
why did you two do *that*?
you can't do *that*
you can't
and you can't go with Stephen
why do you go running and running running and anyplace?
I don't want you to go
don't want you to run outside

(30;3)
suppose I have (giraffe)
suppose I have giraffe to Dad
suppose we (give giraffe) to me and to Jackie and Carl and Emily
if I did *that*

(31;3)
Peter . . . (gave) . . . his car
I bought *it* (??)
and he loved *it*
then he honked kong honked
got out of the car car
drived to
got into the car

(32;0)
tomorrow we wake up from bed
first me and Daddy and Mommy you eat breakfast
eat breakfast like we usually do
and then we're going to play
and then soon as Dad comes Carl's going to come over
and then we're going to play a little while
and then Carl and Emily are both going down the car with some-
    body
and we're going to ride to nursery school
and then we when we get there we're all going to get out of the car
    go in to nursery school
and Daddy's going to give us kisses
then go
and then say and then we will say goodbye
then he's going to work
and we're going to play at nursery school
won't *that* be funny?

(32;5)
watch the footrace
Danny's daddy's going to run
and his mommy and Danny and Arthur are going to do
I don't
watching watching too
and then I want to have the footrace
I'm going to have the footrace
my mom and dad are just going to watch me
but they my they're going to watch right on the sidewalk there
now while I have the footrace
then when I get done
then Arthur will do *it*
and then when Arthur gets done
child men won't you watch
and kids will run in the footrace
well some men will run in the footrace
and some kids will run in the footrace
but not too many kids can run in the footrace
just a couple of kids like Arthur and Danny and me can run by ourselves
while my mommy and daddy will wait
and I'll run by myself
and Arthur and Danny will
and all the kids will run with their daddies
okay?
and mommies too
and some kids can to run by theirselves
and some kids can't
like Sara and Jimmy
their mommy has to go with them
no
sure!
Arthur and Danny can
Arthur will not be with anybody
and Danny will be with somebody
(I) don't know who
maybe his daddy or his mommy will take care of Danny
but Arthur sure won't do *it* by himself
but there are two tries
Emily and Arthur will do *it* first
two kids at a time
Arthur and Emily do *it* first

and then we hold hands
I don't think Arthur wants to hold hands
but I hold hands
all of Danny Emily Arthur and all the kids can do *it*

(32;8)
today Daddy went trying to get into the race
but the people said no
so he has to watch *it* on television
I don't know why *that* is
maybe cause there too many people
I think *that* is why why
but he couldn't go in *it*
so he has to watch *it* on television
see on Halloween day then he can run in a race
and I can watch him
see I wish I could watch him
but they said no no no Daddy Daddy Daddy no no no no have to
    watch have to have to watch have to watch on television
see on Halloween day
then he can run in a race
and I can watch him
see I wish I could watch him
but they said no no no
Daddy Daddy Daddy
no no no no
have to watch
have to
have to watch
have to watch on television
but Halloween day he can run run in the race
tomorrow he'll run run run in the race
he says yes
hooray my mom and dad and a man says you can run in the foot-
    race
and I said *that*'s nice of you, I want to
so next week I'm going to run to the foot
and and run in the footrace
cause they said I could
it's nice
a week or so Sunday and Saturday and Monday and Tuesday I'm
    going to run in the footrace
because *that*'s fun

oh Tuesday that's Carl's birthday
before it was the footrace
the Saturday and Sunday eeooo Wednesday and Thursday and Fri-
     day Friday
oh wonderful

(32;26)
Carl brought along a lot of food
Carl brought along two bags
one for (?)
one for Seth
one for Uncle Don
and one for (?) and (?)
you don't want to (?)
I don't have anything cause I want a drink
just the other people want a p- (?)
but they just want *it*
so they put *it* in there up there

(32;27)
beautiful day
tomorrow it's going to be day Tanta day Tanta day
all the kids come just home Carl Carl Carl Danny Lance Janet
I don't know about Lance or Jack
I know Janet and Carl k- Carl and Danny
Danny and Carl and Janet come
I don't know about Lance and um Jackie
if they don't come
Lance and Jackie maybe maybe their mommy and daddy won't
     work
I think they like to be home
but certainly are more (?)
and Carl and Janet and Dan I don't (know)
and Jack Jackie and Lance I don't know are coming
I'll ask Tanta if Lance and Jackie are c-
cause I don't know bout Lance and Jackie come
I sure know Danny and Lance and um Carl are coming
I don't know about Lance and Jackie
Carl is coming
and Jack and um Jack's c- gonna be there
and Danny and L- and Carl went too
I know *that*

(33;4)
just before breakfast I changed all of my clothes
just before breakfast put on my clothes
see (in) when I just wake up I first get out of bed
and I get out of my room
and I go in Mommy and Daddy's bedroom
and play awhile
and then it's breakfast
(??) (get in) my clothes
and go down for breakfast
see and I choose what I want
cheese omelet or eggs eggs cheese omelet or yoghurt
so I do *that*

(33;12)
actually it's Stephen's koala bear . . .
when Stephen wakes up I'll have to throw his koala bear in his room
cause *it*'s really Stephen's
as a matter of fact Stephen's
as a matter of fact *it*'s sleeping with me now . . .

(33;14)
but he knows he's not supposed to go in the street
and only his father (says *it*'s okay in the s-)
his mom says (*this? that?*)
what his mom say?
okay to go in the street
his mormor says *that*
and I don't
even I know
and I still
but now he's fine
his mommy and daddy and (father) thought about *it*
and said I don't think *it*'s okay cause your mormor says *it*'s not
      okay
so they zoomed away
and he got in the street
that's okay okay okay
nobody was in the street [singsong voice]
he just (?)
oh that was a nice song

(33;21)
Robertson woke up the next morning
(but) Robertson (care full) up the next morning
got out of bed
dressed herself in new clothes
and Jonathan (could)
Jonathan wakes up (?)
and he woke up the the pants and a dress and a wig and
(handsome) and a and a necklace
she walked out to Jonathan
and Jonathan was already dressed
and they went
and they were walking to school
she talks about *it*
she said I don't think I wanna go to school
the boy said I wanna go to school
so so walked boys to school
and the girl went to nursery school
the boy was the see the girl walked the boy to nursery school
and the girl and then the girl walked to nursery school

(34;8)
but I don't know what happened to the dumpster
it was at the church parking lot
and all the big boys were jumping in *it*
I don't know what happened
it mustav been moved someway
yeah

Chapter 5

Monologue as a Speech Genre

Julie Gerhardt

What is the basis for the meanings of grammatical categories in children's speech? Are semantic categories adequate to the task of representing the child's early meaning system? If not, what are the alternatives? Although critics of strictly formal approaches to language share the view that grammatical forms must be associated with particular meanings, they differ in their proposals for characterizing the relevant meanings. In the literature on children's language, the usual assumption is that grammatical forms are associated with semantic meanings—where the semantic meanings are grounded in one of two ways: either they are claimed to be conceptually basic to the child's early cognitive system, or they are assumed to be conceptually transparent as objective event parameters. While the view that the first grammatical categories that emerge are organized semantically is quite reasonable, its foundational assumptions need to be questioned: typically, semantic categories are construed in terms of distinctions that have nothing to do with the discourse-pragmatic context of the event of communication. That is, in practice, semantic-level accounts tend to discount the possibility that children may organize their early grammars as systems that are sensitive to the communicative aspects of the speech event. Hence, these accounts make no attempt to capture the possible relevance of the discourse context or communicative context to the child's developing grammar.

In this chapter, I will attempt to provide an alternative to the recent cognitivist and objectivist construals of the semantic categories associated with the verb. A more experientially based construal of the very same categories will be put forth based on a child's involvement in different modes of discourse.[1]

The particular concern here is to consider the relevance of certain theoretical proposals in linguistics for research in language acquisition. According to certain functionally based studies of verb morphology, the verb inflections have evolved to serve particular discourse functions, with the implication that the sentence-level semantic categories such as aspect and tense are in part derived from these prior discourse functions (Benveniste 1971; Hopper 1979, 1982; Reid 1980; Givon 1982). I suggest that such claims may be relevant to acquisition research if our task is to understand how semantic-level categories such as aspect and tense emerge for the child. Moreover, this appeal to discourse—both its function and its structure—as a source for semantic categories can provide insight into other basic issues in language acquisition, for example, (a) the nature of early meaning representations, in particular for grammatical meaning, and (b) ways of deriving aspects of linguistic structure from language use.

The prevailing assumption has been that semantic categories such as aspect are derived more or less extensionally—by the child's recognition of certain parameters of real-world events. For example, various researchers (Antinucci and Miller 1976; Bloom, Lifter, and Hafitz 1980; Stephany 1981) have proposed that children initially use verb morphology to mark the lexical aspect of different classes of verbs. In this case, lexical aspect is taken to refer to the verb's natural embodiment of certain objective features of real-world events, that is, whether events have endpoints or not, involve changes of state of an object or not, are durative or not, and so on. Thus the claim that the child's marking of such event parameters is based on and reflects preestablished cognitive categories in fact reduces to a sort of correspondence claim in which the child's first use of verb morphology is taken to represent certain objective, perceptible features of events.[2] Moreover, the distinctions to be learned are presumably those to which the child is attuned independent of her interactions with others.[3]

The point of departure for the present research is to suggest that if we can rid ourselves of the lure of correspondence theories, which basically attempt to map language onto our pictures of the world, a discourse perspective offers a way of deriving the meanings of the verb inflections, in part, from the meanings implied by the distributional regularities in the child's discourse. That is, the situatedness of the inflections in particular discourse contexts provides conditions for these markers to become anchored in meanings initially encoded by the discourse configuration.

The focus of this chapter is on Emily's use of verb morphology in her spontaneous speech during the six-week period from 22;16 to 24;2. Given the controversy in the literature over the early status of this paradigm—whether it is first used to express aspect and/or tense (Bronckart and Sinclair 1973; Antinucci and Miller 1976; Bloom, Lifter, and Hafitz 1980; Smith 1980; Stephany 1981; Weist et al. 1984; Weist 1986)—I will examine Emily's use of the inflections with respect to the empirical predictions of the "aspect before tense" hypothesis and the counterpredictions of the "tense as well as aspect" hypothesis. The point in doing so is not to attempt to resolve the controversy as formulated but to reorient the discussion concerning the early meanings of these forms away from purely perceptual-cognitive accounts in favor of an account that recognizes their potential discourse-pragmatic values. Indeed, since the Emily data include sequentially organized monologues and self-assertive dialogues, each of her descriptive utterances when interpreted *in situ* can be claimed to harbor a discourse value as well. The further claim to be developed here is that even with respect to her use of verb morphology, each morpheme is itself initially indexically reliant on the discourse contexts in which it occurs. This dependency exists both at the level of form and at the level of function. With development, certain meanings once carried by the context are abstracted and become associated with the forms themselves. Thenceforth, the inflections are freer to migrate to new contexts.

More particularly, concerning form, I will show that initially the verb morphology systematically co-occurs with other forms in the discourse (such as the forms of self-reference *I* versus *Emmy-my*) suggesting that the forms work together as devices to encode a particular type of meaning. We can think of this as a mode of "configural encoding," since a configuration of forms, rather than a single morpheme, is used as signifier to signify a particular type of meaning. Concerning function, I will suggest that initially each of the verb inflections refers to an *undifferentiated functional cluster*. This is not equivalent to the claim that the first meanings assigned to these forms are discourse meanings in the adult sense (such as *-ed* for "in sequence"). Rather, the incipient discourse and semantic potentials are undifferentiated from each other. Nevertheless, these functional clusters display a sensitivity that exceeds the sentence-level meanings of aspect and/or tense, and in this sense they can be considered discourse-conditioned.

These claims have implications for the nature of early meaning representations. As Bowerman (1985) points out, there are at least two types of error data that can be used to make inferences about the child's system of grammar: errors of commission (such as *goed*) and errors of omission (that is, applying a form in a more limited context than would be predicted from adult usage). The restricted use of a form by a child implies that to the child it has a restricted meaning. What are these restricted meanings like? I will suggest that at least with respect to Emily's use of verb morphology (where each form initially exhibits errors of omission), each form, rather than being associated with a particular meaning narrowly construed, appears to be associated with a *meaning schema* such that a particular value on one dimension of meaning implies a particular value on another dimension of meaning. For example, a particular value with respect to aspect has implications for the dimension of agency: the child does not initially have access, so to speak, to the notion of perfectivity independent of a particular mode of agency. Thus, from the analyst's point of view, the child seems to have a cluster of interrelated meaning components associated with each form. For the young child, however, I will claim that the different meaning components are functionally undifferentiated as schematized wholes. With development the child learns to isolate and operate independently on the different meaning components, so that a particular value on a dimension of aspect no longer implies a particular mode of agency—although certain tendencies continue to exist (Hopper and Thompson 1980). The child's rules become more generalized and less context-determined. The isolable semantic-level meanings eventually ascribed to each form are thus derived from the meanings implicit in these early overly inclusive meaning schemata.

This last proposal implies that aspects of linguistic structure are derived from language use. Thus, rather than view pragmatics as a competence domain in its own right—as merely the third strand of language development (the strands being syntax, semantics, and pragmatics)—in this chapter I seek to characterize various discourse-pragmatic contexts of language use in order to offer a partial account of the emergence of the verb-morphological paradigm in Emily's speech. In other words, it will be proposed that the initial restriction of Emily's verb morphology to particular discourse contexts does not have an adventitious relation to the meanings that eventually accrue to these forms. The earlier context-dependent pragmatic meanings are the basis for the formation of the more discrete event-based semantic meanings that eventually emerge. Indeed, according to Silverstein (1985), semiotic systems such as language are functionally stratified such that semantic categories (those which contribute to the most abstract task of reference and predication) are anchored in a developmentally prior set of discourse-pragmatic categories computed with respect to the context of use through the indexical functioning of particular forms. Thus, in this chapter I attempt, to the extent that developmental progressions of particular morphemes can be traced, to show how later, contextually less restricted, uses of a form are based on Emily's abstraction of a more semanticized meaning from an earlier discourse-based meaning cluster.

Literature Review

From a functional perspective, certain linguists have proposed that the primary function of verb morphology is to mark distinctions inherent to narrative discourse (Benveniste 1971; Hopper 1979, 1982; Reid 1980; Givon 1982). According to Hopper, narrative discourse typically presents events in terms of two types of perspectives: events viewed as thematic in that they are sequentially structured and contingent upon one another are marked as foreground (FG), and material viewed as static and descriptive is presented as background (BG). Since languages often realize this distinction through contrasts in verb morphology (which also realize tense-aspect distinctions) this results in the interesting phenomenon of functional overlap: the same formal means are used as coding devices for the expression of different functional systems. This phenomenon has led linguists to make claims about the historical priority of a particular system and to view the others as derivative. For example, according to Hopper (1979, 217), aspectual categories should be viewed as "DERIVING FROM discourse, rather than as ready-made devices 'deployed' in discourse because they already happen to exist." That is, historically, certain implicatures of the discourse level meanings of the inflections come to be reinterpreted aspectually at the sentence level: "in sequence" becomes "completion." (See Traugott 1982 for the counterclaim that, historically, discourse meanings follow from semantic meanings.) The tendency to treat aspect as a sentence-level semantic category, Hopper considers an artifact of the tendency to treat sentences as independent of their discourse context. Consequently, the speaker's attempt to encode the foreground and background may be (mis)interpreted as the sentence-level marking of aspect and tense. Clearly, the claim that the verb-inflectional paradigm encodes more than a single functional system of meaning poses difficulties for the researcher.

In contrast, the controversy in the child-language literature concerning the early use of these forms hardly mentions discourse-pragmatic factors at all.[4] According to one camp, the use of the verb inflections is determined by the lexical aspect of different classes of verbs (Bronckart and Sinclair 1973; Antinucci and Miller 1976; Bloom, Lifter, and Hafitz 1980; Stephany 1981). For example, according to Antinucci and Miller, children from about 18;0 to 30;0 months restrict their use of the compound past in Italian and the simple past in English to verbs that indicate the present results of a change of state of an object. Similarly, according to Bloom, Lifter, and Hafitz, the use of all three verb inflections in English is determined by the lexical aspect of different classes of verbs: -*ed* for nondurative/completive verbs; -*ing* for durative/noncompletive verbs; -*s* for durative/completive verbs. In other terms, children use the past inflection to mark what have been called "telic" verbs (Comrie 1976) or "accomplishment" verbs (Vendler 1967). The progressive is used to mark what both Kenny (1967) and Vendler (1967) call "activity" verbs. These findings have been interpreted as indicating that children mark aspectual notions (that is, lexical aspect) rather than tense when first using verb morphology. This interpretation is claimed to be in accord with general principles of conceptual development. For example, Antinucci and Miller claim that it is cognitively easier to grasp the physically present results of an object's transformation than to represent a situation displaced in time. In other words, tense marking requires the more abstract capacity to represent displaced events as well as the ability to order the time of the event referred to with the ongoing speech time.

This view has been recently challenged by Weist and his colleagues (Weist et al. 1984; Weist 1986) based on findings from Polish-speaking children of a similarly young age.[5] According to their data, children do not necessarily restrict their use of past morphology to telic verbs expressing completed events; past morphology also occurs with noncompletive/activity verbs for events without a goal. Although the children studied exhibited a tendency to mark telic verbs as past more often than activity verbs, such tendencies do not indicate a cognitive constraint, merely a discourse preference. Thus, Weist and his colleagues claim that the postsensorimotor child is able to represent displaced events that are prior to speech time in a way that is independent of whether or not the events are completed, and hence can use past morphology to order an event as prior to the moment of speaking. In short, Weist claims that aspect and tense are independent notions which can emerge simultaneously for the child.

Nevertheless, Weist proposes that the child operates under another type of constraint in developing a tense system. According to both Smith (1980) and Weist (1986), the child of about 18;0 can coordinate only "speech time" (the interval of the speech act) and "event time" (the time of occurrence of an event relative to speech time). She is not yet able to represent an independent "reference time" (a temporal point established by the linguistic context, often through an adverb). (See Reichenbach 1947 and Comrie 1985 for more on these terms.) In fact, Weist proposes that the child's construction of a fully developed tense system is dependent on her conceptual development, which progresses through four different phases with respect to the marking of tense relations. The initial phase is restricted to the "here and now" context of speech. In the second phase, the child can begin to order events as prior to, subsequent to, or simultaneous with the speech time (ST), using verb morphology to do so. In the third phase, temporal adverbs emerge, which indicate that the child can conceive of an independent reference time (RT); this occurs at about 36;0 for most children, but 30;0 for the Polish children studied by Weist. However, the temporal relations expressed by the adverbs are equivalent to the time period denoted by the verb morphology, so that the event time (ET) is claimed to be "restricted to the RT context" (1986, 357). In the fourth phase, ST, ET, and RT are conceptualized independently of each other and thus "can be related freely" (ibid.).

These issues are pertinent to the research reported here. Since Emily begins to order events with respect to one another using the sequencers *when-then* before she is 30;0, her output is precocious with respect to the age norms suggested by Weist. In addition, since each of Emily's inflections turns out to occur with a semantically heterogeneous class of verbs, her output does not conform to the predictions of the "aspect before tense" hypothesis. However, besides testing these empirical predictions, my intent here is to develop a method for investigating the child's early use of verb morphology in terms of some possible discourse contexts in which this system may emerge. In this sense this research is extremely provisional: I attempt to discover whether any significant regularities obtain with respect to Emily's verb morphology in different contexts of use and, if so, whether these patterns are informative about the eventual emergence of the aspect and tense values of these forms.

The Emily Corpus

The following analysis of Emily's speech covers the six-week period from 22;16 to 24;2. For purposes of comparison with other subjects, it should be mentioned that Emily was a little older than Antinucci and Miller's and Weist's youngest subjects (18;0) though not older than the youngest reported by Bloom, Lifter, and Hafitz (22;0). However, according to Bloom (personal communication), Emily's MLU as inferred from her crib speech is higher than that of any of Bloom's subjects—a point that makes comparisons problematic. I will consider this point further below.

Dialogic and monologic discourse will be compared in the analysis. But these two categories, as analyst's categories, turn out to be too general to capture significant regularities in the verb system. Therefore, once patterns of linguistic and nonlinguistic behaviors are discerned, these will be used to interpret what the functionally relevant discourse parameters are for Emily's speech, and thus we will be able to go beyond the initial functional cuts of dialogue versus monologue.

Phase I: Emily at 22;16–22;20

The analysis begins by focusing on a rather brief period: five days when Emily was 22;16–22;20 (phase I). First I will contrast the dialogues with the monologues as a way of presenting some of the patterns in Emily's speech. Then I will analyze in detail the phase I monologues, followed by the phase I dialogues. For purposes of this investigation, I have tabulated only those utterances which contain a verb and at least a recoverable subject.

MONOLOGUES VERSUS DIALOGUES

Let us consider dialogues 1–3 and monologues 1–3 in the Appendix to this chapter. They are representative of the data for this five-day period, from which there are 18 utterances in the dialogues and 42 in the monologues. Two features of the monologues immediately stand out. The first is their sequential structuring by Emily herself. None of the monologic utterances occurs on its own. In contrast, the dialogues are not sequentially structured by Emily herself. Four utterances are followed by a second turn of Emily's without the addressee having interceded but these are mere repetitions on Emily's part and therefore quite unlike the monologic sequences (for a single example, see D3). Second, the sequentially structured utterances appear to make sense together. Each particular utterance consists of a part of a more or less unified event-type composed of different but related action components. This suggests that one of the cognitive enabling conditions of Emily's monologic speech may be that she have some kind of experientially organized event representation that she can try to project into discourse (see Nelson and Gruendel 1981; Nelson 1986 on children's generalized event representations).

Turning to the grammatical level, there are striking differences between the dialogues and monologues. As indicated in Table 5.1, whereas the progressive occurs in about equal proportions in both contexts, the simple present occurs only in the monologues. "Simple present" refers to both the -s marker, which is just coming in and is not consistently used, and the 0-form (that is, the unmarked form). The 0-form is taken to be a positive choice and not merely an undifferentiated form out of which the other inflections develop for two reasons. First, the -*ing* and 0-forms of the same verbs occur in different contexts, suggesting that they function contrastively, and second, the o-form co-occurs with a restricted set of other forms, suggesting that it is chosen for a particular environment. Thus, the simple pres-

Table 5.1. Percentage of use of verb inflections in phase I.

	Action verbs			Statives[a]	Catenatives
	Progressive	Simple present	Imperative		
Dialogues (N = 18)					
1%	33	0	28	28	11
Number	6		5	5	2
Monologues (N = 42)					
%	38	52	2.5	2.5	5
Number	16	22	1	1	2

a. Stative verbs include *want* and *need* used as main verbs. Catenatives include *wanna, needta,* and *gonna* + verb constructions.

ent seems to be a unique grammatical device reserved for Emily's monologic speech. This suggests that the content of these monologues is in some way special or that this verbal device is governed by the monologic format itself.

Since the verb morphology is not the only grammatical system whose deployment is sensitive to its presence in dialogue versus monologue, a particular pattern of co-occurrences characterizes both contexts. In fact, it is precisely the regularities in the co-occurrence relations between different forms in distinct contexts of use (that is, what is referred to as "configural encoding") that suggests that Emily is using these forms as a means of constructing and organizing different types of discourse.

For example, in contrast to dialogic utterances, monologic utterances often begin with *maybe, when, then,* or other distributionally equivalent terms; for example, see M3: "when Daddy come / then Daddy get Emmy." The simple present tends to occur in a particular syntactic format: sequencer term + N + 0-form verb (+ open term). Although what Emily means by these sequencing terms will not be discussed at this point, it is important to note that a full 86 percent (19) of the simple present utterances begin with sequencers. Moreover, since these structured utterances tend to occur in succession, this gives rise to a particular discourse pattern; for example, see M2: "after my nap / then Carl come over my house / then Emmy go Caldor's in the mall / when Daddy wake Emmy up / when Emmy wake up." In contrast, dialogic utterances do not begin with sequencing terms. Nor do the monologic progressive utterances. Instead, when progressive utterances in the monologues begin with temporal expressions, they are from a different semantic class; for example, *now, not now, and, in morning time.*

Let us consider another grammatical system that is sensitive to monologic versus dialogic context: the self-reference system in subject position. In the dialogues, Emily refers to herself as sentence subject 13 times and uses *I* 85 percent of the time (11 times) to do so. In the other two instances she drops the self-reference term altogether. Similarly, all progressive utterances from the earlier dialogues[6] employ the I-form of self-reference. In contrast, in the 15 monologic utterances that feature Emily as the sentence subject, 87 percent of the time (12 times) she refers to herself as *Emmy* while in the remaining 13 percent she uses *my.* These two forms remain functionally equivalent in subject position for some time. In short, Emily selects different forms of self-reference in subject position for the monologues versus the dialogues.

In addition to the grammatical differences between monologue and dialogue, there are grammatical differences within the monologues themselves. Of the 16 progressive utterances, 13 (81 percent) occur without any type of verb complement. This contrasts with the 22 simple present utterances of which 15 (68 percent) are followed by either a locative complement or, much less frequently, a patient. When the verb occurs with a complement, the event is presented as having a boundary and is therefore represented as being more structured than if the verb had no complement. Moreover, the presence of a second argument suggests that the activity is directed toward that argument. These frequencies suggest that even *within* the monologues some type of distinction is being forged between different ways of viewing events: the simple present is used in utterances that present events as sequentially ordered, bounded, and directed, while the progressive is used in utterances that present events as lacking these structural properties and hence as more static.

Even at this early stage in the analysis, the consistency of these patterns is suggestive. First, Emily's early use of verb morphology is sensitive to distinct discourse parameters. Hence, any attempt to characterize her output in terms of a traditional context-free grammar would fail to capture the regularities in her speech. Second, distributional analyses directed toward accounting for patterns in the child's linguistic output may be better indicators of the system the child herself is developing than a priori decisions about what constitutes grammatical productivity (see, for example, the 90 percent criterion in required contexts in Brown 1973). The formulation of what counts as a productive use of an utterance in a required context rests on adult-centered judgments prescribing how certain forms should be used and thus forfeits the possibility of accounting for the child's system in its own terms.

At this point, I will examine the claim that Emily's verb morphology is sensitive to different discourse parameters. To figure out what these parameters are I will need to go beyond the analyst's categories of monologue versus dialogue and interpret the particular formats Emily imposes on the events she describes (in the monologues) or engages in (in the dialogues). I begin by noting two points. First, the finding that the simple present does not occur in the dialogues suggests that it may be a form that is not used for negotiatory speech.

Second, that Emily refers to herself in the monologues by a unique pair of subject forms suggests that the speaker stance referred to by these forms may be associated with a different view of the self from that represented by *I* in the dialogues. Both findings lead to the question of whether other characteristics of the monologues reveal other clues as to the way Emily views her self with respect to the events described.

SIMPLE PRESENT DISCOURSE IN THE MONOLOGUES

The most surprising feature of these early monologues is the dearth of transitive verbs—and the total absence of transitive verbs with Emily as the agentive subject. In other words, the many transitive verbs typically found in children's early corpora—*take, give, open, hit, drop,* and so on (Bloom, Lightbown, and Hood 1975; Slobin 1981, 1985)—do not occur in these early monologues. Hence, Emily is not representing herself as a causal agent who volitionally executes a particular act. Of the few transitive constructions that do occur *Daddy* is typically the subject. However, transitive constructions are infrequent: 19 percent of the utterances are transitive, 77 percent are intransitive, 2 percent are copula constructions, and 2 percent are mixed (transitive verb without its object).

Now at first blush, characteristics of Emily's earlier crib speech (see note 6) appear to contradict these findings: in the earlier contexts Emily does represent herself as a transitive agent (see Appendix, M4–M6). However, these examples do not represent the same type of monologic speech as M1–M3. Instead, M4–M6 are "enactment sequences": sequences in which Emily acts out the events she describes. For example, in M4, she seems to address her doll (hence the *I* form). In M5 and M6 the occurrence of the deictics *this, right here, this one,* and so on suggests that she is referring to objects in her immediate context. Therefore, she can be assumed to be referring to ongoing activities rather than to temporally remote or displaced events. Indeed, her language use here seems to be an example of what Vygotsky (1962) means by "self-regulative speech"—speech used to organize and set goals for ongoing play. Thus, since these early monologues refer to ongoing events and serve a different function from those in the later period, they do not constitute counterexamples to the claim that in her earliest monologues about decontextualized events Emily does not represent herself in the role of causal agent.

How *does* she represent herself in these early monologues? Since she does not make herself the subject of transitive verbs, she does not represent herself as "in control of" or having "primary responsibility" for actions on objects (Lakoff 1977; Slobin 1981; Comrie 1981; DeLancey 1984). Furthermore, when she makes herself the subject of an intransitive verb, the particular verb always represents an action where she is perforce the recipient (undergoer) of someone else's agency toward her. Although she states that she goes various places, in each case she must be taken by others (for example, to the Peabody Museum, to Caldor's shopping mall, in her father's car). Thus even when she represents herself as the subject of a verb of motion, Emily is not really the executor or initiator of the activity described. This generalization applies to her friend Carl as well: of the five occasions when his name appears in subject position, he is nevertheless the beneficiary of others' actions toward him (for example, "When Carl comes" requires that someone bring him). Moreover, even when Emily represents events in her life that do not involve other people, they are events that do not presuppose much control on her part ("When Emmy wake up"). These findings contrast with those from the dialogues, where Emily represents herself as the subject of both intransitive and transitive verbs where she is indeed the independent actor or agent. Instead, in the early monologues, her father is the only consistent agent. Whether or not this reflects a belief that only her father is all-powerful is beside the point. The point is that Emily herself is not an agent or an actor in these early monologues.

A further interesting generalization about the early monologues is their repetitiveness. Table 5.2 reflects this by reporting verb frequencies. We find that Emily describes variations on the same or similar

Table 5.2. Frequency of the verbs that occur in phase I monologues.

Simple present		Stative		Progressive		Modal		Imperative	
go	7	has	1	sleeping	9	gonna	2	don't turn on	1
come	8			coming	4				
wake up									
(trans.)	2			not turn-	3				
(intrans.)	2			ing on					
get									
(trans.)	2								
(intrans.)	1								

events. What she talks about is that Daddy gets her or wakes her up, or that she goes somewhere or wakes up, or that someone comes, or someone sleeps, and so on. The slight variations in these utterances suggest that they are not merely rote-learned phrases. In terms of the information we have about Emily's life, it is plausible that this verbal repetitiveness is partially motivated by the nature of the events represented. That is, Emily seems to be referring to routine events in her life rather than to unique episodes. This interpretation is interesting in light of recent claims in cognitive science that recurrent events are cognitively represented in a generalized and schematized format such that the details of individual instances are fused (see Minsky 1981; Schank and Abelson 1977; Nelson and Gruendel 1981 for an application to children). Following this lead suggests that Emily may not have a distinct representation of each instance of her daily routines but only a generalized schema. Given this, I will argue that she uses her simple-present discourse to represent routines—recurrent events in her life that are themselves cognitively represented in a generalized format.

Although attempting to solve a different problem—how to characterize different literary genres—Frye (1964) provides an insightful account of the urge to depict recurrent, routine events:

> The historian makes specific and particular statements, such as "The Battle of Hastings was fought in 1066." Consequently, he's judged by the truth or falsehood of what he says—either there was such a battle or there wasn't, and if there was, he's got the date either right or wrong. But the poet, Aristotle says, never makes any real statements at all, certainly no particular or specific ones. The poet's job is not to tell you what happened, but *what happens:* not what did take place, but the kind of thing that *always does take place.* He gives you the typical, recurring or what Aristotle calls the universal event. (1964, 63; italics added)

I do not mean to suggest that we see in Emily the making of a poet. Frye's characterization of the poet nicely captures a mode of speech that is devoted to expressing the way events typically go, in contrast to the narrative mode, which recounts the way events did go. My present claim is that oral speech types are also sensitive to the same functional distinction. And so it seems that Emily has forged a distinct mode of speech with unique grammatical properties to represent the typical events in her life. Moreover, I propose that the later generic-normative meaning encoded by the simple present (see phase IV) derives from its contextualization in this early mode of discourse to represent routine events.

In terms of the pattern of grammatical forms that characterizes these early monologues, the co-occurrence of the following properties needs accounting for: simple-present verb forms, *when-then* sequencers, *Emmy-my* forms of self-reference, and intransitive verbs—each of which contrasts with the speech forms chosen for the dialogues. My provisional interpretation is that Emily has selected these forms to organize a distinct type of decontextualized discourse, namely, the representation of "what happens" in two different senses: (1) events that are routines and not specific occurrences, and (2) events that happen to Emily rather than actions that she executes.

If we focus more specifically on verb morphology, the use of the simple-present construction seems to be implicated at two linguistic levels. Grammatically, the simple present typically co-occurs with *when-then* sequencers, *Emmy-my* forms of self-reference, and intransitive constructions. At the level of meaning, the simple present is used for explicitly sequenced, multipropositional discourse about decontextualized events, for the representation of routine events, and for the absence of speaker agency. Before proposing any generalizations, we need to know to what extent and at which linguistic level each of these factors is responsible for Emily's selection of the simple present. However, if we consider the possible yet non-occurring uses of this form, the tendencies exhibited by the data do not seem arbitrary: (1) The simple present tends not to be used for events in which Emily is the agent; (2) it tends not to be used to describe specific events; (3) it tends not to be used to express a single event; and (4) it tends not to be used to express ongoing events. (All four of these possibilities are within Emily's competence, as can be seen in the dialogues.) These restrictions support the claim that Emily has organized a distinct type of discourse to represent "what happens" in the two senses mentioned above.

Given these findings, my provisional interpretation is that these various factors coalesce to form a distinct mode of discourse, which I will call simple-present (SP) discourse. This discourse type serves as the developmental basis for Emily's phase IV use of the simple present, which occurs in a wider range of contexts. As I will argue, features of SP discourse also provide the starting points for the simple present's expression of aspect and tense.

It is notable that Emily's use of the simple present is in the same semantic field as adult usage described by linguists.[7] For example, according to Lawler (1972), the simple present is used to present a "generic" description of events; according to Calver (1946) it expresses "the essential constitution of things"; according to Goldsmith and Woisetschlaeger (1982), it expresses the structural judgment that an event conforms to a regularity or a pattern. In addition, when 3-year-olds want to downplay their own intentions as motivators of action in favor of a norm, they use the simple present (Gerhardt and Savasir 1986; see also Bowerman 1986, 294). Of course, the correspondence between Emily's usage and adult usage suggests that Emily has picked up some of the characteristics of her SP discourse from adult input. Unfortunately, the data are not detailed enough to determine how this occurs.

Before I focus on the semantic potential of the simple present, it should be noted that this analysis necessarily contains a certain amount of circularity. In brief, certain patterns in the speech are used to infer the existence of higher-order speech genres, which then are used to account for certain tendencies in the use of grammar. This method is inherent to the analysis of spontaneous speech, which does not consist of two sources of data to compare as does a more experimental task (such as instructions to tell a story and the language used, as independent and dependent variable respectively). Indeed, one of the main purposes of this chapter is to suggest that such an approach is the only way to proceed if our goal is to go beyond objective contextual descriptions (such as monologue versus dialogue) and to attempt to characterize the higher-order discourse contexts that are functionally relevant for the child.

DECONTEXTUALIZED TEMPORAL REFERENCE AND
RELATIVE TIME

Clearly, the monologues (except enactment sequences) refer to events that are not ongoing in the speech context. That is, their temporal reference is decontextualized. It is not clear, however, whether Emily intends to refer to past or future events, or whether she is merely representing a generic type of event that is not situated on a time line. Since Emily's parents sometimes tell her, before she goes to bed, what she is going to do when she wakes up (material that occasionally coincides with the monologic material, as will be seen), it has been suggested that her early monologues are future-referring (Nelson 1983b). If so, the fact that they also represent routines would support

Harner's (1982, 143) claim that children "first understand the future as a recurrence of the past." But, given the difficulty of determining the temporal status of these early monologues, I shall adopt the most conservative interpretation, which is that they consist of decontextualized generic event representations not intended to represent the past or the future.

Instead, the temporal task Emily seems to be engaged in is that of *ordering* events with respect to one another. Although the precise meaning of the form *when-then* is unclear, because it co-occurs with references to events that themselves are strictly ordered, it appears to function as a "sequencer," used in the attempt to make this ordering explicit. In other words, Emily uses sequencers to order events with respect to other events, while not caring to specify how the events are ordered with respect to the moment of speech. From an analytic perspective this means she uses sequencers to express relative time—a lexically expressed form of relative tense. Relative tense is itself defined in contrast to absolute tense. According to Comrie, whereas with absolute tense the "reference point for the location of a situation in time is the present moment," with relative tense it is "one which is interpreted relative to a reference point provided by the context" (1985, 56). Since the contextual reference points chosen by Emily are lexical, not grammatical (*when-then*), strictly speaking her use of sequencers expresses relative time and not relative tense. Nevertheless, the point is that the entire "SP + sequencer" construction seems to be used to express relative time relations, but not deictic tense relations.

This finding is surprising given recent claims that relative time emerges only after deictic tense (Smith 1980; Weist 1986; Weist and Buczowska 1986), and that this can occur as early as 30;0 for Polish children. Now since Emily uses the progressive to represent her ongoing activities in the dialogues before the *when-then* sequencers appear in the monologues, the findings support the claim that a deictic system is established before a relative time system. The anomaly is Emily's precocity: she begins to use *when-then* as early as 22;5, suggesting that some type of relative time system has been established. However, it is important to note that Emily's expression of relative time is *constrained* to the representation of these generic event scenarios. Thus, rather than assume that her ability to order these events presupposes a mental time line on which all the events of her life are ordered, it is sufficient to assume that she has a particular *locally or-*

ganized frame within which events are ordered. There is no evidence that events are ordered across frames. In other words, instead of the development of temporal systems depending only on the child's ability to decenter in time—with time conceived as a single linear dimension independent of event frames (Cromer 1971)—perhaps the child is aided in this task by first learning to coordinate events within and then between frames.

THE MONOLOGIC PROGRESSIVES

The major distributional finding for the progressive is that it never occurs with the *when-then* sequencers (see M1 and M3). Hence this construction is not used for explicitly ordering events with respect to one another. Also of note is its contrast with the simple present with respect to taking locative complements: whereas the simple present tends to co-occur with complements, verbs in the progressive do not. Thus the progressive occurs neither with forms that lead on to the next event nor with complements that delimit the event. As such, progressive utterances are less structured than those in the simple present. Moreover, new information is introduced in the subject while the predicate is topicalized: for example, in M1, Emily repeats the verb *coming,* inserting different actors as subject. The same pattern holds for M3, where ten different subjects co-occur with *sleeping.* This type of thematic organization renders the utterances more static. Therefore even though it is more difficult to figure out what Emily is talking about when she uses progressive utterances (and whether they refer to remote events as the simple-present utterances do), these three distributional properties suggest that she is indeed setting up a contrast to the events presented in the simple present: that events presented in the progressive are viewed as less structured, more static. This interpretation has implications with respect to the expression of aspect and to the narrative-like organization of these early monologues.

ASPECT

Note the configural differences between the progressive and the simple present mentioned above. In that the progressive utterances occur without sequencers and without verb complements, contextual conditions exist for the progressive to become associated with *imperfective* aspect. In contrast, since the simple present occurs in sequenced formats and with verb complement constructions—properties that function to close off the event and move the discourse forward—conditions exist for it to become associated with *perfective* aspect. In other words, Emily seems to use the *entire phrasal config-uration* as a way of setting bounds to the event and in effect express-ing perfective aspect (that is, boundedness). Moreover, the use of the simple present to represent routines provides the conditions for it to become associated with habitual aspect as well. Thus these two verb constructions occur in different types of discourse configurations, which provide conditions for them to become associated with differ-ent aspectual values.

This proposal differs from the "aspect before tense" hypothesis, which is based on the claim that each of the inflections is used to mark a distinct class of verbs. No such restriction obtains in the Emily cor-pus. As is evidenced in Table 5.2, the simple present occurs with the telic verb *wake up* and the activity verb *come*. The progressive also occurs with an aspectually heterogeneous set of verbs. In fact, both constructions occur with the very same verb, *come*, but in different discourse contexts: "then Carl come over my house" (M2); "and Carl coming" (M1). In accordance with my proposal concerning the in-dexical value of Emily's verb morphology at this phase, I suggest that in these two utterances the very same verb gains a perfective value when embedded in a contingent sequence of events and an imperfec-tive value in the more open-ended sentence construction. In other words, the aspectual value of the different verb constructions is ini-tially carried by the discourse context—not the lexical aspect of the verb. Moreover, the contrast afforded by these two utterances sug-gests that the inflections are used to encode different perspectives on events, rather than objective features of events. For example, Emily may well have the same real event in mind when she utters "then Carl come over my house" as when she says "and Carl coming." However, she presents the event from a different perspective in each utterance (perfective and imperfective, respectively) by using different discourse features—including the different verb constructions. (See Smith 1983, 1986 for a discussion of the perspectival nature of sentence aspect in adult speech.)

THE PROGRESSIVE TENSE

The last interesting distributional difference is that 38 percent (6 out of 16) of the progressive utterances co-occur with the temporal ad-verbs *now* and *not now* (M1). This co-occurrence suggests that in using the progressive Emily attempts to relate events to the *now*-time of speech. If so, the progressive should be organized with respect to deictic tense. This proposal gains support from the dialogues, where the progressive is used to represent events that are concurrent with the moment of speech—and thus once again in Emily's phenomenological present. Thus whereas Emily seems to use the simple present to order events relative to one another, she seems to use the progressive to order events with respect to the moment of speech. However, since the *-ing* morpheme does not yet occur with auxiliaries, the extent to which she means to locate events in the past or future above and beyond the *now* and *not now* is not clear. What does seem clear is that at this phase she is working out the binary grammatical contrast of *now–not now* through the use of the progressive.

THE NARRATIVE-LIKE PROPERTIES OF THE
EARLY MONOLOGUES

The following narrative-like properties can be found in Emily's monologues: (1) successive sequencing of propositions that are interdependent thematically and syntactically; (2) an apparent expression of something like speaker-stance (that is, the absence of agency on Emily's part); (3) local point of view shifts (for example, "when Daddy wake Emmy up/when Emmy wake up"); and (4) event differentiation within the monologue. In other words, the fact that Emily's SP discourse consists of the representation of routine events does not bar it from being considered as a type of protonarrative. Indeed, according to Stein and Kilgore (1987), the discursive representation of events in terms of a script is a discourse type that is developmentally prior to the ability to tell a narrative story (see also Nelson 1986). The first three properties have already been demonstrated as characterizing Emily's SP discourse; a short discussion of the fourth property follows.

The finding that the simple present and the progressive are associated with different aspectual values in the context of sequentially structured discourse cannot but call to mind Hopper's (1979) claim that narratives are organized into foreground-background format where FG utterances tend to be perfective and BG utterances tend to be imperfective. To be sure, such a schema proposed for adult narrative cannot be automatically assumed to be relevant to a child's connected discourse. And indeed, Emily's monologues are particularly recalcitrant, since her progressive utterances do not seem to be thematically connected to her SP discourse. How could they then serve as background material? In fact, the occasional occurrence of progressive utterances with *now–not now* plus their propositional content suggests that Emily uses them as a way of stepping out of the more remote SP discourse into describing more contextually relevant events. Nevertheless, if we focus exclusively on the formal-distributional properties of the progressive utterances it is notable that they are similar to Hopper's characterization of BG utterances: that is, nonsequentiality, imperfectivity, new information introduced before the verb. Hence, from a distributional perspective the progressive utterances are like BG utterances. Given this, the most cautious interpretation of the binary format found in Emily's early monologues is the proposal that even within the monologues Emily is forging a distinction between different ways of representing events and is using contrasts in her verb morphology to do so. Moreover, that she conceives of the progressive utterances as part of the same discourse type as the simple present utterances rather than merely as successive but unrelated utterances is suggested by the fact that they too employ *Emmy-my* forms of self-reference. These two subject forms are not used in nonnarrative crib speech, as will be discussed below.

Given Hopper's characterization of adult narratives, it would seem that Emily's linguistic patterns must in some way derive from the adult input. Unfortunately the corpus does not contain stories or other narrative forms that Emily is being exposed to at this age, and contains very few examples of *when-then* constructions as input. FD1 in the Appendix (part of a presleep dialogue) presents the only relevant input recorded for this period. In FD1, Emily's father projects her postnap activities in a future-narrative-like format. Her M1 monologue follows about two minutes later with no intervening speech. Comparing the two reveals that Emily does appropriate certain lexical items and the future-narrative-like format from her father: both FD1 and M1 contain *Carl, go* and a *when* clause with a verb in the simple present. Yet even more noticeable is the way Emily restructures the material—in terms of both form and content—such that M1 is by no means a direct copy. For example, of the 42 times Emily's parents explicitly address her (as her father does in FD1), 98 percent of the time they use *you*; only once is *Emily* used. Yet, Emily selects *Emmy* and *my* as her monologic forms of self-reference. Thus, while her father's future-narrative-like formulations may be the catalyst for Emily's crib speech and may give her certain material to work with, her output is by no means a direct or passive copy.

THE DIALOGUES[8]

The overarching goal of Emmy's presleep dialogues (D1–D3) is to keep her father engaged so she will not be left alone to sleep. Her statements and requests are often tactics in the service of this goal. I shall focus on three grammatical properties of the dialogues that contrast with the monologues: verb morphology, subject forms of self-reference, and transitivity.

Of the 18 tabulated utterances for this period, 12 are used in first-person modal requests (such as "I want / I need") or imperatives ("go close shades!"). Six are progressive utterances in the first person: *I* plus *running, laying, sleeping,* and so on (with the copula omitted). On the one hand, each progressive utterance functions as an assertive speech act to describe Emily's ongoing activity. On the other hand, once the utterance is evaluated in context, in each case the progressive utterance counts as a *challenge:* Emily consistently describes herself as doing what she should not be doing, and predictably her father protests (see, for example, D1 and D2). The 10 first-person progressive utterances from the earlier sessions function this same way. For example, Emily states: *I* plus *throwing away blanket / going on my back / jumping* (which she has reason to believe she should not); *I* plus *sitting / laying like this* (where she should not be); *I* plus *getting my book* (she has explicitly been told not to); *I* plus *dawdling* (a general form of disapproved behavior), and so on. All 16 of her earliest progressive utterances function similarly—as challenges.

The question that must be considered is whether this finding is merely happenstance and thus not related to the meaning of the progressive for Emily or if it indeed reveals something about her understanding of this inflection. What is a challenge? Challenges serve a more affect-laden purpose than mere information exchange: the speaker has a stake in what is said and attempts to force the interlocutor to side with her—usually against the interlocutor's inclination. In this way, challenges are potentially discordant discourse phenomena, as they force the interlocutor into some kind of immediate resolution. From the speaker's point of view, challenges are inherently short-lived, as they provoke an unstable discourse situation. Indeed, I propose that the progressive is used at this early phase to encode something like "discourse instability" (see Ochs 1986; Ochs and Schieffelin 1987; Clancy 1987 concerning the grammatical coding of affect in language acquisition).

This characterization of the progressive in terms of "instability" is compatible with the temporal meaning "temporary duration" ascribed to the progressive for adults (Twaddell 1968; Joos 1964; Leech 1971). In fact, Brown (1973) observes that at stage II, Eve uses the progressive to refer to temporary situations in the present. Yet, Brown argues against crediting Eve with this meaning until stage IV, when the progressive is used contrastively with the simple present. Since Emily does give evidence of using the simple present as a contrasting form, following Brown's logic, it would be appropriate to character-ize her use of the progressive in terms of "temporary duration." Nevertheless, I resist this interpretation on theoretical grounds. Since "temporary duration" is an event-based description (a semantic-level meaning) rather than a discourse-based meaning, the perspective adopted in this chapter suggests that "temporary duration" is more likely to emerge from a prior discourse meaning.

Therefore, it is reassuring that the linguistic literature provides other characterizations of the progressive which also accord with its occurrence in challenges in Emily's speech. For example, the progres-sive has been claimed to express the quasimodal judgment of "how things *seem* to the speaker." More particularly, according to Gold-smith and Woisetschlaeger (1982, 80), the choice between the simple present and the progressive is sometimes based on "two rather differ-ent types of knowledge about the world": its long-term structure (simple present) versus its phenomenal appearances (progressive). In other words, the progressive expresses the "metaphysical judgment" that what is being described is just how things seem to the speaker and not how things tend to be or should be in the world. Similarly, Hatcher (1951) characterizes the progressive as a construction that implies that the speaker is affected by or involved in what she is de-scribing.

Given these characterizations, I propose that Emily uses the pro-gressive to indicate that the activity described is grounded not in the way things are supposed to be, but in the way they just happen to be—in her passing perception or desire. As such, the progressive is set up to contrast with the simple present. The difference between this description and that of "temporary duration" is twofold. First, the meaning "this is how things are—but they could change" (that is, "instability") is based on an experiential schematization of events, and not on objective properties of events. Second, the interpretation of instability is discourse based: there is nothing in the events them-selves that renders them unstable (for example, "I sleeping here"). They acquire this status through Emily's anticipated reaction. That is, in each case where Emily is challenging her father she can anticipate that he will protest, and indeed he does. Hence, "instability" is a discourse parameter. In contrast, "temporary duration" is not discourse based but is a sentence-level category that is meant to apply to the description of the event itself.

Indeed, I propose that there are potentially two functional systems, which are undifferentiated at this phase and coded by one linguistic form (*-ing*): the discourse-sensitive meaning ("instability"), which arises indexically by the occurrence of *-ing* in the discourse context, and a semantic meaning ("temporary duration"), which at this phase is merely an implication of the discourse meaning. I further propose that the semantic meaning develops out of the discourse meaning— although the data are not extensive enough to decide on this either way. In other words, Emily will come to understand the more objective notion of "temporariness" in terms of her experience that certain events are not grounded in the way things are supposed to be, and thus are more likely to be temporary (note Silverstein 1985 for theoretical grounding for the claim that semantic categories emerge from discourse categories in language acquisition).

Now to turn to Emily's selection of self-reference forms for subject position: she consistently uses *I* in these negotiatory sequences. The fact that she chooses *I* as opposed to *Emmy-my* for her dialogues (N = 23) and that she uses it with semantically modal forms (*want*) suggests that *I* is chosen as part of the communicative function and/ or to express Emily's more subjective states. According to Lyons (1982), languages often make a distinction between the subjective self of first-person reference and the objective self of third-person pronominal reference or proper-name reference. Although this distinction is difficult to apply noncircularly, the fact that Emily uses *I* in the dialogues to express desire and ongoing negotiated activity and uses *Emmy-my* in the monologues to refer to displaced events that are fixed (whose status is not up for negotiation) suggests that the intersubjective-objective distinction may be relevant to her selection of self-referring forms. A similar distinction underlies the choice between the use of pronominal forms and the child's own name in early possessive constructions (Deutsch and Budwig 1983).

Perhaps a more helpful way of thinking about Lyons's distinction and what Emily's linguistic distinctions might reflect is by considering the notion of "direction of fit" (Searle 1979). In brief, assertive-type utterances function to describe what is the case, while directive-type utterances function to bring about a change in the world in accordance with what is linguistically represented. Hence, assertives and directives have different directions of fit: different ways of relating language to the world. Since Emily's narratives consist of assertive utterances, while her dialogues contain direct or indirect directives or challenges, another way of viewing the selective occurrences of *I* versus *Emmy-my* is in the following terms: Emily selects *I* when she is using language to get what she wants. It expresses her role as a negotiator of ongoing events. She selects *Emmy-my* when the events represented are already settled or fixed and thus there is nothing to negotiate. As such, she uses *Emmy-my* when she takes a more passive or distanced stance toward the events she represents. In other words, she uses *I* for more instrumental purposes (language as social action) and *Emmy-my* for more representational purposes (language as fixed description).

In the majority of the 23 dialogic utterances under consideration, *I* is used intransitively to express the role of actor, although occasionally it is used transitively to express the role of agent. Furthermore, when she uses *I* as the subject of an intransitive verb, Emily no longer casts herself in events where she is actually the recipient of others' actions (as in the early monologues). She now represents activities that she herself independently carries out, so that she is really their actor. Thus, although *I* and *Emmy-my* are used to express the same semantic case role (actor), Emily is an independent actor only when using *I* in the dialogues.

This finding suggests that Emily deploys different forms of self-reference depending on the roles she sees herself as playing in different discourse contexts: her experience as an involved negotiator who plays an active role in defining various aspects of her social reality (*I*), versus her experience as a more distanced narrator who submits to experience being more or less as it is, and tries to represent it (*Emmy-my*). That a young child alights on the self-reference system in subject position as a way of indicating different roles *qua* different modes of involvement in events has also been found by Budwig (1984). According to Budwig, children aged 20;0–30;0 can "use Self reference forms to linguistically mark their involvement as prototypical agents, as well as deviations from this prototype." For example, with respect to a 30-month-old child, Budwig finds that "at both the semantic and pragmatic level, *my* is found in utterances where notions of control and volition are central. The use of *I* marks a deviation from this prototypical agentive perspective" (Budwig 1985, 5).

Note that Emily's selection of forms is almost the converse of what Budwig reports: Emily uses *I* for negotiatory-agentive involvement and *Emmy-my* for events that are fixed and cannot be negotiated but

Table 5.3. Phase I clusters.

Dialogues	Monologues
Monopropositional	Multipropositional
I-form of self-reference	*Emmy-my* forms of self-reference
Verb constructions used: progressive, modal	Verb constructions used: simple present (0-*s*) progressive Simple-present utterances: 1. plus sequencers (*when, then*) 2. plus verb complements (an argument after the verb—usually oblique argument) Progressive utterances: 1. plus terms such as *and, now, not now, cause* 2. typically no verb complements 3. subject encodes new information; verb is topicalized as old information (same verb plus different subjects)
Dominant case role: actor/agent (volition)	Dominant case role: actor-qua-recipient (no volition)
Language used to negotiate events to change things	Language used to represent events as already settled or fixed
Open text/the progressive: events could be otherwise	Closed text/the simple present: events are highly regular and recurrent

only narrated. Furthermore, whereas Emily's early use of *Emmy-my* in intransitive utterances suggests that the selection of these forms depends on the intransitive status of the utterances, in the later monologues she uses *Emmy-my* even in highly transitive utterances. At the same time, she still uses *I* in transitive utterances in the dialogues. Thus, the absence of agency in the early monologues is not an invariant property when *Emmy-my* is selected as the subject form. What remains invariant for all cases of *Emmy-my* is the narrative-like discourse context. Nevertheless, what both sets of findings indicate is that the child may choose the self-reference system in subject position to set up contrasts not marked with similar forms in the adult language. With development, these same contrasts will most likely be absorbed by other grammatical systems (such as modals).

I will conclude this discussion of phase I by observing the *clustering of forms* and the *clustering of functions* that appear in Emily's speech. Table 5.3 presents the findings discussed so far. The consistency of these patterns suggests that Emily imposes different interpretive formats—or types of discourse—as she participates in dialogic and monologic speech.

Phase II: Emily at 22;22–23;5

THE MONOLOGUES: SIMPLE PRESENT DISCOURSE

Phase II can be considered a transitional phase, for two reasons. First, in this phase Emily's crib speech becomes more diverse and exhibits discourse formats other than the SP discourse. The SP discourse does remain the dominant type, however, and the second type of change occurs within the SP discourse itself. Restrictions on SP discourse heretofore observed begin to loosen; the simple present begins to be generalized to a wider range of contexts.

There are 54 interpretable utterances in Emily's SP discourse in phase II (M7–M11).[9] Table 5.4 displays the frequency of Emily's verb

Table 5.4. Monologues: Verb frequency in simple-present discourse.

Phase I 22;16–22;20		Phase II 22;22–23;5	
go	7		9
come	8		9
wake up	4		10
get	3		8
has	1		2
Total	23		38
		ask	1
		remember	1
		help	1
		walk in	1
		put	4
		drinked up	1
		take	1
		eat	1
		make	1
		bring	1
		told	1
		take out	1
		clean up	1
		Total	16

use for phases I and II. The table informs us that 70 percent (38) of the verbs in SP discourse at phase II are the same as those which tend to be repeated at phase I. Combining the verbs across both phases reveals that 79 percent (61) of Emily's simple-present utterances represent the same sort of routine events. Moreover, of these 61 verbs, 75 percent (46) are intransitive. The transitives that do occur are predicated on Emily's father, or, when Emily is the subject, the verb is stative (*has*). Hence, SP discourse at phase II is similar to phase I at its core.

But, what about the novel verbs in the simple present—those in the bottom section of Table 5.4? The hypothesis is that they represent a transitional mode of discourse because they have features of both the SP generic discourse mode and the more particularized recounting mode which begins at the next phase. Although these verbs (such as *make, eat*) tend to occur in the *when-then* formats, they are more specific than before in their denotational content and they tend not to be repeated. From these two properties it is possible to infer that Emily might have a more specific event in mind than the generic routines claimed to underlie her earlier discourse. Other changes in Emily's SP discourse seem to support this claim. Of the 16 new verbs, 88 percent (14) are causative transitive. Half continue to occur with *Daddy*— who is now an agent of many more diverse actions than in the previous monologues (*make, bring, hold, clean up, put,* and so on). However, for the first time Emily represents herself as the causal agent of a few decontextualized activities (*take, eat, put,* and so on). Note that these activities are also more specific in their reference than before, while remaining part of a larger, explicitly sequenced event representation. Thus there seems to be a developmental correspondence between the emergence of Emily's ability to refer to more particular decontextualized events and the representation of herself as an agent of events. Nevertheless, these new trends in the SP discourse consist of only 30 percent of the phase II SP monologues, and thus represent an emerging form of speech at best.

The problem these novel constructions pose is whether they falsify the attempt to demonstrate form-function relations as the principle defining Emily's use of the simple present. In phase I, it was claimed that the primary determinants of the use of the SP are the *when-then* sequencers for decontextualized events, multipropositional discourse, generic event references, and the absence of transitive utterances with Emily as the agent. Then at phase II, SP discourse begins to contain some transitive constructions with Emily as their agent and some references to specific events. However, there is reason to assume that the SP will never be the preferred form to represent the speaker's agency or uniquely occurring events. According to other research, the simple present is used to represent events as generic or habitual, and for events that downplay the speaker's own agency (Calver 1946; Bloom, Lifter, and Hafitz 1980; Gerhardt and Savasir 1986). Thus, the claim here is that, although Emily can come to refer to herself as an agent or can come to refer to uniquely occurring events using the simple present (in an "old forms represent new functions" fashion—Slobin 1973), she will tend not to, as the simple present has already become associated with a different semantic domain. Hence, at some point this old system will have to give way and another means of representing agentive action and specific, unique events will have to develop—which is precisely what happens in phase III.

Regarding the forms of self-reference, of the 54 utterances in SP discourse for phase II, 27 represent Emily as the subject. *Emmy* and *my* are still the preferred forms of self-reference in subject position (with one use of *I*). Since other monologic discourse at phase II does employ the *I*-form (see below), the claim here that the selectional restriction against *I* is based on the particular narrative genre described above and not on crib speech per se.

NON-SP DISCOURSE

Examples M12–M15 illustrate another type of crib speech, in which self-reference is achieved using *I*. These examples demonstrate that it is not crib speech or monologic speech per se that selects for *Emmy-my* in SP discourse but the particular interpretive formats Emily imposes on the events described. It is for this reason that I have argued that as analysts we must go beyond the starting-point descriptors of dialogue versus monologue and use the linguistic regularities to define what the contextual parameters are for Emily herself. In other words, Emily's speech genre cannot be defined extensionally in terms of the presence or absence of an interlocutor in the real world, but must be defined in terms of the type of discourse she is trying to forge.

For example, M12, M13, and M15 seem to have more affinities with the dialogues than with SP monologic discourse: they contain modals and other predicates describing ongoing states that function as reasons why the situation should alter (for example, "I need drink this little bitty more juice," used to call for assistance). In this example, even though Emily is alone, the utterance counts as an attempt to solicit her parent's attention. Hence it is no wonder that *I* is chosen, as *I* tends to be the form that is used in instrumental language: language as social action to effect change.

Another point to note is the absence of sequencing terms in M14. This suggests that the sequenced utterances are not conceived as being contingent upon each other in the same fashion as SP discourse. In fact, an examination of this monologue suggests that Emily is not really talking about independent events, but about different aspects of the same event and her own reaction to it. Furthermore, these examples contain a few irregular past forms. We cannot, however, assume that Emily's system for past-tense reference is productive until phase III, when she begins to use the *-ed* marker and many irregular past verb forms.

Phase III: Emily at 23;6

Given the striking differences between Emily's monologue when she is 23;6 (M16) and the preceding monologues, I propose that M16 represents a new phase of her linguistic development. More particularly, I shall try to show that at the grammatical level Emily has productive control over past-tense morphology, and that at the level of discourse she is forging a different genre of speech.

Accordingly, the first major change in this monologue (which contains 49 decipherable utterances with verbs) is the tendency to replace *Daddy* as sentence subject. Emily herself is referred to in 87 percent of the preverbal constituents. Hence, she is now talking about her own doings. The second major change is that transitive verbs occur in a majority of the utterances: transitives, 55 percent; intransitives, 37 percent; transitive verbs without an object, 6 percent. Third, even though Emily still refers to decontextualized events, she now represents herself as the causal agent 76 percent of the time. We can think of this new mode of self-involvement as a new stance taken toward events: the stance of an agent making things happen in the world. Since differences in speaker stance are one of the defining criteria of different types of discourse idioms, the fact that Emily now casts herself in a new and distinctive role is the first clue that she is attempting to forge a new type of monologic discourse. The fourth change is reflected in the verbs themselves: according to Table 5.5, there are more novel verbs, which represent more specific semantic content

Table 5.5. Frequency of verbs in monologue M16 (23;6).

Simple past		Simple present		Progressive	
woke up	2	get up	1	coming	2
took out	5	make	1	sleeping	3
crashed	1	sick	1	running	6
slept	2	throw	1	getting	4
put	1	play	5	doing	1
played	3	hold	1		
said	1				
went to sleep	1				
wanted	1				
didn't feel	1				
lost	1				
got	1				
ate	1				
sat	1				

than before (for example, *crashed, throw*). Not only does she select semantically more saturated verbs, but the verbs themselves are now not repeated. From these two properties it would seem that Emily's discourse now refers to more specific and individuated events than before. It is as if she now has specific events in mind, which she tries to recount. In fact when repetition does occur (for example at the beginning of M16), it is part of a new topicalization format in which information is introduced after the verb. This differs from the previous tendency to repeat variations on the same event.

The fifth and most notable grammatical change in monologue M16 is in Emily's use of verb morphology. Verbs are now formally marked for the past 68 percent of the time—most often with irregular stem changes, occasionally with the fixed *-ed*. As in findings reported for other children, irregular verbs in the past have appeared earlier in Emily's speech. However, there is no reason to interpret the earlier instances as productive or contrastive morphological options, rather they are frozen forms whose past referring function is equivocal. In contrast, M16 exhibits the following properties: a greater frequency of irregular verbs marked for the past; novel irregular past verbs; and, most important, the beginning productive use of *-ed*—not to mention the other changes just listed in other parts of the grammar. In addition, the events that are sequenced are now distinct past events rather than repeatedly recurring routines. Based on this *pattern* of changes,

I propose that Emily's past morphology becomes productive at this phase, and that she employs it similarly to the simple present in the sequencing of interrelated events.

However, beyond the grammatical changes that characterize this phase (others will be mentioned below), it is proposed that Emily's monologue reflects another more encompassing change: a new type of discourse genre has emerged in her speech. This genre is a distinct type of narrative idiom: the oral recounting of specific past events— events that are interrelated, that have occurred in the past, of which Emily is the agent. Thus, rather than reciting a scripted discourse about what tends to happen, Emily can finally begin to narrate about what did happen. Recall that at phase II Emily had just begun to refer to herself as an agent of decontextualized events, and to refer to more discrete events. Not only have these tendencies become dominant at phase III, but now Emily can make explicit reference to the past. This suggests that the earlier developments may have led to a process of conceptual differentiation (that is, variation within the parameter of agency between other versus self, and variation within the parameter of event generality-specificity), and that this process has served as one of the enabling conditions for her newly emergent ability to recount specific past events.

For purposes of this chapter, the importance of claiming that a new mode of speech exists—the recounting of particular past events—is not to argue for Emily's competence in a new discourse genre, but to consider its implications for the development of Emily's verb morphology. In short, Emily's past morphology becomes productive in a very *restricted* context of use. As stated earlier, restrictions in use are one type of evidence that the child's conceptualization differs from that of the adult. Given this restriction, there is no warrant to conclude that Emily is marking pastness as a deictic notion per se. Instead, since her use of *-ed* or *-irreg* is restricted to these narrative-like sequences where events are ordered with respect to other events, her notion of pastness (as the notional space that is delimited and referred to by *-ed* or *-irreg*) must be similarly restricted. More will be said about this below.

It is notable that, across the board, the data from the Emily corpus disconfirm the predictions of the aspect-before-tense hypothesis. With respect to past morphology, recall that Bloom, Lifter, and Hafitz (1980) found that past forms were used to mark verbs that represented completed events, and that Antinucci and Miller (1976) found that *-ed* was used to mark verbs that represent the present resultant states of past actions. But since Emily's crib narrations are about events that have occurred out of the speech context, there are no resultant end states for Emily to attend to. Moreover, the verbs with which *-ed* initially co-occurs do not constitute a semantically homogeneous class: *-ed* occurs with the stative verb *want,* with the activity verb *play,* and with the accomplishment verb *crash.* Irregular stem changes occur with an aspectually heterogeneous set of verbs as well. Thus we find that Emily's initial use of past morphology is *not* governed by the lexical aspect of the co-occurring verb as predicted by the aspect-before-tense hypothesis. Nor does she limit her use of past forms to describing immediate past events before referring to remote past events—a claim implied by the notion that children conceptualize pastness by backwards inference from the present results of causally determinant actions. Instead, Emily first uses regular and irregular past morphology to represent remote, decontextualized events. Past forms do not occur in the dialogues to represent recent events until three weeks later. With respect to the rest of the verb morphology, neither *-ing* nor 0/-*s* co-occurs with aspectually restricted classes of verbs. Given these findings, we must conclude that Emily is not using her verb morphology to mark the lexical aspect of the verb (that is, objective event parameters).

Nevertheless, the findings on Emily do accord with the most basic insight of the aspect-before-tense hypothesis: children's first use of verb morphology is initially restricted to a narrower range than that found in adult speech. That is, even though Emily's past morphology is not aspectually restricted, another type of restriction does obtain: it is restricted to these narrative-like formats in which events are conceptualized and ordered in terms of other events. This implies that the discourse sequencing of interrelated events may serve as part of the supportive context for reference to the remote past even when there are no concrete traces left in the present.

The provisional conclusion warranted by these findings is that Emily's initial use of past morphology is indeed chosen to mark the deictic relation of pastness, but in a very restricted context. Rather than describe a single, isolated past event, she refers to events that are part of a larger event structure. Moreover, different parts of the event structure must be thematically interrelated in a way that makes sense to Emily. In other words, her understanding of pastness as it emerges with respect to grammatical marking is part of her understanding that certain events go together and form part of a conceptual whole. These restrictions constrain the particular type of tense system she is acquiring. According to the data, when -*ed* and -*irreg* are first used to mark the deictic notion "prior to the speech event" they occur in a relative time context as well: events must be ordered with respect to other nonspeech time events, as well as ordered with respect to the moment of speech. Again we must appeal to the notion of a frame rather than a time-line to model Emily's usage. Similarly to phases I and II, events within a thematic frame are ordered with respect to each other. What distinguishes phase III is that Emily can now explicitly locate the frame in the past. However, there is no evidence that she can yet interrelate different event frames or freely interpolate events within these frames. Therefore, there is no support for the assumption that Emily is conceptualizing the events in her life in terms of the absolute distinction between past and not-past (as the time-line metaphor implies). Instead, the conceptualization of an event as past seems to be frame-bound, such that an event is viewed in its inherent sequence with other events.

Concerning the observed differences between the findings on Emily and those supportive of the aspect-before-tense hypothesis, two factors need to be considered. First, given the complexity of Emily's crib speech, her linguistic competence may be more advanced than, and thus not comparable to, that of children of a similar age studied by Bloom, Lifter, and Hafitz. However, even if this is generally so, M16 does contain Emily's first reliable recorded use of -*ed* (and seemingly productive uses of -*irreg*), and hence the particular findings on -*ed* and -*irreg* are comparable to the other findings. Even the intermittent earlier uses of irregular past forms (such as *saw* in M13) are similar to M16 in not being confined to telic verbs. Thus these data do serve as counterexamples to the predictions of the aspect-before-tense hypothesis. Another factor, however, which may account for the observed differences, concerns the effects of context. Speech that is collected in a context where children are playing with toys tends to concern what happens to those toys. Consequently, such speech requires telic or change-of-state verbs. Instead, the monologic context seems to be less influenced by the immediate surroundings and thus to be topically more open-ended. This observation suggests that studies of children's use of verb morphology and its relation to different classes of verbs need to be sensitive to the possibility that different speech situations may condition different types of verbs (see Bowerman 1984 for a similar claim).

In terms of the perspective of this chapter it is important to note that the finding that *-ed* and *-irreg* are not used as redundant markers of lexical aspect does not disqualify these forms as potential coding devices for the expression of aspect. Of the verb tokens marked for the past, 77 percent (17) occur in transitive utterances: in constructions where events are presented as bounded by the presence of an object. In addition, they tend to co-occur with sequencers, which also function as boundary markers by leading on to a different event. Thus, as in the case of the simple present, the claim here is that the past morphology is situated in a context where the event represented is bounded on both sides. As such, conditions exist for these forms to become associated with perfectivity. However, at this phase of their use, the perfectivity is carried by the discourse context, not the aspect of the verb.

To buttress the claim that Emily's past morphology emerges as part of a new type of discourse idiom, two grammatical changes will be noted for this phase. First, Emily begins to use different sequencers for different discourse purposes. The new sequencer *and* tends to be a within-theme connective, typically used with topicalized (and deleted) subjects, whereas *when-then-yesterday* are used with nontopicalized subjects. It is as if Emily has become sensitive to the relevance for sequenced discourse of the distinction between new and old information. Similarly, this distinction is reflected in the overall topicalization structure of her narrative: the first mention of a referent is lexicalized with a proper noun or pronoun while subsequent mentions are presupposed and deleted. For example, in "then Emily got the blanket / and set the dinner," Emily omits the topic in the second utterance. This omission and the tendency to "maintain one particular referent as topic in several successive clauses" (DuBois 1985, 350) is a common feature of narrative discourse (Halliday and Hasan 1976; Levy 1984; DuBois 1985). What is remarkable is that Emily already seems to be acquiring this narrative technique. Also, note that "When my woke up" is used to introduce and conclude the first section of speech. The use of the same phrase at the beginning and end of a section may indicate Emily's recognition of the convention that narratives have a canonical form including a beginning and an end.

THE PROGRESSIVE

M16 also contains utterances in the progressive (see Table 5.5). Recall that previously the progressive tended to occur without sequencers, without verb complements, and with new topics in subject position.

Progressive utterances were also situated in a clump separated from the simple-present utterances. These properties functioned to render the progressive utterances more static—in contrast to the contingently sequenced simple-present utterances. In M16 the progressive utterances are structurally similar to this. Their purpose, however, is even more opaque than before. In the last stanza of M16 (beginning "Daddy coming up and running downstairs"), are the progressives meant to describe an inference from an ongoing auditory experience, or are they meant to describe a different kind of event, one that does not lend itself to sequencing? In other words, when Emily switches to the progressive, it is not clear whether she has abandoned her attempt to recount or whether she is recounting a different type of event. What is clear is that the progressive continues to be the form chosen when events are not sequentially ordered with respect to one another.

Progressive utterances do exhibit one important structural change in phase III: *-ing* can now co-occur with an object—a property that has been associated with the simple present and simple past constructions and that has been interpreted as functioning as a boundary marker. Nevertheless, when it does co-occur with an object, it also occurs with epistemic qualifiers such as *maybe* and *I don't know*. It has been claimed for adult speech that the use of such irrealis markers is a way of attenuating the event-like status of a reported action (Hopper and Thompson 1980). Hence, even though in Emily's speech progressive utterances begin to break frame and occur with objects, the utterances still retain the trappings of imperfectivity, namely the partitive *some,* the irrealis mode, the tendency for locatives rather than true patients. Given this, there is still reason to maintain that the progressive inflection is used for events that are less event-like, less ordered, and less individuated, that is, for structural features of back-grounded utterances. Also, the co-occurrence of *sleeping* in the first stanza with *now* and *not now* supports the claim that, with respect to the organization of tense, the progressive is used to relate (order) events to the moment of speech—in other words, to code deictic tense.

SELF-REFERENCE

The final property to be considered is Emily's retention of *Emmy* and *my* as her forms of self-reference in subject position even though she now represents herself as a causal agent rather than a passive recipient. This suggests that these forms are not chosen on the basis of the case role assigned to the subject, but are chosen as part of the narrative-reportative discourse idiom. What the generic SP monologues and the recounting monologue have in common is the word-to-world direction of fit (Searle 1979): the discourse is used to represent what has occurred or will occur, but not to bring about or negotiate any changes. Hence in both kinds of discourse Emily's role is more of a representor (one who documents) than a negotiator (one who changes).

Phase IV: Emily at 23;8–24;2

Rather than present the diversity in Emily's crib speech for this phase, I will now present data that reveal how Emily's use of verb morphology has developed. There are 389 decipherable utterances in the 10 monologues for this phase, about one-third of which function analogously to dialogic speech (for example, "I want Daddy," "Come and get me," and other phrases used to call out for help). Of the remainder, most are generic utterances in the simple present describing how things tend to be. There are also two monologues that manifest Emily's emergent ability to recount specific past events using past morphology. I will first focus on these recounting monologues, and then on Emily's use of the simple present.

RECOUNTING THE PAST

M17 and M18 are the two recounting monologues that occur during phase IV. Table 5.6 displays the verbs in both monologues. Once again *-ed* and *-irreg* are not restricted to lexically perfective verbs. Nevertheless, their spontaneous use is still restricted to narrative-like recounting sequences where events are ordered with respect to other events. This suggests that rather than assume that these monologues consist of decontextualized speech, we can better consider decontextualization itself as the capacity to use language as its own context. In this case, Emily's connected discourse about thematically related events seems to provide the necessary representational support for her to reconstruct the past.

But M17 and M18 display suggestive differences from M16. First, concerning the transitivity of the utterances that are explicitly marked for the past, in M16 77 percent (17) of the explicit past utterances are transitive, whereas only 44 percent (8) are in M17, and 66 percent (9) in M18. Second, whereas in M16 89 percent (31) of the utterances

Table 5.6. Frequency of verbs in monologues M17 (23;8)
and M18 (23;21).

Past		Nonpast	
		M17	
slept	3	make	1
came	7	come	2
woke up	1	wake up	3
said	4	bring	1
shouted	1	put	1
dressed up	1	sleeping	2
sat	1		
		M18	
took	3	sleep	1
didn't like	1	put	2
liked	1	has	1
didn't go	1		
wished	1		
came up	1		
bought	1		

have Emily as sentence subject, only 24 percent (7) do in M17, and
15 percent (2) in M18. Although these figures do not reveal absolute
differences, they suggest that the context that characterizes Emily's
earliest use of past morphology is even more restricted than that described above. The *-ed* and *-irreg* forms tend to emerge in the context
of predominantly transitive utterances with Emily as their agent
(M16). It is as if explicit reference to the past is facilitated when an
event is represented as being directed toward an outcome (that is, as
transitive) and when it depicts Emily's own doings. In other words,
what seems to help Emily reconstruct the past as past (and not past
as script for a continuing routine) is her sense of her own effective
actions on objects. Then, as M17 and M18 reveal, her use of past
morphology quickly generalizes along two parameters: from transitive constructions to intransitive constructions, and from utterances
with Emily as doer to utterances that refer to the past activities of
another person.

Thus, even though the data do not provide absolute differences, the
findings permit us to entertain the following proposal: Rather than
see semantic development in terms of the acquisition of discrete
meanings acquired at particular ages, perhaps we should view what
eventually becomes a semantic concept (like "pastness") as initially a

general schema of interrelated potential concepts (like agency and boundedness) and a distinct type of discourse use (narrating short episodes). If this is so, development then consists of the conceptual differentiation of initially fused concepts. Of course, according to the rules of scientific discourse, so much cannot legitimately be made of so little. So at this point I can merely offer such an interpretation, which awaits further support from analyses of other children.

It might also be noted that Emily does not use irregular past morphology to represent an immediately prior event or a single past event until eight days after M10 (see D10). The ending *-ed* is not used for these purposes at all in phase IV.

ASPECT

Phase IV presents evidence for the beginning semanticization of aspect. In phase III, past morphology tended to occur in transitive utterance frames with sequencers. Since objects function, in effect, to represent an event as bounded, and sequencers function to lead on to a different event and thus also convey a sense of boundary, conditions exist for the past morphology to become associated with the meaning of perfectivity in these utterance frames. At phase IV, however, transitive utterances are not as frequent. This suggests that the meaning of perfectivity may have become associated more with the forms themselves than with the entire discourse context. In other words, even in less transitive contexts, past morphology may now be functioning more independently to signal completion. In terms of the above discussion, it encodes both aspect (boundedness) and tense (pastness in terms of a whole event schemata).

PROGRESSIVE

Progressive utterances (of which there are only two in M17) no longer occur in a clump separated from the rest of the discourse. Also, for the first time, their thematic content seems to be integrated with the rest of the discourse. Given this, it is difficult not to interpret "I sleeping Tanta house" (M17) as Emily's attempt to state that she was *already* sleeping at Tanta's when her mother came to get her. If this interpretation is correct, the progressive is now functioning to represent events as being out of order with the main events of the narrative—rather than merely unordered. This is the first time that the progressive may be being used as a true background marker to interrupt and reorder the ongoing sequence of events.

Lastly, in M17 note that *now* is contrasted with *yesterday* as *sleep-*

ing is with *slept*. Whereas the progressive was previously imple-
mented with respect to the binary distinction *now–not now*, its contrast with *yesterday* and the simple past suggests that it may now be
ordered in relation to a more differentiated set of temporal values.
That is, if *now* finally contrasts with *yesterday* (not just with *not
now*), the co-occurring progressive may express present tense in opposition to the past.

Once again note that *Emmy* and *my* remain the dominant self-
referring forms in these monologues. In fact there is evidence that
these forms have become functionally equivalent, as *my* occurs as direct object ("then Mommy woke my up").

SIMPLE-PRESENT MONOLOGUES

For the first time, the simple present no longer occurs in the *when–
then* formats to explicitly sequence events. Nor does it tend to describe activities where Emily is not the agent. However, even though
the simple present has generalized to new contexts, it can do so only
because it has come to encode part of the meaning it previously in-
dexed in the SP discourse. In other words, its greater contextual free-
dom is a consequence of its greater semanticization. The simple present still tends to present events from the perspective of a generic or
normative event-type and thus tends not to represent single or distinct
events, but now this is due to the meaning that has become associated
with the simple present itself, and not to additional discourse co-
occurrences.

M20 and M21 demonstrate some of the new contexts of this form.
Note that in both these monologues the simple present is still used to
convey generic information ("That what Babar do," "sometimes").
Indeed, two types of generic information seem to be encoded by the
simple present: a judgment about what is characteristically done
(M20), and a generalization induced from specific instances of what
typically occurs (M21). What the two types of generic statements
share is that they do not refer to a distinct occurrence of a specific
event in time. The use of noninflected *have* in M22 to list who owns
what and where is similar, as Emily is not individuating specific
events. Thus, across all three examples, the simple present is not used
to represent a unique event that is deictically located with respect to
the moment of speech.

Besides the nonspecific temporal reference, these monologic utterances also convey a particular mode of speaker involvement: namely,

Emily renders an "impersonal" description of events. She seems to choose this verb construction to convey her sense that certain events are motivated by customary routines rather than personal desire or intentional action. This interpretation receives support from other studies, which have found that children of the same age use the simple present to indicate that an object "belongs" in a certain place (Bloom, Lifter, and Hafitz 1980), and that slightly older children use the simple present as a stance operator that conveys that an action is being done to conform to a norm rather than to manifest a personal desire (Gerhardt and Savasir 1986).

Therefore it is proposed that by phase IV Emily has abstracted a core meaning out of the previous SP discourse context: "There is a way that things are done." Even though the contexts of its occurrence are now more diverse, this generic meaning is present in all of the phase IV uses of the simple present. In fact, there seem to be two aspects to this core: (1) that the event represented is not merely a singular or distinct event, and (2) that the event is motivated by some kind of impersonal norm. Moreover, this core constrains the type of tense relation projected through the use of the simple present so that even when this construction is used to denote ongoing or future events, in each case, the event is viewed as an instance of a more overarching pattern.

In M23, for example, Emily uses the simple present as she tries to spell her name. In this case, two different levels of temporal reference are combined: reference to an ongoing event (present tense) and reference to an enduring norm (generic reference). Thus, even when the simple present is recruited for deictic purposes to mark present tense, it does so in a context similar to its previous use to mark relative time: the present event is viewed as being related to an established pattern. Therefore in both its earlier use and its phase IV use, this construction exhibits the tendency to refer to one event in terms of something else.

Moreover, the tendency to refer to something recurrent allows the simple present to be used with lexical expressions of future reference to express a future possibility. In M24, the co-occurrence of the simple present with *maybe, another,* and *come back* suggests that Emily can now refer to the future, but in this case the future event consists of the recurrence of the past. The earlier use of the simple present to represent routines rather than specific instances seems to serve as the basis for its present use to represent a future possibility that is a recurrence of the past.

As a final illustration, turn to M25, Emily's monologue following FD2, her father's speech to her before he leaves the room. M25 consists of Emily's reformulation of what her father has said. Most notably, the catenative *gonna* is omitted from Emily's rendition. However, in lieu of *gonna*, Emily seems to use her father's phrase *on Saturday* plus the simple present to express that an event is to occur in the future. Yet once again, what is projected in the future is something predetermined by the past. Thus, much as in M24 she projects a recurrence of a previous event, in M25 Emily projects a plan already represented by her father, similar instances of which have occurred in the past. This suggests that for Emily the notion of futurity is bound up with that of recurrence (what Benveniste 1968 calls the "future of predestination") rather than with her own sense of making things happen (Benveniste's "intentive future"). Thus, although Emily seems to be able to use the simple present plus other lexical items to make explicit reference to the future, futurity itself seems to be a projection from the past.

The point of presenting these diverse examples is to show not only that the simple present now occurs in different contexts of use but that in each case there is evidence that an aspect of its earlier use has been retained. This is the essence of what has been called the core meaning. Thus, even though monologues M20–M25 are more diverse than SP discourse, they represent events that are in some way nonactual and normatively based. These findings suggest not only that the phase IV use of the simple present develops out of the previous SP discourse context, but that the core semantic meaning itself consists of the crystallization of various meaning components of SP discourse. More particularly, the previous tendency for the speaker not to be the agent corresponds to the phase IV sense of a norm, and the previous tendency to refer to routines corresponds to the phase IV tendency to refer to specific events in terms of the patterns they manifest. Even traces of its earlier use as a relative time marker remain, in that the simple present never functions as a pure and simple deictic tense marker. The expression of tense is always combined with reference to something beyond the moment of speech. In sum, the development of Emily's use of the simple present reveals the semanticization of a meaning that is initially a function of the discourse context.

Before turning to the development of the progressives in the dialogues, let us examine Emily's intermittent use of *I* in subject position in these simple-present monologic utterances. Although *Emmy* and *my* remain the dominant forms, *I* begins to be sporadically used. *I* always occurs in utterance-initial position, and never follows a sequencing term (see M19, M25). Presumably its occurrence in first position is related to its utterance-initial position in the dialogues, suggesting that Emily's emerging rule is based on a syntactic generalization and not a functional distinction: namely, self-reference in first position should be expressed through *I*.

The Dialogues, Phases II–IV: Emily from 22;22–24;2

Examples of D4–D8 are representative of the later dialogues. Basically, Emily attempts to engage her father to prevent him from leaving her room and uses the progressive in challenges as one of her tactics. Of the 30 progressives that occur in this later period, 27 co-occur with *I* to serve the same discourse function as in phase I, to describe Emily's ongoing inappropriate activities and thereby challenge her father over the bedtime routine: *I* is combined with *sleeping here, laying here, waking up, standing up,* and so on. (The present auxiliary begins to occur during this period: "I'm sleeping here.") These examples support the earlier finding that in the dialogues the progressive occurs in challenges. I interpret this finding as indicating that the progressive is used to mark "discourse instability," that is, Emily's understanding that her challenges will provoke a negative response and will ultimately be overriden.

The important change for this period is the progressive's occurrence in a new discourse context: it is used twice in questions to inquire about her mother's activities ("What Mommy doing?" "Where Mommy going?"). Not only has the progressive migrated to a new context, but the nature of this context suggests that Emily has generalized the discourse meaning of this form. That is, it occurs in another relatively unstable discourse context. These questions in the progressive contrast with the simple-present question that occurs in this period (D9): "Does this blank[et] go like this?" In the simple-present question, Emily seems to know that a convention exists and is only checking to see whether her actions conform. In contrast, questions asked through the progressive are much more open-ended, indicating a lack of knowledge on Emily's part, which she seeks to remedy. In effect, the discourse function of such questions is to invite full uptake from the discourse partner. Both the challenges and the more open-ended questions constrain the interlocutor to intervene and in some way complete the transaction. Hence, the term "discourse instability" still pertains to the progressive, as it captures the negotiatory and up-for-grabs status of the content in all uses of this construction.

The contrast between the questions in the progressive and the question in the simple present is notable in that the previously identified distinction between these two construction types is played out again in a new context. The progressive is still used for less certain or less structured content while the simple present is used for more defined or routinized content. The fact that these constructions occur in a new context suggests that their discourse meaning has become less indexically reliant on a single mode of discourse and more reliant on the forms themselves. With respect to the mechanism that promotes this change, it may be that generalizations such as these across contexts serve as the opening wedge to dissociate the meaning of the form in a particular context of use from the meaning of the form itself. In other words, we may be witnessing the beginning semanticization of these two verb constructions.

Lastly, irregular past forms just begin to occur in the dialogues (D10–D12). In D11, Emily refers to a past event that has just taken place in the speech context. This is the only example for the six-week period under scrutiny in which past morphology is used to refer to an event that has just occurred. In D10 and D12 Emily uses irregular past morphology to describe more distant past events. In D12, we actually witness her appropriation of her father's past-tense form, which preempts the use of her previous present-tense form. The adoption of semantically appropriate preemptive forms has recently been claimed to serve as the mechanism whereby children learn to cut back on overgeneralized (and inappropriate) uses of forms (Bowerman 1987; Clark 1987; Fodor and Crain 1987). In this case, Emily's father's use of *did,* which presumably matches Emily's semantic intent, provides the conditions for Emily to appropriate this form in lieu of her overly general use of *do.*

Of course, there are utterances in the dialogues that the present analysis cannot account for. In D4, why does Emily follow "I'm sleeping here" with "Emily sleeps here"? Although it is tempting to argue that she deliberately substitutes a third-person form in the simple present for a first-person form in the progressive to present the event as fixed or immutable (in accord with the use of such utterances in the monologues) in order to get what she wants, there is no independent evidence for this claim. Even more recalcitrant is the following sequence: "Emmy standing up / I stand up / I standing up." Nevertheless, these are isolated instances and the analysis does capture the majority of Emily's dialogic output for this six-week period.

Conclusions

Although the term "context" has become the shibboleth of much contemporary work in language acquisition, the problem of specifying context *qua* structuring principle in language development remains. In the tradition of research inaugurated by Brown (1973), "context" is invoked as a methodological aid for the investigator to assess whether the child's grammatical output is "appropriate" with respect to the alleged constraints of a set of contextual criteria. In that these criteria are posited independent of any ethnographic description, no attempt is made to ascertain what counts as the appropriate context for the child. Indeed, Brown's assumption of a "required" context that determines the appropriate use of select grammatical forms betrays an impatience with the developmental problem itself. What is required for an adult must be worked out by the child, often through a developmental process that reveals initial tendencies that differ from the adult model. Shouldn't our goal be to discover what these tendencies are?

The analysis in this chapter is an attempt to work on the problem of context for a set of target grammatical forms by establishing patterns of regularities in the child's speech. This method was chosen on the assumption that such regularities could be used as a means of discovering the appropriate context for the target items in terms of the child's way of organizing their use. Of course, because of the nature of the data, it was not possible to determine which co-occurrences were causally implicated with respect to a particular form, and which were merely adventitiously associated with a particular form. This problem must be deferred until similar data from other children are collected and analyzed; perhaps comparisons across children (as well as more extensive data) will enable us to sort out the different types of relations that obtain between co-occurring linguistic phenomena.

It is important to note that my reason for pursuing the contextual analyses in this chapter differs dramatically from Brown's reason for invoking the notion of a "required context." Brown was concerned to establish criteria in terms of which it would be possible to assess when the child had attained an adult-like use of particular grammatical constructions (assuming that the criteria are correctly described for the adult system). Hence, he adopted the following measure: 90 percent occurrence in a required context. Instead, the reason for attempting to discover the discourse context for each of Emily's early uses of her verb inflections is to see whether and how these discourse contexts might be implicated in the eventual semantic notions ascribed to each of the target forms. In short, the problem is how certain tokens in language use might influence the development of language structure. For example, the interpretation of phase I SP discourse as talk that describes "what happens" in two different senses (routines rather than specific instances, and events that happen rather than actions that are undertaken) is important only insofar as it provides a basis for the construction of the generic meaning found in Emily's more developed phase IV uses. Similarly, recall the finding that both the simple present and the simple past initially tend to occur in a discourse context with sequencers and object complements—two constructions that render the event as being delimited or bounded. Again, the importance of describing such contextual factors is that, given the necessary conceptual prerequisites (Slobin 1981, 1985; Rispoli and Bloom 1987), an understanding of these factors may provide one of the developmental bases from which the eventual semantic concept of "perfectivity" (that is, boundedness) can emerge.

In the same vein, Emily's use of the progressive is interesting in light of the characterization this construction typically receives from linguists for adult speech: temporary duration and imperfectivity (nonboundedness). Recall that in the dialogues Emily's use of the progressive was interpreted as expressing discourse instability. But in the monologues, where the progressive occurs in contexts that lack a structured contour and an interlocking structure, conditions exist for this construction to acquire the discourse value of nonstructured event. The point is that both of Emily's early discourse contexts provide the conditions for the emergence of the semantic values that have been independently ascribed to this form by linguists: that is, discourse instability could give rise to temporary duration, and nonbounded or nonstructured event could give rise to imperfectivity.

Now of course, the details of these proposals may be incorrect. More important is the attempt to develop a *method* for characterizing the early contextual sensitivity of the child's speech in a way that provides a basis for subsequent development. In addition, what I have tried to demonstrate is that a child may first step into language by adopting a set of meanings or functions other than semantic meanings propositionally construed. This is the essence of my objection to the aspect-before-tense hypothesis—a position that seems to be based on the idea that children use verb morphology to mark objective event parameters. Instead, if the interpretations in this chapter have any merit, their value lies in providing a basis for semantic development that is based not on objective event parameters but on certain distinctions to which the child is sensitive because of her involvement in early modes of discourse.

Two serious difficulties emerge from the above analysis. First, I have claimed that Emily's early use of verb morphology is contextually restricted and that this provides evidence as to the nature of Emily's early meaning representations: that is, I have suggested that, rather than any one meaning operating on its own, Emily's early meanings presuppose a schematization such that certain meanings imply other meanings. For example, the meaning dimension of aspect is related to that of agency, event specificity or genericness, and direction-of-fit, and so on. I suggested that these early meaning dimensions be thought of as functionally undifferentiated components of a larger whole. In other words, the different meaning dimensions are not yet conceptually independent of one another, but are understood in terms of one another. Thus Emily cannot yet operate with them as discrete meanings on their own. Given this claim, development consists of the differentiation of these initially fused components—a position for which the Emily data provide minimal support.

The problem with such a model is that it vies with the claim that children will tend to formulate the simplest rules—where simplicity entails generality (see Fodor and Crain 1987). It seems that Emily selects for her early representations not the most general formulations, but highly specific formulations. However, rather than equate specificity with complexity as would a feature notation model, we do not need to assume that these early meaning schemata, though more detailed in one sense, are necessarily more complex. Feature notation models offer "etic" descriptions based on the assumption that units that differ for the analyst also differ for the system under analysis. However, according to the interpretation in this chapter, the different meaning components of Emily's early representational structures initially function as a *system with systemically inherent links*. This means that although we as analysts can extrapolate independent meaning dimensions from Emily's early schematizations, there is no reason to attribute these dimensions to Emily. Clearly, we need to devise some form of notation to represent the child's early meaning schemata in terms of conceptually fused components rather than bundles of discrete features.

The second difficulty is even more serious than the first. Given a child who speaks in long strings of connected discourse, we must assume that she is being exposed to some type of similarly structured input in her environment. How determinant is this for the patterns observed? For example, does Emily invent the pattern in which the progressive inflection occurs in an imperfective configural context (no sequencers, no complements) or does this restricted use mirror that of her parents? As noted above, although Emily's parents tend to address her as *you* in their pre-bedtime speech, she seizes on *Emmy* and *my* as her forms of self-reference for her monologues. Thus with respect to the grammatical system of self-reference, she seems to have established her own basis for the deployment of *I* versus *Emmy* or *my*. What about her use of verb morphology? Unfortunately, the data are not sufficient to provide an answer to this question, and thus we must end with the anxiety of knowing how incomplete this analysis is and the optimism of assuming that further research will be able to address the necessary questions.

Appendix

KEY
___

[//   simultaneity
(   )   uncertain transcription
((   )) very uncertain transcription
.....   a few lines omitted

E: Emily   M: mother   F: father   D: dialogue
M: monologue

DIALOGUES
___

D1 (22;15)
    E: I um running like anything
    F: You certainly are. But now I think it's time for a nap

D2 (22;18)

    E: I sleeping here!

    F: I think that's not the place that Daddy put the blanket on you

D3 (22;16)

    F: I think we have two [of the clean ones//

    E: [I want that//

    F: somewhere. [to M] Did you throw them down?

    M: No I didn't throw them down honey, I just—

    E: Aaa—I want that closed! (I want) that one closed [refers to shades]

    F: What do you want?

    E: I want that one

    M: This one closed too? Okay

FATHER'S DIALOGUE

FD1(22;16)

    F: I'll put a blanket—

        You lie down

        Daddy'll put a blanket on you

        and when you wake up

        we're going to go to Carl's

        but you have to go to sleep now

        you're such a good girl, Pookey

MONOLOGUES

M1(22;16)

    Maybe when my go—come

    maybe my go in Daddy's (blue) big car

    maybe maybe when Carl come (again)

    then go to back home

    go Peabody

    Carl sleeping

    not right now—the baby coming

    and Carl coming

    my house

    Aaaaaaaaaand Emmy Emmy ((everything)) (???) coming

    after my nap

    not right now—cause the baby coming now

M2 (excerpt) (22;17)
    (Then)—when Emmy wakes up
    Carl come
    after my nap
    then Carl come (over) my house
    then Emmy go Caldors in the mall
    when Daddy wake Emmy up
    not not—um um—( )
    when Emmy wake up
    Emmy has—has something on my face
    . . . . .
    When Mommy—when Mommy comes in
    Mommy go in my room
    then go get me ((sleep)) (??) baby

M3 (excerpt) (22;19)
    When D-Daddy come
    then Daddy get Emmy
    then Daddy wake Emmy up
    then—then—Carl come (play)
    Emmy
    not right now—Emmy sleeping
    Emmy sleeping
    . . . . .
    Carl sleeping
    and ((Emmy)) sleeping
    and Lance sleeping
    and Alex sleeping
    and Uncle Dick and Aunt (Sam) and Carl and Emmy and Daddy
        and Mommy and (Oh-ten) and Uncle (Joe) all go sleeping

QUASI MONOLOGUES: ENACTMENTS

M4 (excerpt) (21;7)
    I got baby
    I put blanket on baby
    (I'll) put the baby—I'(ll) put the—um
    change the baby's diapers
    put the baby nap
    I change the baby's diapers
    Then put—take it—take the baby—put the baby nap
    Hi! baby!

M5 (22;1)

> I getting this
> And putting this just here—right here
> then Emmy put this one right here (on my doll)
> and get Rocky Raccoon
> put here by me (little one) here
>
> . . . . .
> Get this
> Emmy get this
> put this up
> put this up
> sometime Emmy make this (one feel better) [talks to doll]
> sometime Emmy make that one feel better

M6 (22;4)

> Emmy put this here
> then this
> My blanket—up in crib
> Emmy put in this
> Emmy can't get out
> Emmy put blanket on
>
> . . . . .
> When Daddy comes
> then Daddy come and get Emmy
> then—when Daddy (???)
> then Daddy come and play with me

MONOLOGUES

M7 (22;24)

> When Daddy comes in
> then Daddy get Emmy
> then Daddy get Emily (??)
>
> . . . . .
> When Emmy wake up
> Emmy has ( )
> then Emmy go over library
> then (???)

M8 (23;2)

　　When my wake up [crying]
　　then Daddy don't (get my) . . .
　　when my wake up
　　(then Daddy maybe my)
　　and (??) go visit my baby sleeping
　　my go my bed (??)
　　(go bed)
　　when my wake up into (my buta)
　　then Daddy ((my won't go do that))
　　then Daddy—then Daddy (when my) wake up
　　not now (??)
　　Mommy sleeping (??) [crying]
　　I needed that
　　I need the (??)
　　this one Daddy
　　my Daddy coming
　　my Daddy coming
　　Daddy

M9 (23;2)

　　And . . . when Daddy comes [crying]
　　I put that (there)
　　then my eat my (waffles)
　　then Daddy make my bed
　　[unintelligible]
　　and then maybe—maybe. . . . .
　　when Daddy comes
　　[unintelligible]
　　. . . . .
　　and when Daddy comes up
　　Emmy sleeping on this
　　when Daddy comes
　　then Daddy gets Emmy
　　and bring my waffles
　　then Daddy (maybe perhaps) and—and hold Emmy . . . ummm
　　that not now
　　Emmy (sleepy head)
　　Emmy sleeping
　　that next day
　　Emmy do that
　　Emmy
　　Ummmmmmmm
　　Emmy wake up

M10 (23;6)

> When Daddy comes in
> then Emmy come in
> then take my out
> then (leave my sleep)
> then clean baby up
> now Emmy can (leave)

M11 (excerpt) (22;22)

> (Morrow) morning when my wakes up
> then Daddy (???)
> (morrow) morning when my wake up
> then Daddy (???)
> and puts some juice and cups
> then Emmy (have) cock-party
> then Emily drinked her cocktail up

M12 (22;25)

> I blew my nose [crying, calling for help]
> I blew my nosey
> Daddy clean my nose
> clean my nosey
> I need clean my nose

M13 (22;22)

> I saw Daddy
> I want Daddy to . . .
> I want go to Daddy

M14 (22;22)

> Daddy did(n't) make some cornbread for Emmy (??)
> Daddy didn't make that—cornbread
> (but) then Emmy eat
> Daddy make (??)
> not that bread for corn . . . Emmy
> that bread not for Emmy
> Emmy like cornbread and toast
> I don't like (??) apples and (??)
> food I like and noodles too
> I don't like anything cept—cept for that—that bread Daddy has
> I don't like that bread (something)
> Daddy don't like
> Emmy don't like
> Daddy and Mommy d-d-d-d-d

M15 (22;29)
> I don't like what Mommy or Daddy
> I don't—
>
> . . . . .
>
> I don't know who take (?) (bath)
>
> . . . . .
>
> I didn't drink my [crying out for help]
> I drink this little bitty juice (???)
> I need drink this little bitty more juice!

M16 (23;6)
> When my woke up
> then Daddy took my friends out
> and took the boat out
> and took Emmy out in—
> Emmy crashed the boat
> when my woke up
>
> . . . . .
>
> Emmy took the boat out
> when my get up
> [unintelligible]
> now sleeping time
> now not sleeping time
> Emmy make it bedtime
> not sleeping time
>
> . . . . .
>
> Yesterday my (swep/slep) all the blankets
> and on the wall
> and on the floor
> and in the dining room table, with the baby
> and in the hallway like my pretty
> and Emmy (swept/slept) the hallway
> and make pretty
> and throw the baby
>
> . . . . .
>
> Put my jamas on
> and then my play
> and my said—play and play in a boat and play with my boat
>
> . . . . .
>
> and then Emily went to sleep
> and played—um—the blanket
>
> . . . . .
>
> Then Emily got the blanket

and set the dinner
Emmy ate one time
and one time, Emmy sick
Emmy wanted dinner
Emmy (??)
and Emmy ate the ice
and took dinner
and (Emmy) played and played
. . . . .
Da-Da-Daddy coming up and running downstairs
Daddy running and running and running downstairs
Daddy running and running downstairs
get some dinner
(   )
maybe Daddy getting some books or nothing
maybe
I don't know what Daddy getting downstairs
maybe Daddy getting some books or getting blankets
I don't know what Daddy doing
maybe Daddy getting some books

M17 (excerpt) 23;7
When Mormor (???)
when Mormor make pretty
(when my bring Tanta house)
(when my slept)
and Mommy came
and Mommy said
"Get up/time go home" [*alters her voice as if to mimic another's*]
When my slep
and (and Mormor came)
and Mommy (come in)
then get up
time t'go home
time t'go home drink p-water [Perrier]
yesterday did that
now Emmy sleeping in regular bed
yesterday my slept
(??) um, in Tanta house
(and) Mommy woke my up
(??) "Go/time go home"
. . . . .
When Mormor came in

and Mommy shouted "Make my bed"
when—when Mommy came in
when my (bed)
((wh-wh)) I sleeping Tanta house
Mommy came wake my up
because time t'go home
drink P-water
. . . . .

M18 (23;20)

Carl sleep in bed
and Carl's daddy took the blanket back
and Carl didn't like that
Carl liked his blanket a whole bunch in the bed
then Carl didn't go in the—
then Mommy, Daddy (put) bed
and Carl took a really nice, long nap
and Mommy and Emmy's daddy and Emmy wished that
Emmy came up and (??)
. . . . .
Daddy Mommy put that blanket
Emmy has and also Mommy and Daddy, all my friend . . . in my bed

M19 (24;2)

I put Danny my can go my horse
and Arthur put (like) one bike
but Danny said: "No I can't get on bike"
Danny said: "Yes! I can go my horse
but not in the bike"
but, but "Yes, yes (???) bike"
getting on the horse
but, but Danny said: "No my can go on the . . ."
but Mormor came to watch my horse

M20 (excerpt) (23;9)

Lessons! Get lessons and come back
that (???)
the Babar lessons!
that what Babar do!
Babar come from the lessons
then come on the town

M21 (excerpt) (23;10)

Sometimes (Daddo) (in table) and put my down

sometimes Mommy Daddy put Emmy down (with h-)
sometimes Momma—sometimes Tanta puts Emmy down with (the h-)
sometimes Jeannie and Annie and Tanta and Emmy Mommy and my Daddy and Carl Daaaaddy and Carl Mommy
sometimes Tanta and Jeannie come over
and sometimes Jeannie take my old changing table at home
and my get that diaper
and put it on
sometimes—sometimes Emmy change diaper
and sometimes Emmy (help Jeannie change) diaper
sometimes Jeannie change my diaper

M22 (23;9)
    Dana have this bedroom (her) house
    D-Dana (??)
    Dana (this) have bed in the hall, Dana house
    Dana have her toys in bed and toys and play with
    and Danny have toys in Danny's room
    Carl have toys in (her) room where Emmy play with
    Carl have bed and toys and toys and that (all) Carl have
    and then for Emmy play with
    Lance (too) got bed in Lance's room
    and toys for play with

M23 (23;28)
    M-O-Y
    M-O-Y
    That spells Emmy
    [unintelligible]
    M-O-Y
    M-O-Y
    M spell and spell Emmy

M24 (24;1)
    Maybe tow-truck come back
    And then tow-truck another car (??)
    Maybe my stand by the tow-truck with the (??)
    Maybe tow—the tow—tow (woooo-h go) back
    (And then) yellow car (come back)
    And thennnn leave the blue car
    It's broken
    Now the (pink) tow-truck come back with the blue car

FATHER'S DIALOGUE
***

FD2 (23;15)
    F: You know what we're gonna do?
       You know what we're gonna do this weekend?
       We're gonna go to Childworld
       and we're gonna buy some diapers for Stephen
       and some diapers for Emily
       and we're gonna buy an intercom system
       so that we can hear Stephen, in different parts of the house
       I think you're gonna like it
       because we'll be able to hear Stephen downstairs when Stephen's
           upstairs
       It's gonna be a neat gadget
    E: Say that again
    F: When we, on this weekend, we're going to Childworld
       and buy diapers for Stephen and diapers for Emily
       and what is called an intercom system
       that we plug in—and Stephen—into Stephen's room
       and then we go downstairs and we plug it in
       and we get to hear Stephen—making a—when Stephen wakes up
           we'll hear him cry, through the intercom system—it's a neat
           gadget
    E: Say again
    F: One more time and then (we'll) go to bed
       On Saturday we're gonna go to Childworld
       and get diapers for Emily and diapers for Stephen and an inter-
           com system so we can hear Stephen in different parts of the
           house
       Okay Hon, I love you

MONOLOGUE (THIS FOLLOWS FD2, 30 SECONDS LATER)
***

M25 (excerpt) (23;15)
    I went to sleep
    Daddy said: buy diapers for Stephen and Emmy
    and buy (some)thing for Stephen
    plug in and say ahahah
    and put in, the—in
    on Saturday go Childworld
    buy diaper for Emmy
    and diaper for the baby
    and then buy (something) for the—

and (see) for that baby plug in and get—
diapers for anybody!

D4 (22;25)

 M: Good night Honey. Have a good nap
 E: I'm sleeping here!
 M: Okay, well you and Daddy can resolve that
 E: Emily sleeps here!
 F: I think we'll sleep down here Sweetie!
 . . . . .
 E: I'm waking up!
 . . . . .
 E: I'm standing up [3 times]
 F: What do you want, Hon?

D5 (22;29)

 E: What Mommy doing?
 F: Taking a bath
 . . . . .
 E: I'm laying here
 F: I know you're laying there, but it's time for sleeping, isn't it?
 . . . . .
 F: Well, that's enough of the game, so I'll see you in the morning
 E: Emmy standing up!
  I stand up!
  I standing up

D6 (4 different dialogues from 23;2 to 23;10)

 E: I sleeping here!

D7 (23;2)

 E: I standing up!

D8 (24;1)

 E: I'm not standing
  I'm sitting up!
 F: Well, I know you're sitting up, but you know what . . .

D9 (24;2)

 E: Does this blanket go like this?
  Put the best way
 F: Okay, night-night

D10 (28;10)

> F: Maybe we'll go to the library
>   it may be snowing too
>   maybe some more snow outside
> E: And (???)
>   Mommy said—n—maybe go library
> F: Maybe go to the libr—
>   we'll go to the library
>   unless it's very bad weather

D11 (24;1)

> E: Eeeeeehh!
> F: Oh sorry
> E: What Daddy did?
> F: I almost (hurt) your hand again
>   I gotta be careful with that, huh?

D12 (24;1)

> E: What we do today
> F: What did we do today? Well we went to Tanta's today and you saw a tow-truck. Then we came back here and we painted, and we read *Hansel and Gretel,* and we had, and you helped Daddy make pasta (gucoe), and tortellini, and Daddy played the tortellini man, the pasta man, and Emmy played the pasta girl. We had a good time
> E: What we di-?
> F: And Daddy had a little nap, just now, huh?
> E: What we did just now?

Chapter 6

Monologue as Reenvoicement of Dialogue

John Dore

The history of child-language studies can be seen as a struggle toward clarity about two major issues. The first concerns the conceptualization of language itself: Which terms best describe the phenomenon of language?—or in other words, Whose theory will hold sway? The second issue is, given some set of theoretical terms, how do we know what a child's language abilities are at any given moment of development? This concerns the methods we rely upon to reveal exactly what is changing in the speech produced by a child at the time we are analyzing. In this book we have the opportunity to apply somewhat differing viewpoints on aspects of language to the same corpus of data—the pre-sleep monologues of a prolific little girl. Although we all agree in general that language must be described in light of its social conditions, we vary in which aspects of language we describe and in how extensively we are committed to the social determination of the child's language development.

In this chapter I propose one of the more extensive accounts of how language emerges out of a social matrix. Regarding our corpus of a child's monologues and dialogues with her parents, my central claim is that her monologues "reenvoice" the features of dialogue that she experiences. This notion of "reenvoicement" is taken from a theory of the social determinants of language, called "dialogism," articulated by Bakhtin (1981, 1984, 1986). Reenvoicement is a concept that replaces the reliance upon imitation (Skinner 1957) on the one hand, and upon "sentence creativity" (Chomsky 1965) on the other, for describing language development. And such reenvoicement takes place in terms of the unit of analysis called the "genre" (Bakhtin 1986). Thus, developments in this child's monologues are described here in terms of changes in the features of genre they manifest. One implication of this analysis is that language acquires children as much as children acquire language.

A general concern of this chapter is to show how language functions and how it is structured in a recurring scene from one family's daily life. This concern dovetails with the other chapters in this book insofar as it contributes to our understanding of the development of narrative in the mind of the child being studied. I begin by discussing some perspectives as background to the kind of theory that informs the data analyses. (The theoretical perspective proposed here derives primarily from insights proposed by Bateson, Vygotsky, and Bakhtin.) Then I describe the scene of putting the child to sleep from an ethnographic viewpoint. In large part the scene is a social struggle between the parents, who require that their child sleep alone, and the child, who resists this.

The data to be analyzed here are the speech productions of a little girl, Emily. They are in the form of conversations between Emily and her parents before she goes to sleep, and her talk to herself after her parents leave the room. The conversation is referred to as dialogue and the crib talk to herself as monologue. After proposing the units of analysis, I describe the features of the adults' talk in the dialogues. These features are primarily from the father's conversations with Emily, and they do not change much throughout the corpus. Then I analyze a pivotal example of narrative from one of Emily's monologues in terms of the same units, and compare it to the features in the dialogue preceding it. This comparison shows the influence of dialogue on Emily's monologues at this transitional period of her development. I then analyze three months of her earlier and her later monologues to specify what changes in the course of her development. After summarizing some of the findings, I conclude with some implications of this kind of approach.

Background: Mind as Social System

Gregory Bateson (1972) conceived of "mind" as a cybernetic system of "messages" defined as transforms of differences traveling in circuits around the system. He described mental systems in general as having several properties: they process information by trial and error; they operate via feedback loops and mechanisms of comparison which allow for adaptive change; they are hierarchically organized in terms of levels of learning and signaling; and they are self-corrective. But the "total self-corrective unit which processes information, or thinks and acts . . . is a system whose boundaries do not at all coincide with the boundaries either of the body or what is popularly called the 'self'" (p. 319). Rather, mind is immanent in the larger system of man plus environment, and "large parts of the thinking network are located outside the body" (p. 320).

To illustrate a total "thinking" system, Bateson used the example of a blind man tapping his way along a street with a stick. He argued that the "stick is a pathway along which transforms of difference are being transmitted." If we are to explain the blind man's behavior, the total system of man, stick, and street must be involved. And "the way to delineate the system is to draw the limiting line in such a way that you do not cut any of these pathways in ways which leave things inexplicable" (p. 459). Regarding the status of the "self" in such systems, Bateson made two points of crucial importance for this chapter. First, that a "human being in relation with another has very limited control over what happens . . . He is part of a two-person unit, and the control which any part can have over any whole is strictly limited" (p. 267). And second, at the higher levels of learning to act in terms of the contexts of contexts, the "concept of the 'self' will no longer function as a nodal argument in the punctuation of experience" (p. 304).

Depending on whether they are inside or outside of the body, the pathways along which "messages" travel differ, but not absolutely so. There is a certain amount of compartmentalization segmenting the system. But there is also a "'semipermeable' linkage between consciousness and the remainder of the total mind. A certain limited amount of information about what's happening in this larger part of mind seems to be relayed to what we may call the screen of consciousness" (p. 432). What gets into consciousness is highly selected. Bateson thought that there was little known about the rules and preferences of selection by consciousness, but that the limitations of language must play a role (p. 444). Using the analogy of the map to its territory, he claimed that the "process of representation will filter it [the territory] out so that the mental world is only maps of maps of maps" (p. 454). But he felt it was dangerous to attempt "to separate intellect from emotion" or "to separate the external mind from the internal" (p. 464).

Bateson's notion of mind is useful in describing language, especially as language is involved in "thinking" and as it develops in the child's mind. Bateson himself spoke of language occasionally, usually as a symbol system (along with art, ritual, myth, and others) for organizing cultural experience. Although he offered no structural account of language itself, he stressed the need to describe "meaning" within a hierarchy of contexts: "the word only exists as such—only has 'meaning'—in the larger context of the utterance, which again has meaning only in a relationship . . . without context there is no communication" (p. 402). As discussed below, this view fits nicely with Vygotsky's theory of how language develops in the child's mind, and with Bakhtin's notions about how language functions. But here it is most useful to speculate about how some of Bateson's notions might apply to the language of our corpus. The following discussion is not a set of claims about the Emily data so much as a larger-scale theoretical framework in terms of which the claims I will make below can be understood.

Emily and her parents form a kind of cybernetic system of feedback loops. They form a sort of "collective mind," a "mind" that strictly circumscribes whatever is "in" Emily's mind. "Messages" circulate among them in the forms of words, tones, and narrative story-lines. These forms are transformed as they move among the members of the system. From this perspective Emily's monologues can be viewed as trial-and-error productions, hierarchically organized in terms of certain linguistic units, operating as self-corrective feedback mechanisms, and adapting to related models of language forms used by her parents in the wider system of language they all share. Emily is only one part of the three-person language system of her family. Any control she may be able to exercise over her monologues is strictly constrained by the properties of the larger family system. Her consciousness is at least "semipermeable" to the expressed features of this system. Her monologues will inevitably be "maps" of her parents' larger "maps."

Now let us extend this discussion to include the work of a thinker who focused on child development. Vygotsky (1978) proposed a theory of how any higher intellectual function, such as language, could appear in the child's mind. He offered the example of how an infant's grasping for an object becomes the communicative act of pointing. At first the infant struggles alone to reach an object by grasping toward it. When a parent observes this, she interprets the gesture as indicating something. She assumes that the infant is pointing to a particular object and that he wants to receive it. "Consequently," Vygotsky argued, "the primary meaning of that unsuccessful grasping movement is established by others. Only later, when the child can link his unsuccessful grasping movement to the objective situation as a whole, does he begin to understand this movement as pointing" (p. 56). For Vygotsky the meaning of any language unit can emerge in the child's mind only by means of such social collaboration in objective situations.

Vygotsky theorized that "the process of internalization consists of a series of transformations." First, "an operation that initially represents an external activity is reconstructed and begins to occur internally" (pp. 56–57). Second, "an interpersonal process is transformed into an intrapersonal one." And third, this transformation is "the result of a long series of developmental events" (p. 57). That is, intellectual functions that take place at first between individuals are transferred to inner processes and "are incorporated into a new system with its own laws" (p. 57). A recent retranslation of Vygotsky (1987) clarifies his position and provides an important vantage point for viewing the Emily data: "Speech for oneself has its source in a differentiation of an initially social speech function . . . The central tendency of the child's development is . . . a gradual individualization that emerges on the foundation of the child's internal socialization" (p. 259).

Elsewhere I have argued that this model of development accounts for the emergence of word meaning in the child's mind based on the process of dialogue with parents (Dore 1983, 1985). Although the present case concerns larger units of language, I suggest that Vygotsky's theory applies, to a point, here as well. The "initial external activities" that serve as models for Emily's monologic narratives are her parents' narratives in their dialogues with her. Emily tries to "reconstruct" these internally, transforming what was an external process of narrative in dialogue into an internal process of monologue. But, in order for her to establish "a new system" of her own narrative structures cognitively, she must undergo "a long series of developmental events," namely successive attempts at reformulating monologic narratives. The challenge here is to show the "gradual individualization" of her narratives—to show how her monologues are reflections on dialogues, sometimes reproducing dialogic segments almost exactly, while at others refracting (or otherwise assimilating) them through her own newly emerging internal system.

Speech Genres: The Organization of Discourse Meanings and Functions

Speech has most often been analyzed structurally, with reference to language as an abstract system, most notably as a grammar. But speech, of course, serves numerous functions; and a grammar is not a theory of these functions. The structural properties of sentences tell us little about how utterances express intentions, acts, and social conventions, much less how they express emotions, motives, attitudes, and social stances. Yet since speech works simultaneously as both structural knowledge and social function, we need a unit of analysis that captures both structure and function simultaneously. Vygotsky (1962) proposed that the minimal unit of the analysis of thought and language that met this criterion was "word meaning," since it reflected both conceptual and linguistic aspects of words. Beyond the word level, previous analyses have usually kept structural and functional analyses separate: for example, an utterance might be seen as having a sentence containing a proposition on the one hand, while expressing a speech act (attitude or intention) on the other (Searle, 1969).

For describing the Emily corpus we need a larger unit, one that provides for the analysis of narrative sequences in monologues and dialogues. A unit that captures the overall functioning of narrative and conversational sequences is the "genre." Some ethnographers have identified different types of genres. Hymes (1974), for example, described the "complex genre of a church service" in terms of "elementary genres" such as sermons, hymns, litanies, psalms, and so on. Goffman (1974) apparently had a similar notion in mind when he spoke of "frames" of talk, where some "key" will shift the frame in terms of how some strip of talk is done. And a genre in this sense functions as one of the kinds of context that Bateson had in mind when he argued that an utterance can have meaning only in terms of its relationship to a larger communicative context (1972, 402).

But the most extensive treatment of the genres of everyday speech is to be found in the work of Bakhtin (1986). According to him, "speech genres" are "relatively stable types" of organization for the "thematic content, style and compositional structure" of utterances as expressions (p. 60). A set of speaker assumptions and expectations, of emotions and attitudes, are expressed, primarily through intonation, by the genre in which one speaks. A speech genre is in the central functional mode for the analysis of sequences of speech. In scope a genre may range from a single retort in conversation to the tone of an entire formal speech. But in the data analyzed here the same speech genre will cover several successive sequences of utterances. In the literature on child language the phenomenon that comes closest, at least to the stylistic aspect of a genre, is "baby talk." That is, the register of talk in which adults simplify, repeat, differentially intone (with higher pitch, elongation, emphatic stress, and so on), and otherwise tailor their speech to young children. But baby talk has not been proposed as a unit that organizes the style, content, and structure of adult speech to children. Moreover, in our corpus the adults mix baby-talk features with those of a more adult-like talk. So a certain weave of genres occurs.

A genre in Bakhtin's sense is a functional format for organizing content, style, and structure simultaneously. It is a routine means, sometimes even a ritual way, of accomplishing a verbal interaction. The dialogues of our corpus manifest a strictly circumscribed set of styles, contents, and structures—the forms of this talk are determined by the kind of social scene they are motivated to achieve. The actual scenario of putting Emily to bed is enacted through several genres. These are complex genres, which are made up of several kinds of elementary ones. These genres are not strictly ritualized, but they are fairly routine. And genre, I propose, is what most deeply organizes Emily's speech.

This notion of genre must be distinguished from the social orders of the scene and the scenario on the one hand, and from the internal states of individuals on the other. When a scenario is actualized in a scene, the actualization is typically performed in terms of varying mixes and levels of genres. An individual may bring any number of conscious intentions and strategies to a scene, and probably brings many unconscious motives and needs as well. For example, in the dialogues to be analyzed it seems to me uncontroversial to say that Emily's father is motivated to get his child to go to sleep, and that he often uses the strategy of promising her rewards if she does so. Similarly, Emily is presumably motivated (though perhaps less consciously) to keep her father in the room, possibly for fear of being alone; and she accomplishes this by continually questioning him, eliciting repetitions, crying, pleading, and otherwise delaying him.

These internal phenomena are not the object of study when we analyze the genres of speech. Nor does the specification of genre appeal to any pragmatic explanation of the participants' purposes for interacting. A genre is (before it can be internalized) a social performance, requiring recognition, uptake, and collaboration in order to be sustained. It is thus explicitly displayed by interacting members—even when the "speaker" is writing to an "audience." Genres orchestrate the themes, styles, and discourse structures and functions of a scenario. And in the case of a child's emerging monologues with herself, various pieces of content, structure, and style are what gradually evolve into the organized format of a recognizable genre.

The notion of genre proposed here is the functional counterpart to grammar. While sentence structures are organized in terms of grammar, discourse functions are organized in terms of genre. However, a grammar operates with a fixed set of syntactic rules, a systematic set of semantic meanings, and a narrow array of phonological realizations. Genre, in contrast, organizes dynamically shifting sets of fluctuating meanings, of situated messages, and of varying discourse functions.

Genre can be viewed as analogous to Wittgenstein's (1953) notion of "family resemblances." When we look for the common meaning among the uses of the same word form, as with the word "game" for example, we do not find an exclusive set of conceptual criteria or semantic features shared by each use of the word. Rather we find something like "fuzzy family resemblances," enabling us more or less to recognize a meaningful use of the word when it is extended to refer to a new object. Similarly, the set of thematic, stylistic, and structural features that constitute a genre often vary widely from one occasion to the next. For instance, while content and structure may vary, a speaker may persist in the style of the same genre nevertheless.

This is so because there seem to exist wide arrays of options available to be actualized in the three components of genre. Within each component of theme, structure, and style there are elementary genres that together constitute the larger and more complex genres. Moreover, unlike the rather limited variations of grammatical speech, genres are less fixed formats for organizing the situated functions and momentary meanings in a conversation. Also, in everyday speech grammatical expressions are rarely too complex to be decoded, and speakers of the same dialect rarely have difficulty in understanding one another grammatically. But multiple genres are typically woven together in ordinary conversation; and the quality of experience needed to recognize the more subtle features of genre shifts differs from one person to another. Because of all this complexity, it takes years for a child to acquire consistent control over genre formats. In fact, it is not likely that such complex formats could be acquired at all without enormous amounts of specific socialization in the ways that speech can be used. This subtlety of genre formation is quite challenging, not only to the child learning language, but to the analyst trying to describe it.

The Family Scene and Its Emotional Significance

In order to appreciate fully the relations between dialogue and monologue in these data, we must understand the nature of the scene in which this talk occurs. The central fact is that Emily is being put into her crib for a nap or a night's sleep. It is a necessary scene of family life. The activity to be accomplished is that Emily lies down to sleep and her parents leave the room. We must appreciate that this entire activity could be accomplished silently: placing her in the crib and exiting through the door could do it. And this scene must indeed be done this way in other cultures, in other families, and perhaps at times in this family. However, the encouragement of talk is a primary ethnographic fact in this family's life.

We can ask, then, what these dialogues accomplish. And the prima facie answer is that the dialogues negotiate the conditions for going to sleep. The central fact for Emily is that she must sleep alone; and the father, whose "job" this is, must leave the room. Many other conditions are also negotiated. Among the required conditions are that the door be closed and the light put out, that Emily stay in her crib, and that she not cry. There are optional conditions as well: she may lie down at one end of the crib or the other, may have a blanket on, may have "friends" (toys) with her, and may request other conditions, such as having the shades shut.

All of the above facts are explicitly discussed by family members, but much else also goes on. The parents answer Emily's questions; they perform naming routines (of her "friends," of objects in the room, of their colors, and so on); they make lists (of who is sleeping, of who is "big" versus who is a "baby," of who is coming to visit, of where they will be going when she awakes, of what they will buy, and so on); they engage in baby talk, apparently for solidarity and emotional alignment; they describe events, sing songs, explain rules, and so on. Moreover, the parents sometimes cajole, indulge, and placate Emily. They make promises of "fun" to come after she sleeps; they try to convince her of the rationale for sleeping. Emily often cries in anticipation of the parent's departure, and she persists in asking questions, naming things, requesting repetitions, and, in general, resisting being left alone to sleep.

Obviously a good deal more is being done in the dialogues than the verbal pleasantries of taking leave of one another. The emotional significance of being left alone to sleep is great for Emily, as is evidenced by her frequent crying, delaying their talk, lingering on topics, refusing conditions of sleep, changing her mind, and much else. The practical necessity of getting his daughter to sleep is uppermost in her father's mind; this is evidenced by his persistence at the task, his occasional exasperation, and his frequent ignoring of what Emily says.

But there is a tacit contract, as it were, that the negotiation of the scene will be done civilly, even affectionately. The parents want it to be pleasant; for Emily it is often threatening. And herein lies the struggle at the heart of the discourse: how to accomplish the practical task at hand, and at the same time preserve positive relations. In this respect the scene is like many other social encounters. But the emotional significance for Emily here is enormous. It is not only that she may feel abandoned by her parents each time she must sleep; at a critical, transitional point in the collection of our data a baby boy is born into the family. The mother is nursing him, which is apparently why the father is handling Emily at sleep time. All of this contributes to the considerable emotional impetus motivating Emily's talk, in both the dialogues and the monologues. Descriptively then, if metaphorically, the music of the father's rational rhythms (alternating with the sweet sounds of baby talk) clashes with Emily's plaintive cries and pleas, even screams, in their dialogues as well as in her monologues. I suspect that the emotionally charged style of her monologues is due to these conflicts, which may accelerate her growth.

Throughout these data, a certain scenario is played out in the dialogues before Emily goes to sleep. That scenario may be schematized as follows:

1. *Negotiatory*	*Obligatory*	*Promissory*
2. (First/now)	(When/if)	(Then/after)
3. We talk about X	You/Em sleep	We go/do Y
	I/Dad leave	They come/go Y

The first line labels phases of the drama that is often played out in the Father-Emily dialogues. The three phases are: optional talk about an array of routine topics, an obligatory component about sleeping conditions and the father's departure, and a promise of things to come. The X on line three represents several kinds of talk routines (naming colors, labeling toys, answering questions, and so on). The negotiation of the conditions for sleep (blanket, toys, and so on) is virtually obligatory. And the Y at the end stands for such promises as going shopping, visiting playmates, making breakfast, and several others.

I call this the "sleep-bargaining scenario," and it is often actualized by a complex weave of genres. At this level of generality the pre-sleep talk genres might be comparable to "meal talk" genres, or "shopping talk" genres, and so on, where different rules and means for talking apply. That is, each complex genre can combine different structures and styles. The pre-sleep talk, for example, contains elaborate narrative, descriptive, explanatory, and promissory structures. These can be delivered in varying styles of singing, baby talk or a more business-like adult talk, or even a mixed style of "adult-baby cajoling talk." As a further subdivision within this intermediate level, there occur even more basic elements of genre, such as naming, questioning, answering, listing routines. Thus a shifting set of features of theme, style, and structure constitute each genre.

Genre Descriptions of Our Data

When Emily was 23½ months old a remarkable shift took place in the coherence of her monologues. Before that time, though she produced many word forms in several of her monologues, the words that appeared in coherent sequences of narrative were far fewer than occurred later. A coherent narrative sequence is defined as any stretch of words that contains two or more clauses related semantically. These could range from "when Emmy wakes up, Carl come" at 22½ months to "Oh mother, no hat, mother. I am not wearing a hat. I got fancy clothes, see, mother" at 25½ months.

Figure 6.1 displays the first three months of this data analysis, at half-month intervals, in terms of the percentage of words that occurred within coherent sequences in Emily's monologues. That is, the number of words that occurred within coherent sequences was divided by the total number of words produced in each monologue. So, for example, of 147 words produced at 22;18, only 48 occurred in the 5 coherent sequences in that monologue, yielding a .33 ratio of words-in-coherent-sequences. Compare this to the 157 words pro-

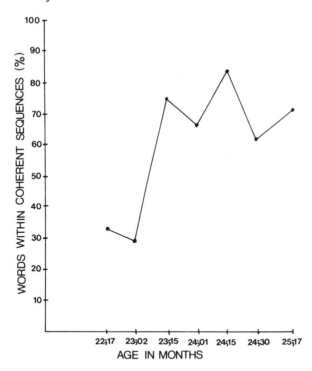

Figure 6.1. Percentage of words appearing in coherent sequences, Emily's monologues, 22;17–25;17.

duced at 25;20, of which 114 occurred in 12 coherent narrative sequences, yielding a ratio of about .70.

The dialogue and monologue of 23;15, at exactly the time when the shift in Emily's coherence took place, are especially revealing. This point in her development shows the closest connections between the dialogue she hears and the monologues she produces. Before this time she can barely reenvoice in her monologues what she hears in dialogue. After this time she becomes more and more able to reenvoice the features of dialogue in her own monologues. A thorough analysis of the features of genre in the data for 23;15 will show how closely monologue can reenvoice dialogue. After this is clearly shown, I will look at Emily's early and later monologues to see how reenvoicement develops.

Following Bakhtin, we can describe the features of genre of the father's speech in the dialogue at 23;15 (called the Childworld episode) in terms of content, style, and structure. Now, for the sake of coherent analysis, I propose that for these data the three components of genre are construed as follows. Content concerns the primary "propositional themes"; in this case the father's first long narrative is about "buying" and the second is about "crying." These predicates of "buy" and "cry" organize the content of his utterances about what is to be bought and who does the crying. The two major themes of his talk, then, might be concisely stated as follows: "we buy X on Saturday at Childworld"; and "little kids cry, but big kids don't." Example 6.1 in the Appendix to this chapter codes the dialogue.

For these data two styles of talk are systematically identifiable: baby talk and (for lack of a better contrasting term) adult talk. These styles are manifested primarily through prosody, but at times the lexicon and syntax also mark a style shift. For example, looking at the father's first Childworld narrative we see these features of baby talk (called the BT style): he whispers "we're gonna go"; repeats "we're gonna" four times; uses a slow rhythm of speech, with unusually long pauses between and within phrases; sustains a cadence with emphatic stress on words like "diapers" and "Stephen"; elongates the ("wavy") intonation of words like "house" at the end of clauses and so on. However, there is a shift away from this slower, simpler, cadenced BT style toward a more rapid and complex adult talk (AT style) when he introduces the word "intercom," follows it with the "so" clause, and then gives the "upstairs-downstairs" explanation. The successive repetitions of the "buy at Childworld" theme have closely analogous patterns of BT rhythms punctuated by occasional AT features. In a still more subtle mix, in the third round of the Childworld narrative, the father uses an extremely wavy intonation on the "inter" syllables of "intercom," as if to make it more accessible to Emily through the BT style.

The third component of genre, what Bakhtin called "compositional structure," is close to what is referred to today as discourse structure. There are two sorts of discourse structures. Narrative structures are those relations which connect the parts of long speech monologues or of written prose, ranging from causal, temporal, locative, and so on connections among clauses in sentences up to the plots and story-lines that organize paragraphs and larger units. And the second sort of discourse structure is the exchange structures found in conversation; for example, question-answer, summons-response, statement-acknowledgment, command-compliance, and the other "adjacency pairs" that organize conversation (Sacks et al. 1974).

In the first part of the Childworld episode Emily's father structures his discourse in the following way:

Question   You know what we're gonna do this weekend?
State   We're gonna go to Childworld, and we're gonna buy . . .
List   . . . diapers for Stephen . . . and Emily . . . an intercom
            system
Explain   . . . so that we can hear Stephen . . . downstairs
Evaluate   . . . it's neat. You're gonna like it.

So in three repetitions of this Childworld narrative we see the "buy" theme take various objects ("diapers," "intercom"), various temporal phrases ("this weekend," "on Saturday"), and various explanations of how the intercom system will work. Stylistically, these narratives are delivered primarily in the BT register, punctuated briefly by the AT style around the "intercom" object. And structurally the five discourse categories described above are repeated, but Emily supplies the initial request or question in the last two rounds.

This kind of organizational format, integrating theme, style, and structure, is a clear and fairly simple example of a speech genre. It can be labeled a "promissory genre" because of the simple thematic content, the predominance of BT, and the structural boundaries of promising to take Emily to an interesting place she will like, *if* she goes to sleep.

Example 6.1 in the Appendix is a transcript of the entire Childworld dialogue, coded for style and structure. The themes are clear from the text itself. The father initiates the two major themes of buying and crying. Emily collaborates in these themes with requests, questions, repetitions, and extensions. She also repeats a "sleep" theme five times; and she mentions blankets and alligators. Stylistically, only the father's speech is coded: each time his tonal features shift between baby talk (BT) and adult talk (AT), this is coded. For example, he begins with BT features in his repetition and agreement with Emily about sleep, using a high-pitched, slow, sing-song intonation while elongating the first and last syllables of "Y-e-s you a-r-e"; then he shifts to the more tense, clipped, and rapid tones of AT in explaining the intercom system. The exchange and narrative structures in the speech of both Emily and her father are coded. They begin with the standard exchange of the "state-agree" type, and then the father goes on to produce a "state-list-explain" narrative sequence.

The dialogue of this pre-sleep scenario exemplifies a complex weave of genres on the father's part, and Emily's minimal participation in these genres. Both of his extended "buy" and "cry" narratives begin when Emily is crying: his talk is at least partly motivated to stop her from crying. The genre function of the "buy" narrative is to promise Emily the reward of shopping at Childworld if she stops crying and goes to sleep (or, more precisely, if she allows him to leave the room without crying and talks to herself before sleeping). So I call this a promissory genre of speech, since it is organized to prevent her from crying by supplying the entertaining information in the promise of shopping.

The second set of narratives, the "big kids don't cry" sequences, also begins as Emily is crying. But these do not entertain or make promises. Rather, they are in a more explanatory genre, containing as they do so many categorizations, contrasts, arguments, and explanations. Whereas the "explain" structure in the "buy" narratives is a secondary addendum to the "buy" theme, the "explain" structures at the end of the "command-state-list-contrast-explain" sequences of the "cry" theme are primary. Not only are the discourse content and structure of the "cry" narratives more complex, but stylistically there are more AT and more rapid alternations of BT and AT in them. Thus, while some of the same features appear in both sets of the father's narratives, the first "buy" theme is articulated in a promissory genre and the "cry" theme in an explanatory genre. The overlap of features weaves the two genres together.

Example 6.2 in the Appendix is a transcript of Emily's monologue after the Childworld dialogue. It is not coded for style and structure, because although Emily's narratives do contain many of the empirical features of her father's genres, they are not yet stabilized in conventional genre formats. The purpose here is to compare the features of the Childworld dialogue and monologue in order to specify how Emily's monologue reenvoices features of the dialogue. An obvious early reenvoicement occurs when Emily reproduces her father's line, "we're gonna buy some *dia*pers for *Steph*en and some *dia*pers for *Em*ily and we're gonna buy an *int*ercom system . . .", as her own " . . . buy *dia*pers for *Steph*en and *Em*my and buy *soke*thing . . ." This is neither an imitation nor a creation of her own, but intermediate between the two. Emily reenvoices the theme of buying diapers, the structural feature of listing names, and the stylistic feature of emphatic stress on names of people and objects. She substitutes "sokething" for the complex word "intercom," and introduces all this with an apparently indirect quotation, "Daddy said."

Moreover, a subtler version of reenvoicement can be seen if we compare Emily's opening lines, "I member the . . . e- *D-a-d*dy said," to the father's "member what we said about big kids" in the dialogue. This example illustrates a different degree of reenvoicement, involving the blend of features in monologue from different genres in dialogue.

More globally, notice that this monologue reproduces first, in 1a and 1b, the minor theme of "sleep," which was one of Emily's own contributions to the dialogue. Then she reenvoices the father's "buy" theme (in 2), followed by a fragment (3), and her own "broken seat" narrative (4). And the monologue ends with her version of the father's "cry" theme (5 and 7), with a slight interruption by another fragment (6).

In terms of style Emily not only reenvoices the frequent emphatic stress on the same nouns stressed by her father, but she adopts the cadence of most of his phrasing; for example, the rhythm of 2d ("buy *dia*pers for Emmy and *dia*pers for the baby") is virtually identical to the father's version, despite minor differences in content. Furthermore, Emily reenvoices close analogues of her father's exaggerated, elongated, and "rippled" intonation patterns. However, she often produces these patterns with words of her own. For instance, the father says "Y-e-s you a-r-e!" and "*house*" and "N-o-o-o" with quite dramatic melodies. Emily reproduces similar melodies in her monologue on "*T-a-n*ta's" (4a and d), "*any*body" (2g), and "*bl-a-n*kets" (1a), respectively.

In general Emily preserves her father's two major themes while varying the content within them; for example, she inserts word forms like "sokething" in 2b, "chocolik" in 2e, and "croutes" in 2j into phrase structures provided by her father. She places the "Saturday" and "Childworld" phrases later in the narrative, she drops complicated explanations, and she inserts her own "broken seat" theme.

Beyond the obvious borrowings of style and theme from dialogue in this monologue, there are numerous reenvoiced discourse structures, as well as a few structures that Emily introduces herself. Among the latter is her opening complaint in 1a: "I can't sleep with the *bl-a-n*kets." (Her father had put a blanket on her, and in the past this complaint had often brought him back into the room.) It appears at this point that Emily addresses this monologue to her father, but her "*D-a-d*dy said" mitigates this probability. Semantic anomalies such as this occur repeatedly in Emily's monologues up to this date. See, for example, "I went to sleep" in 1b. These anomalies, along with syntactic and narrative fragmentations in the monologues, make it difficult to track her speech for discourse structures. In fact, overall, the utterances in her monologues fluctuate between reenvoicements of parental genres, attempts at her own themes, and fragmentations of both of these.

The reenvoiced structures in the monologue's segment 2 are evident: the lists of people, the repetition of "plug in," the paraphrase of "say ahhh" for the father's "we'll hear Stephen cry," the reduced statement "on Saturday go Childworld," the repeating of the predicate "buy" with lists of items, and the recycling of the whole narrative theme. Similarly, in segments 5 and 7 we see reenvoiced lists of "big kids" names (5a), statements (5b, 7c), contrasts (7a, 7f, and so on). Moreover, line 5a represents in microcosm the essence of the reenvoicement phenomenon. Emily begins with an apparently interrogative structure (the auxiliary verb "do") as if to ask a question, then lists kids' names, but ends with the statement form "don't cry." Notice how this one utterance reproduces in fragmented miniature the father's dialogic sequence of structures: question-list-state. Yet in 7a she reproduces an almost flawless version of the father's argument—the contrast of "big" and "little kids" ("babies") and the explanation of who cries.

As to her own contributions, Emily says "the big kids at Tanta's cry" in 7d, but then she contradicts this in 7f: "but the big kids don't cry." In addition, she attempts her own narrative, a conventional version of which might be "the infant seat was broken at Tanta's." But she is not yet able to sustain this theme in a conventional way, that is, to organize all the features of theme, style, and structure that a recognizable genre requires. This attempt is infiltrated by the father's stresses ("one") and tones ("*T-a-n*ta's") and is syntactically fragmented.

Even when Emily does not reproduce the same thematic content as her father (as in the "buy" and "cry" themes), she sometimes reenvoices his prosodic style with other content. The theme, style, and structure components of genre are separable in this sense. Each component is produced in the father's dialogues in a certain "shape"—a certain semantic, prosodic, and discourse shape. These are the inputs to Emily's hearing. Her monologues are characterizable as mixtures of repeated features of her parent's genres. She recreates these in terms of her capability of the moment. And, of course, she permutes the order of genre features in less conventional ways than her parents do.

More important, in order to understand the reenvoicement of the features of genre in monologue, we must see how the processes in monologue are analogous to the processes in dialogue. For example, Emily's Childworld monologue recreates processes that are analogues of the processes in the Childworld dialogue: the successive rephrasings of the "buy" and "cry" themes; the successive listings of names; the same cadence and rhythm and distributions of emphatic stress and dramatic melodies; even the mix of question, answer, and statement processes of dialogue is partially reproduced and permuted in monologue. So it is not the case that Emily merely imitates part of what her father said, or that she creates something entirely different from what was said. Rather, her monologues conflate these two overall processes of imitation and creation. She blends her own "voice" with that of her father.

Reen*voice*ment involves combinations of what Bakhtin called the "voices of authority" and "one's own internally persuasive voice." In this case we have the "official" conventional versions in the father's voices (his BT cajoling, his AT explanatory argument, and so on) and Emily's own efforts (her fairly clear contributions to the dialogue, and her underdeveloped genres in the monologue). In the dialogue she asks "who cries?"; she categorizes herself as "I big kids," extends her father's argument in "babies cry at Tanta's," adds "Lise" to the list of names, and so on. Her monologic efforts not only are longer and more complex but mix pieces of her own dialogic contributions with those of her father; for example, segment 4 mixes her introduction of "Tanta" with her "broken seat" theme *and* her father's dramatic prosodic style.

Emily's own contributions to her monologue, apart from closely analogous reenvoicements of her father's features, are best described not as mistakes but as efforts to learn how to weave the features of genre together. For example, she generalizes the list of names to *any*body, combining her own content ("any") with the father's stress style (*any*). Recall also that Emily asks the questions during the dialogue. So, in terms of the genre hypothesis proposed here, even a line like her "do big kids like Emmy and Carl and Linda don't cry" is not a grammatical error. Rather, it is a blend of her voice (the questioning voice) and her father's stating-and-listing voice ("*big* kids like Donny and *Leslie* and *Carl* and Emily and Neil, they don't cry").

This analysis of the reenvoicement of the features of the genres in the Childworld dialogue in Emily's monologue of the same night reveals Emily's speech ability at that point in her development. What develops is not only the components of grammar (phonology, syntax, and semantics) but also the processes of genre (of thematic construction, of stylistic rendering, of discursive processes). If we look for fixed products, such as repeated sentences, or exact prosodic rhythms or imitated story-lines, we will be misled. Features of genre are more fluid than the more stable features of grammar. One can produce a perfectly grammatical sentence (as occasionally happens in Emily's monologues of the first three months), but a perfect genre performance is a misnomer. Rather, speech is performed only as approximations of "ideal" genre formats.

Analysis of Earlier Monologues

The first monologue in the transcripts I analyzed was as follows:

> Seven and eight-nine-ten . . . (little bit) seven *and* eight (?) ring around the rosey pocketful of posey . . . ashes ashes w- all fall *down* [Emily banging crib] boom . . . boom pocka . . . and posey . . . ring around the ro-ey rosey pocketful of rosey . . . ashes ashes . . . all . . . fall . . . *d-o-w-n* ring around-a- . . . pocketful of rose . . . ashes-all-fall-down p- . . . f- . . . oh pocka . . . pocketful of po-ey . . . ashes as- (?) all fall down boom boom boom. 22;16

This monologue has several features that are essential for understanding Emily's monologues in general. It is entirely sung. It seems as if a melodic rhythm is established and then words are "backfilled" into it, as it were. In this monologue there is also an action corresponding to the words ("all fall down" followed by the banging of the crib), then an echo of that action ("boom boom"). This suggests that there is some amalgamation of word-action-echo in Emily's system of mental representation at this time.

Also, the initial phrase of the song, the conventional one, had to be imitated. In this sense it must be an imitation of the "voice" of another. Yet the singing of the numbers may not be taken from another, and the words sung at the end of the monologue are almost certainly not imitated. Thus we have the first weave of voices in our data. Another musical feature is the variations on a theme here: the two "number" phrasings vary, as do the "all fall down" phrases. We also see abbreviations ("p- . . . f- . . .") and other rearrangements ("pocketful of rose") of elements. Further, a few days later Emily's mother sings the first line of "ring around the rosey" in the midst of their dialogue before sleep, thereby weaving the voice of that song into their conversation. The mother reports that she and Emily had sung this song before.

Example 6.3 in the Appendix gives some of the dialogue of the next day. After they negotiate the "blanket" condition, the father promises: "and when you wake up, we're going to go to Carl's, but you have to go to sleep now." This is produced in a very high pitched, rapid, sing-song intonation. Emily's monologue that night follows the dialogue in Example 6.3. I suggest that at least part of Emily's monologue here is an attempt to reenvoice the father's promissory sequence. And, further, other sequences are being worked out at the same time. That is, in addition to the core clauses of the promissory genre (Emmy wake, Daddy and Emmy go to Carl's, Emmy sleep now), there seem to be elements like "Emmy go / come in Daddy's car"; "Carl come then go (?)"; "Carl sleeping"; "the baby coming"; "Emmy coming after my nap." Table 6.1 presents an abstract schema for comparing their talk.

In Table 6.1 the clauses of the father's promissory sequence are numbered consecutively; we might abbreviate these as the "Emmy," the "go," and the "sleep" clauses. Emily uses these in her monologue as three frames in the narrative sequence. Her first two clauses use a reference to herself ("my") and the "go" from the second narrative frame; the third to fifth clauses reflect the "go" frame also, but she

Table 6.1. Schema for comparing Emily's talk with that of her father.

Father's dialogue	Abstract schema	Emily's monologue	
1. and when you wake up	when Emmy (verb)	when my go come	1–2
		my go in Daddy's (?) car	2
2. we're going to go to Carl's	X go/come Y	when Carl come	2
		then go to (?)	2
		go [Peabody]	2
3. but you have to go to sleep *now*	X sleep	Carl sleeping	3
		not right now	1–3
	X come	the baby coming	2
	Y	Carl coming m' house	2
	Z	Emmy coming	2
		after my nap	1
		not right now	1–3
		the baby coming *now*	2–3

substitutes "come" for "go"; and the sixth and seventh clauses reflect the "sleep" and "now" of the third frame. Then her monologue roughly recycles the theme again. It seems she is struggling toward some formulation of a sequence that would be an analogue to her father's theme, but here she does not approximate it closely.

The theme produced by the father is in a promissory genre. But in the monologue Emily is trying instead to work out the theme of who is going (coming) where, and who is sleeping. Operations to note in the monologue are the following: She produces semantically opposed verbs in the same predicate slot ("go come") and then alternates them. She seems to paraphrase the father's "when you wake up" with "after my nap," adding the formulaic expression "not right now." She has "Carl come" instead of her father's "we're going to Carl's." She says "Carl sleeping" instead of her sleeping, and "Emmy coming" instead of Carl. Then she lists names of who is "coming" (the baby, Carl, Emmy). Instead of the father's "sleep now," she produces "not right now" and "the baby coming now." In sum, in her monologue Emily doubles the verb slot, substitutes one object phrase for another, reverses directionality ("Carl come"), lists several names before her verb slot of "coming", interjects a formula ("not right now"), and introduces the theme of her brother's birth ("the baby coming now"). What is more, she ends with the same word and with the same emphatic stress on it as her father does in his version. These latter borrowings from her father, and the different analogues of the father's model in dialogue reveal how this early monologue of Emily's reenvoices only small parts of the preceding dialogue.

In addition to more singing and people coming and going, waking and sleeping, the monologues, at 22½ months, show Emily both calling out to her parents and working out various statements to herself. At the end of that week, for example, a monologue begins with "I blew my nose [crying] I blew my nosey . . . Daddy clean my nosey. Clean my nosey! I need clean my nosey." So here she calls out to her father again and she also refers back to their nose-wiping routines. Although this routine is not mentioned in our data, we can safely suppose that Emily is here again reenvoicing a family ritual.

By the end of the next week there are several new developments. She fantasizes that someone other than her parents will get her ("Dindo come and get Emmy"), thereby beginning to mix the imaginary ("Dindo") with her actual wishes (for her parents to get her). She recounts family scenes that may not have been discussed with parents; for example, referring to her mother's morning showers, she says, "so Momma all clean." She works toward formulating for herself descriptions and statements about other family rules: "I didn't drink my . . . this little bitty juice . . . I need drink my little bitty more juice . . . I need my juice." She begins to state her wishes clearly in her monologues: "I don't want to go nap!" And to relate these to "argument-like" structures, as in "I don't need go nap today."

At almost 23 months, we hear her working out her next day's agendas: "pretty soon Emmy get up and go Mormor's . . . Tanta's . . . house or Mormor's Tanta . . . maybe afternoon when my wake up." Compare this to the preceding dialogue: the father says: "you've got to be rested for tomorrow cause it's a Tanta day tomorrow"; Emily replies, "a Mormor day"; and the father concludes, "maybe you'll see Mormor later but mostly a Tanta day tomorrow." It is this kind of collaboration with her father about the next day's events that becomes transformed into the apparently confused material of Emily's monologues ("Mormor/Tanta," and so on).

In the next night's monologue we see a shift back to more emphasis on melody (as a prosodic style) than on narrative continuity. Emily produces clear beats in melodic lines; for example, "kiss . . . kiss . . . kiss . . . mmm . . . mmm . . . mmm." She spells out the letters of words in song: "B-i-n-g-o." But in the same monologue she fails to sustain semantically coherent narrative lines. It is as if the melody (prosodic style) is worked out here partly independently of the narrative content (theme).

The next night's dialogue, 23;9, shows how Emily modulates her linguistic forms in line with her father's input. A dialogic exchange goes as follows:

> E: I don't want boat
> F: You don't want a what?
> E: Boat
> F: You don't want a boat.

The father provides the conventional form of the noun phrase with the "a" determiner, which Emily adapts to in her monologue of that night. And she elaborates: "when my woke up, then Daddy come my went . . . out and took the boat out and took Emmy out in . . . Emmy the boat." In this monologue we also see the reenvoicement of conversational exchange structures: after she mentions "alligator," she says "No-o-o . . . no . . . no . . . no . . . n- . . . n," which is the frequent response of the parents in the dialogues. Moreover, we see further signs of the opposition of Emily's voice to the parent's voice blended in rapid monologic succession. She says "Now sleeping time. Now *not* sleeping time" as if to disagree with her parent the way she does in the dialogues.

The closest Emily comes to sustaining more than three semantically coherent clauses in the same narrative theme during this part of the analysis occurs a few days before the Childworld episode, when she says "Now Emmy fix the bed. Tuck it down. And tuck it down. Tuck it down. Now over here." This reflects how she reenvoices talk rituals in monologue. The last phrase must be a part of how her mother or father talks while making a bed. Her monologues to this point, though they pervasively reenvoice bits of the parents' speech in all the ways described above, are still fragmented in terms of recognizable genre performances.

Later Developments in Emily's Monologues

In the opening lines of the monologue after the Childworld episode, at 23;15, Emily finally succeeds in sustaining a coherent narrative for a familiar theme: "Oh Carl sleep in bed and Carl's daddy took the blanket back . . . and Carl didn't like that . . . Carl liked his blanket (a whole bunch) in the bed." There had been talk that night of blankets, as usual, but not of Carl's blanket or Carl's daddy or what Carl liked. Rather, Emily spoke of her own blankets, Daddy, and likes. So at this point she can systematically substitute multiple items from dialogue in her monologues. The mother reports that they had talked about a "special blanket" that Carl had but Emily did not. Also in this monologue she first distinguishes several of her own blanket designs (another standard dialogic routine): "This is kinda blanket . . . Emmy blanket . . . her bear blanket and star blanket . . . mother goose goose blanket and some *n-e-w* blanket Daddy Mommy put the bl-." This list having been performed, however, she can not yet add on coherent related clauses.

But at 24½ months related narrative themes begin to become woven together. For example, "Later when I wake up we put my jamas in the laundry and down in the basement they get *washed* . . . These okay but they're dirty . . . It's okay but they're dirty . . . and down in the laundry my (?) . . . After I take these jamas off I wear my red pajamas to *bed* so Mamma can wash these jamas." This narrative combines, first of all, a description of the clothes-washing scene with some dialogue typical of that family scene ("These okay but they're dirty"). Secondly, it makes a transition from the washing scene itself to a pajama-changing scene, while still preserving narrative continuity about washing.

Two weeks later, at 25;0, Emily struggles in a monologue to internalize some of her father's evaluations: "cough really makes my better here . . . on my tomach. My back is *this* and my tomach is *this* . . . Oh good tomach ache oh . . . This is . . . good really good side my because it's really good . . . for Emmy . . . for Emmy *likes* this side." This monologue would be incomprehensible had we not had the father's talk in the dialogue: "It's better for your cough on the other side . . . That side is not good for your cough because what happens is that the stuff in your nose drips down into your throat and makes you cough and if you are on your *stomach* it's better." Not only does Emily work out the contrast between stomach and back and evaluate which side is better, she also internalizes the father's preference by claiming to herself which side she "likes" better.

Two months after the Childworld transition, at 25;18, we hear Emily weaving several voices in a dramatic reading. She had taken a book called "Dandelion the Lion" to bed with her, and it happened to be raining outside at the time. She begins: "I am Dande- (?) and it's raining outside and you better come outside with me. I am Dandelion. I want to come with you . . . 'Why don't you take out (?) because it's not raining' . . . 'I'll keep Dandelion, Mother' . . . 'Mother, you *cannot* keep it' (?) . . . 'Now Mother' . . . Dandelion, I am coming to your party. I came already. It was good." So Emily merges lines from the book, facts from the context (rain), and dialogue she addresses to both her mother and the Dandelion. Moreover, her voice tones shift to impersonate other characters in the book, and some utterances narrate other facts about the story in a more neutral voice.

These sophisticated developments far surpass Emily's efforts of her twenty-third month. At that point she could only minimally reenvoice a few features of genre components at a time. At the Childworld episode she reached a maximum of reproducing the complex sets of features she had heard in the preceding dialogue. After that she had apparently internalized enough of the abstract format of some genres to reenvoice them while using her own content or style or structure. By her twenty-sixth month her monologues weave together many voices, and Emily begins to coordinate more than one genre at a time.

Some Implications of Genre Theory

The theory of the speech genres of everyday life I propose here is meant to help us discover the "deep functions" of language. It provides some reliable tools for examining the functional organization of talk beyond the level of single utterances. It is a rich theory of discourse, capable of describing any exchanges in conversation as well as the narrative lines of monologue to oneself (perhaps even those chains of mental events we call "verbal thinking," insofar as such data is available). In this sense the genre theory of language functioning fulfills Foucault's (1970) definition of language: "discourse . . . is the concrete link between representation and reflection . . . the path by which representation communicates with reflection" (p. 83). This is a theoretically useful way to understand Emily's monologues in particular: she is using discourse genres to work through what she can already represent on the one hand and her reflections on those representations on the other hand.

I propose the notion of speech genre as the largest manageable unit of linguistic functioning. It is Wittgenstein's "language game" writ large. The features of genre performance will be partly determined by the particulars of the social scene and the scenario in which it occurs. Each performance is actualized with a different set of features. This accords with Wittgenstein's point that the applications of word uses to new situations will continually vary. And it meets Bakhtin's sense of the "live utterance" as ever renewing itself. Genre attempts to describe the experience of speaking, not knowledge of language.

Apparently, the formatting of speech genres emerged in this child's mind in at least partial separation from grammatical development. We saw how Emily's monologues developed more sophisticated genre formats across time. Yet even in her later monologues there is a good deal of syntactic fragmentation, semantic anomaly, and phonological inconsistency. Also, one can imagine a child acquiring the structural properties of a grammar on the basis of limited speech input. However, learning something as subtle and variable as a genre seems to require much more "practice," that is, the ongoing experience of being in dialogue with others, and of reprocessing the voices of dialogue in one's own monologic versions. Genre performance is less fixed, less stable, and less computational than grammar. It seems that the learning of genre requires more repetitions and routine productions, indeed even ritualizations, of varieties of talk in context than does grammatical learning.

Given the emphasis on the social determination of genre learning, if this theory has merit, we will have to reconsider one of the basic premises of our field. We all readily believe that "children acquire language" in some sense. We are less ready to believe that "language acquires children." Yet the genre conceptualization of what language is requires some such principle: that the agency that enables a child to speak ever more appropriately must extend beyond the child's cognitive capacity; genre meanings and functions are first coconstructed with more fully socialized agents of language (parents). The voices of others in close coproduction and coarticulation are involved not only in the child's social talk but in her thinking itself.

Our field needs at least a more deeply interactionist view of language development. Obviously, interaction must occur between the patterns of speech the child hears and the ability to internalize knowledge and skill about these. But many of the nuances of genre performance emerge in the child's speech long before she can assimilate them to any knowledge structure—see, for example, the many "frozen" voices of others appearing in Emily's early monologues, long before they are integrated into her own versions of talk. Utterance meanings and functions become most alive when they pass from passive hearing to active speaking. We need a theory of what happens *between* speakers and, especially, a theory of the interaction between how the child acquires language cognitively and how a society acquires the child functionally.

Appendix

Example 6.1. The "Childworld" Text Coded for the Elements of Genre

Dialogue	Style	Structure
E: I sleep in here [crying]		State
F: You know—		
You're gonna sleep right there! Yes you are.	BT	Agree
You know what we're gonna do		
[Emily crying] . . .		
you know what we're gonna do this weekend?		Question
We're gonna go . . . to Childworld . . . and we're		State
gonna buy some *dia*pers for *Ste*phen, and		List

Dialogue	Style	Structure
some *dia*pers for *Emi*ly, and we're gonna buy		List
an *int*ercom system, so that we can hear	AT	Explain
Stephen in different parts of the *house* . . .		
I think you're gonna like it because we'll be		Evaluate
able to hear Stephen downstairs when Stephen's		Explain
upstairs . . . It's gonna be a neat gadget . . .	BT	
E: Say that 'gain.		Request
F: When we . . . we're goin' to Childworld and buy		State
*dia*pers for *Ste*phen, and *dia*pers for Emily,		List
and what is called an *int*ercom system, that		
plug in . . . Stephen, into Stephen's room . . . and		Explain
then we go downstairs and we plug it in . . .		
and we get to hear Stephen . . . we'll see who		State
wakes up . . . we'll hear him cry . . . through the	AT	
intercom system . . . It's a neat gadget.		Evaluate
E: Say again.		Request
F: One more time . . . and then we go to bed.		Comply/Command
On *Sat*urday . . . we're gonna go to Childworld	BT	State
and we're gonna buy *dia*pers for *Emi*ly and		List
*dia*pers for Stephen and an *int*ercom system		
so we can hear Stephen in different parts of	AT	Explain
the house . . .		
Good night . . . Hon. I love you.	BT	Leavetake formula
E: I sleep in here		State
F: Yeah . . . I love you Sweety.		Leavetake
E: [crying] I want [crying]		
F: You want . . . you want that right like that?		Question
That's fine . . . Hon.		Evaluate
E: [crying]		
F: Okay, night-night.		Leavetake
E: [crying] I wanna sleep in there . . .		Request
F: Night-night . . . Sweety . . . I'll see you in the morning.		Leavetake
E: I wanna sleep in there [crying].		Request
F: Now, remember, y-, remember, Emily what we	AT	Command
said about . . . member what we said about big kids?	BT	Question
Big kids don't cry, do they?	AT	Tag question
E: I big kids, the b-l-a-nket.		?Request
F: What do you want Daddy to do with the blanket?		Question
E: [crying]		
F: You know *Carl* doesn't cry . . . Hon	BT	State
E: [crying] (?) Alligator		
F: N-o-o-o. There's no alligators. You know . . .		Disagree

Dialogue	Style	Structure
would you like to have the blanket on *top* of you?		Question
Would that be fun? Let me show you . . .		Request
I can take this pretty blanket and put it on top of you.		State
E: [crying]		
F: Now remember, Em. Know when I say	AT	Command
[whisper] *Carl* doesn't cry, and *Carolyn*, and *Neil* doesn't cry.	BT	List
E: Neil		Repeat
F: Neil doesn't. You know who cries when they go to bed?		Contrast
Stephen cries, cause Stephen's a little baby.	AT	Explain
But *big* kids like you and Neil	BT	Contrast
and Carolyn and *Carl*, they don't cry.		List
They just go to sleep.		Explain
E: The big . . . what do- . . . *what* do *one* do?		Question
F: Carol . . . Carol who's still a little bit of a baby . . .		Answer
she's kind of a still a baby, and Stephen,		State
they cry . . . and Angela cries sometimes . . . and Lilly, they cry.		List
But *big* kids, like Donny and Leslie		Contrast
and *Carl* and Emily and Neil, they don't cry		List
cause they're big kids . . .		Explain
Mommy and Daddy don't cry and Mormor doesn't cry . . . Tanta doesn't cry . . .		List
You could talk to yourself a little bit before	AT	
you go to sleep if you want.		Suggestion
E: Th- th- th- th- *ba*bies *cry* at *Tan*ta's when baby		State
F: *Yeah*, but *big* kids *don't*.		Agree/Contrast
E: Eh- th- th- *one* at . . . house. Eh . . . who cries?		Question
F: The babies cry, huh, but not the big kids.		Answer/Contrast
E: Um . . . who cries . . . at . . . who cries?		Question
F: Lilly . . . and Angela . . . and Stephen	BT	Answer/List
E: And Linda		List
F: No . . . Linda's a big kid . . . Carol, the little girl	AT	Disagree
who was here tonight . . . *she* cries sometimes		Explain
E: Oh . . . baby!		Exclaim
F: Yeah . . . Okay, Sweetie . . .	BT	Agree
Well I'll see you in the morning. [Emily crying]		Leavetake
F: Now remember . . . no crying . . . remember?	AT	Command
E: I sleep in . . . up this!		?
F: Yes . . . Okay, I love you. I'll . . . [Emily crying]	BT	Agree/Leavetake
F: Now remember what I said about crying, Hon!	AT	Command

Dialogue	Style	Structure
E: Tell me what . . . buy at Childworld!		Request
F: We're goin a Childworld on . . . S-a-turday	BT	Comply
So you have a good sleep Hon . . . I love you.		Leavetake

Example 6.2. Emily's Monologue after the Childworld Dialogue

1a. I can't sleep with the *bl-a-n*kets [crying] . . .
  b. I member the (?) . . . [crying] I went to sleep . . .
2a. e- *D-a-d*dy said buy *dia*pers for *St*ephen and Emmy
  b. and buy *soke*thing for 'tephen . . .
  c. plug in . . . and say ahhh . . . and put . . . the . . . in . . .
  d. on *Saturday* go Childworld . . . buy *dia*pers for Emmy and *dia*-
     pers for the baby
  e. and then buy (chocalik) for the . . . and . . .
  f. see . . . for . . . that baby plug in and
  g. get diapers for *any*body . . .
  h. and buy more (?) that day . . . at Childworld . . .
  j. and buy (croutes) . . .
3a. and my *blank*et . . .
  b. Childworld cause . . .
4a. that *one* is broken at *T-a-n*ta's . . .
  b. the one (is) broken . . . the one that broken . . . here
  c. the . . . infant seat . . . bed (actually) and (?) . . .
  d. Oh, they . . . at *Tant*a's . . .
5a. do . . . big . . . big kids like Emmy and Carl and Linda don't cry.
  b. *They* big kids. *They* sleep like big . . . kids
  c. the baby cry at Tanta's.
6a. And the (next over) the next people that came. Then . . .
7a. babies can cry but—big kids like Emmy don't cry . . .
  b. they go sleep but the *bab*ies cry . . . (?)
  c. everbod- the big kids like Emmy don't cry.
  d. The big kids at Tanta's cry
  e. and (say d-a-h)
  f. but the big kids don't cry.

Example 6.3. Excerpts from the Father-Emily Dialogue of 22;17 and from Emily's Monologues of 22;17 and 22;18

FATHER'S DIALOGUE

F: I'll put a blanket . . . you lie down. Daddy'll put a blanket on you.

E: [muttering under her breath]

F: [higher-pitched, "optimistic" tone] And when you wake up we're gonna go to Carl's, but you have to go to sleep now. You're *such* a good girl, Pookey.

E: I sleeping on my *bun*ny.

F: That's okay.

E: [Tearfully, emphatically] I don't *want* sleep on my . . .

F: [Quickly] Oh, I know you don't want to sleep on your bunny. No! Okay.

E: The bad *bun*ny!

F: Okay. Have a good . . . Hon. I love you.

E: The bad—[Father exits, closing door]

MONOLOGUE OF 22;17

Maybe when my go come, maybe my go in Daddy's (blue) big car maybe maybe when Carl come again go to back home go Peabody Carl sleeping. Not right now. The baby coming and Carl coming m-house . . . *a-n-d* Emmy (???) coming after my nap. Not right now cause the baby coming *now* . . .

EXCERPT FROM MONOLOGUE OF 22;18

Because then Emmy go to sleep Emmy have go to sleep. When Emmy wakes up, Carl come after my nap then Carl come over my house. When Daddy wake up sleep when Emmy wake up Emmy has—then alligator come get me.

Part III

Constructing a Self

Chapter 7

Monologue, Dialogue, and Regulation

Rita Watson

An overwhelming characteristic of Emily's talk, evident even from our initial attempts to grasp its nature, is that it reveals much about her inner states, and about the virtuosity of her struggle to map these states into forms that will have some currency in discourse. Her pre-sleep dialogues and monologues reveal a compelling drama in the life of a 2-year-old: saying goodnight, separating from her parents and her waking reality, and facing aloneness with the tumultuous residue of her day's experiences. When she is alone, she talks aloud, even though there is no one to hear but herself.

Emily's monologues are not a unique phenomenon. This form of talk has been observed in other children, most notably, although not exclusively, by Weir (1962). Weir's masterful linguistic analyses of crib monologues only begin to give an indication of their richness and complexity. What place do the myriad forms and elusive functions of such monologues have in a child's life, and what can we know, or infer, about the meanings and intentions that underlie them?

Solitary speech has usually been analyzed in the context of goal-directed activity, that is, in the form of the vocalizations that often accompany the actions of the young child. Piaget (1959) argued that it was egocentric, that it stemmed from insufficient socialization, and that while it accompanied action and thought, it was not functionally related to either. Vygotsky (1962, 1978) argued that it was a transitional phase from social to inner speech, that it stemmed from insufficient individuation, and that it was an integral part of thought. Further, he argued that it served a regulatory function in thought: children use words to create plans, to express intentions and goals, and sometimes to substitute for actually attaining a goal. Of course, the notion of regulation was not absent from Piagetian theory. Piaget (1977) argued that the prelinguistic child is subjected to regulations by the parent "from the cradle," and that once language is acquired it can be used to stipulate and revise rules, as in peer play. Importantly, he differentiated between the application of a rule and consciousness of it. He argued that autonomous regulation occurs as part of any act of knowing, from the earliest stage of the child's cognitive life, that this is followed by regulation that simply accompanies cognitive activity, and that finally regulation comes under conscious control (see Brown 1987 for a fuller discussion).

The link between early solitary speech and self-regulation, however, was made by Vygotsky. The standard Vygotskian account of regulation is that it occurs first in the social domain and only subsequently in the intracognitive domain. That is, an adult first provides the regulatory function for the young child, and the child subsequently develops the ability to regulate her own cognitive activity (Brown 1987; Vygotsky 1962, 1978; Wertsch 1985c). The transitional function of solitary speech is quite obvious on this account: it is like social speech, in that it is voiced, but it is like inner speech, or thought, in that it is not communicative. Piaget's and Vygotsky's interpretations of solitary speech thus differ both in the direction of the transition (social to intracognitive versus intracognitive to social) and in its regulatory status.

If we accept, as Weir (1962) did, that crib monologues are a transitional form of inner speech, this would suggest that they are regulatory in nature. However, this would still leave unanswered the question of what form of activity Emily is engaged in that is in need of regulation. Most studies of self-regulation have focused on the child's ability to monitor his or her own problem-solving activity (Brown 1987; Brown and DeLoache 1978; Flavell 1979; Wertsch 1985c; Yussen 1985). The other chapters in this book evidence a range of linguistic and cognitive problem-solving activity in the monologues. Yet the monologues probably are not regulative of this activity in the same way that, say, solitary speech while playing with marbles might be viewed as regulative. Emily's problem-solving activity is more representational than enactive. She appears to be sorting inconsistencies and contradictions between aspects of her representations that are clear and those which are fuzzy, as Flavell (1979) suggested in a discussion of early cognitive monitoring of person knowledge. The regulation of enactive problem-solving through solitary speech does not appear to strictly parallel the functions of the monologue. It seems, rather, that Emily's inner states, cognitive and affective, form the ground of her activity.

There is, however, an affective problem that dominates the dialogues that precede the monologues, which may shed some light on the regulative function of the monologues. Separation from her parents and her waking reality presents a problem for Emily, or so it would seem from an examination of the dialogues. Once she has been taken to her room in preparation for sleep, she tries to delay the impending separation from her father. She indicates this primarily by her talk and activities. For example, she initiates a color-naming game. She points to and comments on objects in the room. She refers to the presence of imaginary objects (alligators under the bed) or to the absence of real objects (toys) which will prevent her from sleeping. She deliberately gets her foot "stuck" in her crib (it is not really stuck) and, when all else fails, flatly refuses to lie down in her crib.

As long as her father is present, he regulates this conflict through dialogue. He responds to and anticipates Emily's reactions to the impending separation and makes some attempt to contain them. He does this in part by providing articulate forms for Emily's diffuse and sometimes intense affect. For example, when Emily runs out of articulate devices for keeping him in the room, she simply refuses to lie down. This physical noncompliance is not met with a physical reaction by her father. Instead he introduces a new device. He states that Emily has a choice: *either* she lies down and allows him to put the blanket on, *or* he goes out without giving her the blanket. On another occasion, he responds to her tears by saying "Big girls don't cry, only babies cry." Much discussion ensues on this and subsequent occasions to establish that Emily is a big girl, and big girls don't cry. When future crying episodes threaten, her father appeals to this co-constructed form: "Remember what we said? Big girls don't cry."

When her father is no longer present, Emily must provide this regulation for herself. The relevance of regulation in the dialogues for understanding the regulative aspects of the monologues is suggested by the view that patterns of social interaction are constitutive of intracognitive activity (Bruner 1983; Vygotsky 1962; Wertsch 1985a, 1985b). Stern (1985) in particular argues that affective regulation provided by another becomes integrated with the infant's own self-regulation. On Stern's view, self-regulation incorporates other-regulation through the activation of memories of past interactions, in the form of a generalized other evoked from memory.

In what follows, I will first examine the regulative function of dialogue in the resolution of the separation conflict. I will then argue that the very explicit regulative function of the dialogue is continuous with the less obvious regulative function of the monologue. The segment of the data used for this analysis is from age 22;16 until age 23;15. The analyses focus on the dialogue between Emily and her father, who usually puts her to bed. The total number of utterances analyzed is 793, about equally divided between Emily and her father. Unusual texts, such as one episode recorded in the kitchen not related to bedtime, are omitted from the analysis.

Regulation in Dialogue: The Choice Routine

From the earliest stages of life, joint regulation of affect by the caretaker-infant dyad is a central feature of the development of early social interaction (Bruner 1983; Stern 1985; Trevarthen 1979). From early abilities to match the timing of the occurrence of their behaviors (Beebe et al. 1985), to manage gaze and joint attention (Murray and Trevarthen 1985; Scaife and Bruner 1974), to match intentional states (Trevarthen 1979) or affect states (Stern 1985), dyads display highly developed reciprocal structures. These regular patterns of interaction have been implicated in both socialization and some aspects of language acquisition (Bruner 1983; Kaye 1982; Stern 1977, 1985), and the perturbation of these patterns leads to distress in the infant (Murray and Trevarthen 1985). While both partners contribute to the regulation of interaction, in the case of conventional or cultural forms such as play or language games, the adult partner often arranges the context to render the form accessible to the child (Bruner 1983; Kaye 1982). This arranging of context, or formatting (Bruner 1983), is characterized by simplification and repetitiveness. The realization of this pattern of interaction involves routinization, elaboration, and eventually a role reversal in which the child becomes the initiator. All are evident in the routines developed by Emily and her father in their pre-sleep dialogues.

Emily's repertoire of devices for keeping her father in the room range from the articulate (requests for toys and initiation of games and conversational topics) to the primal (crying). On several occasions, perhaps when her repertoire is exhausted or when tiredness dulls her inventiveness, she simply refuses to lie down in the usual place in her crib, sometimes accompanying her action with the expression "I standing up!" Her refusal to lie down appears on the face of it to be unmanageable. Her requests for toys, descriptions of anticipated events, a color-naming game, or an open window fulfill her objective of delaying separation. However, these articulate requests specify conditions for her compliance. They are justifiable, or at least manageable, within the established bedtime routine. Her refusal to lie down also demands a response from her father but, in contrast to her requests, provides no indication as to the conditions for her compliance. Her father responds by introducing an ultimatum: Emily has the *choice* of either lying down in her crib and accepting her blanket, or having her father leave without putting on the blanket. This "choice" quickly develops into a routine that becomes incorporated into the pre-sleep dialogues.

In the period analyzed here, the first introduction of the choice occurs at 22;16. As her mother leaves the room, her father asks whether Emily wants a blanket on; then he attempts to disengage: "Okay, have a good nap, Sweetie." This leads to an inarticulate cry of protest from Emmy: "Aah! . . . Aah! . . ." Her father then gives a direct request for her to lie down: "Put your head down there, probably be better, huh?" He repeats this a second time. Emily raises the intensity of her protest by using an articulate form and repeating it three times: "Aah . . . not now, not now . . . not now!" This intensification of conflicting agendas, indicated by both speakers' repetitions and by Emily's apparent refusal to lie down, leads to her father's introduction of the choice: "Not now? Well then Daddy's going to leave, Sweetie. You have two choices. Either you can lie your—lay your head right there and Daddy will put a blanket on you . . ." At this point Emmy laughs and relents, and her father says "That's a girl, okay. Have a good nap, Hon. I'll see you in a little while."

Then her father leaves. His strategy has worked. At this point, the choice has not emerged as a routine, and has not assumed the canonical structure that it will eventually have. The first alternative (father leaves, no blanket) was not expressed in the either/or structure after the introduction of the choice proposition, but was rather stated before the choice as an ultimatum in response to Emily's behavior. Emily was probably reacting to this earlier expression when she complied. Yet this early episode has most of the components of the choice routine, as it is repeated and elaborated.

The structure of the choice routine, as it emerges in the subsequent dialogues, can be roughly characterized as follows:

1. Precipitating event	(1a)	F: attempts to disengage
	(1b)	E: protests: (a) behavioral (refusal to lie down) (b) vocal (cry of protest) (c) verbal ("Not now! I standing up!")
2. Frame	(2)	F: introduces choice routine, usually with the expression "You have (a, two) choice(s)," and specifies
	(2a)	alternative A (E resists, F leaves, no blanket)
	(2b)	alternative B (E complies, blanket on)
3. Choice	(3)	E: chooses
	(3a)	E: no blanket (to repetition of F's turn 2, or feigned enactment of 2a and repetition of E's turn 3)
	(3b)	E: compliance (to termination, 4)
4. Termination	(4)	F: disengagement.

The precipitating event for the routine is always Emily's noncompliance with her father's attempt to disengage. Her father then frames the choice for Emily: she can continue to resist, in which case he will leave without putting the blanket on (alternative A); or she can comply and get the blanket (alternative B). Emily then must respond, and this is where most of the variability in the routine is observed. If she chooses A, which she sometimes does by continued refusal to lie down or by saying "no blanket," her father either repeats his turn with some variation or feigns departure. This invariably (although not always immediately) leads to Emily's choosing B, and to the termination of the routine in positive disengagement.

The full text of the introductory episode at 22;16 contains most of these elements, although not in the sequence they later come to assume:

1. Precipitating event	(1a)	F: Okay, have a good nap, Sweetie.
(Repeated)	(1b)	E: Aah! . . . Aah! Hah! Um-m.
	(1a)	F: Put your head down there, probably be better, huh?
	(1b)	E: Um.
	(1a)	F: (That's probably) better to put your head down there?
	(1b)	E: A-a-h! . . . not now, n-o-t n-o-w . . . not *now!*

2. Frame	(2a)	F: Not now? Well then Daddy's going to leave, Sweetie.
	(2)	F: You have two choices.
	(2b)	F: Either you can lie your—lay your head right there and Daddy will put a blanket on you—
3. Choice	(3b)	E: [laughs]
4. Termination:	(4)	F: That's a girl, okay. Have a good nap, Hon. I'll see you in a little while. [F leaves the room.]

The second occurrence of the choice routine happens three days later (22;19) at naptime. The canonical structure of the routine emerges on this first repetition. It is atypical of all subsequent instances of the routine in that Emily's mother is present and interjects one turn. But in all other respects it is typical:

1. Precipitating event	(1b)	E: I...I...(?) here.
	(2)	F: No. I think that's not the place that Daddy puts the blanket on you, is it? Well you have ... you remember you have two choices ...
2. Frame	(2a)	F: Would you like to (?) for Daddy to just go out,
	(2b)	F: or do you want to put your head down here so Daddy can put the blanket on you?
3. Choice	(3a)	E: No.
		M: No blanket today?
	(3b)	E: [compliance implied, by F's next speech]
4. Termination	(4)	F: I think so ... that a girl.
		M: [says something unclear]
	(4)	F: You're a good girl, Sweetie. [request for toy, dialogue continues]

In this first repetition of the choice, which marks its emergence as a routine, the father provides a full expression of the choice frame (2, 2a, 2b). What was originally expressed as an ultimatum (2a) is here incorporated as an alternative dependent on Emily's choice. The other development is the articulation of choice by Emily. She initially chooses the first alternative before ultimately complying.

The next instance, five days later (22;25), has the same structure:

1. Precipitating event	(1a)	F: Okay, well, we'll see you in the morning ...
	(1b)	E: Uh, no-o-o ...
2. Frame	(2)	F: Okay, you have two choices.

(2a) F: You can either just lie like that and Daddy'll leave,

(2b) F: or you can lie down, the other way, and Daddy'll put a blanket on you.

3. Choice   (3a) E: (Da-da) leave.
                   F: Daddy just want to leave? [repetition of 2a]
             (3b) E: (?) (Put) the blanket.

4. Termination (4) F: I . . . I . . . I think so . . . t-h-a-t's the best.
                     [color naming, dialogue continues]

The choice routine occurs 29 times in the corpus between 22;16 and 23;15, at both naptime and bedtime. As the examples illustrate, it occurs sometimes in the middle of the pre-sleep dialogues and sometimes at the end, but the internal structure is relatively constant.

Changes within the routine can be attributed to both handover and elaboration. Handover of the routine occurs at 22;26. After six recorded episodes of the routine have occurred, Emily produces a version of the choice alternatives in response to her father's direct question. Both "alternatives" she expresses here are actually the same (alternative 2b). Still, she does use the *either-or* structure, even if the arguments aren't quite worked out.

1. Precipitating   [M leaves and says good night]
   event   (1b) E: Emily sleeps here.

2. Frame   (2) F: I think we'll sleep down here, Sweetie. Okay. You have two choices . . . we . . . you know what the two choices are?
            (2b) E: Either Emmy go to sleep or put blanket at either side.
            (2) F: Right, so what do you want?

3. Choice   (3a) E: Nothing!
                   F: Nothing, okay. [starts to leave, enacting 2a]
             (3b) E: A-n-d yes!

4. Termination (4) F: You want the blanket, don't you? Yeah.

Later in the conversation on the same occasion, her father states the choices, and Emily spontaneously produces a correct, truncated form of the alternatives A and B:

2. Frame   (2) F: You want the two choices again?
                 E: . . . I . . . yeah . . .
            (2a) F: Okay, I can either leave . . .
                  E: I . . . Da-da . . .

	(2b)	F: or I can put a blanket on you.
(Repeated)	(2b)	E: Emmy go sleep or
	(2a)	E: nothing, to let Daddy put blanket on.

This illustrates a very explicit handover of the routine to Emily from her father. Emily first produces the expression of alternatives in response to a direct question from her father. Subsequently, his expression of the frame itself is sufficient for Emily to produce the discourse forms introduced by him. She is now able to "co-construct," or take an active part in the routine. At 22;30, she again produces the alternatives 2a and 2b in response to a direct request (much as at 22;26), and then again (later in the same dialogue) spontaneously:

1. Precipitating event	(1a)	F: . . . it's time for sleeping now isn't it?
2. Frame	(2a)	E: Put blanket on
	(2b)	E: or go out.
	(2)	F: . . . That's right. And what do you want Daddy to do?
3. Choice	(3a)	E: No blanket.
		F: Okay [feigns departure, enacting 2a]
	(3b)	E: Yes, blanket on . . .
4. Termination	(4)	F: Okay.

Here, Emily clearly expresses both alternatives before any framing or expression of choice is offered by her father. She initiates the routine on her own. This leads to her father's expression of 2 *after* rather than *before* her expression of alternatives 2a and 2b, a pattern that becomes frequent as Emily takes the initiative more often. Thus, handover of the routine leads to some variation of the order of turns within the framing of the choice. The sequence of the macrostructure, defined by the four components of (1) precipitating event (impending separation and noncompliance), (2) framing, (3) choosing, and (4) termination (which is dependent on Emily's compliance), remains constant.

Elaboration of the routine occurs in a number of ways. As the anticipatory structure of the routine becomes well established, each partner begins to "stretch" the routine, apparently relying on shared expectations to maintain cohesiveness. One example is Emily's testing of the sincerity of her father's threat to leave (2a). At 22;30, Emily says "No blanket on" at 3a and her father feigns leaving. She then feigns compliance (3b). Her father attempts positive disengagement (4), but Emily then begins the routine again with the utterance "I stand up" (1b). Her father initially just kisses her goodnight, not joining in the reinitiation of the routine, but she persists and repeats "I stand up." Her father then gives a nonstandard repetition of alternative A, and Emily responds with genuine compliance (4) (Appendix 7.1 contains the text of this example).

Emily continues to experiment with reinitiation: on two subsequent occasions she shouts "I standing up," attempting to begin the routine again after one cycle is complete (23;2; 23;4). Her father also experiments with feigning departure without expressing the alternative 2b (23;2). It is unlikely he would leave without the implicit (2b, blanket on) alternative, since doing so would be inconsistent with positive separation. This is substantiated by Emily's subsequent call "Put blanket on": she voices the implicit choice (2b). Her father then reenters, puts on the blanket, and disengages: "I thought so, Sweetie. Okay . . . you're a good girl."

The foregoing illustrates the routinization, elaboration, and handover of the choice format. Her father provides a structure, repeats it, and "hands it over" to Emily by using direct questioning. Emily then begins to express the alternatives herself, and becomes an active partner in the routine, rather than a passive one. Later in the month, she introduces the routine, never actually using the word *choice* but expressing the alternatives "Put blanket on or go out" prior to any framing by her father (23;5). Both partners elaborate the routine. Emily tests the sincerity of her father's expression of alternatives, and attempts reinitiation of the routine, again in what is apparently an attempt to prolong the interaction. Her father enacts his verbal ultimatum, feigning departure. Elaborative variations appear restricted to who initiates, whether the choice is stated prior to or subsequent to the expression of alternatives, whether the father enacts 2a or not, and the number of turns and/or reinitiations that precede Emily's ultimate compliance. The choice routine appears to be a repetitive, reciprocal structure in the pre-sleep dialogues.

The Regulative Function of the Choice Routine

The pre-sleep interaction between Emily and her father presents a conflict of intentions: Emily wants her father to stay, while he wishes to disengage. The routine he introduces, when faced with Emily's simple noncompliance, bears an intrinsic relation to sleeping: putting her blanket on. But its purpose appears to be to regulate the interaction rather than to determine anything about the status of the blanket, such as whether it is necessary or desired. The latter never seems to be in doubt, as much of the routine seems predicated on the shared assumption that the blanket will be on when separation occurs. Several features of the routine indicate that its function is regulative rather than simply communicative or affiliative.

The content of the choice routine is the whereabouts of the blanket (on or off) and Emily's choice of her position in the crib (standing or lying), on which the presence of the blanket is contingent. But the ostensible goal of negotiation—the blanket's being on or off—is never really in question. In none of the episodes does Emily genuinely and finally choose to sleep without the blanket. In fact, if the blanket's status were open to genuine negotiation, the father's threat to leave without supplying it would not have the highly predictable consequence that it does. Second, Emily is not simply asked to say whether or not she wants the blanket. She is asked instead to indicate her choice by her position in the crib. She is more than capable of verbally expressing her desires in regard to the blanket, but this is never requested. Third, the introduction of the routine occurs in response to a noncompliant action, not in response to the temperature of the room or an expression of discomfort, which would provide a primary motivation for introducing discussion about the blanket. Thus, neither Emily's actual preference regarding the blanket nor the blanket's objective necessity is at issue. The issue is compliance. The propositional content of the routine is independent of this pragmatic intent, even though the content is ostensibly related to sleeping. This independence allows the routine to provide a way of arriving at a coordination of goals without ever confronting the conflict at hand.

Emily's father does not respond to her utterance "I standing up" with a simple request for her to lie down, although this is clearly what he wants her to do. Direct expression of his intent would emphasize the actual conflict of intentions: Emily's intent to delay separation is irreconcilable with his intent to disengage. Instead, the introduction of a routine that is to some degree removed from this head-on conflict allows for agreement to occur without the conflict ever being directly expressed, and successfully regulates the conflict.

The regulative function of the choice routine is most evident when its assumptions are violated, or simply speaking, when it doesn't work. This happens at 22;30, later the same night after the exchange quoted in Appendix 7.1 to this chapter. On this occasion, the affective content seems to overflow the boundaries of the conventionalized interaction patterns (see Appendix 7.2). This is the night Emily's new baby brother comes home from the hospital. The format proceeds normally, although the start is a little unusual: Emily claims she is already asleep. The first clue that things are not the same as usual is when her father, at the second termination (4), explicitly mentions that what they are doing is independent of the actual situation and emotion (compare Bateson 1979): "that's enough of the game." Emily protests vigorously. She tries to reinstate the routine by three utterances in quick succession: "Emmy standing up! I standing up! I standing up!" Her father continues to appeal to "reality," again implying that the routine in which they are engaged has a status that is different from ordinary talk: "I'm serious now . . ." At this point the regulative function of the routine breaks down. Emily begins to cry, and both partners repudiate the routine as its regulative function ceases:

> E: [begins to cry] I don't want the b-l-a-n-k-e-t! [sound of kiss]
> F: You don't have to have the blankets. [kiss]
> E: Throw ('em) [tearfully] throw—I didn't . . . throw way!
> F: Okay, we'll just throw the blankets out . . . okay?
> E: M-m-m.
> F: Okay, Sweetie [E crying] . . . why don't you s- . . . why don't you
>   stay up for just a couple more minutes while Daddy's [kiss]
>   goes and . . . gets the baby, okay?

This is not the end of the effectiveness of the routine in regulating presleep interactions; it reappears in its full form on subsequent nights. This is rather a situation-specific failure of the routine to successfully regulate the interaction.

This event points to a number of critical features that clarify how the routine functions in regulation. First, it requires the consensus of both partners. Second, its independence from the actual situation and emotion must be kept implicit—both partners must act as if the routine is the *actual* rather than the *displaced* content of the interaction. When this is violated by explicit reference to the routine as a game, it can't work. Third, the consensus is fragile. It can be sustained when the level of the conflict to be managed is ordinary, but it breaks down under conditions of high arousal. Finally, *both* partners recognize when it is not working. This suggests that the routine is coconstructed, a conventionalized format within which the dyad can interact and achieve consensus without any explicit reference to the actual conflict.

Self-Regulation in Dialogue

On one occasion (22;20; see Appendix 7.3), the conflict that is in evidence throughout the dialogues does not arise, and the pattern of interaction is strikingly different. With no prompting from her parents, Emily says "Night-night." She repeats this three more times in succession, and as her delighted parents take leave of her, she makes no attempt to delay their departure. There are two remarkable features of this episode. First, Emily is compliant and displays no attempt to delay separation. Second, the prosodic contour of her expression "night-night" is identical to that used by her father in the termination phase of the choice routine.

Her father has several utterances that he uses at the end of the routine. These include:

> Night-night, Hon.
> You're (such) a good girl (Hon, Sweetie).
> I love you (Sweetie, Hon).
> Okay (Sweetie, Hon).
> Have a good nap (sleep).
> I'll see you in the morning (when you wake up).

These are invariably marked by a terminal falling pitch contour, in some cases quite pronounced. This contour has been associated with coaxing (Stern, MacKain, and Speiker 1982) and soothing (Papousek 1987), and it is generally accepted that prosody can convey meaning that is independent of morphogrammatical structures (Bolinger 1986; Cruttendon 1986). This is consistent with the father's regulative function in the interaction. The same pitch contour occurs across a range of his utterances but appears to convey a consistent regulatory intent, or meaning.

Emily's expression "night-night" has a similar falling pitch contour. Several things may influence this production. First, it is reasonable to claim that Emily's prosody in this utterance context is not constrained by limitations on production, since her utterances display a wide-ranging prosodic variability. Second, it is not likely that her production is a delayed imitation of one of her father's separation utterances in combination with his typical prosody. She is not imitating a form, she is conveying a meaning. In fact, her father uses the same separation utterances when he *feigns* departure, and on these occasions, his utterances occur *without* the terminal falling pitch contour. The situational meaning on these occasions, feigned departure rather than genuine separation, appears to be carried by the prosody rather than by the morphogrammatical structure of the utterance. Emily's expression "night-night" reflects both a morphogrammatical structure and a prosodic contour, which appear independently in her discourse environment, to convey her compliance. Thus imitation cannot explain why Emily uses both the expression *and* the prosody in a situationally appropriate way.

The similarity of Emily's prosody with that of her father, and a comparison of her father's genuine and feigned separation utterances, were tested with acoustic analysis.[1] Weak signals and overlapping voices made acoustic analysis difficult, but one of Emily's "night-night" utterances and a number of her father's genuine and feigned separation utterances were analyzable. Pitch contours of Emily's utterance and of three of her father's utterances are presented in Figure 7.1. It is clear from the figure that Emily's utterance and her father's separation utterances have similar pitch contours. The fourth utterance occurs during a feigned departure in the choice routine. Its contour is markedly different from the other three. Six of the father's additional termination utterances and several additional feigned separation utterances were subjected to acoustic analysis. These were selected on the basis of the quality of signal: from a sample of 45 utterances of both types, only 16 were clear enough to obtain contours. Of the eight analyzable termination utterances, six had clear terminal falling pitch contours. Of the eight nontermination utterances with similar semantic content, only two had such contours.

A systematic contour can thus be identified with the father's diverse separation utterances, a contour consistent with his regulative role. Emily's production of this contour co-occurs with her compliance, on the only occasion when she seems able to successfully regulate her own reactions to the impending separation. It cannot be coincidence that Emily's use of both her father's expression and his prosody occurs on the only occasion when she manages this. And she repeats the same expression with the same contour in her subsequent monologue.

Regulation in Monologue

Two characteristics of the monologue that follows this exchange (Appendix 7.3) are of interest here. First, the expression "nighty-night" is repeated three times at the beginning of the monologue. It is immediately followed by a short narrative of Emily's next anticipated experience with her father. "When Daddy come, then Daddy get

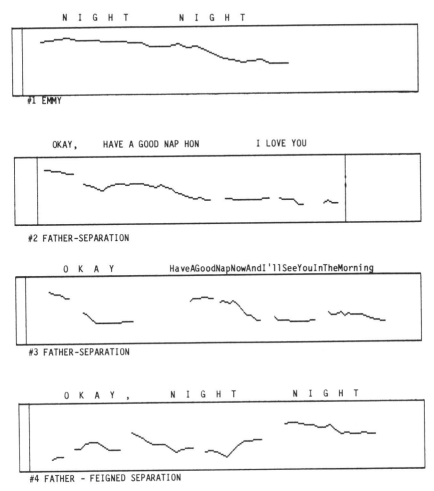

Figure 7.1. Pitch contours of Emily's and her father's utterances.

Emmy then Daddy wake Emmy up . . ." This is followed by a single reference to playing with her friend Carl, and then an extended description of herself and others sleeping. There is thus a juxtaposition in the monologue of the other's (her father's) expression with the next anticipated reexperiencing of the other. This is consonant with Stern's (1985) notion of the role of the "evoked other" in self-regulation.

Second, Emily's use of this expression occurs when she is compliant, when she has accepted that she must go to sleep. But her acceptance is not limited to acquiescence to her parents' wishes. The monologue, in the sequence beginning with the expression "nighty-night," expresses not simply her decision to comply, but an apparent generalized understanding that it is time for *everyone* to sleep. Beginning with herself, "Emmy sleep," she lists all others in her experience who are sleeping—"Carl sleeping and Lance sleeping," and so on—ending with another reference to herself sleeping. Her father has, on previous occasions, explained to her that everyone has to go to sleep at night, so again, this generalization is not a solitary accomplishment. But it demonstrates that her compliance is not a capitulation. In her talk, she relates her own particular experience to one that is canonical for other children and other people in general. She does not seem to be simply repeating or imitating what she has heard, or simply listing experiences in a random way. In this monologue, she casts her experience in relation to a social reality. Her effective self-regulation co-occurs with her expression of shared patterns of action, of a given version of the way things are.

Conclusions

Regulation in the pre-sleep dialogues is directed toward Emily's attempts to delay the impending separation. The conflict is regulated by interactive patterns such as the choice routine, which operates through displacement, consensus, and convention. The choice routine is ostensibly related to sleeping, but it is actually concerned with compliance. It requires a consensus between Emily and her father that the blanket is the actual, rather than displaced, content of the conflict. The violation of this consensus by reference to the routine as a "game" by the father leads immediately to a breakdown of its regulative function, and it is quickly repudiated by both partners. The routine shifts the focus of the interaction from a direct unresolvable conflict to a conventionalized one in which agreement can be attained. The choice gives Emily a ritual agency, when in fact she has no choice. Delay as she will, separation must inevitably occur.

This conventional or ritual choice is always followed by a termination of the interaction by the father. He has a group of usual expressions, and these are almost invariably marked by a falling terminal pitch. One of his typical expressions, together with his characteristic prosody, is used by Emily in the dialogue on the only occasion when she demonstrates no delaying tactics and no resistance to the impending separation. On this occasion, she appears to be effectively regulating the interaction herself, and thus there is no need for regulation by her father. She uses the same expression in the immediately subsequent monologue. Emily's successful regulation of her own inner states thus appears to co-occur with expressions originally occurring in dialogue with her father.

In the same way that the regulative aspect of the dialogues is directed toward attempts to delay separation, the regulative aspect of the monologues may be directed to Emily's actual experience of separation. That is, the choice routine in the dialogue gives her a ritual agency in a situation she actually cannot change. Similarly, she cannot change her outward state of separateness, but she can create a narrative that displaces or diminishes it (see also Chapter 9). Her narrative monologues can be seen to accomplish this in two ways.

First, the monologues are concerned with others, and her experiences of being with others, in contrast to her outward state of separateness from others. The monologues are not typically descriptions of herself or her surroundings as she lies in her crib, but rather of herself in relation to others and to events that constitute her waking life. In the example discussed above, she uses her father's expression and his prosody, and immediately recounts her next anticipated experience of him. She describes her present experience (going to sleep) in terms of a general social reality, by recounting the same event occurring at the same time for "everybody." The monologues thus express a shared rather than a private reality, and may function to displace her experience of separateness by recounting her experiences of belongingness in a social reality.

Second, the monologues are largely concerned with reconstruals of past experiences and voicings of anticipated experiences. Emily's expression "When Daddy come, then Daddy get Emmy," for example, is frequent throughout the monologues. But it describes a virtually invariant event, a given rather than a new fact. Its repeated expression must reflect a significance beyond the working out of aspects of her cognitive or linguistic representations of this event. The importance of the event may lie rather in the fact that it marks the end of separation. It is the temporal demarcation of her present experience, and is the point at which her narrative monologues often begin. She has no way of *knowing* that this will actually happen, that her separateness is not a permanent state. She rather has an expectancy, based on past experiences. Voicing this expectancy may be a conviction she has established for displacing the uncertainty of her present state. In this way, listing past and future events may regulate her experience of separateness. Her narratives of what will be and what has been may help her deal with the vicissitudes of the present.

This account suggests that crib monologues have a regulative aspect. This regulative aspect is probably more autonomous than explicit, in that self-regulation is probably not represented as an intention by Emily as she speaks. But a regulatory intention need not be explicitly represented in order for regulation to occur. In fact the opposite case seems to hold in the dialogue: the regulative function of the choice routine breaks down when explicit reference to the routine is made.

What does appear to be explicitly represented in the monologues is Emily's social reality: others, events, reunions and farewells. Thus, although the monologues occur in the absence of an interlocutor, they are not truly solitary in nature. They are more like expressions of belongingness in what Wittgenstein (1953) would call forms of life. In voicing these forms of life Emily appears to be construing her inner reality in relation to the broader social reality of which she is a part. It is in this process of construal that the autonomous regulation of her inner states is accomplished.

Appendix 7.1 (22;30)

1. Precipitating event	(1b)	[E prolongs color-naming more than usual]
2. Frame	(2)	F: W-e-l-l, what is your choice tonight, Hon?
	(2b)	E: Either put blanket on,
	(2a)	or go out.
	(2)	F: Which do you want me to do?
3. Choice	(3a)	E: No blanket on.
		F: No blanket! Okay. [F feigns leaving, enacting 2a.]
	(3b)	[E apparently makes a nonverbal indication of compliance]
4. Termination	(4)	F: No-ho-ho-ho-! I think so! Well, you have a good night's sleep, you say "Good morning, Daddy, good morning, Mommy" in the morning.
1. Reinitiation attempt	(1b)	E: I stand up.
		F: Have a big kiss, h-m-m?
	(1b)	E: I stand up!
2. Frame	(2a)	F: Well, you stand up, then I can't put the blan-

ket on you, and then I'll just have to go out, huh?

| 3. Choice | (3b) | [sound of E lying down] |
| 4. Termination | (4) | F: R-i-g-h-t. |

Appendix 7.2 (22;30)

1. Precipitating event	(1b)	E: I already sleeping! F: O-h-o, I don't think so! . . .
2. Frame	(2a) (2a)	F: Okay, well I'm just going to leave then. F: You want Daddy to go, with no blanket?
3. Choice	(3b)	E: N-n-
4. Termination	(4)	F: N-o-o-!
1. Second precipitating event	(1b) (1a)	E: I not already . . . I laying here. F: I know you're laying there but it's time for sleeping, isn't it?

2. Frame	(2b)
	(2a)
	(2b)
	(2a)
	(2)
		E: Put blanket on
		    or go out.
		F: Do what? Put blanket on
		    or go out. That's right.
		    And what do you want Daddy to do?

3. Choice	(3a) (3b)	E: No blanket. F: Okay . . . [F moves toward door, enacting 2a] E: Y-e-s, blanket on.
4. Termination	(4)	F: Okay, well, that's enough of the game. So I'll see you in the morning, Sweetie.
1. Reinitiation attempt	(1b)	E: Emmy standing up! I standing up! I standing up!
2. Frame (nonstandard)	(2a) (2b) (2)	F: Well, you know, I'm gonna have to go out, Sweetie, *I'm serious* now unless you want to to— unless you want Daddy to put a blanket on. Do you want Daddy to put a blanket on?
3. Choice	(3)	E: [no response]
4. Termination attempt	(4)	F: Okay, night-night, Hon—I love you, night-night.

E: [begins to cry]
   I don't want the b-l-a-n-ket!
[sound of kiss]
F: You don't have to have the blankets. [Kiss]
E: Throw ('em). [tearfully] Throw—I didn't . . . throw way!
F: Okay, we'll just throw the blankets out . . . okay?
E: M-m-m.
F: Okay, Sweetie. [E crying]
F: Well why don't you s-, why don't you stay up for just a couple more minutes while Daddy's [kiss] goes and gets the baby, okay?

Appendix 7.3 (22;20)

DIALOGUE

M: What happened?
E: (wonder where the boat go?)
M: Oh the boat? Oh this is in your bed.
F: The boat's in your bed, Honey.
M: Have a really good night's sleep.
E: *N-i-g-h-t–n-i-g-h-t.*
   [M and F both react simultaneously]
M: Night-night. I love you, Honey. [M exits]
F: Night-night, Sweetie. I love you.
E: *N-i-g-h-t–n-i-g-h-t.*
F: You're such a good girl.
E: Night-night.
F: See you in the morning. Night-night.
E: *N-i-g-h-t–n-i-g-h-t.*
   [F exits, closing door]

MONOLOGUE

E: Nighty-night. Nighty-night. Nighty-night . . . [sighs]. When D-daddy come then Daddy get Emmy then Daddy wake Emmy up then . . . t-h-e-n . . . then Carl come play, Emmy not right now. Emmy sleep [kiss], Emmy sleep(ing) . . . next y-e-a-r, next y-e-a-r, [whispers] Carl come [in strong voice] and the baby come . . . Carl sleeping and the—(I'm) sleeping and (Lance) sleeping and

(Allen) sleeping and (Meg) sleeping a-n-d . . . Uncle (Jack?) and Aunt (Sam) and Carl and Emmy and Daddy and Mommy and (Ohten) and Uncle (Ben). All go sleeping and Emmy and Daddy and Mommy have go sleep.
[whispers softly, briefly]
Sleeping, sleeping, sleeping
[sings something—words unclear]
[soft whispers—content unclear] . . .

Chapter 8

Monologue as the Linguistic Construction of Self in Time

Katherine Nelson

Many of the previous chapters have focused in different ways on the question of how Emily uses language to organize and make sense of her experience. It is evident from these discussions that the world she is so transparently trying to come to terms with is a social-cultural world; problems involving only physical objects, space, and causality play little or no part in her monologues. In this chapter I explore the proposition that the central problem with which Emily grapples over these months is how to situate herself within the world of other people engaged in activities organized in time. In so doing, I consider her effort to use language as a socially constituted symbolic form to represent her own experience, and thus to "make sense" of her social experience on an individual personal level. The larger and more ambitious goal of the chapter (as indeed of the whole undertaking) is to characterize how social experience is reconstructed and transformed in the process of internalization, and how the individual perspective of the unsocialized child becomes the social perspective of the child in a social world.

The problems examined in this chapter are familiar ones to students of infant development. Development of a self-concept, of the self in relation to significant others, of the coordination of actions and vocalizations in time with others—these have all been the focus of important theoretical and empirical work (for example, Mead 1934; Werner and Kaplan 1963; Trevarthen 1980; Stern 1985). What this analysis contributes is a direct view into the process of how the child uses linguistic representations to construct a self that is coordinate with other selves and that is capable of coordinating actions and interactions with others within quite large activity frames through time.

As many others have argued, the construction of a self-concept is dependent upon the organization of self in a social space. Here I emphasize the importance of the temporal as well as the spatial organization of the social world, and the necessity of organizing temporal concepts in order to understand one's self in relation to others. What is important here is the emphasis on language as the medium through which these understandings are brought about.

As I have suggested, the social dynamic of the child's world demands particular perspectives. The child must represent herself as a person within a social nexus, not simply as an ego with wants and needs. She must also come to understand and represent how events unfold through time and space, because these are essential defining dimensions of socially constituted activities. These two critical perspectives are reflected in language in the system of self and other reference and in the linguistic system of temporal reference using verb morphology and time adverbials. The development of these two systems reflects an evolving sense of the place of self in relation to the social world. Both involve the terms in which activities are described. In one case, reference to self and others reflects an understanding of what roles are played in activities and by whom, that is, how one relates to others within events. In the other case, activities themselves are described in relation to the temporal position of the describer. Thus both reference systems require that the narrator take a perspective on events that reflects the way those events are socially organized.

In Chapter 5, Gerhardt traced the developments of these two systems over the course of one developmentally significant month, demonstrating both the interrelations of the two systems and their role in differentiating among Emily's discourse intentions, as these functioned to reference different perspectives on events. In this chapter I extend this analysis to examine the use of self-reference over the succeeding months and the further development of devices for temporal expression that enable Emily to construct increasingly complex relations among events.

Self-Reference

As seen in Chapter 5, Emily used three different forms for reference to herself from the outset: *I, my,* and *Emmy.* Gerhardt suggested that *Emmy* was used in contexts in which the child was the recipient of action, the passive participant in other people's activities, while *I* was used in active, volitional, and interactive intentional contexts. A slightly different analysis of the data from the same period has been proposed by Watson (1983), who focused on the subjective case use of the three terms in the monologues. Like Gerhardt (and similar to Budwig's 1985 analysis of self-reference by six children), Watson notes that *Emmy* and *I* tend to be used consistently in different contexts, representing distinct discourse styles within the monologues.

Watson showed that at 23 months Emily uses *I* only in the subjective case, while *Emmy* and *my* occur also as possessives and as objects of the verb. *I* occurs most frequently in the here-and-now situation of the dialogue, and only half as often in the monologue. *Emmy* and *my* occur most frequently in monologue and only occasionally in dialogue. *I* is used to express immediate wants and needs (volition), actions (agency), and cognitive states expressed by verbs such as *know* and *remember; Emmy* and *my* are almost always used to express actions and occasionally with the statives *have* and *be* and with causatives.

The difference between this account and that in Chapter 5 is that Watson (1983) does not distinguish between agent and recipient or passive participant in action as Gerhardt does. According to Watson, shifts in the form of self-reference are associated with different "text types" or genres that vary on dimensions of here-and-now versus there-and-then situational reference, and the degree of lexical cohesion within, and subjective involvement with, the text. This suggestion clearly connects self-reference and the temporal dimension as they are becoming mutually defined, and implies that the self is being differentiated in relation to different temporal contexts.

Although their emphases differ, it is not surprising, given the common data base, that Watson and Gerhardt converge on a description of the distinction between uses of *Emmy* or *my* and *I* in what can be termed objective versus subjective views of self, respectively. *Emmy* is viewed objectively as the recipient of action, or the actor in an event displaced in time or space, while *I* takes part in ongoing activities or expresses wants and needs. This distinction in self-perspective accounts for the different verb forms associated with the two self-referent forms. *I* partakes of ongoing *-ing* forms, while *Emmy* is viewed in past or normative present forms.[1]

Given the striking differentiation apparent in the use of these self-referent forms at this early point, the question naturally arises whether the language that Emily *hears* provides a basis for such a contrast. To evaluate this possibility, I examined her parents' personal references in the dialogue. A tabulation of reference to self and child by mother and father during four sessions of Emily's twenty-third month revealed a predominant use of pronominal forms by both parents to refer to both self and child. In referring to Emily, both parents used *you-your* about two-thirds of the time, and *Emmy* or *Emily* very infrequently (less than 3 percent). Other uses included pet names such as *Honey* (10 percent) and *we* (20 percent). They also referred to themselves most frequently by the use of *I* rather than *Daddy* or *Mommy*. *I* was used 75 percent of the time by the mother and 56 percent of the time by the father. In references to third persons (usually references to mother or father by the other) they predominantly used nominal forms rather than pronominals, however. There is nothing in this pattern that appears to be a model for Emily's uses in the monologue. In particular, her dominant use of *Emmy* (or *my*, not used at all by her parents) in preference to *I*, reserving *I* for volition and ongoing action, reflects neither parental reference to themselves nor to Emily, both of which predominantly involve the pronominal.

The view that has emerged of Emily's two types of self-reference at 22–23 months has significant implications for her emerging sense of self, on the one hand as actor and experiencer, and on the other as a person within a social nexus in which her role is defined in terms of the expectations and actions of others. It may be inferred that because the monologues apparently serve the function of representing Emily's emerging conception of an objective social world, *Emmy* is the most appropriate form for this representation.

But what happens to these forms over time? The initial contrast that Emily develops does not map onto contrasts of the adult language, either in terms of abstract grammar or as the forms are used by her parents. A tension is thus set up between expressive contrasts that apparently serve an important definitional function for the child, and the system that she must internalize based on linguistic uses by others. Thus some change in the system can be expected as it accommodates to the forms dictated by adult usage. These changes can in turn be expected to necessitate a reorganization of other parts of the linguistic system to take over functions previously served by contrasts in the self-reference system. The resolution of these tensions takes place over the succeeding four months.

The long-term development of Emily's self-referent forms can be seen in terms of their relative uses in the monologues over the first eight months of this study, as shown in Figure 8.1. As already noted, although at all points between 21 and 28 months *I* was used predominantly in the dialogues, in the earliest transcripts *Emmy* was the most frequent term used for self-reference in the monologues. At 22 months *Emmy* and *I* were used with equal frequency while *my* was used less than 10 percent of the time. *Emmy* predominated again at 23 months.[2]

Further developments shown in Figure 8.1 reveal that the proportion of the use of *Emmy* in the monologues drops by more than half between 23 and 24 months, from 48 percent to 22 percent, as *I* becomes the most frequently used term. However, two other shifts in the system also occur: *my*—originally an alternative in *Emmy* contexts—*increases* in frequency, and *we* emerges in discourse contexts that were previously occupied by singular reference. As noted above, Emily's father used *we* as an alternative to *you* quite frequently; thus

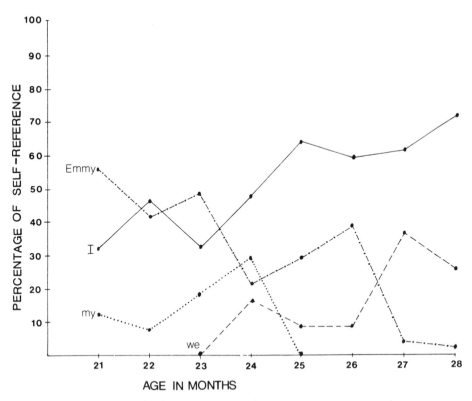

Figure 8.1. Use of self-reference terms in subject position, 21–28 months.

Emily's adoption of this form may represent a new attempt to incorporate parental distinctions into her own system. After 24 months *my* drops out completely. *Emmy,* following the *my* pattern, first rises again to a peak at 26 months and then drops to virtually zero, while *I* and *we* become established as the canonical forms.

There is some indication that *we* is used first in normative or group contexts. For example, at 24;4 Emily says "But in the morning we put jamas on" (see Episode 1.6 in Chapter 1 for the full passage and discussion). Yet in the same normative description she also uses *I* ("I sleep with jamas") and *my* ("but afternoon my wake up and play"). This alternation is also seen in talk about going to the doctor at 24;8 (Episode 1.4), in which she speculates about whether her jamas will come off: "maybe, maybe we take my jamas off." But later: "*my* have get my checkup, so *we* take my jamas off." Thus at this point the use of *we* does not seem to be a consistent substitute for the earlier *Emmy* or *my* (indeed, *my* is still used, as the quotation shows). It may be that the earlier system is beginning to break apart at this time, to be replaced by an *I-we* contrast.

The later established normative use of *we* can be seen in the "airport rule": "If ever we go to the airport we have to get some luggage" (29;18, Episode 1.8); and again at 32;0 when she describes her Friday morning routine (Episode 1.9), where "what we do" is the theme and *we* is used almost exclusively throughout (see Chapter 1 for discussion of these examples). However, *we* is also used at 33 months to describe the group activity of buying a doll (Episode 1.12): "we bought a baby." In contrast, in recounting Daddy's failure to get into a race (32 months; see Chapter 3) she uses *I* exclusively. In this passage she uses *I* to reflect on the problem with verbs of mental state: "I don't know," "I think," "I wish," "I said," "I want." But in the same passage there is also the possibility of action expressed by *I*: "I can watch him," "I'm going to."

Thus, by 32 months *I* and *we* do appear to be used in different discourse contexts, reflecting a reorganization of the self-reference system from its original organization in terms of objective *Emmy* and subjective *I.* There may be a residue of the earlier system in the apparent normative or group assignment of *we* in contrast to the subjective volitional or active *I.* A complete analysis of the contexts of Emily's uses of these forms over the entire period would be necessary to sustain this suggestion, and this has not been carried out. Nonetheless, these observations are sufficient to indicate that the system has become reorganized over time into something more closely resembling the adult model. Just as important, this model incorporates Emily as agent, and as coparticipant in activities ("we bought a baby") that involve others (father, mother, brother, and friends) as well as herself. Her evolved self-referent system thus reflects an evolved representation of herself as actor within a complex social world.

It would be foolish to argue on the basis of these developments that, after having established a contrast between objective and subjective self, Emily abandons her original notion of an objective self as she adopts canonical linguistic usage that requires the deictic subjective *I*. Rather, the changes in the self-reference system would seem to require that she find some way of making these distinctions outside the self-reference system. The coincidental rise of *my* and *we* as *Emmy* first drops from dominant use suggests an initial groping for substitute distinct forms. But *my* will not do at all as a subjective pronoun, given its assignment to the possessive case, and the *we* contrast eventually established is not primarily objective but is rather used for normative or group contexts.

Thus other discourse devices must be called upon to preserve the distinctions previously encoded in the *Emmy-I* contrast. I suggest that among these distinctions is the evolving temporal reference system, which enables Emily to place an account of an event within an objective frame without having to rely upon a particular form of self-reference for this purpose.

The Temporal Reference System

Temporal Concepts and Their Linguistic Expression

The development of temporal reference in Emily's speech is integrally related to self-reference in the initial phases of its mastery, as described in Chapter 5.[3] Here I focus on how Emily uses her emerging linguistic contrasts to express temporal relations within and among events, and to construct an account of an event that combines the subjective and objective perspectives. Temporal perspective is coded grammatically in English (as in most other languages) in terms of tense forms expressing past, present, and future. In addition to tense there are other ways of marking temporal relations, in particular the temporal adverbials, prepositions, and conjunctions. It has frequently been noted that terms such as *yesterday, today,* and *tomorrow* are acquired only after tense marking has been established (Bloom, Lifter and Hafitz 1980; Weist 1986) and are at first used inaccurately. *Yesterday,* for example, has often been observed to be used to reference any time other than the present (Harner 1982). The timing of the development of these temporal terms in relation to the acquisition of tense forms and other linguistic developments may be taken as evidence for the development of temporal concepts.

I wish to argue that Emily uses her developing temporal language to construct the relations of past, present, and future. This argument may seem problematic because of the apparent circularity of the evidence, but I shall set forth reasons why it should be taken seriously. As with all of the analyses of these data, evidence for the proposals made here comes entirely from Emily's verbal productions, supplemented for some purposes by her mother's comments on her memories. Because the claims I make with respect to Emily's developing ideas about temporal relations depend so closely on the evidence from her linguistic forms, it is necessary first to consider the issues involved in drawing conceptual conclusions from language data.

The close relation between developing language and developing conceptual systems has most often been seen as one of linguistic dependence upon developing concepts (see, for example, Cromer 1968; Sinclair 1971; Slobin 1982; Weist 1986). That is, the assumption has been that the linguistic devices for expressing particular concepts are acquired only after the child has achieved those concepts. Because there is evidence that some forms are used before the child has acquired the "full meaning" associated with them, this general position has been modified to indicate that forms acquire their adult meaning only after the child has achieved the requisite concepts. For example, there are a number of claims that children who use causal terms such as *because* and *so* do not understand their full causal implications (Piaget 1974; Emerson 1979). Similarly, the common observation that children may use *yesterday* at first to refer to any time in the past, or even in the future, is taken as an indication of a defective understanding of time measured in terms of days.

The appropriate conclusion from these and many other observations is that one cannot infer from a child's use of a particular linguistic form that the child has acquired the adult meaning of that form, or that the child has developed the conceptual structure necessary to understand its meaning. This is the implication as well of Slobin's (1973) famous dictum (based on Werner and Kaplan's 1963 formulation) that with development "old forms come to serve new functions, and old functions take on new forms." Thus caution indicates that one cannot simply view the child's acquisition of, say, past-tense inflections as an indication that the child has a *concept* of past in relation to present events.

There are, however, two puzzles that deserve more attention than they usually get in these discussions. First, why does the child acquire forms that at first have little or no conceptual underpinning, or that are at best mapped onto concepts or functions that are irrelevant to their adult meaning? The usual answer is that there is another concept in the child's repertoire that may be conveniently expressed through the new form; in the case of past *-ed* the proposal is that the child's focus on completed action finds expression in this form (what Weist et al. 1984 refer to as the "defective tense hypothesis"). A more interesting and potentially more profound proposal is put forth by Gerhardt (Chapter 5), who sees the child as operating within discourse structures that require the differentiation of intentional states in order to make her meaning clear. She then acquires contrastive forms for the expression of different discursive attitudes.

But is it always the case that children attach new forms to newly discovered distinctions? "New forms serve old functions" implies not. If the functions are old, how were they expressed previously? Do new forms compete with old ones? Gerhardt's analysis suggests that these questions are too simplistic. Rather, the emerging system of discourse functions consists of a large complex of distinctions that are served by a very few contrastive verb forms backed up by adverbials. Because of the complexity of the discourse system, the child's emerging forms may begin by expressing only parts of it, and these possibly idiosyncratically. Pragmatic functions may at first dominate semantic ones.

There is a further important question to be addressed. What is the impact on the child's emerging conceptual system of the acquisition of linguistic devices for expressing concepts that are not yet part of that system? Assume for the moment that the defective-tense hypothesis is true for at least some children (see, for example, Antinucci and Miller 1976). We might then ask: Does acquiring a past-tense marker that is used to code completed action in any way advance the child's understanding of deictic temporal relationships? Or does the use of the form in a deictic sense wait on the independent emergence of a conceptual distinction between past and present? That is, are the developing conceptual and linguistic systems independent of one another, or do they interact, such that the acquisition of a form opens up the potential for the acquisition of the concept that it references in the adult language? (See Levy's analysis of the use of *do it* and *do that* in Chapter 4 for a related discussion.)

In addressing these issues we must account for the critical point that children infrequently use terms inappropriately in their productive language. That is, they may use terms for a restricted set of functions, or in restricted contexts, but, for example, when they use *because* and *so* they use them in contexts that adults find appropriate (French and Nelson 1985). There may be several explanations for this observation. One (the one favored by French and Nelson) is that the child uses the terms meaningfully in restricted contexts, which are a subset of those used by the adult. Another possible explanation is that the child is simply copying the adult's use in particular contexts without at first attaching semantic force to the terms. Still another possibility is that the child has mapped the term onto a pragmatic function that coincides with some of the possible semantic uses of the term in the adult language. In summary, appropriate uses may not indicate conceptual understanding, but rather may index a continuum of concept mastery from "not at all" to "full command."

Still, the use of a language form may alert the child to potential distinctions that she has not yet herself worked out on a conceptual level. Emily's use of *so* in the early months to string discourse units together without any of the semantic causal entailments of the term is an example. As discussed in Chapter 1, *so* is used first as an empty pragmatic device for connecting two strings, later drops from use, and emerges again with the more fully developed system of relative terms at 24 months, then carrying a causal sense in contrast to other connectives. The fact that the term drops from use even as Emily is establishing connected narratives and adopting other conjunctive and adverbial forms suggests that at some level she recognizes its semantic force but does not yet have the conceptual wherewithal to utilize it.

A nagging problem here is that for complex concepts such as time we have no way of assessing a prelinguistic concept. We can show that children prelinguistically respect sequential order and relative temporal duration (such as the time between feedings), but nonlinguistic concepts of *past* and *future* do not appear to be assessable. Is it then the case that language is *necessary* for the very formation of these concepts and not merely for their expression?[4]

There are at least four logical possibilities that need to be considered with respect to the relation between the linguistic expression of time and the mastery of time concepts:

1. Concepts of present, past, and future are innately given in the human conceptual system. When language development has reached a particular developmental level (such as Brown's Stage 2 with the beginning acquisition of grammatical morphemes including *-ed* and *-ing*) these concepts will be expressed in the language. Thus expression depends only upon the status of development of the linguistic system.

2. Concepts of present, past, and future are an inherent part of the human conceptual system, but depend on maturation of that system independent of linguistic development. Thus, expression in the language may be delayed relative to other forms of equal linguistic complexity. In particular, grammatical morphemes such as *-ed* and *-ing* may be acquired late and may at first be used for meanings or functions other than the past-present distinction. Their acquisition may be variably ordered for individual children with respect to other language forms, reflecting their dependence on the state of the conceptual system rather than the linguistic system.

3. Concepts of present, past, and future need to be constructed in the human conceptual system, and thus their expression in the language may be relatively delayed. The acquisition of *-ed* and *-ing* may facilitate the construction of the temporal system by flagging potential deictic distinctions in adult uses, even if these forms are at first used to code aspectual distinctions. However, the concepts are not wholly dependent upon linguistic expression. Both linguistic and conceptual development may therefore contribute to the timing of the emergence of the relevant concepts.

4. Concepts of present, past, and future are dependent upon language expression for their construction in the human conceptual system. Thus the acquisition of *-ed* and *-ing* forms is an important and necessary advance toward conceptual distinctions that previously were not made. Prior to the acquisition of the relevant concepts the child may not use temporal inflections at all, or may use them for distinctions that are nonexistent or peripheral in the adult language, for example for aspect rather than tense, or as part of a pragmatic marking system.

I will consider these possibilities here in relation to the development of Emily's temporal marking system.

Evidence for Temporal Concepts in the Monologues

Emily refers to episodes from her past life in the earliest monologues recorded, at 21 months. The question raised here is: Did she have a notion of pastness at 21 months as distinct from a general sense of "not nowness"? For example, in the "broken car" narrative at 21 months (see Episode 1.1 in Chapter 1), does Emily represent this as a unique episode at a specific point in time in relation to other events that took place before and after it, and differentiated from other possibly similar or associated happenings? In a previous report on these data (Nelson 1984) I suggested, based on her use of language forms, that Emily moves from a state of the undifferentiated nonpresent to a specific representation of past, future, and general. Gerhardt (Chapter 5) has documented that during the period from 22 to 24 months Emily develops a present-past-progressive system of contrasting tense and aspect. She also suggests that the system first reflects only a contrast between *now* and *not now,* but that by 23;6 it takes on direction by specifically coding pastness. The question at this point is whether there is evidence that the emergence of pastness (and futureness, which I have suggested may emerge prior to the past) reflects a conceptual advance or whether it is simply a linguistic coding of the already available distinction. In part the evidence on this issue rests on a comparison of the development of the tense system with other aspects of Emily's developing language.

As described in the Introduction, Emily's language development was not only precocious but, on the evidence in the monologues, somewhat unusual. Her acquisition of many of the 14 grammatical morphemes in Brown's (1973) Stage 2 was delayed in relation to her acquisition of devices for combining clauses and forming intersentential relations (Stages 4 and 5). When compared to Bloom and Lahey's (1978) scheme, her pattern of acquisition order also appears unusual. In particular, according to both schemes, one would have expected her to acquire the past inflection some months earlier than she actually did. Most children begin to acquire -*ed* and -*ing* forms when their MLUs average 2 to 3 morphemes. In contrast, Emily's MLU averaged 3.6 in the dialogue and 5.4 in the monologues during the period when she was acquiring these forms.

It is noteworthy, however, that both Bloom, Lifter, and Hafitz (1980) and Weist (1986) place these developments within the age range of 22–28 months. Emily's acquisition of these forms is then in line with expectations based on age rather than on language stage. This fact suggests either possibility 2 or 3 above, namely the late maturation or the late construction of a system of temporal concepts in comparison to other aspects of language development. Neither possibility 1 (an innate conceptual system already in place) nor possibility 4 (a system directly derived from linguistic representation) would be expected to result in a relative delay in temporal forms compared to developments in other aspects of the grammatical system.

As noted in the Introduction, inflected verbs (irregular past and *-ing* forms) are scattered through the transcripts from 21 and 22 months, but they are not used consistently or systematically. Rather, the forms appear to have come to Emily's attention and then to be used somewhat haphazardly, although usually in relevant contexts of talking about past events. We can speculate that she is modeling her use on her parents' use; her language has by this time developed to the point that she can note the existence of forms for which she has as yet no relevant conceptual distinctions.

Now note what happens as she begins to map these forms onto distinctions in her own language. She makes a number of semantic and pragmatic distinctions based initially on her role in the referenced activity and only later on a temporal coding of *now–not now* and later still on coding of *now* versus the past. The evidence for a *now–later* coding is less substantial; it may come in earlier than past (as I originally claimed), or it may remain undifferentiated, as a kind of irrealis "not here, not now" form. This uncertainty reflects the relatively ambiguous coding of future in English.[5] Emily, like other speakers, might talk about future events using present tense (tomorrow we have waffles for breakfast); or the *-ing* form (on Saturday Daddy's taking me to Childworld); or the *going to* form (tomorrow I'm going to go to the doctor); or the *will* form (after lunch we'll go to the park). During the period in question Emily is just beginning to use *-ing* forms, including *gonna*. Thus interpreting her references in terms of future time is inherently ambiguous. When she repeats at 22½ months "Carl coming after my nap" does she intend the future reference (as I am inclined to argue), or is she simply talking about a *not now* occurrence, perhaps one that is recurrent (as Gerhardt argues)? The evidence on this point remains inconclusive.

To return to the question at hand, how can we explain the striking omission from Emily's earlier development of linguistic forms those which code temporality? Why does she not develop these at the time she is acquiring other grammatical morphemes, such as her extensive repertoire of prepositions (see Introduction)? One clue is that for Emily temporal adverbials appear at the same time as the tense system is being organized, during her twenty-fourth month. Before 23 months temporal adverbials and conjunctions (with the exception of *when* and *then,* used to connect two statements) are infrequent. But after 23;0—when the contrast of *now* and the past is established—they appear in considerable numbers: *then, when, and then,* and *yesterday* were recorded 6 to 8 times each within a two-week period. In addition, other terms are used once or twice each: *again, today, after, and now, one day, the day, that day, one time, because,* and *next.* In contrast, most children master irregular and regular past tense many months before they acquire temporal adverbials. Emily's uses of these terms appears to be in the service of her concerted attempt at this time to make clear that temporal relations are involved, even though her uses are not always semantically accurate.

Additionally, it is precisely at this point that her monologic recounts take on a more organized, sequential form. We begin to see her moving through a narrative directly from its beginning point to its end (see, for example, Episode 1.3), in contrast to the circular free-associative character of the earlier recounts, such as the "broken car" narrative. Taken together, these developments suggest that it is only at 23 months that Emily acquires a singular notion of pastness, that is, a notion that experienced events can be ordered in relation to the present.[6] At this point a number of linguistic devices previously neglected are called on to express this relation.

It is worth noting that when past-tense forms emerge as a system in Emily's discourse they are used to reference "far" as well as "near" past, that is, to describe what happened hours, days, and weeks ago, as well as what happened just now. The distinction between far past and near past has sometimes been invoked as the basis for early restriction of the past tense to just-completed events. Emily's monologues are largely concerned with past events that occurred more than a few minutes ago; thus uses for the far past are easily observed in this context. This point underscores a continuing theme throughout this book: the monologues may reveal more extensive linguistic and conceptual knowledge or competence than is revealed in dialogic contexts. The restriction of past to near-past events that has sometimes been observed may be an artifact of the usual here-and-now context of observation in which far-past events are not discussed (Lucariello and Nelson 1987).

It is interesting that after the development of past and future reference Emily begins to formulate rules and norms explicitly using the general "timeless" present, such as "in the morning we put jamas on." She also begins to note exceptions to the general case: "Sometimes Tanta puts Emmy down with the home. Sometimes Jeanie and Annie and Tanta and Emmy and Mor" (23;10). Moreover, she begins speculating, on the basis of general knowledge and past experiences, about what might happen, as various passages from 24 months demonstrate, for example, whether the doctor will take jamas off (Episode 1.4) and which boy will bring a book to Tanta's (discussed in Chapter 3). These developments, which emerge simultaneously or just subsequent to the emergence of the past-present-future system of reference, during months 24 and 25, indicate that she is developing a fully articulated temporally organized system of events that includes not only the specific past, the anticipated future, and the general norm, but also notions of the unusual, the possible, the frequent and infrequent, as well as the contingent (when x then y) and the necessary (you have to x). These notions have been discussed in various ways in the preceding chapters. I refer to them here to point out that they begin to emerge in temporal concert with the system of temporal reference, suggesting that they are conceptually and linguistically related to that system.

The conclusion I advance here, then, is that temporal concepts are constructed in response to linguistic coding (possibility 3). The argument can be summarized on the basis of the foregoing observations. First there is the relatively late emergence of linguistic coding of temporal relations already noted, ruling out possibilities 1 and 4. Secondly, there is the correlated linguistic development of the many related notions just outlined, including far and near past, future, timeless general norm, frequency, contingency, and possibility—suggesting that a system of mutually defining temporal and causal relations is in the process of being established. Third, there is the simultaneous appearance of the many temporal adverbs, prepositions, and conjunctions that help to establish the system. The fact that linguistic components of the system appear in contrastive pragmatic use before they are used for their conventional temporal referents indicates that the linguistic forms precede and guide the acquisition of the concepts. In turn, the emerging temporal conceptual system may recruit forms for its own semantic purposes (as in the use of *yesterday* to refer to any not-now event). Subsequent experience with the uses of these forms may be expected to refine their meanings. However, the entire conventional system of temporal concepts is highly complex and is not established until well into the school years (Harner 1982).

There are many indications in the data from the months preceding these developments that both linguistic and conceptual fragments of such a system are in place. On the conceptual side, there is the early effort at 21 months (traced in Chapter 1), to lay out the account of an event in order by stringing together related utterances. At that early period neither verb form (tense) nor relational terms, nor for that matter, order of propositions, provides an adequate framework for making clear the relations involved, or for Emily to place herself in relation to the event recounted. On the linguistic side, there is the unsystematic use of irregular past verbs within these accounts, alternating with zero tense of the same verb (*come, came*), indicating that she has begun to suspect that these forms may play some useful role within such accounts, but does not yet know what role they play.[7] As another example, there is her use at 21 months of the term *so,* which subsequently drops from use and then emerges again within a causal-temporal system. This progression seems to indicate sequentially awareness of the linguistic form, some guess about its usefulness in discourse contexts, an attempt to use it in those contexts, failure to identify its specific function (thus its dropping out), followed by the placement of it within an appropriate system. Thus on both sides, at 21 and 22 months there are already fragments of the system to come: on the conceptual side, the felt need to order events; on the linguistic side, the beginning uses of forms that will fulfill some of the needed functions.

The argument can be summarized as follows. Assume that there is a natural (not language-dependent) system for understanding sequence and duration (as emerging evidence from infants affirms; see, for example, Mandler 1988). The linguistically organized temporal system builds on this by providing the particular forms that are needed for organization in culturally appropriate ways. For Emily, learning the English system of temporal distinctions, it is not a far step to acquire the forms that establish present activity as a fixed point in a sequence of events such that events that happened before that point are designated past and events that happen after that point are designated future.

It need not be this way, however. As Whorf (1956) argued based on evidence from Hopi, time is not treated in all linguistic systems as a system of linearly arranged units, but may be alternatively treated as a stream of recurrent events. It may seem overly speculative to suggest that Emily's early protonarratives could as well be organized within that system as within the "Standard Average European" (SAE) "time-line." I base this suggestion on the total lack of evidence that Emily distinguishes in these early passages whether events happened on one occasion or on many occasions, were or were not distinct from one another, might or might not happen again. Rather, her monologues up to the middle of her twenty-fourth month suggest that her notion of events in time is quite undifferentiated.

It may be concluded therefore that there is a dialectic relation between the linguistic forms Emily encounters and the natural underlying system of event organization she brings to bear on them. She both adjusts the linguistic system of contrasts to fit her conceptual roles and in turn adjusts her conceptual organization to fit the linguistic system. As a result she moves from a prior state in which she views events in terms of the objective and subjective roles she plays in them within an undifferentiated "now–not now" time scheme—to a state in which there is one subjective-objective self within a differentiated temporal order where different roles can be designated by different grammatical distinctions of subjects, objects, verbs, and adverbs, and relative times can be established through a variety of grammatical mechanisms. Thus has her represented world expanded in its possibilities.

Establishment of the SAE Time-Line

There is a further development in Emily's system of temporal relationships that remains to be described, namely her emerging ability to organize speech time, reference time, and event time (Miller 1978; Smith 1980; Weist 1986; see discussion in Chapter 5). Surprisingly, this ability to manipulate complex temporal relationships begins to emerge at about the same time as her mastery of tense and temporal adverbials.

The system of ordered temporal relationships that is realizable in

English follows the linear ordering that Whorf (1956) laid out in characterizing SAE languages as following a time-line that moves from future to past. This metaphor has been discussed extensively by linguists, philosophers, and psychologists (see, for example, Miller and Johnson-Laird 1976; Lakoff and Johnson 1980). It appears to have considerable psychological reality among those who speak SAE languages, even though the actual temporal relationships that may be invoked are far more complex and subtle than such a scheme allows. The investigation of Emily's capacity for representing relationships along a time-line permits a glimpse of both her organization of events and the considerable complexity involved in even such a seemingly simple metaphor.

The speech time (ST), event time (ET), and reference time (RT) system was originally outlined by Reichenbach (1947). It has been utilized in the analysis of child language by Weist (1986) and by Smith (1980). In this scheme, it is held that sentences may encode ST, ET, and RT independently. Further, according to Weist, the child develops the system gradually, being at first confined to a system where ST, ET, and RT coincide (the "here and now" system). Weist relates the subsequent linguistic development of the child's time system to general conceptual development. The child is seen as first entering into an *ET system* at about 22 months (plus or minus 2 months). At this point the child may reference ET and ST independently, and is thus able to code past versus nonpast.[8] Of temporal adverbs at this point, there is only a possible *now,* according to Weist's analysis of child data from both English and Polish. Next a *restricted RT system* emerges at about 36 months (plus or minus 2 months), signaled by the onset of temporal adverbs, the use of temporal adverbial clauses such as "when *x* then *y,*" the use of *today, yesterday,* and *tomorrow,* but the absence of the temporal adverbs *before* and *after.* With this system the child can establish RT that fixes ET in relation to ST, by the use of terms such as *yesterday.* Not until sometime between 3½ and 4 years is the child capable of dealing with all three times simultaneously, and entering into a full *free RT system.* Then the child can establish RT at some point prior to or subsequent to ST and fix ET at a third point in relation to it. At this point the child uses *before* and *after* and the present perfect form of the verb to achieve these complexities.

Note that Weist's scheme refers to the development of temporal relations at the sentence level. In comparison, the ordering of events within even a very simple narrative consisting of several related statements can become quite complex, and it might be expected that the ability to handle temporal relations at this level would be delayed still further (see Karmiloff-Smith 1986). Considering the complexities of Emily's system of expressing temporal relations, it is of interest to examine her expression of RT-ET-ST relations in her narratives to see how her development relates to Weist's scheme.

Consider first the following portion of a narrative from 23;8:

My sleep	$ET_1 = RT_1$
Mommy came	$ET_2 = RT_1$
and Mommy "get up, get up time go home."	ET_3
When my slep and	$RT_1 = ET_1$
and Mormor came.	$RT_1?$
Then Mommy coming	$ET_2 = RT_1$
then "get up, time to go home."	ET_3
Time to go home.	ET_3
Drink p-water.	ET_4
Yesterday did that.	$RT_1 = ET\{1,2,3,4\}$
Now Emmy sleeping in regular bed.	$ST = RT_2$
	$= ET_5 > RT_1$

Here ET_1 indicates the first event in the activity sequence, ET_2 the second, and so on, while RT_1 indicates the reference time of the first event.

As noted in Chapter 1, this monologue circles back again and again. However, the segment quoted here provides sufficient data for the purposes of the present analysis. My gloss on this narrative is straightforward, although not without its ambiguities: Yesterday (actually earlier the same day) Emily was sleeping at Tanta's (or perhaps Mormor's) when Mommy (or Mormor) came and told her to get up because it was time to go home. They went home and she drank p-water (Perrier). (The alternative interpretation that Mommy said to drink p-water is ruled out by later versions that establish this as a separate action.)

Emily displays several characteristics of Weist's Stage 2 (restricted RT): she uses both temporal adverbs (*yesterday, now*) and adverbial clauses (*when my slep*) to establish RT separately from ST. This puts her considerably in advance of the age norms Weist projected. More interestingly, it indicates that she can manipulate these relations with minimal mastery of the tense system itself. Note the inconsistent use of tenses in this segment: Mommy *came*, Mommy *coming*; my *sleep*, my *slept* (and in another version, *my sleeping*). Yet from another perspective, she appears to be attempting to contrast tenses to set up temporal relations.[9] For example, in the first two lines: my *sleep* (RT) followed by Mommy *came* (ET); and in lines 4 and 6: my *slep* (RT), then Mommy *coming* (ET). The last three lines here also contrast in an interesting way: *drink* (ET3), *did* that (RT = ET {1,2,3,4}), *sleeping* (ST = ET5). Present is used for the event time in the narrative, past to indicate reference time for the narrative, and progressive to indicate now, speech time.

From the point of view of sentence structure, then, this segment represents an imperfect attempt at restricted reference time. But when viewed in terms of extended discourse, namely as an attempt to construct a narrative, the effort is much more impressive. In the narrative, the speaker must go beyond sentential relations to relate events to one another over time. In this simple segment, what Emily accomplishes is to set up a reference time, not for one event, but for a sequence of actions that are ordered in relation to one another. We can envision this in terms of positions along a time-line, as follows:

$$RT = ET_1 \rightarrow ET_2 \rightarrow ET_3 \rightarrow ET_4 \longrightarrow ST$$

Given these relations, the narrator must first refer back in time to establish the beginning point (my sleep) and then move forward toward the present in the order of the actions (events 1, 2, 3, and 4), finally moving to the present to reestablish speech time in relation to the totality of the events recounted (yesterday did *that,* now Emmy sleeping). When viewed in this way it is clear that Emily is not restricted to an RT = ET system, but rather is able to use events as references for subsequent ones. That is, "Mommy coming" serves as the RT for the ET of Mommy saying "get up," which serves in turn as the RT for the ET of "Drink p-water." The RT system may not yet be quite free, but it is already quite complex.

Consider next a fragment from five months later at 28 months. Here a portion of the dialogue is first reproduced to provide context (the only reference in the dialogue to a race) for the monologue that follows (produced here in virtual entirety).

Dialogue
F: . . . and Daddy went for a race,
     and we went to Childworld,
        bought an easel,
E: And then you were a tiger racing!

Monologue
Race . . .
and he ran in a race . . .   (RT1 = ET1)
a race, a regular race,
and and John's daddy went with him   (RT1 = ET2)
but when he came back then John's daddy was going
back,   (RT2 = ET3 = ET4)
and he did . . .

In this segment the focus is not on Emily but on two male participants—her own father, presupposed as "he," and "John's daddy."
Here it is clear that Emily has control of simple-past-tense forms and
is able to manipulate two past forms in relation to each other ("when
he *came* back, then John's daddy *was going* back"), consistent with
the adverbial clause structure setting up RT and ET (when . . . then).[10]
(Other examples from this period support this claim; see Chapters 2–
5.) Of course, as a report this segment is hardly adequate, leaving
many ambiguities. To what and whom does the final "he did" refer?
But as an example of increasing control over grammatical devices for
ordering events in discourse it is of considerable interest.

Consider next a segment of the doll-buying account at 33 months:

(but) when we went to the s-s-store we didn't have our jacket
on   (RT1 = ET1)
but I saw some dolly   (ET2)
and I yelled at my mother and said "I want one of those
dolly."   (ET3)
So after we were finished with the store,   (RT2 = ET4)
we went over to the dolly,   (ET5)
and she bought me one.   (ET6)

At this age Emily has acquired more of the devices she needs for
establishing relative order among events in a narrative. In addition to
the control of past tense and relative adverbial clauses, she uses *after*
to establish event time separately from reference time. It seems quite
clear that at this point she has reached Weist's stage of free RT, if she
had not before. Yet I would claim that, despite her incomplete mastery of linguistic devices in the first segment, she was attempting there
the same sort of conceptual temporal ordering that she achieves here.

Indeed, the argument I would like to make is that it is precisely this
struggle to order events conceptually that drives Emily to the mastery

of the complexities involved in tense usage, adverbial clauses, temporal adverbials, and all the rest of the armamentarium that she displays by the age of 3 years. But the argument is incomplete. It is precisely the availability of the linguistic devices that enables her to construct this neat story. At 23 months her linguistic immaturity drives her to construct and reconstruct the same account four times, each time reworking the relations. By 33 months she is able to manipulate the grammar to produce a coherent account the first time around. Thus it is the conceptual need in conjunction with the linguistic framework that enables her to reconstruct her experience and make it available for further reflection.

Conclusion

In the first section of this chapter I traced the reorganization of a system of self-reference, beginning at 24 months. At approximately the same period the system of temporal reference emerged, and over the succeeding months it underwent significant development. By 33 months Emily had acquired most of the grammatical devices necessary to construct narratives that related events in which she and others took part within a well-organized temporal scheme. Although the evidence is circumstantial and indirect, my claim is that these two systems—self-reference and temporal reference—developed over the same period of time because they are both essential to the construction of self within a temporally organized social world. Beyond this, this overview of the development of some of the elements of the system for constructing connected discourse and expressing notions of self and time therein has established some important points, beyond the particular systems under examination, that deserve particular emphasis.

One point that has been made repeatedly here is that Emily's speech in the monologues reveals competencies that are not revealed in her dialogic speech. There are two probable interacting reasons for this. First, the purpose of discourse in the monologue is different. Clearly part of the purpose is to recount and account for different types of experience, and this requires the connected discourse in which her special competencies are expressed. In dialogue she contributes to but does not sustain connected discourse. Second, the cognitive and linguistic demands of the two situations are different. In the dialogue she must adapt her speech to the other speaker(s), maintaining relevant comments on established topics. An analysis of her ability to do this with increasing competence would show a different type of pragmatic development from the one traced here. In monologue, she is free from the interactive requirements and can follow her own path without the need to take a listener into account.

This point has important methodological implications. It may be that most children possess greater linguistic ability than is revealed in their dialogic contributions. We are accustomed to thinking of the dialogic partner as helping the child to achieve communicative competence through framing and scaffolding (Bruner 1983). We tend to forget that the conversational format is a demanding one, placing restrictive requirements on the participants for taking turns, maintaining topic, taking account of the listener's perspective, and so on (Bloom, Rocissano, and Hood 1976; Levinson 1983; Jarvella and Klein 1982). Clearly, child-language studies need more data from children talking while they are alone in order to test the hypothesis that in the general case children may have important competencies that are masked in interactive situations.

This point is related to the next one. The particular competencies revealed in Emily's monologues are specifically those relevant to the construction of connected discourse, as virtually all of the previous chapters have documented. The title of this book reflects this emphasis. But these findings go against the conventional wisdom in child-language research, which views the development of language as proceeding from word to phrase to sentence to discourse, each larger unit building on the preceding smaller one,[11] and within the sentence morphological marking preceding transformations and complex clause combinations. Karmiloff-Smith (1986) suggests in fact that prior to the age of 5 the child is building a "practical" sentence grammar, which then becomes reorganized during the succeeding years to reflect the requirements of connected discourse.

Emily's progress seems quite different from this common description. As noted in the Introduction, in her monologic language her sentence grammar reflects complex clausal structures before morphology. More strikingly, her monologues reveal from the beginning the effort to connect related clauses in sequence, and the developments traced in this and other chapters reveal the sustained progress she makes. There is no waiting here for the completion of a sentence grammar before a discourse grammar becomes the focus. Rather, the two progress together, and we can argue that many aspects of the sentence-level grammar, including the system of temporal reference that is the focus of this chapter, are constructed on the basis of their role in connected discourse.

Again, this point has implications for methodology in the study of child language. As we have found in studying preschool children's scripts (French and Nelson 1985), when called upon to produce a connected account of an event, young children display a command of relatively complex language structures that are not usually found in their interactive speech. Thus there is precedent for the finding here that Emily's efforts at exposition and narrative reflect greater competencies in many of the more complex aspects of language structure than are found in her interactive speech. More studies of young children talking about their own experience (for example, Peterson and McCabe 1983) without the use of props or pictures, without the requirement of "telling a story," and without the demand of a turn-taking conversation, are called for to uncover now-unsuspected capacities for constructing connected discourse.

Finally, the intriguing interplay of the conceptual and linguistic levels that I have discussed in this chapter demands further intensive study. It is hard to escape the conclusion that Emily has a strong conceptual *need* to express certain relations, a need that drives her to acquire the relevant linguistic forms and structures. But at the same time, we see the linguistic forms in dialectical interaction with the conceptual structures, reshaping them and setting up new distinctions. The mutual determinism of concept and linguistic form is a vital topic in the contemporary focus on semiotic mediation (Mertz and Parmentier 1985; Wertsch 1985a, 1985b). More research of this kind is needed to trace similar developments in other children.

But this brings us back to a beginning point. To what extent can Emily's development be generalized to other children, even within her social class and culture? To what extent are the developments traced here unique to her practice of talking to herself about her experiences? Or to her parents' similar practices? Without further research we cannot know. We do know that not all children talk to themselves when alone, although many do. Are there differences in language development between those who do and those who do not? Emily is a very bright and highly verbal child, but we do not believe she is unique. Only further research can provide a definitive answer to these questions.

But even if the particular course of Emily's development were to turn out to be unusual or even unique in some way, this would not negate the lessons that her talk has taught us: the importance of observing noninteractive speech, the relevance of connected discourse to early language development, and the interdependent relationship of the conceptual and linguistic levels in early development.

Chapter 9

Crib Monologues from a Psychoanalytic Perspective

Daniel N. Stern

When Katherine Nelson first introduced us to Emily and her monologues from the crib, a potentially new "royal road" into the workings of the psyche seemed revealed. I felt as if we were observing, almost for the first time, mental transformations with considerable import for psychoanalysis, as well as for language and concept development.

In this chapter I shall try to view Emily's monologues from a psychoanalytic point of view, and equally try to view several psychoanalytic concepts from the newly permitted point of view of Emily's productions.

The central question that all of us address in these chapters, in one way or another, is why does a child engage in bedtime monologues when alone? And what purpose do they serve? Strictly speaking there can be no psychoanalytic answer to these questions because Emily has not, and could not have at her age, entered into the analytic process that discovers and constructs psychoanalytic explanations. Nonetheless, several issues central to psychoanalysis and Emily's monologues can be addressed.

The Role of "Major Life Events"

Emily has experienced at least four life events that are major in the sense of being (presumably) very affective, novel, unexpected, rare, and suddenly transforming of her social and affective world. These are: (1) a change in her bedroom at age 21 months, in preparation for (2) the birth of her brother at 23 months (including the pregnancy before and her mother's two-day absence in the hospital for delivery),

309

(3) a long plane trip to visit her grandmother at 29 months, and (4) entering nursery school on a regular basis at 31 months. All these qualify as potentially traumatic events.

The importance of these life events and the themes associated with them in psychoanalysis rests on the specialness given them by patients in reconstructing their life histories and equally on theoretical grounds related to basic sources of anxiety such as separations, threatened loss of love, and sibling rivalry. Psychoanalysis is not alone in marking these kinds of events as being of major importance.

One might have predicted that these "important life event themes" would be well represented in Emily's monologues. And that one of the functions of her monologues would be to rework and work through these events or—had they been truly traumatic—to repeat or relive them. (Or perhaps that is the work of dreams and not bedtime reveries.) But in fact these life events and their themes are not heavily represented, as several authors have commented (for example, see Chapter 1). And when they are, they are not especially marked with affect. A good example of how such an event is handled is the first monologue about Emily's room change and her brother's arrival.

> Daddy didn't bring in the baby room. Cause the baby (?) and diapers the baby room, but Daddy must Emmy in this room, cause the baby sleeping in um . . . room. Daddy brought this (in the magoo). Emmy sleeping in this (magoo-goo) cause the (bath) this in the baby in there. Then Emmy's stay other room that's where the baby. This is Emmy room. This where Emmy sleeps. (Nap) time Emmy go bed and napped. Sometimes Emmy take napping. Sometimes Emmy take bed(room). Time go bed. Emmy sometimes take nap . . . nap sometimes (my bed . . . room). (23;11)

It has been argued that when Emily's affect is too high (such as on the very night her mother and new brother come home from the hospital) her monologue is disrupted by affect and she cries out for her father rather than elaborate a monologue.

Even when her affect is not so high as to disrupt the making of monologue, these important life event themes are not well represented in the monologue corpus. But might not they be present in a disguised form? If they were disguised (displaced, condensed, reversed, and so on), that would imply that Emily already had the capacity for that kind of transformation among symbols—and that she had a defensive reason for the disguise, such as to mitigate their affective force (more on this below).

In any event, I cannot make a convincing case that the thematic material of the monologues consists to any predominating extent of the major life themes in disguise. The vast majority of the monologue material is about things other than these themes.

Might not, however, the questions and uncertainties raised by major life events be the nonspecific engine behind Emily's searchings and questionings and problem solving about almost everything? Feldman (Chapter 3) raises and dismisses the idea that Emily's daily engagement with the "puzzles" around her is a substitute for the major puzzles posed by life events, especially the puzzle of why her new brother arrived on the scene and displaced her from her room and from her parents' unshared attention. And I am inclined to agree with Feldman. If Emily's bursts of questioning and searching in her monologues were triggered by or reflective of the presence of perturbations from major life events, we would expect some systematic association between the two. The advent of potentially perturbing life events is fairly discrete in some cases and limited in time—at least their novelty is. The production of monologues, however, is quite continuous. In sum, no convincing evidence exists that major life events are *the* trigger, *the* engine or *the* subject matter of Emily's monologues. However, like other less dramatic (from our point of view) events they may be included in the monologue process.

There is one other way to consider a special role for major life events in monologue. And this concerns the question just raised: From whose point of view do we judge a life event to be "major" or "important"?

"Sibling rivalry," "threatened loss of love," and other major life themes that have earned a privileged place in psychoanalytic thinking are from our point of view general themes. A child of 2 or so years could never abstract such general life themes. Children would get caught up in the many diverse lived events that taken together and abstracted could become these general life themes. The lived events that Emily chooses for narration are not these larger themes disguised but rather smaller daily events that are intertwined with other daily events. We cannot know, from her point of view, which small lived events will ultimately contribute to her construction of these life themes (assuming they are one day to be so constructed with or without the help of the psychoanalytic process).

In short, the thematic material is present for a construction after the fact (après coup), built upon and around these major life events, as a psychoanalytic perspective might predict. However, at this point

Emily gives no strong evidence that she is starting to build these kinds of constructions. It looks as if such construction will be après coup, if at all, and not contemporaneous with the events when lived.

The Role of Nightly Separation

Separation is another major life event and theme. However, it requires different treatment because it occurs nightly—at bedtimes. And it is exactly at this moment that the Emily data are collected. The potential psychological importance of this moment in the day is well appreciated. During the second year of life, sleeping disturbances are far and away the most common reason for psychological consultation among the "psychofunctional" problems of childhood. And the majority of these include a going-to-sleep problem as well as repeated awakenings, nightmares, and so on. Extended going-to-sleep rituals or "sleep ceremonials" are generally part of the clinical picture, but these in themselves are usually little more than exaggerated normal rituals. The going-to-sleep ritual is very widely used to help the child make the transition to sleep—or to simply being alone.

Watson in Chapter 7 describes the basic elements of Emily's sleep ceremonials during the *dialogue,* which includes the deploying of various strategies to get her parents to remain in the room (these are part of the ceremonial) as well as formulaic terminations such as "I love you, Hon." And I believe she is right in arguing that the dialogues that precede the monologues must be seen primarily as going-to-sleep rituals, where the fact that the dialogue is leading up to separation is almost never out of Emily's or her parents' minds. I would also agree that this particular dialogic sleep ritual is well suited to transforming an insoluble affective conflict (separation) to a "soluble" or negotiable psycholinguistic interaction, and in so doing reducing the affective force of the situation.

The above discussion leaves unaddressed the question of what direct role the actual separation and its preceding ritualized interaction in dialogue plays in determining the monologues that follow. An appealing psychodynamic hypothesis is that separation distress or anxiety (after the parents have left the room) is the trigger and engine for the monologues, which serve to "hold on to" the parent in some manner, thus permitting Emily to pass into sleep without being fully alone. To push this hypothesis further, if the dialogic sleep ritual is totally successful Emily will fall asleep without having to elaborate a monologue. (Indeed, many nights she does go right off to sleep without a monologue. However, there is no independent way, besides her elaboration or not of a monologue, to determine the "success" of a dialogue in reducing her separation distress.) Most times, then, the ritual dialogue is successful enough to permit the parents to leave the room, but the remaining—though reduced—separation anxiety is still high enough to produce the monologue that will continue or finish, so to speak, the work of the dialogue.

What evidence exists for this hypothesis? Several authors have noted that Emily, in her monologues, will repeat words or phrases used just before by her parent in the dialogue (see, for example, Chapter 1). And this taking up of their words seems to have a reassuring effect. Similarly, does repeating or taking up topics and themes from the immediately preceding dialogue and bringing them into the monologue act as a form of "carrying" the absent parents into the monologue? Here the evidence cuts in both directions. Anticipations, or future talk, in Emily's monologues are based in large part on the parental dialogue. However, this is not true for memories or past talk (see Chapter 1). Do memories or past talk, compared to future talk, only follow upon a very successful reduction of separation anxiety during the dialogue, or are they just a different way to recreate the presence of the parents, or neither of these?

Besides taking up the parents' phrases or topics from the dialogue, there is a third way to bring them along into the monologue. This is to envoice the parent—to take on the parent's voice. (Dore deals with this in Chapter 6.) This process seems to come closest to a direct form of identification which "holds on to" the parents or "brings them along" into the monologue world.

There is yet another way that the monologue can "hold on to" the presence of others. A tenet of current self-psychology is that the maintenance of the self-system is a continuous process, and that the "presence" of internalized others is a requisite of self-regulation. To put this most simply, one is very rarely all alone, mentally. Other persons who help to regulate our momentary states of being are internalized in various forms depending on one's theoretical persuasion (introjects, in traditional psychoanalysis; self-objects, Kohut 1977; self-regulating-others, Stern 1985). These internalized others are always activated to some extent so that self-regulation (even when physically all alone) occurs in the representational context of relatedness with others. Under stress or distress or anything that threatens the equilibrium of the self-system (such as separation) the internalized others are that much more activated. From this point of view, one can construe both Emily's future talk and her past talk as types of activation of internalized others to help her self-regulate under the anxiety of separation. This kind of self-regulation need not be very specific. She does not have to activate a self-regulating-other in the act of holding and soothing her—that is, the specific complementary action to resolve her separation distress. Rather, a nonspecific mental peopling of her world will do. And she can accomplish this through future talk or through evoking others by activating memories of being with them.

At this point it is worth noting that in the preverbal, prenarrative period of life toward the end of the first year and in the second year of life, it is not at all uncommon for infants to "sing" to themselves at bedtime after the parents have left the room. This "singing" can take several forms or genres. There is the repetitive, rhythmic, low-tension groaning that accompanies each expiration—almost like a motor idling. There are the often quite melodic lines sung with the mouth open—containing a simple few-note melody that undergoes variations, or rather that wanders. There is the humming of something like scales up and down. And there is the regular repetition of two notes, high-low, high-low. (This list is from anecdotal reports and not the product of a systematic examination.)

The developmental relationship between these forms and the different genres of monologue merits study. It seems likely that some "songs" are self-regulating in the sense of creating a reassuring surround of sound. Other songs may accompany certain kinds of mental activity and/or affective state. Within this context, it is worth raising an unlikely possibility: Suppose Emily is sleep-talking during part of some of the monologues—or for all of a selected group of them. We think of the different states of sleep and wakefulness and drowsiness as distinct categorical semistable states of the central nervous system during which different types and processes of mental operations occur. In this light, could some of the differences in types of monologues be due to differences in states of consciousness during the fluctuating and quantal shifts between waking and sleep—each with its own functions and forms and even, possibly, antecedents in prenarrative crib songs?

To summarize the situation with regard to the context of nightly separation, it would seem that some monologues, or parts of some monologues, may be designed to "hold onto" the parents, via their

words, phrases, topics, or "voices." However, the majority of monologues do not seem to be especially designed for this purpose. But
whatever the other purposes of monologue, if it recreates the "presence" of others by activating internal representation of self-with-
others, it will have served the self-regulating function of mitigating
separation anxiety to some extent.

At times, in the monologues, not only does it appear that Emily is
not struggling with separation, it appears that she may even enjoy
being alone. Once the bedtime ceremony is closed, she can settle com-
fortably into the different world of monologue to do something else,
on her own. Some older children savor this moment of the day. We
can now consider some of those other things she may be doing with
monologue.

The Role of World Making and Problem Solving

It may seem disappointing to holders of some versions of the psychoanalytic perspective that no strong convincing evidence has emerged
to implicate major life events and their traditional psychoanalytic
themes, separation in particular, in the form and function of Emily's
monologues. But this is fully compatible with the psychoanalytic notion of thematic construction après coup.

Instead, in much of this book a major emphasis has been placed on
world making and problem solving. A consideration of these two activities from a psychoanalytic perspective may be fruitful. By way of
introduction, I would like to take up one of Freud's most basic formulations of psychic functioning, the pleasure principle.

The pleasure principle in psychoanalysis can be interpreted very
narrowly in terms of excitation which disturbs a resting equilibrium
by adding a quantum of energy which is experienced as unpleasure
and pushes the psychic system to discharge energy equal to that introduced into the system. The discharge of energy and the return of the
system to equilibrium will be experienced as pleasure. Or, the pleasure principle can be interpreted more broadly and without the energy metaphor in terms of psychic systems at equilibrium, in states of
perturbation and disequilibrium, and in terms of the motives and
moves to reequilibrate the system at an old or new point of equilibrium. And this, of course, brings us to the narrative, its elements and
its engine. As described by Bruner and Lucariello in Chapter 2, the
engine of the narrative is "trouble," and trouble is an imbalance or

disequilibrium among the elements of the narrative pentad (the actor, the action, the goal or intention, the scene, and the instrumentality). How far is this from the pleasure principle or something very like it?

In Freud's original conceptualization, he was largely concerned with disequilibrium in psychosomatic systems such as hunger and sex. In this context the more narrow, energic (that is, related to discharge of libido) interpretation may suffice. However, when dealing with disequilibria in the representational world alone, the broader interpretation is needed. In this light, it is relevant that in arguing that Emily's main purpose is to make sense of events, Feldman says "Emily is *driven* by a *need* to explain . . ." and "Every puzzle involves a challenge to some stipulation of a *steady state*." Or, in Bruner's terms, *trouble*. But trouble in the narrative for Bruner and Lucariello and for Feldman is like excitation in the psyche for Freud. While this is not explicitly stated, disequilibrium in the narrative pentad is seen as a drive, in the sense of an inherent motivating force.

Is this drive different from the desire to know, from curiosity, from the tendency to avoid or resolve cognitive dissonance, and so on? Perhaps not, but it arises in a different context, namely, it is situated entirely in the internal world of representations and concerns the coherence of a story. And here we rejoin a central theme in current psychoanalysis.

Much current thinking in psychoanalysis has been influenced by the work on narrative and by the realization that almost all psychoanalytic data is in the form of narratives (Ricoeur 1977; Spence 1976; Schafer 1981). When so considered, the clinical work of psychoanalysis becomes the co-construction (between patient and analyst) of a life story (the narrative) that is most coherent, comprehensive, continuous, commonsensical, and so on. The center of gravity switches from reconstructing the past *accurately*, to creating a story of the past *coherently* and helpfully.

Once the child has reached the stage at which narratives of her own experience are possible, such narratives become obligatory. And the mental system involved in the construction and reconstruction of narratives functions like other motivational subsystems such as hunger, sex, or curiosity. Narratives do not simply tell about motivational forces in other aspects of life (like hunger or love); the narrative system has its own built in motivational forces. What Bruner and Lucariello mean by the need or desire to tell a narrative "well" is an aesthetic problem from one point of view. From another, it is the goal of a motivational force.

(There is something optimistic about this viewpoint. Hermeneutic psychoanalysis has struggled o've the issue of how many different adequate—that is, therapeutic—life histories could be co-constructed from the same life material, in a psychoanalytic process, and what are the criteria for choosing the best: coherence, comprehensiveness, or continuity of life story, or functional grounds such as helpfulness in current life. The notion of a narrative system that inherently seeks the best balance between the elements of the narrative pentad is encouraging. It does not, however, resolve the issue.)

One might argue that in considering the narrative system we are largely discussing the domain of cognition, not that of affect, motive, or action. In fact we are dealing with the domains of affect, motive, action, and cognition as represented, that is, with lived experience as represented. This is the stuff of psychoanalysis and can hardly be considered affectively "cold."

There are two aspects of the above that have interesting implications for psychoanalysis. The first is the conceptualization of a motivational system operating in the representational world itself, independent of the motives and affects that are represented. The workings of this motivational force is particularly clear in Emily's monologues, where one can see (hear) her being pushed to solve the problems posed by the narrative form.

The second concerns the role of developmental history in psychoanalysis. One of the implications of the narrative view of psychoanalysis is that the importance of actual historical happenings in childhood is relatively small. After all, historical truth has given way—in great part—to the balance, cohesion, continuity, and so on, of the narrative. One unfortunate effect of this shift is that, among some hermeneutic psychoanalytic thinkers (Schafer 1981; Green 1975), developmental psychology including developmental psycholinguistics has been determined to be less and less relevant to the central concerns of psychoanalysis proper. From this perspective, developmental studies are considered to be no more relevant than anthropology, mythology, and so on. Data like the Emily data reopen this question on two levels. First, we can now look at the developmental history of the child's construction of an event—not the event itself, but its representation as revealed in narrative. This kind of ontogenetic history does not run into the same epistemological problems as the more traditional search for the association between earlier "fact," or historical truth, and later construction (après coup) or reconstruction, which exist at different levels. Now we can compare early (pre-oedipal) narrations with later ones, when both exist at the same epistemological level. Secondly, we can now examine the developmental history of the basic unit of hermeneutic psychoanalytic theory—the narrative. Certainly that reexamination cannot fail to have special relevance for psychoanalysis.

The Narrative Self

I have argued in detail elsewhere (Stern 1985) that different senses of the self emerge in the first few years of life. In brief, a "core" sense of self starts to emerge after the second or third month. It consists of a sense of agency, coherence, continuity, and affectivity. It is a sense of self that is nonreflective and not conscious.

Beginning around the ninth month of life a "subjective" sense of self starts to emerge. It consists of the appreciation—again nonreflectively and nonconsciously—of having subjective states of mind that may or may not be shared with others, who, also, are perceived as having separate subjective experiences. This new subjective sense of self permits intersubjectivity and intersubjective exchange. Contents of mind such as the focus of attention, intentions, and affective states can now be shared.

Beginning around 15–18 months a "verbal" sense of self begins to organize. This is the sense of self that is self-reflective and permits an objectivation of the self as evidenced in use of pronouns, in mirror behavior, in deferred imitation, and in symbolic play.

Each of these senses of self is viewed as organizing subjective perspectives about the self. At points of developmental discontinuity there are thought to occur major "bio-behavioral shifts" (Emde et al. 1976). These are roughly between 2–3 months, a lesser one around 7 months, again at 9–12 months, and again at around 15–18 months. At each shift there is the maturational unfolding of many new capacities in the domains of cognition, affect, motivation, and motor activity. With the advent of these new capacities the infant must create a new subjective perspective about herself that organizes her new abilities. This is what is meant by an organizing subjective perspective. And each new sense of self is a new organizing subjective perspective. Each new sense of self opens a new domain of experience, but does not necessarily fully absorb, or obliterate or encompass, the previous senses of self. All senses of self are viewed as coexisting together.

Sometime after the second year—earlier in Emily's case—a new sense of self emerges, the narrative sense of self. This too is the result, in part, of new capacities in language and conceptualization. Many of the chapters in this book have focused exactly here, on the nature of the development of new conceptual and linguistic capacities and the dialectic between them. These new capacities force Emily to reorganize her subjective perspective about who she is, and how she is in relation with others—but now she does it in the domain of narrative.

This reorganization requires that she learn to represent in narrative form the basic senses of self that she has already sensed in a different domain of experience. Thus, much of the "work" that she performs in her monologues transforms experiences of agency, coherence, continuity, affectivity, intersubjectivity, and self-reflection into the domain of narration. This process clearly need not be a dialogic one and is probably best done in monologue, which is free of the many constraints of the dialogue form.

The task Emily is undertaking in these monologues is the creation of her narrative self. And it is this self—that is, this same epistemological form—that she will build upon for the rest of her life in explaining herself to herself and to others. She is crossing the great gulf, in psychoanalytic terms, between a reconstructable and an unreconstructable past.

Notes

Introduction. Monologues in the Crib

1. The ease of making these recordings may be compared with the complex apparatus arranged by the Weirs in the early 1960s.
2. Weir's analysis utilized phonemic transcriptions of her own son's speech. The primary problem she noted in transcription was in identifying "functionally significant units unequivocally" (1962, 29). Kuczaj (1983) does not discuss the transcription problem or the problem of identifying units or utterances in the monologues. He reports high (99–100 percent) agreement between two transcribers based on samples of 100 utterances. Although we recognize the ambiguities such data present, we are quite confident that these have not resulted in gross distortions of the analyses.
3. This characteristic is not unique to children's speech or to monologue but obtains in normal adult discourse as well (Brown and Yule 1983). These characteristics of Emily's monologues are similar to those identified by Weir (1962) and discussed in terms of "paragraphs."
4. Kuczaj (1983) found no significant difference in MLU between social-context speech and crib speech for the 14 children in his sample; their average MLU was 2.4 for social-context speech and 2.3 for crib speech. There were, however, individual differences among children in the relation between crib speech and social-context speech over time on this measure. From the graphed data Kuczaj presented there did not appear to be any child in that sample who exhibited the significant discrepancy between the two contexts that we find for Emily. Because all of the social-context speech recorded for Emily was in pre-bed talk with her parents, it might be that the difference was exaggerated, and that a wider scan of speech contexts might have revealed a lesser difference or even none at all. It must be borne in mind, however, that Emily's language skills, by the MLU measure, were more advanced than those of any of the other children whose crib speech has been reported.

5. Brief reports of crib monologues by other investigators include Black (1979), Britton (1970), Jesperson (1922), and Pickert (1981). These are summarized by Kuczaj (1983).
6. The six functions are the emotive, conative, referential, phatic, poetic, and metalingual. See Bruner (1975) for further explanation and discussion in relation to child speech.
7. See Nelson and Levy (1987) for a more complete analysis of the development of functions in Emily's discourse using Halliday's scheme.
8. There are also data demonstrating that 2-year-olds engage in non-social speech in the presence of others (Furrow 1984); thus Vygotsky's presumptive age of onset may in general be late.
9. But, as noted in Chapter 5, her speech in play sequences with her "friends" in the crib may be viewed in terms of a self-regulatory function. These sequences play a minor role in the monologues as a whole and are not a major focus of our analyses. Also see Chapter 7 for a discussion of the relation between other-regulation in the dialogue and self-regulation in the monologue.
10. "Event" is used by different authors in different ways. Some (e.g., Gerhardt, Chapter 5) use "event" in a micro sense to refer to any action: for example, "Daddy get Emmy." In my use, the term generally refers to rather long sequences of related actions, such as the event of having lunch, although I recognize that such events can be decomposed into smaller event units (Nelson 1986). Familiar event sequences form the basis for the formation of generalized event representations, or scripts.

1. Monologue as Representation of Real-Life Experience

1. I use the term "narrative" here in a loose rather than a technical sense, for lack of any better term. We could use "protonarrative" to indicate that Emily's productions do not meet some criteria of narrative organization, but this would leave us with the problem of deciding just when a protonarrative becomes a narrative. Here I use "narrative" to refer to all of her productions that reference sequenced events. Similarly, I use the terms "topic" and "proposition" informally and not in a technical sense applicable to the analysis of adult discourse. My concern here is not to set up formal criteria, but to uncover important aspects of this unusual developmental data set.
2. There is little evidence that Emily distinguishes memory for a specific event from the general category of "not now" in the early months (Nelson 1985; also see Chapters 5 and 8). That is, past, future, and general events may be undifferentiated, forming a global category of events displaced from the ongoing reality of the phenomenological present. This possibility and the difficulty of viewing the development of specific time

concepts independently of the acquisition of temporal language are considered in Chapter 8.

3. The selection of tenses is more complex than this statement implies and is integrally involved in the development of narrative form (see Chapter 5).

4. Of course what was novel for Emily might be quite routine for an adult. A trip on a bus was counted as novel, as were airplane trips, although neither would be novel for most readers of this book.

5. An additional analysis took into account the extent of such episodes in terms of number of turns in the dialogues and number of intonation units in the monologues. The two analyses revealed the same trends.

6. At 29–30 months there is a low frequency of all types; this was a time when Emily spent much of her naptime looking at books and reciting stories and songs.

7. Of course I do not claim that Emily has control of an explicit deductive logic system, but it is clear from these constructions that she works within an implicit system of inferential logic.

8. Lieberman (1967, 1984) hypothesizes that the breath-group is a phonological construct with perceptual, physiologic, and linguistic reality. He suggests that "human speakers usually segment the flow of speech into sentences, or other syntactic units, by grouping words in complete expirations" (1984, 118). See also Crystal (1975) and McNeill (1979). Thus at 2 years Emily apparently was using the same basic speech-production unit that adult speakers use.

9. Chafe measured length of IUs in words, but the morpheme measure provides a way of indicating increasing grammatical competence over time as Emily acquires the various grammatical inflections. This difference means that the length of Emily's units is overstated in comparison to those identified in adult speech by Chafe.

10. I do not mean to imply here that efficiency is necessarily a desirable end in itself. However, it may be an important dimension of development. See also Peterson and McCabe (1983).

11. As will be seen later, this does not imply that each IU tended to express half a proposition; rather, it measures the prevalence of repetition, false starts, paraphrasing, and returning to an earlier point in the narrative.

12. The structure of this and the next episode seems similar in some ways to those described by Weir: "the paragraph at times is not only delimited by a change of topic or by a change of linguistic exercise, but by a larger circular, rondo-like construction. Frequently, it ends just as it began. Moreover, smaller closed constructions occur, as part of the larger circle, and, after we have been led back to the beginning, a new round just like the completed one may be started, a structure parallel to rounds in songs" (1962, 146). Recall that Anthony was 28–30 months old at the

time of Weir's recordings, but in many ways was at an earlier stage of language development than Emily was at 21 months.

13. This practice might eventually lead to the immature structure posited by Chafe of no intermediate closures within a narrative. This is speculation only, however, since we have no evidence of this and no data for Emily beyond 36 months.

14. Recall that I analyzed the most coherent narratives from each time period. Thus circular organization may not disappear from the data, but may continue to be typical of problematic or less well organized episodes.

15. This is not to be taken as a claim that narrative in general does or should move forward in this relentless way. However, for a child just gaining control over this mode of discourse the observation seems reasonable.

2. *Monologue as Narrative Recreation of the World*

1. This research was facilitated by grants from the Spencer Foundation and by a Postdoctoral Fellowship from the National Institute of Mental Health (National Research Service Award 1-F32-MH09296) to the second author.

2. After this chapter was completed, additional Vygotsky manuscripts became available. It turns out that Vygotsky was indeed interested in the socialization of affect, and concerned himself with the manner in which affective arousal becomes shaped by the linguistic account the child develops to "make sense" of the affect-arousing situation. His discussion, however, does not deal directly with the issues we are addressing here (see Bruner's Prologue, in Vygotsky 1987).

3. *Monologue as Problem-Solving Narrative*

1. "Well-formed, extended monologic sequences" are sequences that meet certain somewhat inexact criteria. By "extended" I mean longer than two or three propositions, long enough to try to tell a story. "Well-formedness" is harder. One matter at issue is whether there is a story-like pattern: whether the narrative begins with something that sets up a story context, has a middle that develops details within it, and an end that looks like an effort toward resolution or meaning. Another matter is whether the narrative includes markers of Emmy's mental states, or perspective—a landscape of consciousness as well as of action. But both narrative types analyzed here have more specific features that are described in the text.

2. The sample of dialogue was randomly selected. It consisted of 59 words from 21;0, 128 words from 23;10, 222 words from 26;2, and 153 words from 33;9. The monologues were *all* of the well-formed type that we

identified. The monologues cover a period from 22;11 to 34;9, nearly the full range of the sample. They are distributed by month as follows:

Age (months)	Temporal monologues	Problem-solving monologues
22	2	0
23	7	5
24	1	2
25	2	2
26	2	2
27	0	1
28	1	1
29	1	3
30	1	1
31	0	0
32	1	1
33	2	2
34	0	1
35	1	0

3. *Editor's note:* Emily's mother reported that "mole" was a game they played in which Emily's mother covered Emily's head with her sweater.
4. *Editor's note:* Carl's mother's name is Chris; thus if Emily is (pretending to be) Carl, her mother's name must be Chris.

4. Monologue as Development of the Text-Forming Function of Language

1. Weir notes that the names in this passage are those of close family friends. The father's name is Bob, sometimes called "big Bob" by Anthony to distinguish him from his son, Bobby; the mother's name is Nancy.
2. The following passage from Weir (1962) is also striking as a chain of associations:

    1. Alice (calling)
    2. Mommy (4x—calling)
    3. Mommy's too weak
    4. Alice strong
    5. Alice too weak (2x)
    6. Daddy's too weak
    7. Mommy's too weak
    8. Too weak with Barbara
    9. Be careful Barbara

10. Barbara can broke
11. Careful broke the (rami)
12. Careful broke Anthony
13. Careful broke it (2x)
14. Careful broke the
15. Broke the finger
16. Broke the Bobo
17. Broke the vacuum clean
18. The broke
19. (begi phu)
20. Get some broke
21. Broke the
22. Alice broke the baby fruit
23. Alice almost dropped
24. It's David fruit
25. Look (2x)
26. All right
27. Lady
28. Mama

3. Note that in addition to the use of formulaic phrases, discourse units are undoubtedly bounded as well by paralinguistic devices (such as intonation contours) and extralinguistic cues (gestures, shifts in body motion, and so on). All of these provide structural cues for Emily to use both in segmenting her father's speech and in creating her own discourse units.

4. This seems to be based in part on "Rockabye Baby." Note semantic and lexical similarities: "when the bough breaks the cradle will fall, and down will come baby, cradle and all." Note also that this progresses for the most part from more to less explicit NPs.

5. Weir (1962) noted a third type of nonreferential linkage. She observed pronominal usages in Anthony's speech based on formal parallelisms with earlier utterances, as in:

> find *it*
> with juice
> drink *it* (2x).

Here the pronoun in the last line is produced to match the pattern established in the first line. On Weir's interpretation the pronoun's co-occurring verb, *drink,* is evoked by the preceding nominal, *juice.*

6. It should be noted that this model—of the highlighting of formal properties on the basis of metalinguistic procedures—does not imply that the earliest uses of pronouns lack a functional basis. Rather, the introduction of the forms into the child's repertoire suggests that there may be an

initial functional basis to their use. (Otherwise, one would need to ask why these particular forms have been acquired and not others.) The child-language literature supports this conjecture. Observations of young children's participation in dialogue, for example, suggest that children's single-word utterances serve a relatively consistent function relative to adult speech. Specifically, there is evidence that children's utterances in dialogue tend to reflect that which cannot be presupposed on the basis of the remarks of other interactional participants; single-word utterances tend to mark "new information" (Greenfield 1979; Keenan and Schieffelin 1976), as in the following example (from Keenan and Schieffelin 1976):

> Mother: (trying to put too large diaper on doll, holding diaper on)
> Well we can't hold it on like that. What do we need? Hmmm?
> What do we need for the diaper?
> Child: Pin.

From this point of view, the task that awaits the child at this early stage of language development is to produce utterances in which "old information" is formally marked as well—an ability that underlies the appropriate use of cohesive pronouns.

5. Monologue as a Speech Genre

1. A different version of the material in this chapter appeared in the Journal of Child Language 15, no. 2 (1988):337–393, under the title "From Discourse to Semantics: The Development of Verb Morphology and Forms of Self-Reference in the Speech of Two-Year-Olds." Copyright © 1988 by Cambridge University Press; reprinted with the permission of Cambridge University Press. I would like to thank Richard Beckwith, Lois Bloom, Nancy Budwig, Michael Leyton, and Katherine Nelson for providing feedback on an earlier draft. Extensive critical commentary was also generously provided by Melissa Bowerman and Annette Karmiloff-Smith. Of course, none of the above should be assumed to agree with any of the claims made herein. The research was supported by two Post-Doctoral Research Fellowships in Child Development: NICHD #HD07196–04 and 05 at the City University of New York, and NICHD #07307-01 at the University of Chicago.
2. The most explicit version of this position is to be found in the work of Bronckart and Sinclair (1973), who claim that in French children differentially deploy verb morphology depending on objective features of real-world events (for example, the clause "a truck goes into a garage" receives a different inflection from that of "a fish swims around in a bowl"). Although the remaining studies in support of the "aspect before

tense" hypothesis are based on the child's marking of the lexical aspect of the verb, my impression is that this reduces to the same thing, since lexical aspect is taken to encode the inherent aspect of certain event-types objectively construed. Hence, if the child uses verb morphology to mark lexical aspect, this is, in essence, a transparent way of marking objective event features.

3. In a notable exception, de Lemos (1981) proposes that children are socialized into the aspectual notions relevant for their language through structural properties inherent in prelinguistic mother-child interactive formats.

4. An exception is the work by Antinucci and Miller (1976), who claim that the Italian imperfect first appears in storytelling discourse, where the child is both "pretending" and referring to a "succession of events."

5. Kuczaj 1977, Smith 1980, and Harner 1981 report results for slightly older children that are similarly inconsistent with the aspect-before-tense hypothesis.

6. This analysis does not begin with the onset of data collection, but I also partially analyzed the earlier sessions. I will refer to them when they have any bearing on the discussion.

7. I must appeal to the linguists' characterization of adult usage, rather than to child-directed caretaker speech, because so little parental speech containing the target inflections was recorded. The grammaticality judgments used by linguists can yield quite different results from an investigation of the speech patterns found in actual usage. For an insightful discussion of this problem, see Ochs (1985).

8. The dialogues are much richer than they might seem from the selected examples—which are chosen only because they contain one of the target constructions.

9. This figure is a conservative judgment based only on decipherable utterances. For example, on the evening of 22;29, Emily's newborn brother comes home from the hospital. Her crib speech is prolific, but because she is crying throughout, her speech is impossible to decipher reliably (especially her verb morphology), and thus only one utterance from this session is included in the count.

7. Monologue, Dialogue, and Regulation

1. This analysis was done by Dr. Stephen Eady, at the Centre for Speech Technology Research, University of Victoria, Canada.

8. Monologue as the Linguistic Construction of Self in Time

1. See Gerhardt's Chapter 5 for a more detailed explication in terms of discourse intentions and perspectives.

2. This was the period analyzed by Gerhardt and Watson. These quantitative estimates for the earliest months must be taken as rough approximations because of the frequent difficulty of distinguishing the articulation of *Emmy, I,* and *my* in this period.

3. Children's mastery of temporal reference is a topic that has been the focus of much research in child language and one that has produced a number of conflicting claims. Gerhardt discusses a number of these issues in Chapter 5, and I will not review them here except as they may bear on my argument.

4. Whorf's (1956) discussion of the different conceptions of time in different languages appears to implicate such a conclusion, and it is a conclusion that should not be dismissed out of hand. Subsequent cross-cultural and cross-linguistic studies of temporal concepts and relations have provided further support for the proposal that such concepts are linguistically constructed (for example Fraser 1987; Hall 1983).

5. Many linguists (for example Lyons 1977) assert that English has no real future tense, both the *will-shall* and the *be-going-to* forms encoding notions of modality to a greater degree than futurity.

6. Gerhardt in Chapter 5 claims that the emergence of the specific past does not indicate an absolute distinction between past and not past, but rather a relative positioning of events within a frame. As the subsequent analysis of the "Mommy get me" monologue will indicate, I am not in total agreement with this claim. In my view, positioning events in sequence within a larger event frame requires conceptualizing them along a timeline, as does the distinction among future, present, and past. Moreover, the entire frame must be conceptualized as positioned along this line in the past. Event frames (or episodes) need not be positioned relative to one another (for example, Emily need not be capable of knowing that going to the beach took place before or after a trip to Caldor's), but they are positioned in the past relative to *now,* and the component actions within an event are positioned relative to their linear sequence in time. Thus the time-line does appear to be psychologically meaningful, even if its extent from the present into the past or future before events become jumbled along it—their places unclear or confused—is limited.

7. Since an account such as that of the broken car is situated in the past, there is no past-present contrast to be established within it; thus the function of the past marker might be hard for the child to identify.

8. The child at this point, according to Weist, also codes continuative-noncontinuative, complete-incomplete, and realis-irrealis—contrasts I am not concerned with here.

9. Or from another perspective to set up foreground and background relations (see Hopper 1979).

10. It is interesting with respect to discourse reference that John's daddy receives full nominal treatment in both mentions, whereas the presumed

topic, Daddy, is realized pronominally. This accords with normal adult usage (Karmiloff-Smith 1979; Levy 1982).

11. As Clark (1974), Fillmore (1979), Nelson (1981), and Peters (1983) have shown, this is not always the neat progression for the construction of sentence grammars, which may involve the reverse, the analysis of smaller parts (words) from the whole (the phrase or sentence).

References

Abelson, R. P. 1981. Psychological status of the script concept. *American Psychologist* 36:715–729.

Antinucci, F., and R. Miller. 1976. How children talk about what happened. *Journal of Child Language* 3:169–189.

Astington, J. 1988. Children's understanding of the speech act of promising. *Journal of Child Language* 15:157–173.

Austin, J. 1962. *How to do things with words*. Cambridge, Mass.: Harvard University Press.

Bakhtin, M. 1981 (original 1975). *The dialogic imagination*, ed. M. Holquist. Austin: University of Texas Press.

———— 1984 (original 1963). *Problems of Dostoevsky's poetics*. Minneapolis: University of Minnesota Press.

———— 1986 (original 1976). *Speech genres and other late essays*. Austin: University of Texas Press.

Bates, E., and B. MacWhinney. 1982. Functionalist approaches to grammar. In E. Wanner and L. Gleitman, eds., *Language acquisition: The state of the art*. Cambridge: Cambridge University Press.

Bateson, G. 1972. *Steps to an ecology of mind*. New York: Ballantine Books.

———— 1979. *Mind and nature: A necessary unity*. Toronto: Bantam.

Bauer, P. D., and C. M. Shore. 1987. Making a memorable event: Effects of familiarity and organization on young children's recall of action sequences. *Cognitive Development* 2:327–338.

Beebe, B., S. Feldstein, J. Jaffe, K. Mays, and D. Alson. 1985. Interpersonal timing: The application of an adult dialogue model to mother-infant and kinesic interactions. In T. Field and N. Fox, eds., *Social perception in infants*. Norwood, N.J.: Ablex.

Benveniste, E. 1968. Mutations of linguistic categories. In Y. Malkiel and W. P. Lehman, eds., *Directions for historical linguistics*. Austin: University of Texas Press.

——— 1971. *Problems in general linguistics.* Coral Gables, Fla.: University of Miami Press.

Black, R. 1979. Crib talk and mother-child interaction: A comparison of form and function. *Papers and Reports on Child Language Development* 17:90–97.

Bloom, L. 1987. On acquiring language. Colloquium talk, New School for Social Research.

Bloom, L., and M. Lahey. 1978. *Language development and language disorders.* New York: Wiley.

Bloom, L., K. Lifter, and J. Hafitz. 1980. Semantics of verbs and the development of verb inflection in child language. *Language* 56:386–412.

Bloom, L., P. Lightbown, and L. Hood. 1975. Variation and reduction as aspects of competence in child language. In A. Pick, ed., *Minnesota Symposia of Child Psychology.* Minneapolis: University of Minnesota Press.

Bloom, L., L. Rocissano, and L. Hood. 1976. Adult-child discourse: Developmental interaction between information processing and linguistic knowledge. *Cognitive Psychology* 8:521–552.

Bolinger, D. 1986. *Intonation and its parts: Melody in spoken English.* Stanford: Stanford University Press.

Bowerman, M. 1984. Looking at the development of temporality with diary data. Manuscript, Temporality Workshop, Max-Planck Institute.

——— 1985. Beyond communicative adequacy: From piecemeal knowledge to an integrated system in the child's acquisition of language. In K. Nelson, ed., *Children's language,* vol. 5, Hillsdale, N.J.: Erlbaum.

——— 1986. First steps in acquiring conditionals. In E. C. Traugott, A. Ter Meulen, J. Reilly, and C. A. Ferguson, eds., *On conditionals.* Cambridge: Cambridge University Press.

——— 1987. Commentary: Mechanisms of language acquisition. In B. MacWhinney, ed., *Mechanisms of language acquisition.* Hillsdale, N.J.: Erlbaum.

Britton, J. 1970. *Language and learning.* London: Penguin.

Bronckart, J. P., and H. Sinclair. 1973. Time, tense and aspect. *Cognition* 2:1–30.

Brown, A. 1987. Metacognition, executive control, self-regulation and other more mysterious mechanisms. In F. E. Weiner and R. H. Kluve, eds., *Metacognition, motivation and understanding.* Hillsdale, N.J.: Erlbaum.

Brown, A. L., and J. S. DeLoache. 1978. Skills, plans, and self-regulation. In R. Siegler, ed., *Children's thinking: What develops?* Hillsdale, N.J.: Erlbaum.

Brown, G., and G. Yule. 1983. *Discourse analysis.* Cambridge: Cambridge University Press.

Brown, R. 1973. *A first language: The early stages*. Cambridge, Mass.: Harvard University Press.

Bruner, J. S. 1975. From communication to language: A psychological perspective. *Cognition* 3:255–287.

———— 1983. *Child's talk: Learning to use language*. New York: Norton.

———— 1986. *Actual minds, possible worlds*. Cambridge, Mass.: Harvard University Press.

Budwig, N. 1984. The grammatical marking of transitivity in early child language. Manuscript, University of California, Berkeley.

———— 1985. I, me, my and "name": Children's early systematizations of forms, meanings and functions in talk about the self. *Papers and Reports on Child Language Development* 24.

Burke, K. 1945. *Grammar of motives*. New York: Prentice-Hall.

Calver, E. 1946. The uses of the present tense in English. *Language* 22:317–325.

Chafe, W. L. 1980. The deployment of consciousness in the production of a narrative. In W. L. Chafe, ed., *The pear stories: Cognitive, cultural and linguistic aspects of narrative production*. Norwood, N.J.: Ablex.

———— 1986. Cognitive constraints on information flow. In R. Tomlin, ed., *Coherence and grounding in discourse*. Amsterdam: John Benjamins.

Chomsky, N. 1965. *Aspects of the theory of syntax*. Cambridge, Mass.: MIT Press.

———— 1975. *Reflections on language*. New York: Random House.

Clancy, P. 1987. The expression of affect in the acquisition of Japanese grammar. Paper presented at the International Pragmatics Association Conference.

Clark, E. 1987. The principle of contrast: A constraint on language acquisition. In B. MacWhinney, ed., *Mechanisms of language acquisition*. Hillsdale, N.J.: Erlbaum.

Clark, R. 1974. Performing without competence. *Journal of Child Language* 1:1–10.

Comrie, B. 1976. *Aspect*. Cambridge: Cambridge University Press.

———— 1981. *Language universals and linguistic typology: Syntax and morphology*. Chicago: University of Chicago Press.

———— 1985. *Tense*. Cambridge: Cambridge University Press.

Cromer, R. F. 1968. The growth of temporal reference during the acquisition of language. Ph.D. diss., Harvard University.

———— 1971. The development of the ability to decenter in time. *British Journal of Psychology* 62:353–365.

Cruttenden, A. 1986. *Intonation*. Cambridge: Cambridge University Press.

Crystal, D. 1975. *The English tone of voice*. London: Edward Arnold.

Danes, F. 1974. Functional sentence perspective and the organization of the text. In F. Danes, ed., *Papers on functional sentence perspective*. New York: Academic Press.

deLaguna, G. 1927. *Speech: Its function and development*. New Haven: Yale University Press.

DeLancey, S. 1984. Notes on agentivity and causation. *Studies in Language* 8:181–213.

de Lemos, C. 1981. Interactional processes in the child's construction of language. In W. Deutsch, ed., *The child's construction of language*. London: Academic Press.

Deutsch, W., and N. Budwig. 1983. Form and function in the development of possessives. *Papers and Reports on Child Language Development* 22.

Dewey, J. 1958. *Experience and nature*. New York: Dover.

Dollard, J., and N. Miller. 1950. *Personality and psychotherapy*. New York: McGraw-Hill.

Dore, J. 1983. Feeling, form and intention in the baby's transition to language. In R. Golinkoff, ed., *The transition from prelinguistic to linguistic communication*. Hillsdale, N.J.: Erlbaum.

——— 1985. Holophrases revisited: Their "logical" development from dialog. In M. Barrett, ed., *Children's single-word speech*. Chichester: Wiley.

DuBois, J. W. 1985. Competing motivations. In J. Haiman, ed., *Iconicity in syntax: Typological studies in language*, vol. 6. Philadelphia: John Benjamins.

Emde, R. N., T. Gaensbaver, and R. Harmon. 1976. Emotional expression in infancy: A bio-behavioral study. *Psychological Issues Monograph Series* 10(1), no. 37.

Emerson, H. F. 1979. Children's comprehension of "because" in reversible and nonreversible sentences. *Journal of Child Language* 6:279–300.

Feldman, C. 1977. Two functions of language. *Harvard Educational Review* 47, no. 3:282–293.

——— 1988. Early forms of thought about thoughts: Some simple linguistic expressions of mental state. In J. Astington, P. Harris, and D. Olson, eds., *Developing theories of mind*. Cambridge: Cambridge University Press.

Feldman, C., and J. Bruner. 1987. Varieties of perspective: An overview. In James Russell, ed., *Philosophical perspectives on developmental psychology*. Oxford: Blackwell.

Feldman, C., and S. Toulmin. 1976. Logic and the theory of mind. *Nebraska Symposium on Motivation* 1975:409–476.

Fillmore, J. 1968. The case for case. In E. Bach and R. T. Harms, eds., *Universals in linguistic theory*. New York: Holt, Rinehart, and Winston.

Fillmore, L. 1979. Individual differences in second language acquisition. In C. J. Fillmore, D. Kempler, and W. S.-Y. Wang, eds., *Individual differ-*

ences in language ability and language behavior. New York: Academic Press.

Firbas, J. 1971. On the concept of communicative dynamism in the theory of functional sentence perspective. *Philologica Pragensia* 8:135–144.

Fivush, R., and J. Mandler. 1986. Developmental changes in the understanding of temporal sequence. *Child Development* 56:1437–1446.

Flavell, J. 1979. Metacognition and cognitive monitoring: A new area of cognitive-developmental inquiry. *American Psychologist* 34:906–911.

Fodor, J., and S. Crain. 1987. Simplicity and generality of rules in language acquisition. In B. MacWhinney, ed., *Mechanisms of language acquisition.* Hillsdale, N.J.: Erlbaum.

Foucault, M. 1970. *The order of things.* New York: Random House.

Fraser, J. T. 1987. *Time the familiar stranger.* Amherst: University of Massachusetts Press.

French, L., and K. Nelson. 1985. *Young children's knowledge of relational terms: Some ifs, ors and buts.* New York: Springer-Verlag.

Freud, S. 1956. *The complete introductory lectures on psychoanalysis.* New York: Norton.

Fyre, N. 1964. *The educated imagination.* Bloomington: Indiana University Press.

Furrow, D. 1984. Social and private speech at two years. *Child Development* 55:355–362.

Gardner, H. 1983. *Frames of mind: The theory of multiple intelligences.* New York: Basic Books.

Gee (nee Gerhardt), J. 1985. An interpretive approach to the study of modality: What child language can tell the linguist. *Studies in Language* 9:197–229.

Gee (nee Gerhardt), J., and I. Savasir. 1985. On the use of WILL and GONNA: Towards a description of activity-types for child language. *Discourse Processes* 8:143–175.

Geertz, C. 1976. From the native's view: On the nature of anthropological understanding. In K. Basso and H. Selby, eds., *Meaning in anthropology.* Albuquerque: University of New Mexico Press.

Gerhardt, J. In press. From discourse to semantics: The development of verb morphology and forms of self-reference in the speech of a two-year-old. *Journal of Child Language.*

Gerhardt, J., and I. Savasir. 1986. The use of the simple present in the speech of two three-year-olds: Normativity not subjectivity. *Language in Society* 15:501–536.

Givon, T. 1982. Tense-aspect-modality: The Creole prototype and beyond. In P. Hopper, ed., *Between semantics and pragmatics.* Philadelphia: John Benjamins.

Goffman, E. 1974. *Frames analysis.* New York: Harper and Row.

Goldsmith, J., and E. Woisetschlaeger. 1982. The logic of the English progressive. *Linguistic Inquiry* 13:79–89.

Goodman, N. 1978. *Ways of worldmaking*. Hassocks, Sussex: Harvester.

Green, A. 1975. La psychoanalyse, son objet, son avenir. *Revue Française de Psychoanalyse* 39:103–134.

Greenfield, P. M. 1979. Informativeness, pre-supposition, and semantic choice in single-word utterances. In E. Ochs and B. B. Schieffelin, eds., *Developmental pragmatics*. New York: Academic Press.

Greimas, A., and J. Courtes. 1976. The cognitive dimension of narrative discourse. *New Literary History* 7:433–447.

Hall, E. T. 1983. *The dance of life: The other dimension of time*. Garden City, N.Y.: Doubleday.

Halliday, M. A. K. 1975. *Learning how to mean*. London: Edwin Arnold.

Halliday, M. A. K., and R. Hasan. 1976. *Cohesion in English*. London: Longmans Group.

Hallowell, A. I. 1960. Self, society, and culture in phylogenetic perspective. In S. Tax, ed., *The evolution of man*. Chicago: University of Chicago Press.

Harner, L. 1981. Children talk about the time and aspect of actions. *Child Development* 52:489–506.

——— 1982. Talking about the past and future. In W. J. Friedman, ed., *The developmental psychology of time*. New York: Academic Press.

Hatcher, A. G. 1951. The use of the progressive form in English: A new approach. *Language* 27:254–280.

Heath, S. B. 1983. *Ways with words*. Cambridge: Cambridge University Press.

Hopper, P. 1979. Aspect and foregrounding in discourse. In T. Givon, ed., *Discourse and Syntax,* 12. New York: Academic Press.

——— 1982. Aspect between discourse and grammar. In P. Hopper, ed., *Between semantics and pragmatics*. Philadelphia: John Benjamins.

Hopper, P., and S. A. Thompson. 1980. Transitivity in grammar and discourse. *Language* 56:251–299.

Hymes, D. 1974. Ways of speaking. In R. Bauman and J. Sherzer, eds., *Explorations in the ethnography of speaking*. London: Cambridge University Press.

Jakobson, R. 1960. Linguistics and poetics. In T. A. Sebeok, ed., *Style in language*. Cambridge, Mass.: MIT Press.

——— 1962. Anthony's contribution to linguistic theory. In R. Weir, ed., *Language in the crib*. Cambridge, Mass.: MIT Press.

Jarvella, R. J., and W. Klein, eds. 1982. *Speech, place, and action*. New York: Wiley.

Jesperson, O. 1922. *Language: Its nature, development, and origin*. New York: Allen and Unwin.

Joos, M. 1964. *The English verb*. Madison: University of Wisconsin Press.

Karmiloff-Smith, A. 1979. Language as a formal problem-space for children. In W. Deutsch, ed., *The child's construction of language*. Cambridge: Cambridge University Press.

———— 1980. Psychological processes underlying pronominalization and non-pronominalization in children's connected discourse. In J. Kreiman and A. E. Ojeda, eds., *Papers from the Parasession on Pronouns and Anaphora, Chicago Linguistics Society.* Chicago: Chicago Linguistics Society.

———— 1985. Language and cognitive processes from a developmental perspective. *Language and Cognitive Processes* 1:61–85.

———— 1986. Some fundamental aspects of language development after age five. In P. Fletcher and M. Garman, eds., *Language acquisition,* 2nd ed. Cambridge: Cambridge University Press.

Kaye, K. 1982. *The mental and social life of babies*. Chicago: University of Chicago Press.

Keenan, E. O., and B. B. Schieffelin. 1976. Topic as a discourse notion: A study of topic in the conversations of children and adults. In C. N. Li, ed., *Subject and topic*. New York: Academic Press.

Kenny, A. 1967. *Action, emotion and will*. London: Routledge and Kegan Paul.

Kohut, H. 1977. *The restoration of the self*. New York: International Universities Press.

Kuczaj, S. A., II. 1977. The acquisition of regular and irregular past tense forms. *Journal of Verbal Learning and Verbal Behavior* 16:589–600.

———— 1983. *Crib speech and language play*. New York: Springer-Verlag.

Lakoff, G. 1977. Linguistic gestalts. *Papers from the Regional Meeting of the Chicago Linguistics Society* 13:236–287.

Lakoff, G., and M. Johnson. 1980. *Metaphors we live by*. Chicago: University of Chicago Press.

Lawler, J. 1972. Generic to a fault. *Papers from the Regional Meeting of the Chicago Linguistics Society* 8:247–258.

Leech, G. 1971. *Meaning and the English verb*. London: Longman.

Levinson, S. C. 1983. *Pragmatics*. Cambridge: Cambridge University Press.

Levy, E. 1982. Towards an objective definition of "discourse topic." *Papers from the Regional Meeting of the Chicago Linguistics Society* 18.

———— 1984. Communicating thematic structure in narrative discourse: The use of referring terms and gestures. Ph.D. diss., University of Chicago.

———— 1987. A Vygotskian perspective on discourse: From complex to concept. *Quarterly Newsletter of the Laboratory of Comparative Human Cognition* 3, no. 3.

Lieberman, P. 1967. *Intonation, perception and language*. Cambridge, Mass.: MIT Press.

—— 1984. *The biology and evolution of language.* Cambridge, Mass.: Harvard University Press.

Lucariello, J., and K. Nelson. 1987. Remembering and planning talk between mothers and children. *Discourse Processes* 10:219–235.

Luria, A. R. 1961. *The role of speech in the regulation of normal and abnormal behavior.* New York: Liveright.

Lyons, J. 1977. *Semantics,* vol. 1. Cambridge: Cambridge University Press.

—— 1982. Deixis and subjectivity: Loquor, ergo sum? In R. J. Jarvella and W. Klein, eds., *Speech, place and action.* London: Wiley.

Mandler, J. M. 1988. How to build a baby. *Cognitive Development* 3:113–136.

McNeill, D. 1979. *The conceptual basis of language.* Hillsdale, N.J.: Erlbaum.

—— 1988. Linear steps or internal dialectic? Reply to Butterworth and Hadar. Manuscript.

Mead, G. H. 1934. *Mind, self, and society.* Chicago: University of Chicago Press.

Mertz, E., and R. J. Parmentier, eds. 1985. *Semiotic mediation: Sociocultural and psychological perspectives.* New York: Academic Press.

Miller, G. A. 1962. Foreword to R. Weir, *Language in the crib.* Cambridge, Mass.: MIT Press.

—— 1978. Pastness. In G. A. Miller and E. Lenneberg, eds., *Psychology and biology of language and thought: Essays in honor of Eric Lenneberg.* New York: Academic Press.

Miller, G. A., and P. N. Johnson-Laird. 1976. *Language and perception.* Cambridge, Mass.: Harvard University Press.

Minsky, M. 1981. A framework for representing knowledge. In J. Haugeland, ed., *Mind design.* Cambridge, Mass.: MIT Press.

Murray, L., and C. Trevarthen. 1985. Emotional regulation of interactions between two-month-olds and their mothers. In T. Field and H. Fox, eds., *Social perception in infants.* Norwood, N.J.: Ablex.

Nelson, K. 1973. Structure and strategy in learning to talk. *Society for Research in Child Development Monographs* 38, nos. 1–2 (serial no. 149).

—— 1978. How young children represent knowledge of their world in and out of language. In R. S. Siegler, ed., *Children's thinking: What develops?* Hillsdale, N.J.: Erlbaum.

—— 1981. Individual differences in language development: Implications for development and language. *Developmental Psychology* 17:170–187.

—— 1983a. The derivation of concepts and categories from event representations. In E. Scholnick, ed., *New trends in conceptual representation: Challenges to Piaget's theory.* Hillsdale, N.J.: Erlbaum.

—— 1983b. Time talk. Paper presented at the New York Child Language Conference.

———— 1984. The transition from infant to child memory. In M. Moscovitch, ed., *Infant memory*. New York: Plenum.

———— 1985. Memories in the crib. Paper presented at the biennial meeting of the Society for Research in Child Development, Toronto.

———— 1986. *Event knowledge: Structure and function in development*. Hillsdale, N.J.: Erlbaum.

———— 1988. The ontogeny of memory for real events. In U. Neisser and E. Winograd, eds., *Remembering reconsidered: Ecological and traditional approaches to the study of memory*. New York: Cambridge University Press.

———— In press. Remembering: A functional developmental perspective. In P. R. Solomon, G. R. Goethals, C. M. Kelley, and B. R. Stephens, eds., *Memory: An interdisciplinary approach*. New York: Springer-Verlag.

Nelson, K., and J. M. Gruendel. 1981. Generalized event representations: Basic building blocks of cognitive development. In A. Brown and M. Lamb, eds., *Advances in developmental psychology*, vol. 1. Hillsdale, N.J.: Erlbaum.

Nelson, K., and E. Levy. 1987. Development of referential cohesion in a child's monologues. In R. Steele and T. Threadgold, eds., *Language topics*. Amsterdam: John Benjamins.

Ochs, E. 1985. Variation and error: A sociolinguistic approach to language acquisition in Samoa. In D. I. Slobin, ed., *The cross-linguistic study of language acquisition*. Hillsdale, N.J.: Erlbaum.

———— 1986. From feelings to grammar: A Samoan case study. In B. Schieffelin and E. Ochs, eds., *Language socialization across cultures*. Cambridge: Cambridge University Press.

Ochs, E., and B. Schieffelin. 1987. Language has a heart. Paper presented at the International Pragmatics Association Conference.

Papousek, M. 1987. Models and messages in the melodies of maternal speech in tonal and non-tonal languages. Paper presented to the Society for Research in Child Development, Baltimore.

Pavlov, I. P. 1929. *Lectures on conditioned reflexes*. New York: International Publishers.

Peirce, C. S. 1960. *The collected papers of Charles Sanders Peirce,* ed. C. Hartshorne and P. Weiss. Cambridge, Mass.: Harvard University Press.

Peters, A. 1983. *The units of language acquisition*. New York: Cambridge University Press.

Peterson, C., and A. McCabe. 1983. *Developmental psycholinguistics: Three ways of looking at a child's narrative*. New York: Plenum.

Piaget, J. 1926. *The language and thought of the child*. Rpt. New York: World Publishing, 1955.

———— 1959. *The language and thought of the child*, 3rd ed. rev. Thetford, Norfolk: Lowe and Brydone.

———— 1974. *Understanding causality*. New York: Norton.

———— 1977. The moral judgement of the child. In H. Gruber and J. Voneche, eds., *The essential Piaget.* New York: Basic Books.

Pickert, S. 1981. Imaginative dialogues in children's private speech. *First Language* 2:5–20.

Propp, V. 1968. *The morphology of the folk tale.* Austin: University of Texas Press.

Reichenbach, H. 1947. *Elements of symbolic logic.* New York: Macmillan.

Reid, W. 1980. Meaning and narrative structure. *Columbia Working Papers in Linguistics* 5:12–19.

Ricoeur, P. 1977. The question of proof in Freud's psychoanalytic writings. *Journal of the American Psychoanalytic Association* 25:835–871.

Rispoli, M., and L. Bloom. 1987. The conceptual origins of the transitivity/ intransitivity distinction. *Papers and Reports on Child Language Development* 26.

Sacks, H., E. Schegloff, and G. Jefferson. 1974. A simplest systematics for the organization of turn-taking in conversation. *Language* 50: 696–735.

Scaife, M., and J. S. Bruner. 1974. The capacity for joint visual attention in the infant. *Nature* 253:265–266.

Schachtel, E. G. 1947. On memory and childhood amnesia. *Psychiatry* 10:1– 26. Rpt. in U. Neisser, ed., *Memory observed.* San Francisco: Freeman, 1982.

Schafer, R. 1981. *Narrative actions in psychoanalysis.* Worcester, Mass.: Clark University Press.

Schank, R. C., and R. P. Abelson. 1977. *Scripts, plans, goals and understanding.* Hillsdale, N.J.: Erlbaum.

Schiffman, R. 1985. Discourse constraints on "it" and "that": A study of language use in career counseling interviews. Ph.D. diss., University of Chicago.

Searle, J. 1969. *Speech acts.* Cambridge: Cambridge University Press.

———— 1979. *Expression and meaning.* Cambridge: Cambridge University Press.

Silverstein, M. 1985. The functional stratification of language and ontogenesis. In J. Wertsch, ed., *Culture, communication and cognition: Vygotskian perspectives.* Cambridge: Cambridge University Press.

———— 1987. Cognitive implications of a referential hierarchy. In M. Hickmann, ed., *Social and functional approaches to language and thought.* Orlando, Fla.: Academic Press.

Sinclair, H. 1971. Sensorimotor action patterns as a condition for the acquisition of syntax. In R. Huxley and E. Ingram, eds., *Language acquisition: Models and methods.* London: Academic Press.

Skinner, B. 1957. *Verbal behavior.* New York: Appleton-Century-Crofts.

Slobin, D. I. 1973. Cognitive prerequisites for the acquisition of grammar. In C. A. Fergerson and D. I. Slobin, eds., *Studies of child language development.* New York: Holt, Rinehart and Winston.

———— 1981. The origins of grammatical encoding of events. In W. Deutsch, ed., *The child's construction of language*. London: Academic Press.

———— 1982. Universal and particular in the acquisition of language. In E. Wanner and L. R. Gleitman, eds., *Language acquisition: The state of the art*. Cambridge: Cambridge University Press.

———— 1985. The cross-linguistic evidence for the language-making capacity. In D. I. Slobin, ed., *The cross-linguistic study of language acquisition*. Hillsdale, N.J.: Erlbaum.

Smith, C. 1980. The acquisition of time-talk: Relations between child and adult grammar. *Journal of Child Language* 7:263–272.

———— 1983. A theory of aspectual choice. *Language*.

———— 1986. A speaker-based approach to aspect. *Linguistics and Philosophy*, 97–115.

Snow, C., and B. Goldfield. 1983. Turn the page please: Situation-specific language acquisition. *Journal of Child Language* 10.

Spence, D. P. 1976. Clinical interpretation: Some comments on the nature of the evidence. *Psychoanalysis and Contemporary Science* 5:367–388.

———— 1982. *Narrative truth and historical truth: Meaning and interpretation in psychoanalysis*. New York: Norton.

Stein, N., and K. Kilgore. 1987. The development of the story concept. Manuscript, University of Chicago.

Stephany, U. 1981. Verbal grammar in Modern Greek early child language. In P. Dale and D. Ingram, eds., *Child language*. Baltimore: University Park Press.

Stern, D. N. 1977. *The first relationship*. Cambridge, Mass.: Harvard University Press.

———— 1985. *The interpersonal world of the infant: A view from psychoanalysis and developmental psychology*. New York: Basic Books.

Stern, D. N., K. MacKain, and S. Speiker. 1982. Intonation contours as signals in maternal speech to prelinguistic infants. *Developmental Psychology* 18:727–735.

Todorov, T. 1977. *The poetics of prose*. Ithaca: Cornell University Press.

Traugott, E. 1982. From propositional to textual and expressive meaning: Some semantic-pragmatic aspects of grammaticization. In W. P. Lehmon and Y. Malkiel, eds., *Perspectives in historical linguistics*. Amsterdam: John Benjamins.

Trevarthen, C. 1979. Communication and cooperation in early infancy: A description of primary intersubjectivity. In M. Bullowa, ed., *Before speech: The beginnings of human communication*. Cambridge: Cambridge University Press.

———— 1980. The foundations of intersubjectivity: Development of interpersonal and cooperative understanding in infants. In D. R. Olson, ed., *The social foundations of language and thought: Essays in honor of Jerome Bruner*. New York: Norton.

———— 1983. Emotions in infancy: Regulators of contacts and relationships with persons. In K. Scherer and P. Ekman, eds., *Approaches to emotion.* Hillsdale, N.J.: Erlbaum.

Turner, V. 1975. *Revelation and divination in Ndembu ritual.* Ithaca: Cornell University Press.

———— 1982. *From ritual to theatre: The human seriousness of play.* New York: New York Performing Arts Journal Publications.

Twaddell, W. F. 1968. *The English verb auxiliaries.* Providence: Brown University Press.

Vendler, Z. 1967. Verbs and times. In Z. Vendler, ed., *Linguistics and philosophy.* Ithaca: Cornell University Press.

von Humboldt, W. 1885. On the verb in American languages. *Proceedings of the American Philosophical Society* 22:332–354.

Vygotsky, L. S. 1962 (original 1934). *Thought and language.* Cambridge, Mass.: MIT Press.

———— 1978. *Mind in society: The development of higher psychological processes,* ed. M. Cole, V. John-Steiner, S. Scribner, and E. Souberman. Cambridge, Mass.: Harvard University Press.

———— 1987. *The collected works of L. S. Vygotsky,* vol. 1: *Problems of general psychology,* ed. R. Rieber and A. Carton, trans. N. Minick. New York: Plenum.

Watson, R. 1983. Reference to self and other in Emmy's pre-sleep monologues and dialogues. Paper presented at the New York Child Language Group.

Weir, R. 1962. *Language in the crib.* The Hague: Mouton.

Weist, R. M. 1986. Tense and aspect. In P. Fletcher and M. Garman, eds., *Language acquisition.* Cambridge: Cambridge University Press.

Weist, R., and E. Buczowska. 1986. The emergence of temporal adverbs in child Polish. Manuscript, SUNY, Fredonia.

Weist, R., H. Wysocka, K. Wrtkowska-Stadnik, E. Buczowska, and E. Konieczna. 1984. The defective tense hypothesis: On the emergence of tense and aspect in child Polish. *Journal of Child Language* 11:347–374.

Werner, H. 1948). *The comparative psychology of mental development.* New York: International Universities Press.

Werner, H., and B. Kaplan. 1963. *Symbol formation: An organismic-developmental approach to language and the expression of thought.* New York: Wiley.

Wertsch, J. V., ed. 1985a. *Culture, communication and cognition: Vygotskian perspectives.* Cambridge: Cambridge University Press.

———— 1985b. *Vygotsky and the social formation of mind.* Cambridge, Mass.: Harvard University Press.

———— 1985c. Adult-child interaction as a source of self-regulation in children. In S. Yussen, ed., *The growth of reflection in children.* New York: Academic Press.

Wertsch, J. V., and C. A. Stone. 1985. The concept of internalization in Vygotsky's account of the genesis of higher mental functions. In J. V. Wertsch, ed., *Culture, communication and cognition: Vygotskian perspectives.* Cambridge: Cambridge University Press.

White, H. 1981. The narrativization of real events. In W. Mitchell, ed., *On narrative.* Chicago: University of Chicago Press.

Whorf, B. L. 1956. *Language, thought and reality: Selected writings of Benjamin Lee Whorf,* ed. J. B. Carroll. Cambridge, Mass.: MIT Press.

Wittgenstein, L. 1953. *Philosophical investigations.* New York: Macmillan.

Yussen, S. 1985. Review of Langer's reflections. In S. Yussen, ed., *The growth of reflection in children.* New York: Academic Press.

Contributors

JEROME S. BRUNER
   Russell Sage Foundation

JOHN DORE
   *City University of New York Graduate Center
   and Baruch College*

CAROL FELDMAN
   New York University

JULIE GERHARDT
   California School of Professional Psychology

ELENA LEVY
   University of Connecticut at Stamford

JOAN LUCARIELLO
   The New School for Social Research

KATHERINE NELSON
   City University of New York Graduate Center

DANIEL STERN
   Brown University and University of Geneva

RITA WATSON
   University of British Columbia

Index

Action, 73, 74, 75, 78, 95
Adjectives, 148
Adult talk, 243, 244, 245, 248. *See also* Baby talk
Adverbs, 61; temporal, 11, 28, 81, 177, 189, 285, 297, 298, 300, 301, 305; epistemic, 102–103
Affect and affectivity, 73, 74, 75, 78, 90, 95, 310
Antinucci, F., 176, 178, 202–203
Appropriateness marking, 82, 83
Articles, 8, 10
Austin, J., 75–76

Baby talk, 237, 239, 240, 243, 244, 245, 248. *See also* Adult talk
Bakhtin, M., 231, 232, 236–237, 242, 255
Bateson, Gregory, 232–234, 236
Benveniste, E., 212
Bloom, L., 9, 10, 11, 76, 178, 202, 204, 295
Bowerman, M., 174
Brother, birth of, *see* Events
Brown, R., 8, 9, 11, 192–193, 215–216, 294, 295
Bruner, Jerome S., 1, 21, 75, 98, 104, 106, 315, 316
Budwig, N., 195, 286
Burke, K., 76, 106

Calver, E., 186
Causal expressions, 81
Chafe, W. L., 42–43, 45, 49, 51, 54, 61
Chain complexes, 138, 139

Challenges in discourse, 192, 195, 213
Choice routine, *see* Dialogue, purpose
Chomsky, N., 101
Classification process, 106, 109, 110–111
Clustering of forms and functions, 196–197
Cognition, 74, 75, 95; goals of, 99; in problem-solving narratives, 106–107, 317; metacognitive processes, 117; and linguistics, 123. *See also* Thought
Comrie, B., 187
Configural encoding, 180
Conjunctions, 11, 78, 297, 298; in memory episodes, 56; for sequencing, 81
Connectives, 11, 48–49; in memory episodes, 51–53, 54, 58, 60, 61; causal, 83; for sequencing, 83, 86, 100; logical, 102
Consciousness, 233, 234
Correspondence process, 106, 108–109
Courtes, J., 78
Crib speech, *see* Monologues

Defective tense hypothesis, 292
Deictic tense, 187, 189, 202, 203, 204, 206, 211, 212, 290, 292
deLaguna, Grace, 75
Deontic modality, 39, 40
Dewey, J., 73
Dialogism, 231
Dialogues: vs. monologues, 1, 4–5, 12, 19, 22, 100–102, 113–114, 116, 119, 178–182, 231, 232, 239, 297–298,

345

38–41, 60, 84, 86, 91, 95–96, 184–185; analysis of, 30–32, 310–312; separation, 312–315. *See also* Dialogues, purpose; Dialogues, themes of
Thought: and language, 1, 12, 17, 23, 73, 74, 75, 99–100, 236; and development, 1, 12; theoretical, 21; and narrative, 75. *See also* Speech, inner
Time, *see* Temporal organization of dialogues; Temporal organization of monologues
Time-Line, Standard Average European, 300–305
Todorov, T., 77
Transitivity, 192
Turner, V., 77

Variability marking, 82, 83
Verb morphology: and event parameters, 172, 217; and aspect/tense, 172, 173, 175–176, 177–178, 185, 187, 188–189, 200, 202–203, 204, 209, 217, 292, 295, 300; and self-reference, 173; meaning schema, 174, 217–218; restricted, 174–175, 217; function of, 175; contrasts in, 175, 191; and discourse, 177–178, 181–182, 185–186, 189, 218; in dialogues vs. monologues, 179–182, 192; past, 200, 202–205, 208, 214; and verb classes, 204; and temporal reference, 285

Verbs, 21–22, 61; auxiliary, 8; present progressive, 9; irregular past, 9–10, 11, 201, 203, 204, 209, 214, 296, 299; past and simple past, 10, 21–22, 28, 176–177, 200, 216, 297–298; inflected, 11, 176, 296; complex, 11; present and simple present, 21–22, 179–180, 181, 182–186, 188, 190, 191, 193, 198–199, 205, 206, 213, 214; progressive, 21–22, 187, 189–190, 191, 193–194, 205–206, 209–210, 213, 214, 216; units of, 137; chains, 152, 154; undifferentiated function clusters, 173; activity, 176; transitive and intransitive, 182, 183, 185, 198, 205, 207–208, 209; copula constructions of, 182; novel, 198, 200–201; telic, 204; future, 298
von Humboldt, W., 73
Vygotsky, L. S., 17–18, 19, 74–75, 101, 182, 232, 234–235, 236, 263, 264

Watson, Rita, 1, 22–23, 286, 312
Weir, R., 13, 14, 16, 128–129, 130, 138, 157, 263, 264
Weist, R. M., 176–177, 178, 295, 301–302, 304
Wertsch, J. V., 156
White, Hayden, 77
Whorf, B. L., 74, 300, 301
Wittgenstein, L., 238, 280
Woisetschlaeger, E., 186, 193